Mark Nolting's newly-revised *Africa's Top Wildlife Countries* remains the quintessential safari planning guide for travelers to Africa. A comprehensive, concise, and truly indispensable information source.

Joseph V. Kuca
*African Expedition Gazette*

"Out of Africa always something new." Old as that saying is, it's as true today as when Pliny first penned it. Africa is constantly changing and to keep up with those changes, safari goers can turn to the third and newest edition of *Africa's Top Wildlife Countries*. New maps, new photos, the most up to date information about where to go and where to stay that can be found in book form. Have a great trip!

Diana McMeekin
Executive Vice President
African Wildlife Foundation

Nearly as big and as exciting as the continent itself, Mark Nolting's newest edition is certainly must reading for anyone who yearns for the lure and lore of Africa. Take it along with you whether you travel there by air, sea or armchair. You won't be disappointed.

Ed Sullivan
*TravelAge East*

# AFRICA'S TOP WILDLIFE COUNTRIES

BY

MARK W. NOLTING

GLOBAL TRAVEL PUBLISHERS, INC.

*Africa's Top Wildlife Countries* (Third Edition, completely revised and updated).

ISBN: 0-939895-04-8
Edited by Patricia H. Cook
Interior Design by Marilyn Ratzlaff
Cover by Marilyn Ratzlaff
Illustrations by James B. King

Library of Congress Cataloging-in-Publication Data

Nolting, Mark, 1951-
Africa's top wildlife countries / by Mark W. Nolting. — 3rd ed.
p. cm.
Includes index.
ISBN 0-939895-04-8 : $15.95
1. Wildlife watching—Africa, Sub-Saharan—Guidebooks. 2. Safaris—Africa, Sub-Saharan—Guidebooks. 3. National parks and reserves—Africa, Sub-Saharan—Guidebooks. 4. Africa, Sub-Saharan—Description and travel—1981- —Guidebooks. I. Title.
QL337.S78N85 1992
333.95'4'0987—dc20 92-5391
CIP

PUBLISHER'S NOTE: Every effort has been made to make *Africa's Top Wildlife Countries* as accurate as possible. However, things change, especially in Africa, and neither Global Travel Publishers, Inc. nor the author can accept any liability for inaccuracies or omissions.

## DEDICATION

TO ALL THOSE WHO HAVE VENTURED TO AFRICA, AND BY VISITING THE PARKS AND RESERVES, HAVE CONTRIBUTED TO THEIR PRESERVATION AND THE WILDLIFE WITHIN THEM.

OTHER BOOKS BY MARK NOLTING

*TRAVEL JOURNAL AFRICA*

Dear Reader:

As President of The Africa Adventure Company, I have had the pleasure of sending hundreds of people from all walks of life on game viewing (photographic) safaris to Africa.

Why do so many people wish to go to Africa? Some want "to get on the edge of things" and live "where the excitement is!"

More and more people want to take trips which are meaningful and fulfill a greater need or involvement than just doing what others do on vacation.

Some seek the wonderful wilderness of a still primitive African continent where wildlife in its natural and exciting environment still abounds.

In other words, Africa means getting back to basics and feeling the thrill that goes with doing something entirely different from the world in which we live. Such adventures enhance an individual's perspective, refresh, and hone the instincts.

I've also talked to many people who decided to "do Africa before they got any older or the animals got any fewer!"

Population pressures in Africa are causing many parks to be reduced in size, resulting in even further declines in wildlife. African governments must be able to prove to their people that the parks provide more jobs, foreign exchange, and other benefits than if the land were given to their people for farming, grazing, or other uses.

Going on a photographic safari is a donation in itself towards saving endangered wildlife in Africa. This could be the most enjoyable and rewarding donation you will ever make!

Sincerely,
The Africa Adventure Company

Mark W. Nolting
President

P.S. For more information on The Africa Adventure Company, please see page 481.

A REQUEST:

Before booking your trip to Africa, call Mark Nolting *personally* toll free at 1-800-882-9453 (U.S.A. and Canada) or 305-781-3933 to discuss the hundreds of safari options The Africa Adventure Company (a tour operation which specializes in Africa) has to offer. Call today — Mark would love to help!

## ACKNOWLEDGMENTS

The completion and accuracy of this guide would not have been possible without the assistance of many people. Many thanks to all who have contributed to this project, including the following (my apologies to those contributors I have unintentionally omitted): the Embassy of Burundi; Ms. Mulili, David Waweru and Maggie Maranga of the Kenyan Tourist Office; Roger Sylvester of Block Hotels; Cynthia Moss, Conrad Hirsh; The Lesotho Tourist Board; Roselyne Hauchler of the Mauritius Government Tourist Office; Jeremy Pask of the Mauritius Government Tourist Information Service; the Embassy of Rwanda, Géard Pierson; the Digit Fund; Ross Battersby; Namibia Directorate of Trade and Tourism; Maricia Steward, Julian Harrison and Bronwen Redman of SATOUR; Ron Stringfellow of Southern Suns; the Embassy of Swaziland; Edson Tembo of the Zambia National Tourist Board; Mary Hatendi and the Zimbabwe Tourist Development Corporation; Ian Cochrane of Zimbabwe Sun Hotels; Garth Thompson, Benjamin Parker, Jo Pope, Bruce and Neil Davidson, Hugh and Mary Wright, Joe Perreira, Colin Bell, Russel Friedman, Dennis Rundle, Melanie Millin-Moore; Phillip Koboneka; Jill, Gary, Ella and John Strand; and Jeff Trotta for sharing his expertise on SCUBA diving in Africa.

My special thanks to Alison Wright for her invaluable assistance on the entire project.

Photo Credits: All photos are by Mark W. Nolting except the following:

Mike Appelbaum - 44, 45, 49, 102, 110, 122, 126/A-3 (lower right), 126/A-4 (upper & lower), 126/A-5 (upper & lower), 126/A-7 (upper right) & (lower right), 137, 280, 282, 350/B-10 (lower), 350/B-12 (upper), 350/B-15 (lower), 369

Bill Edison - 126/A-2 (lower)

John Haupt - 350/B-9

Ralph Hope - 126/A-8 (upper)

Kenya Tourist Board - 40, 126, 144

Ker and Downey, Inc., Houston, TX - 44, 55, 82, 126/A-8 (lower)

Virginia Misoff - 126/A-1, 126/A-3 (lower left), 126/A-7 (upper left)

SATOUR - 176, 217, 225, 231, 233, 235

Amy Schoeman - 126/A-6 (upper), 185, 189

Sun International - 161, 166, 220

Garth Thompson - 126/A-2 (upper), 126/A-6 (lower)

Wilderness Safaris - 79, 350/B-13 (lower)

Alison Wright - 350/B-11 (upper)

Zimbabwe Tourist Board - 391, 397, 413

## CONTENTS

# MAPS

# CHARTS AND ILLUSTRATIONS

## Charts



## Illustrations

# CALL OF THE WILD

# CALL OF THE WILD

Feature films like *Out Of Africa, African Queen* and *Gorillas In The Mist* have kindled in the hearts of many people the flame of desire for travel to Africa.

A visit to Africa allows you to experience nature at its finest — almost devoid of human interference, living according to a natural rhythm of life that has remained basically unchanged since the beginning of time.

At our deepest roots, the African continent communicates with our souls. Travelers return home, not only with exciting stories and adventures to share with friends and family, but with a feeling of accomplishment, increased self-confidence and broader horizons from having ventured where few have gone. Here's the kind of adventure about which many dream but few experience.

Having visited Africa once, you too will want to return again to the peace, tranquility and adventure it has to offer. I invite you to explore with me the reasons for this never-ceasing pull as we journey to some of the most fascinating places on earth.

**The time to visit Africa is now.** In spite of international efforts, poaching is still rampant. In addition, the continent is rapidly becoming westernized, making it more and more difficult to see the indigenous peoples living as they

# AFRICA

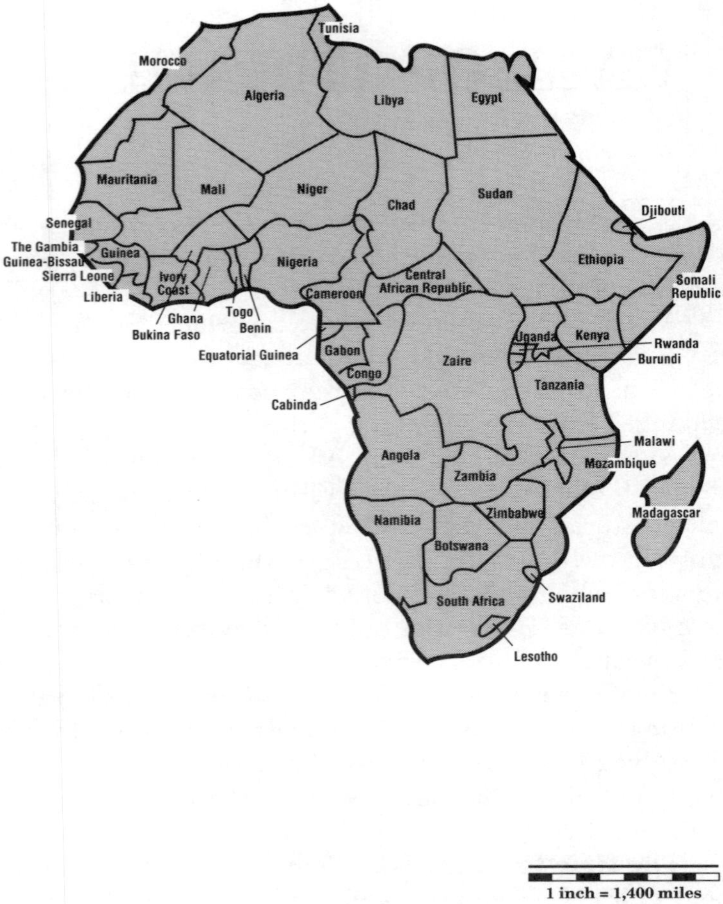
Tunisia
Morocco
Algeria
Libya
Egypt
Mauritania
Mali
Niger
Chad
Sudan
Djibouti
Senegal
The Gambia
Guinea-Bissau
Guinea
Sierra Leone
Liberia
Ivory Coast
Ghana
Bukina Faso
Togo
Benin
Nigeria
Cameroon
Central African Republic
Ethiopia
Somali Republic
Equatorial Guinea
Gabon
Congo
Zaire
Uganda
Kenya
Rwanda
Burundi
Tanzania
Cabinda
Angola
Zambia
Malawi
Mozambique
Madagascar
Namibia
Zimbabwe
Botswana
South Africa
Swaziland
Lesotho
1 inch = 1,400 miles

have for thousands of years. Go now, while Africa can still deliver all that is promised — and more!

Africa has such a tremendous variety of attractions that most everyone can find something fascinating to do. In addition to fabulous wildlife, Africa boasts having one of the world's largest waterfalls by volume (Victoria Falls), the world's longest river (the Nile), the world's largest intact caldera or crater (Ngorongoro), and the world's highest mountain not part of a mountain range (Mt. Kilimanjaro).

Africa is huge. It is the second largest continent on earth, covering over 20 percent of the world's land surface. More than three times the size of the United States, it is also larger than Europe, the United States and China combined. No wonder it has so much to offer!

## HOW TO USE THIS BOOK

*Africa's Top Wildlife Countries* highlights and compares wildlife reserves and other major attractions in the continent's best countries for game viewing.

Most people travel to Africa to see lion, elephant, rhino, and other wildlife unique to this fascinating continent in their natural surroundings. *Africa's Top Wildlife Countries* makes planning your adventure of a lifetime easy.

This guide is designed to help you decide the best place to go in Africa to do what you want to do, when you want to do it, in a manner of travel that personally suits you best.

From the easy-to-read **When's The Best Time To Go** chart (see page 65), you can conveniently choose the specific reserves and country(ies) that are best to visit during your vacation period. From the **What Wildlife Is Best Seen Where** chart (see page 63), you can easily locate the reserves which have an abundance of the animals which you wish to see most. From the **Safari Activities** chart (see page 43), you can choose the reserves that offer the safari options that interest you most.

The **Safari Glossary** contains words commonly used on safari and will define words used throughout the book. En-

# SOUTH, EAST and CENTRAL AFRICA

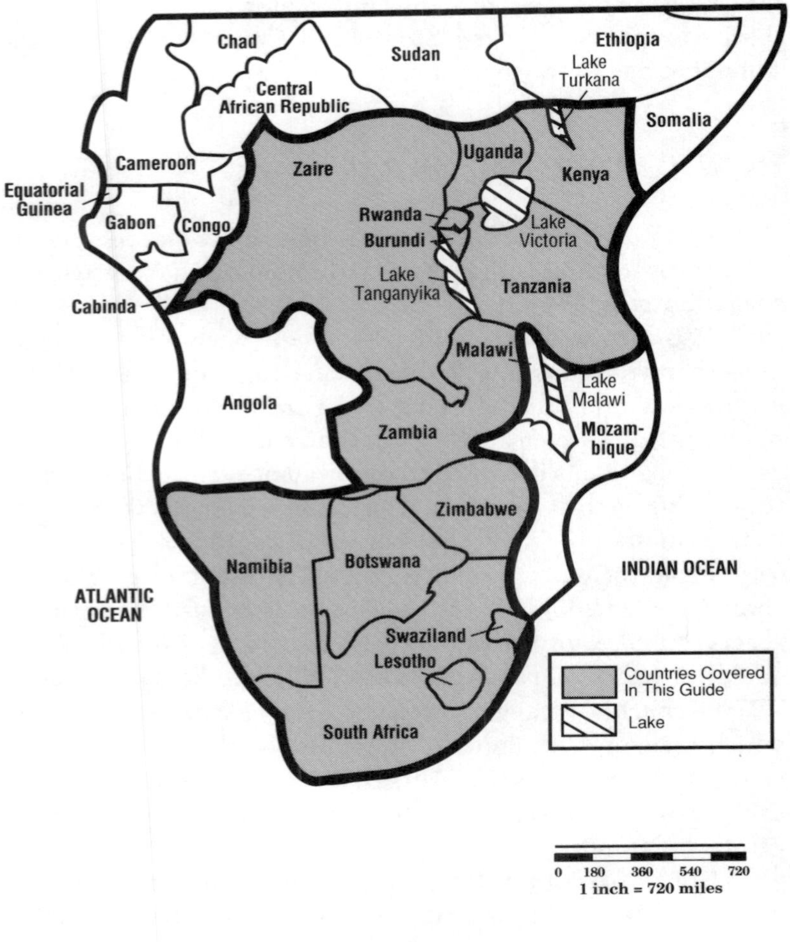

glish is the major language in most of the countries covered in this guide, so language is in fact not a problem. The **Safari Pages** (a safari directory) provide a veritable gold mine of difficult-to-find information and sources on Africa.

First, complete reading this introduction ("The Call of the Wild"). Then read the chapter or chapters on the countries that you feel offer the kind of *experience* you are looking for in Africa. Then call me, Mark Nolting, at The Africa Adventure Company (toll free 1-800-882-9453 in the U.S.A. and Canada) to discuss your thoughts. I will match the experience you are looking for with one of more than 100 safaris we have to offer, putting you one step closer to experiencing the safari of your dreams.

## WHAT IS A SAFARI LIKE?

"Alephaant, allephanntt," the Masai softly said as he escorted us to dinner that evening. Neither of us could understand him until he shined his flashlight on a tree-sized elephant browsing not 50 feet from where we stood. It was then I realized why we were requested to wait for the spear-wielding Masai assigned to our tent to escort us to dinner. The pathway to the dining tent was covered with giant pizza-sized footprints that were not there 45 minutes earlier. Carrying a spear in these parts is not a bad idea!

The dining tent was filled with people from the four corners of the earth, reveling in camaraderie and sumptuous cuisine by candlelight. An excellent selection of wines and desserts complemented the meal.

After dinner we sat around a roaring fire, listening to bush lore from our entertaining host. Later we watched hippo grazing only a few feet from our tent. The night was alive with the sounds and scents of the Africa we had dreamed of — the untamed wilderness where man is but a temporary guest and not a controller of nature. Only then did we retire to our comfortable deluxe tent with private facilities to sleep that gentle sleep which comes with a sigh of contentment.

What happens on safari? What is a typical day like?

Most safaris are centered around guests participating in two or three activities per day, such as game drives in minivans or four-wheel-drive vehicles. A game drive simply consists of having your guide drive you around a park or reserve in search of wildlife.

Most activities last two to four hours and are made when the wildlife is most active: early in the morning, often before breakfast, just after breakfast, in the late afternoon and at night (where allowed). Midday activities might include lazing around the swimming pool, reading or taking a nap. After an exhilarating day on safari, many guests return to revel in the day's adventures over exquisite European cuisine in comfortable lodges and camps.

The kind and quality of experience one has on safari varies greatly from country to country, and even from park to park within the same country. For instance, going on safari in East Africa (Kenya and Tanzania) is completely different from going on safari in Zimbabwe, Zambia and Botswana.

Simply watching wildlife anywhere in Africa is an experience in itself. However, more and more people are preferring to travel away from the crowds and wish to personally experience more from the safari than just seeing animals.

How can this be done? By choosing a safari that includes parks which are not crowded and afford the feeling of being more in the bush. Choose reserves that allow you to participate in activities that make you a more integral part of the safari, like walking and canoeing. Choose smaller camps and lodges that are unfenced, allowing wildlife to walk freely about the grounds.

Another excellent way to get the most out of your safari is to have a private safari arranged for you. A private safari immediately becomes *your safari*. You do not have to bow to the wishes of the majority of the group or the strictly set itinerary of group departures. You are basically free to do what you wish during the day (within reason) as long as your guide can get you to your camp or lodge before nightfall.

Depending on the park or reserve, safari activities might include day game drives, night game drives, walks, boat safaris, canoeing, kayaking, white-water rafting, ballooning, mountain climbing, fishing — the options are almost endless. See "Safari Activities" and the **Safari Activities Chart** which follow.

## DISPELLING MYTHS ABOUT TRAVEL ON THE DARK CONTINENT

Many prospective travelers to Africa seem to think that if they go on an African safari they may have to stay in mud or grass huts or little pup tents and eat strange foods. Nothing could be farther from the truth!

Almost all of the top parks and reserves covered in this guide have deluxe or first class (Class A or B by our grading system) lodges or camps (with private bathroom facilities) serving excellent food, specifically designed to cater to the discerning traveler's needs. Going on safari can be a very comfortable, fun-filled adventure!

Many prospective travelers to Africa have voiced their fear of being overwhelmed by mosquitoes and other insects, or the fear of encountering snakes on safari.

However, most travelers return pleasantly surprised, having found that insects and small snakes are a much greater problem in their own neighborhoods than on safari. In over 15 years of travel to Africa, I have only seen about five snakes — and I had to look for them!

The fact is, most safaris do not take place in the jungle, but on open savannah during the dry season when the insect populations are at a minimum. In addition, the best time to go on safari for most of the countries is during their winter, which is when many snakes hibernate. Also, many parks are located over 3,000 feet in altitude, resulting in cool to cold nights, further reducing the presence of any pests.

In any case, except for walking safaris, most all of your time in the bush will be spent in the safety of a vehicle or boat.

# ACCOMMODATION

There is a great variety of styles and levels of comfort in accommodation available in the major cities while on safari, ranging from basic huts to suites with private swimming pools. Options include hotels, lodges, small camps with chalets or bungalows, fixed tented camps and mobile tented safaris.

## CHOOSING ACCOMMODATION

The type of accommodation included in a tour of Africa will have a major influence on the type of experience and adventures you will have on safari.

An important factor to consider when choosing accommodation or a tour is the size of the lodge or camp. In general, guests receive more personal attention at smaller camps and lodges than larger ones. Large properties tend to stick to a set schedule while smaller properties are often more willing to amend their schedules according to the preferences of their guests. However, larger properties tend to be less expensive, making tours using the larger properties more affordable.

Many larger properties (especially in Kenya) are surrounded by electrical fences, allowing guests to move about as they please without fear of bumping into elephant or other wildlife. Travelers (including myself) who enjoy having wildlife roaming about camp should seek properties that are not fenced; these properties are best for travelers who want to experience living in the bush.

Most properties in Kenya and Tanzania have 75-200 beds, whereas most camps in Botswana, Zambia, and Zimbabwe have 16 or less.

## HOTELS

Many African cities such as Nairobi (Kenya), Harare (Zimbabwe), and Kigali (Rwanda) have four- and five-star (first class and deluxe) hotels comparable to anywhere in the

Typical deluxe fixed tented camp accommodation.

world, with air-conditioning and private facilities, swimming pools and one or more excellent restaurants and bars.

## LODGES

Lodges ranging from comfortable to deluxe (many have swimming pools) are located in or near most parks and reserves. Many lodges and camps are located in wildlife areas 3,000 feet or more above sea level, so air-conditioning is often not necessary.

## CAMPS

There is often confusion over the term *camp.* A camp often refers to lodging in chalets, bungalows or tents in a remote location. Camps range from very basic to garishly plush. Deluxe camps often have better service and food, and most certainly a truer safari atmosphere, than large lodges and hotels.

**Fixed tented camps** are permanent camps that are not moved. Besides generally having better food and service than lodges, guests of deluxe fixed tented camps have more of a "safari experience." One is less isolated from the environment than if he were staying in a lodge. **Mobile tented camps** are discussed below under "Types of Safaris."

## HOTEL CLASSIFICATIONS

Hotels are categorized as *Deluxe, First Class* and *Tourist Class*.

*DELUXE*: An excellent hotel, rooms with private bath, air-conditioning, more than one restaurant serving very good food, swimming pool, bars, lounges, room service — all the amenities of a four- or five-star international hotel.

*FIRST CLASS*: A very comfortable hotel, rooms with private bath, air-conditioning, at least one restaurant and bar; most have swimming pools.

*TOURIST CLASS*: Comfortable hotel with simple rooms with private bath, most with air-conditioning, restaurant, bar, and most have swimming pools.

## LODGE AND TENTED CAMP CLASSIFICATIONS

Lodges and tented camps are classified as *Class A-F*.

*CLASS A*: Deluxe lodge or tented camp, many with swimming pools, excellent food and service, large nicely appointed rooms or tents with private bath, comfortable beds and tasteful decor; lodges may have air-conditioning.

*CLASS A/B*: An excellent lodge or tented camp with very good food and service, many with swimming pools; rooms in lodge with private facilities; bathroom facilities in camps may be ensuite or a short walk from the chalet or tent.

The dining room of a typical thatched lodge.

*CLASS B*: A comfortable lodge or camp with good food and service, many with swimming pools. Rooms in lodges have private baths; most tents, chalets or bungalows have private bathrooms.

*CLASS B/C*: Most often a "Class B" property that is somewhat inconsistent with the quality of accommodation, food and service.

*CLASS C*: A simple lodge with private bathroom or tented camp, chalet or bungalow with private or shared facilities, fair food and service, or a "Class B" structure with fair to poor food or service.

*CLASS D*: A basic lodge or tented camp. Lodges, chalets, bungalows and tents seldom have private bathrooms, or a "Class C" structure with poor food or service.

*CLASS F*: Very basic lodge or tented camp without private bathrooms, often self-service (no restaurant).

## FOOD

Most international travelers are impressed with the quality of the food and drink served on their safari — especially on mobile tented safaris.

Excellent European cuisine along with interesting local dishes are served in the top hotels, lodges, camps and restaurants. French cuisine is served in Rwanda, Zaire, and Burundi, while British cuisine predominates in the other countries covered in this guide. Restaurants serving cuisine from all over the world may be found in the larger cities in Africa.

## TYPES OF SAFARIS

### LODGE AND PERMANENT CAMP SAFARIS

Lodge safaris are simply safaris using lodges or fixed camps for accommodation. Some safaris mix lodges with fixed tented camps, or camps with chalets or bungalows, providing a greater range of experience for their guests.

### MOBILE TENTED CAMP SAFARIS

Private mobile tented camp safaris are, in my opinion, one of the best ways to experience the bush. Group mobile tented safaris are also a great way of getting off the beaten track.

Having hippo grazing by your tent at night or elephant walking through your camp by day is an experience not to be missed! When under the guidance of a professional guide, this is not as dangerous as it might sound. Animals will almost never try to enter a closed tent unless tempted by the smell of food. If you keep the tent flaps closed at night, you are generally just as safe as if you were staying in a bungalow or chalet. So why not go where the excitement is!

Tanzania, Zimbabwe and Botswana are excellent countries for mobile tented safaris. These safaris are also available in Kenya and Zambia.

Mobile tented safaris range from deluxe to first class, midrange and budget (participation) safaris.

## Deluxe Mobile Tented Camp Safaris

Deluxe mobile tented camp safaris are the epitome of mobile safaris. Each tent has a private shower and toilet tent. Food and service are excellent. Camp attendants take care of everything, including bringing hot water for your shower. Camp is usually set in remote areas of parks and reserves, providing a true *Out Of Africa* experience. These safaris, however, are not cheap. For a party of four, the cost ranges from $500-$700 per person per day.

## First-Class Mobile Tented Camp Safaris

These are similar to the deluxe safaris in that each sleeping tent has a private toilet tent and shower tent. Food and service is also very good. The main difference is that the tents are a little smaller, yet very comfortable; less expensive tableware is used; and there are not quite as many staff. For a party of four, the cost is around $400 per person per day.

## Midrange Mobile Tented Camp Safaris

Comfortable (and less expensive) midrange mobile tented safaris are available in a number of countries. Like deluxe and first-class mobile tented safaris, camp staff take care of all the chores. The difference is that the tents are a bit smaller but are still large enough (in which) to stand. The food and service is very good, and guests from one to three sleeping tents may share one toilet tent and one shower tent with (hot water) facilities. For a party of four, the cost is usually under $300 per person per day.

A remote mobile tented camp showing sleeping tents and the dining tent.

## Budget (Participation) Mobile Tented Camp Safaris

On budget mobile tented safaris, participants are most often required to help with camp chores. Park campsites with basic (if any) facilities are often used.

The advantage is price. Budget camping safaris are almost always less expensive than lodge safaris. However, these are recommended only for the hardiest of travelers. Most participants are under thirty-five years of age. Hot showers are usually available most nights, but not all. The cost is usually under $175 per person per day.

## PRIVATE SAFARIS

For those who wish to avoid groups, a private safari is highly recommended for several reasons.

An itinerary can be specially designed according to the

kind of experience *YOU* want, visiting the parks and reserves *YOU* wish to see most, and traveling on dates that suit *YOU* best. You may spend your time doing what you wish to do rather than having to compromise with the group.

What few people realize is that, in many cases, a private safari need not cost more than one with a large group. In fact, I have sent many couples and small groups on private safaris for not much more (and sometimes less) than group departures with leading tour operators offering the same or similar itinerary.

If you find this difficult to believe, call or write me with what you have in mind, and I'll be happy to send you an itinerary (see page 481).

## SELF-DRIVE SAFARIS

In Africa, self-drive safaris are a viable option for general sightseeing in countries such as South Africa that have excellent road systems. However, self-drive safaris into wildlife parks and reserves are, in general, not a good idea for several reasons.

One major disadvantage of a self-drive safari is that one misses the information and experience a driver/guide can provide. A good guide is also an excellent game spotter and knows when and where to look for the animals you wish to see most. He can communicate with other guides to find out where the wildlife has most recently been seen. This also leaves you free to concentrate on photography and game viewing instead of the road and eliminates the anxiety of perhaps getting lost.

Self-drive safaris, especially ones requiring four-wheel-drive vehicles, are most often more expensive than joining a group safari. Petrol is generally several times the cost of what it is in the U.S.A. or Canada. Vehicle rental costs are high, especially since most have high mileage charges over and above the daily rental rate.

Finally, self-drive safaris by people without extensive experience in the bush can be dangerous. Lack of knowledge of wildlife and the bush can result in life-threatening situations. For instance, if a lion sees you out of your vehicle changing a tire, it may very well attack.

*Carnet de Passage* is required by most countries to take your own vehicle across borders without paying import duty or leaving a deposit with Customs; a *carnet* must be purchased before arrival.

I suggest you get an International Driver's License from your automobile association, as it is required by most of the countries covered in this book. Contact the tourist offices, consulates, or embassies of the countries in which you wish to drive for any additional requirements.

## SAFARI ACTIVITIES

Africa can be experienced in a myriad of exciting ways. What follows are a number of types of safari activities. For additional information, refer to the country mentioned.

## SAFARI VEHICLES

**Open vehicles** usually have two rows of elevated seats behind the driver's seat. There are no side or rear windows or permanent roof, providing unobstructed views in all directions and a feeling of being part of the environment instead of on the outside looking in. This is my favorite type of vehicle for viewing wildlife. Open vehicles are used in Botswana, Zambia, Zimbabwe, some reserves in Namibia, and private reserves in South Africa.

In **vehicles with roof hatches or pop-top roofs**, riders may stand up through the hatch for game viewing and photography. If the vehicle is full, riders usually must take turns using the hatches, making tours which guarantee window seats for every passenger (i.e., maximum of seven passengers in a nine-seat minivan) all the more attractive. These vehicles are used in Kenya and Tanzania.

Wildlife viewing, and especially photography, are more

# SAFARI ACTIVITIES

## VEHICLES - NIGHT GAME DRIVES - WALKING SAFARIS
## BOAT SAFARIS - CANOE SAFARIS

| COUNTRY | MAJOR PARK OR RESERVE | TYPE VEHICLE ALLOWED | | | NIGHT DRIVES | WALKING SAFARIS | BOAT SAFARIS | CANOE SAFARIS |
|---|---|---|---|---|---|---|---|---|
| | | OPEN | HATCHES | CLOSED | | | | |
| Botswana | Chobe | X | | | | | X | |
| | Moremi | X | | | | *1 | X | X |
| | Okavango Delta | X | | | | X | X | X |
| | Savuti | X | | | | | | |
| Kenya | Masai Mara | | X | | *1 | *1 | | |
| | Mount Kenya | | X | | | X | | |
| | Other Parks | | X | | | | | |
| Namibia | Etosha | | | X | | | | |
| Rwanda | Akagera | | X | | | | X | |
| | Volcano | | X | | | X | | |
| South Africa | Kalahari - Gemsbok | | | X | | | | |
| | Kruger | | | X | | | | |
| | Private Reserves | X | | | X | X | | |
| Tanzania | Selous, Rubondo Island | | X | | | X | X | |
| | Arusha, Gombe St. | | X | | | X | | |
| | Mahale Mts. | | X | | | X | X | |
| | Other Parks | | X | | | | | |
| Uganda | Murchison Falls | | X | | | | X | |
| | Queen Elizabeth N. P. | | X | | | | X | |
| | Kigezi Mountain Gorilla Reserve | | X | | | X | | |
| | Others | | X | | | | | |
| Zaire | Kahuzi - Biega, Bukima and Djomba Gorilla Sanctuary | | X | | | X | | |
| | Rwindi (Virunga) | | X | | | | | |
| | Ruwenzori Mountains | | X | | | X | | |
| Zambia | South Luangwa | X | | | X | X | | |
| Zimbabwe | Chizarira | X | | | | X | | |
| | Hwange | X | | | *1,*2 | *1,*2 | | |
| | Mana Pools | X | | | | X | X | X |
| | Matusadona | X | | | *1 | X | X | X |

*1: Activity is conducted on the outskirts of the park or reserve.

*2: Activity is conducted at Makalolo and Nemba Camps within Hwange National Park.

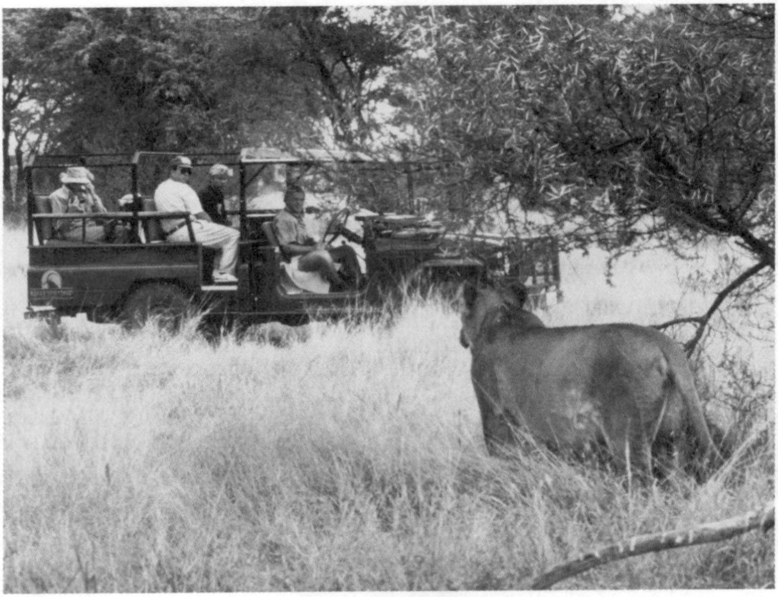

Game viewing by open vehicle.

Game viewing by land cruiser with roof hatches.

Game viewing vehicle with pop-top roof

difficult where **closed vehicles** are required. In South Africa (except private reserves) and the major parks in Namibia, closed vehicles are required.

## PHOTO SAFARIS

The term *photo safari* generally means any kind of safari *except* hunting safaris.

In its strictest sense, a photo safari is a safari escorted by a professional wildlife photographer, especially for the serious photographer. These safaris are mainly about learning wildlife photography and getting the best photos possible. These are recommended only for the serious shutter-bug.

Tracking rhino spoor (footprints) on a walking safari.

## WALKING SAFARIS

Walking safaris put one in closest touch with nature. Suddenly your senses come alive — every sight, sound and smell becomes intensely meaningful. Could that flash of bronze in the dense brush ahead be a lion? I wonder how long ago these rhino tracks were made? Can that herd of elephant ahead see or smell us approaching?

Accompanied by an armed wildlife expert, walking safaris last anywhere from a few hours to several days. The bush can be examined up close and at a slower pace, allowing more attention to its fascinating detail than on a safari by vehicle.

Participants can often approach quite closely to game, depending on the direction of the wind and the cover available. This is experiencing the excitement and adventure of the bush at its best. Zambia and Zimbabwe are the top countries for walking safaris. Walking is also available in some parts of Botswana, Tanzania, Kenya and South Africa.

## NIGHT GAME DRIVES

Night game drives open up a new world of adventure. Nocturnal animals, seldom if ever seen by day, are viewed with the aid of the vehicle's powerful search light. Bushbabies, night apes, leopard, civet, genet and many other species can be seen.

In addition to the chart which follows, night game drives are allowed and often conducted outside of many reserves, including the Masai Mara (Kenya), Hwange, and Matusadona National Parks (Zimbabwe).

## GORILLA SAFARIS

Gorilla trekking is one of the most exciting adventures one can have on the "dark continent" and is certainly one of the most exciting experiences of my life.

Mountain gorillas are best seen in Volcano National Park (Rwanda), Djomba Gorilla Sanctuary and Rumangabo (Bukima) Station (Zaire). Lowland gorillas have been habituated in Kahuzi-Biega National Park in Zaire. Permits for gorilla trekking are limited; gorilla safaris should be booked well in advance.

## BALLOON SAFARIS

At five-thirty in the morning, we were awakened by steaming hot coffee and tea brought to our bedsides by our private tentkeeper. We were off at six o'clock for a short game drive to where the hot-air balloons were being filled. Moments later we lifted above the plains of the Masai Mara for the ride of a lifetime.

Silently viewing game from the perfect vantage point, we brushed the tops of giant acacias for close-up views of birds' nests and baboons. Most animals took little notice, but somehow the hippos knew we were there. Maybe it was our shadow or the occasional firing of the burners necessary to keep us aloft.

Our return to earth was an event in itself. One hour and 15 minutes after lift-off, our pilot made a perfect crash landing. By the way, all landings are crash landings, so just follow your pilot's instructions and join in the fun.

Minutes later a champagne breakfast appeared on the open savannah within clear view of herds of wildebeest, buffalo, and zebra. Our return to camp was another exciting game drive, only a little bumpier than the trip out.

Hot-air balloon safaris are available in Kenya in the Masai Mara National Reserve, at Taita Hills near Tsavo West National Park, and in Serengeti National Park (Tanzania).

## BOAT/CANOE/KAYAK SAFARIS

Wildlife viewing by boat, canoe or kayak from rivers or lakes often allows one to approach wildlife closer than by vehicle. Game viewing by **boat** is available in Chobe National Park and the Okavango Delta (Botswana), Lake Kariba, and along Matusadona National Park (Zimbabwe) and the Zambezi River upstream from Victoria Falls (Zambia).

**Canoe safaris** from three to nine days are operated along the Zambezi River below Kariba Dam in Zimbabwe. Wildlife is best in the area along Mana Pools National Park. This is definitely one of my favorite adventures. In Zambia, canoe safaris are offered above Victoria Falls and below Kariba Dam.

Three-day/two-night **kayak** safaris are operated on the Zambezi River in Zambezi National Park upstream from Victoria Falls, Zimbabwe.

## WHITE-WATER RAFTING

For white-water enthusiasts and newcomers alike, the Zambezi River (Zambia/Zimbabwe) below Victoria Falls is one of the most challenging rivers in the world. Some rapids are *Class Five* — the highest class runable. Rafting safaris from one to seven days are available. No previous experience

Ballooning safaris are available in Kenya and Tanzania.

is required. Just hang on and have the time of your life! See the chapter on Zambia for more details.

## HORSEBACK SAFARIS

Game viewing by horseback is yet another intriguing way to experience the bush. Horseback safaris up to 16 days in length are conducted in Kenya. Half-day horseback safaris are available in Matobo National Park and Kyle Recreational Park (Zimbabwe).

Horseback riding outside of wildlife areas is offered in a number of areas, including Nyanga National Park and Victoria Falls (Zimbabwe) and Arusha (Tanzania).

## BIRD WATCHING

If you are not a bird watcher now, there's a good chance you will be converted before the end of your safari. Bird watching in Africa is almost beyond belief. Some countries have recorded over 1000 different species and some parks over 500.

The best time of the year for bird watching is November-March in most areas covered in this guide. However, bird watching is very good year-round.

Keen birders planning to visit southern Africa (Botswana, Lesotho, Namibia, South Africa, Swaziland, and Zimbabwe) will find *Newman's Birds Of South Africa* by Kenneth Newman invaluable. *Birds Of Eastern And Northern Africa* by C. W. Mackworth-Praed and C. H. B. Grant is excellent for eastern Africa.

## MOUNTAIN CLIMBING

Africa has mountains to challenge the tenderfoot and the expert as well. Mt. Kilimanjaro (Tanzania), 19,340 feet in altitude, is the highest mountain in Africa, followed by Mt. Kenya (Kenya) at 17,058 feet. The Ruwenzoris, or *Mountains Of The Moon* (Uganda/Zaire), are the highest mountain chain in Africa, rising to 16,794 feet. All of these mountains lie within a few degrees of the equator yet are snowcapped year-round. Hiking through fascinating and unique Afro-alpine vegetation found on all of these mountains gives one the feeling of being on another planet.

## SCUBA DIVING AND SNORKELING

Kenya, Tanzania, South Africa and Mauritius offer excellent coral reef diving in the warm waters of the Indian Ocean.

In Kenya, Malindi-Watamu Marine National Reserve is probably the best choice. For those willing to rough it, five-day dive trips on a live-aboard dhow are available from the southern Kenyan coast to Pemba Island (Tanzania).

The Natal coast of South Africa has excellent coral reefs, while the Southern Cape offers the ultimate underwater thrill of diving with great white sharks!

## FISHING

Some of the finest **deep-sea fishing** in the world is found in the Indian Ocean off the coast of Kenya, off Pemba and Mafia Islands (Tanzania), and off the island country of Mauritius.

**Freshwater fishing** for Nile perch (200+ pounds) and tigerfish (one of the best fighting fish in the world) is excellent in Lake Tanganyika (especially near Zambia), Lakes Turkana and Victoria (Kenya), and Lake Kariba (Zimbabwe). Trout fishing is very good in parks such as Nyanga (Zimbabwe) and the Aberdares (Kenya). Most freshwater fishing requires a license which can usually be obtained from your hotel, lodge or camp for a small fee.

## OTHER SAFARIS

Additional options for the special interest traveler include anthropology, archeology, art, backpacking, and camel safaris.

# COST OF A SAFARI

African currencies have been historically weak against the U.S. and Canadian dollars, making Africa an especially attractive destination when the value of the dollar is down against the currencies of Europe, the Far East, and other destinations overseas.

The cost per day is most dependent on how comfortably you wish to travel (the level of accommodation), type of transportation used, whether you're on a private safari or on a tour, and the destinations involved. Deluxe accommodations and transportation are normally more expensive in countries off the beaten track than in the more popular tourism spots.

For example, deluxe (Class A) safari camps in Botswana and Zimbabwe are often more expensive than Class A lodges in Kenya. Camps in Botswana and Zimbabwe cater to smaller groups and are generally situated in more remote locations, and charter aircraft are often used to reach them.

Transportation is more costly in Tanzania, for instance, than in South Africa because in Tanzania petrol is more expensive and poor roads give greater wear-and-tear on vehicles.

As in Europe and other parts of the world, general interest tours cost less than tours with more unique itineraries. Getting off the beaten track may dip a bit more into the wallet, but many travelers find it well worthwhile.

For current costs on package tours and tailor-made itineraries, contact The Africa Adventure Company (see page 481).

## LANGUAGE

English is widely spoken in all these countries except Burundi, Rwanda, and Zaire, where French is the international language.

*Travel Journal Africa* (see **Catalog**) has illustrations of 125 mammals, birds, reptiles and trees along with words and phrases in French, Swahili (Kenya, Tanzania), Shona (Zimbabwe), Tswana (Botswana), and Zulu (Southern Africa). Your guide will love it if you start naming the animals spotted in his native language!

## PHOTOGRAPHY

ASA 64 and 100 are best during the day when there is plenty of light. ASA 200-ASA 400 is often needed in early mornings and late afternoons, especially when using telephoto or zoom lenses. With very low light, use a flash or ASA 1000 or higher film.

Bring extra camera and flash batteries and plenty of film as film and batteries are very expensive and difficult to obtain in Africa. At least thirty rolls of film should be brought (per couple) for a two-week safari.

For wildlife photography, 200mm zoom lens is the smallest that should be used; 300mm zoom is preferable. A 500mm or larger lens is necessary for bird photography. A wide-angle lens (28-35mm) is great for scenic shots.

I prefer a 35mm camera with automatic and manual settings. The Minolta 7000i and 8000i have a fabulous automatic focusing feature which is invaluable when photographing moving animals. On my most recent safari, I took the 8000i body, 28-85mm and 100-300mm zoom lenses, and a 500mm mirror lens and was very satisfied with the results.

Consider bringing a small tripod to help steady your camera when shooting from the roof of your vehicle. Monopods (one-legged support) are also useful, especially on walking safaris.

Vehicle vibrations can cause blurry photos, so ask your guide to turn off the engine for those special shots. Protect lenses with UV filters. A polarizer helps cut glare and is especially effective when sky and water are in the photo. Store cameras and lenses in plastic bags to protect them from dust and humidity, and clean them regularly with lens paper or lens brushes.

If you bring a camcorder or video recorder, be sure to bring at least one extra battery pack, a charging unit and converter (Africa uses 220-240 volts). Batteries can usually be recharged at your lodge or camp while the generator is running.

Do *not* take photographs of airports, bridges, railway stations, government buildings, telecommunication installations and offices, military and police installations and personnel. You may have your camera confiscated and waste a lot of time having to explain why you were taking the photos in the first place.

## SAFARI TIPS

Read the **Safari Glossary** to become familiar with the terminology used in the bush. Once on safari, you will notice that when you ask people what animals they saw on their game drive, they might reply, "Elephant, lion, leopard and oryx," when in fact they saw several members of each species. This use of the singular form when more than one of that species was seen is common. However, one exception to this rule is saying *crocs* for *crocodile*. This form of "Safariese" will be used throughout this guide to help separate you from the amateur.

Obtain detailed maps of the countries you intend to visit. This will not only increase your awareness of the geography before and during your safari, but will better enable you to relate the story of your safari to family and friends upon your return. For a catalog of difficult-to-find maps of Africa, please see page 486.

It is often better to sit quietly at a few water holes than to rush around in an attempt to visit as many locations as possible. Don't just look for large game; there is an abundance of reptiles, amphibians, smaller mammals, birds, and insects that are often fascinating to observe. Do not disturb the animals. Remember, we are guests in their world.

Put your valuables in a safety deposit box at your lodge or hotel. Do not call out to a person, signaling with an index finger. This is insulting to most Africans. Instead, use four fingers with your palm facing downward.

Wear colors that blend in with your surroundings (brown, tan, light green or khaki). Do not wear perfume or cologne while game viewing. Wildlife can detect unnatural smells for miles and unnatural colors for hundreds of yards, making close approaches difficult.

The very few tourists who get hurt on safari are almost always those travelers who ignore the laws of nature and most probably the advice and warnings of their guides. Common sense is the rule.

Do not wade or swim in rivers, lakes or streams unless you know for certain they are free of crocodiles, hippos, and bilharzia (a disease). Fast-moving areas of rivers are often safe, but are still risky. Also, do not walk along the banks of rivers near dawn, dusk or at night. Those that do so may inadvertently cut off a hippo's path to its water hole, and the hippo may charge. Hippos are responsible for more human

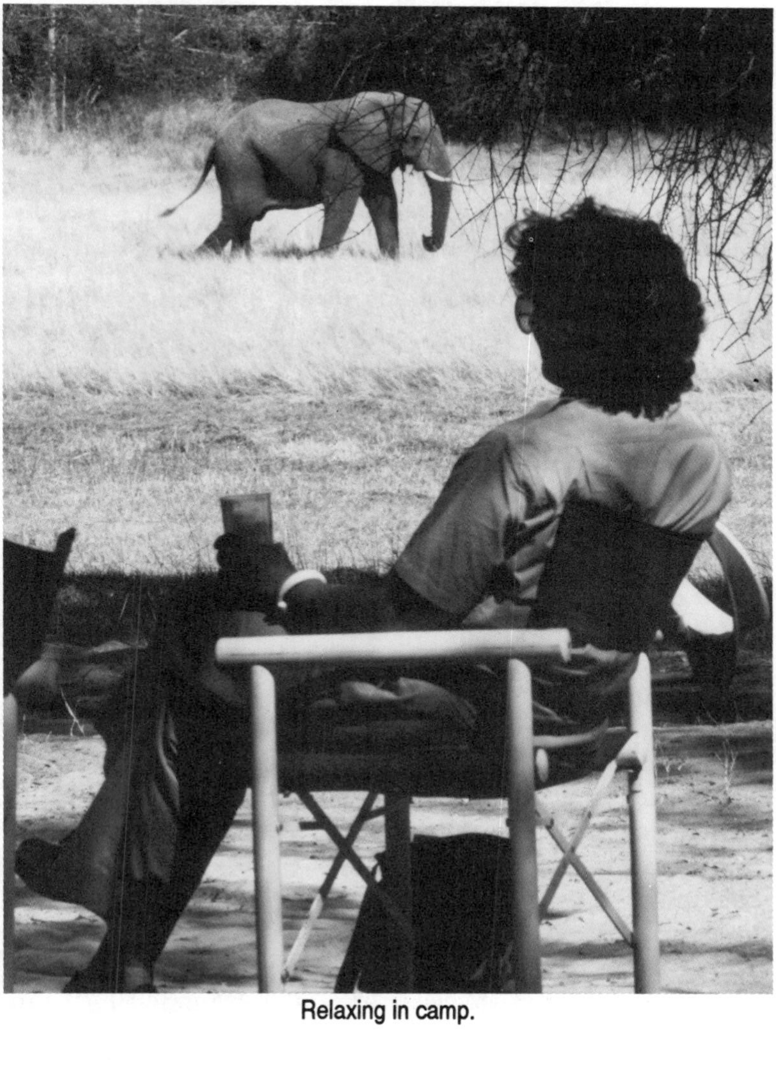

Relaxing in camp.

deaths in Africa than any other game animal, most often from this type of occurrence.

Wear closed-toed shoes or boots at night and also during the day if venturing out into the bush. Bring a flashlight and always have it with you at night.

Don't venture out of your lodge or camp without your guide, especially at night, dawn or dusk. Remember that wildlife is not confined to the parks and reserves in many countries.

Resist the temptation to jog in national parks, reserves or other areas where wildlife exists. To lion and other carnivores, we are just "meat on the hoof" like any other animal — only much slower and less capable of defending ourselves.

## WHAT TO WEAR — WHAT TO TAKE

Countries close to the equator (Burundi, Kenya, Rwanda, Tanzania, Uganda, and Zaire) have small differences in seasonal temperatures, with June-August being the coolest time of the year; the main factor affecting temperature is altitude.

Countries in southern Africa (Lesotho, Namibia, South Africa, Swaziland, Zambia, and Zimbabwe) have more pronounced seasons, often cold (sometimes freezing) in winter (June-August) and hot in summer (October-February).

Casual clothing is usually worn by day. Dresses for ladies and coats and ties for men are only required in top restaurants in Kenya, South Africa, Zimbabwe, and at the Mount Kenya Safari Club (Kenya). In some restaurants, gentlemen's coats are available on request.

Bring at least one camera and lots of film, binoculars, sun block, electric converter and adapter, a copy of *Travel Journal Africa,* alarm clock, insect repellent, brown, khaki or light green cotton clothing including at least two pairs of long pants and two long-sleeve shirts, wide-brimmed hat, rain gear, good walking shoes, flashlight and extra batteries, two pairs of sunglasses, two pairs of prescription glasses (one for contact-lens wearers) and a copy of the prescription, prescription drugs with a letter from your doctor verifying your need, medical summary from your doctor if medical problems exist, Band-aids (plasters), motion-sickness tablets, medicine for traveler's diarrhea, antimalarial prophylaxis, decongestant tablets, laxative, headache tablets, throat lozenges, antacid, and antibiotic ointment.

Each person going on safari should definitely have his own pair of binoculars. I am amazed at the number of Africa travelers who have paid thousands of dollars each for a game viewing safari, yet take with them a poor-quality pair of binoculars which limits the enjoyment of the primary function of the trip.

If your budget will allow, I suggest spending from $250 to $375 for a high quality pair of binoculars that could be used on subsequent Africa safaris and safaris to other continents, and possibly provide you with a lifetime of use. I recommend binoculars with 8 or 9 power, such as Steiner 8X30 or 9X40.

Leave your dress watch at home and buy an inexpensive (under U.S. $50) waterproof watch with a light and alarm. Do not wear or bring any camouflage or dark green clothing; these colors are reserved for the military.

For a more comprehensive packing list and trip organizer for your safari, obtain a copy of *Travel Journal Africa*. To obtain a catalog of valuable books, maps, binoculars and safari clothing, see page 486.

# WILDLIFE

## HABITATS

Animals are most often found in and nearby the habitats in which they feed or hunt. These habitats fall roughly into four categories — savannah, desert, wetlands and forest.

**Savannah** is a very broad term referring to dry land which can be open grasslands, grasslands dotted with trees, or wooded areas. Grazers (grasseaters) and carnivores (meateaters) adept at hunting in savannah are most easily found here. Some browsers (leafeaters) also make the savannah their home.

**Deserts** have little or no standing water and very sparse vegetation. Many desert animals do not drink at all but derive water only from the plants they eat and the condensation formed on them. Some savannah grazers and carnivores can be found in the desert.

African **forests** are thickly vegetated, often with grasses and shrubs growing to about ten feet in height, shorter trees 20-50 feet high, and a higher canopy reaching to 150 feet or more.

It is usually more difficult to spot animals in forests than in the other habitats. Many forest animals such as the elephant are more easily seen in open savannah areas. Forest herbivores (planteaters) are browsers, preferring to feed on the leaves of plants and fruits usually found in forests. Carnivores have adapted to a style of hunting where they can closely approach their prey under cover.

**Wetlands** consist of lakes, rivers and swamps which often are part of a larger savannah or forest habitat. Many rivers wind through savannah regions, providing a habitat within a habitat. Wetlands are good places not only to see wetland species, but also other habitat species that come there to drink.

## ANIMALS BY HABITAT

The animals listed below are classified according to the habitat where most of their time is spent. The animals are listed in order of size by weight.

### SAVANNAH

**Grazers:**
white rhino
eland
zebra
waterbuck
roan antelope
sable antelope
gemsbok (oryx)
topi
hartebeest
wildebeest
tsessebe
warthog
reedbuck
Grant's gazelle
impala
springbok
Thomson's gazelle
gerenuk
klipspringer
steenbok

**Grazers:**
giraffe
black rhino
kudu
dikdik

### FOREST

**Browsers:**
elephant
nyala
bongo
bushbuck
duiker

**Primates:**
gorilla
baboon
chimpanzee
colobus monkey
Syke's monkey

**Carnivores:**
leopard
serval
genet

### WETLANDS

**Browsers:**
hippopotamus
buffalo
sitatunga

## SAVANNAH

**Carnivores:**
lion
hyena
cheetah
African wild dog
jackal
mongoose
bat-eared fox

## WETLANDS

**Carnivores:**
crocodile
otter

## DESERTS

see Savannah grazers and carnivores above

# MAJOR WILDLIFE AREAS BY HABITAT

## Savannah Wildlife Areas

**Botswana**
Chobe
Savuti

**Kenya**
Amboseli
Masai Mara
Meru
Nairobi
Samburu
Tsavo

**Namibia**
Etosha

**Rwanda**
Akagera

**South Africa**
Kruger
Private Res.

**Tanzania**
Mikumi
Ngorongoro
Ruaha
Selous
Serengeti
Tarangire

**Zaire**
Virunga (Rwindi)

**Zambia**
Kafue
South Luangwa

**Zimbabwe**
Chizarira
Hwange
Matopos

## Forest Wildlife Areas

**Kenya**
Aberdare
Mt. Elgon
Mt. Kenya

**Rwanda**
Volcano

**Tanzania**
Arusha
Gombe Stream
Mahale Mountains
Mt. Kilimanjaro

**Zaire**
Kahuzi-Biega
Virunga (other)

## Wetland Wildlife Areas

**Botswana**
Moremi
Okavango Delta

**Kenya**
Lake Baringo
Lake Bogoria
Lake Naivasha
Lake Nakuru

**Namibia**
Eastern Caprivi

**Tanzania**
Lake Manyara

**Uganda**
Murchison Falls
Ruwenzori

**Zambia**
Kafue
Lochinvar

**Zimbabwe**
Mana Pools
Matusadona

## Desert Wildlife Areas

**Botswana**
Kalahari Desert

**Namibia**
Namib-Naukluft
Skeleton Coast

**South Africa**
Kalahari-Gemsbok

# WHAT WILDLIFE IS BEST SEEN WHERE?

| COUNTRY | MAJOR PARK OR RESERVE | Lion | Leopard | Cheetah | Elephant | Black Rhino | White Rhino | Hippo | Buffalo | Eland | Greater Kudu | Sable Antelope | Gemsbok/Oryx |
|---|---|---|---|---|---|---|---|---|---|---|---|---|---|
| Botswana | Chobe | B | D | C | A+ | / | F | A | A | D | B | B | F |
| | Moremi | B | C | C | A | / | F | A | B | F | C | B | / |
| | Okavango Delta | C | D | D | B | / | / | A+ | B | F | D | C | / |
| | Savuti | A | C | C | A | / | F | / | C | D | C | C | / |
| Kenya | Amboseli | B | C | B | A | B | / | A | A | C | / | / | C |
| | Masai Mara | A | B | B | A | B | / | A | A | B | / | / | / |
| | Samburu | B | B[1] | C | A | D | / | / | A | B | / | / | A |
| | Tsavo | B | D | C | A | D | / | B | A | C | / | / | C |
| Namibia | Etosha | B | C | B | A | B | / | / | / | B | B | / | A |
| S. Africa | Kruger | B | C | B | A | C | B | A | A | C | B | C | / |
| | Private Reserves | B | A[2] | B | A | C | A | A | A | C | B | C | / |
| Tanzania | Lake Manyara | B | D | D | A | D | / | A+ | A | / | / | / | / |
| | Ngorongoro | A | C | B | A | A | / | A | A | B | / | / | B[3] |
| | Serengeti | A | B | A | B | D | / | B | A | B | / | / | B |
| | Tarangire | A | C | B | A+ | D | / | B | B | B | / | / | A |
| Zambia | S. Luangwa | B | A[2] | F | A+ | F | / | A | A | C | B | F | / |
| Zimbabwe | Chizarira | B | C | F | B | B[4] | / | / | B | D | B | D | / |
| | Hwange | B | C | B | A | C | B | C | A | C | B | A | F |
| | Mana Pools | B | B | F | A | F | / | A+ | A | B | B | F | / |
| | Matusadona | B | C | / | A | B[4] | / | A | A+ | / | B | F | / |

A+ - Best reserves
A - Almost always seen (seen on almost all game drives)
B - Frequently seen (usually seen on every two - four game drives)
C - Occasionally seen (seen every one - two weeks)
D - Seldom seen (seen every two - four weeks)
F - Present but almost never seen
/ - Not seen in this reserve
[1] At lodges that bait for leopard
[2] On night game drives
[3] In Ngorongoro Conservation Area near Serengeti National Park
[4] Seen more often on walks than on game drives

The major parks and reserves listed above in the **Wildlife Areas By Habitat** chart are classified according to their most dominant habitat. Wildlife in the **Animals By Habitat** chart is classified by the most dominant habitat. Use the **What Wildlife Is Best Seen Where** chart as a guide in finding the major parks and reserves that are most likely to have the animals you are most interested in seeing on safari.

Many of these wildlife areas are composed of more than one habitat, so consult the text of this book for in-depth descriptions. Keep in mind that savannah and forest animals may visit wetland habitats to drink and that many forest animals are more easily seen on the open savannah.

A well-rounded safari includes visits to several types of habitats and parks, giving the visitor an overall picture of wildlife and ecosystems.

## WHEN'S THE BEST TIME TO GO?

The **When's The Best Time To Go?** chart shows at a glance when to go to see wildlife in the countries, parks and reserves of your choice. Alternatively, the chart shows the best places to go in the month(s) in which your vacation is planned. In other words, how to be in the right place at the right time.

For example, your vacation is in February and your primary interest is game viewing on a photographic safari. Find the countries on the chart in which game viewing is "excellent," "good," or "fair" in February. Turn to the respective country chapters for additional information and choose the ones that intrigue you the most. Use this chart as a general guideline as conditions vary from year to year.

Timing can make a world of difference. For example, Hwange National Park in Zimbabwe is well-known for its population of over 25,000 elephant. I once spent Christmas there (during the rainy season), and we didn't see one elephant. But during the dry season, they're everywhere.

In most cases the best game viewing, as exhibited on the chart, also corresponds to the dry season. Wildlife concen-

# AFRICA'S TOP WILDLIFE RESERVES

## WHEN'S THE BEST TIME TO GO?

A - EXCELLENT B - GOOD C - FAIR D - POOR X - CLOSED

| COUNTRY | PARK/RESERVE | JAN | FEB | MAR | APR | MAY | JUN | JUL | AUG | SEP | OCT | NOV | DEC |
|---|---|---|---|---|---|---|---|---|---|---|---|---|---|
| BOTSWANA | MOREMI AND OKAVANGO DELTA | D | D | C | C | B | B | A | A | A | A | B | C |
| | SAVUTI | C | C | B | A | B | B | A | A | A | B | B | C |
| | CHOBE | D | D | C | C | B | B | A | A | A | A | C | C |
| | NXAI PAN | A | A | A | A | B | B | C | D | D | D | B | A |
| | MAKGADIKGADI | B | A | A | A | B | B | C | D | D | D | C | B |
| KENYA | AMBOSELI | A | A | A | C | C | B | A | A | A | A | B | B |
| | TSAVO | B | B | B | C | C | C | A | A | A | C | C | B |
| | MASAI MARA | A | A | A | B | C | B | A | A | A | B | B | B |
| | ABERDARES & MERU | A | A | B | C | C | B | A | A | A | B | C | A |
| | SAMBURU, BUFALLO SPRINGS & SHABA | A | A | A | B | B | B | A | A | A | B | B | A |
| NAMIBIA | ETOSHA | D | D | D | C | C | B | A | A | A | A | C | C |
| RWANDA | AKAGERA | D | D | D | D | C | B | A | A | A | B | C | C |
| SOUTH AFRICA | KRUGER AND PRIVATE RESERVES | D | D | D | D | C | B | A | A | A | B | C | C |
| TANZANIA | LAKE MANYARA | A | A | A | C | C | B | A | A | A | A | B | B |
| | NGORONGORO | A | A | A | B | B | A | A | A | A | A | B | A |
| | SERENGETI (SOUTHEASTERN) | A | A | A | A | A | B | C | C | C | C | B | A |
| | SERENGETI (NORTH & NORTHWEST) | C | C | C | C | C | B | A | A | A | A | B | C |
| | TARANGIRE | C | C | C | C | C | B | A | A | A | A | B | C |
| | SELOUS & RUAHA | D | D | D | D | D | C | A | A | A | A | C | D |
| ZAIRE | VIRUNGA (RWINDI) | A | A | B | D | D | B | A | A | A | B | C | B |
| ZAMBIA | SOUTH LUANGWA (NORTHERN PART) | X | X | X | X | X | B | A | A | A | A | X | X |
| | SOUTH LUANGWA (CENTRAL) | C | C | C | B | B | B | A | A | A | A | B | B |
| ZIMBABWE | CHIZARIRA | D | D | D | D | C | B | A | A | A | A | C | D |
| | HWANGE | D | D | D | C | C | B | A | A | A | B | B | C |
| | MATUSADONA | C | C | C | C | C | B | A | A | A | A | B | B |
| | MANA POOLS | D | D | D | D | C | B | A | A | A | A | C | D |

COMMENTS:

trates around water holes and rivers, and vegetation is less dense than in the wet season, making game easier to find. There are, however, exceptions. For instance, the Serengeti migration often begins at the height of the rains in Tanzania.

During the rainy season the land is often luxuriously green, the air clear. People interested in scenery or with dust allergies may wish to plan their visits shortly after the rains are predicted to have started or soon after the rains are predicted to have stopped. Game is more difficult to find, but there are usually fewer travelers in the parks and reserves.

Most reserves in Africa are simply heaven for bird watchers. The best times for bird watching (usually November-March) are often the opposite of the best times for big game viewing. Bird watching, however, is good year-round in many regions.

Generally speaking, game viewing is best in Kenya and Tanzania mid-December-March and July-September, while the best game viewing in Zimbabwe, Zambia, Botswana and South Africa is June-October.

# AFRICA'S TOP WILDLIFE COUNTRIES

# BOTSWANA

## THE ELEPHANT'S TRUNK

Watching a herd of elephant using their trunks can be a rewarding experience for hours, as this fascinating organ serves many uses. The trunk is a combination of upper lip and nose with the nostrils beginning at the tip and running the entire length. The trunk possesses thousands of muscles, and the tip of the trunk is covered by tiny hairs.

Used as a smelling tool, the matriarchal elephant may hold her trunk up in the air, trying to pick up the scent in the wind of a nearby elephant herd. When the two groups come together, the elephants softly entwine their trunks, caress each other gently, and place the trunk in each other's mouths as a greeting.

During feeding, trunks will first touch the object and then are used to pluck leaves, tufts of grass and branches, shake fruit off trees, tug at roots, or strip tree barks. A foot may gently nudge away the roots of stubborn grass before the trunks swish and flap the soil off the grass and delicately place the food in the small mouth for chewing.

Air will be expelled through the trunk as a trumpet and may be used to chastise a playful calf, to greet another elephant, or as a display of defense.

Young calves may clumsily trip over their trunks, too young to control the muscles, suck the tip like a thumb, but best of all, use the trunk to enjoy the daily visit to a water hole. Water is drawn up the trunk at about seven liters per trunkful, and this is done several times to drink their fill of about 200 liters of water. They will also use water to shower and cool off in the spray. They then might finish with a dust bath by sucking in the dust and blowing it all over themselves.

It is a relief to see sleeping elephant resting their trunks over the tip of one of their tusks after all those muscles have been put to work smelling, touching, feeding, drinking, and talking.

# BOTSWANA

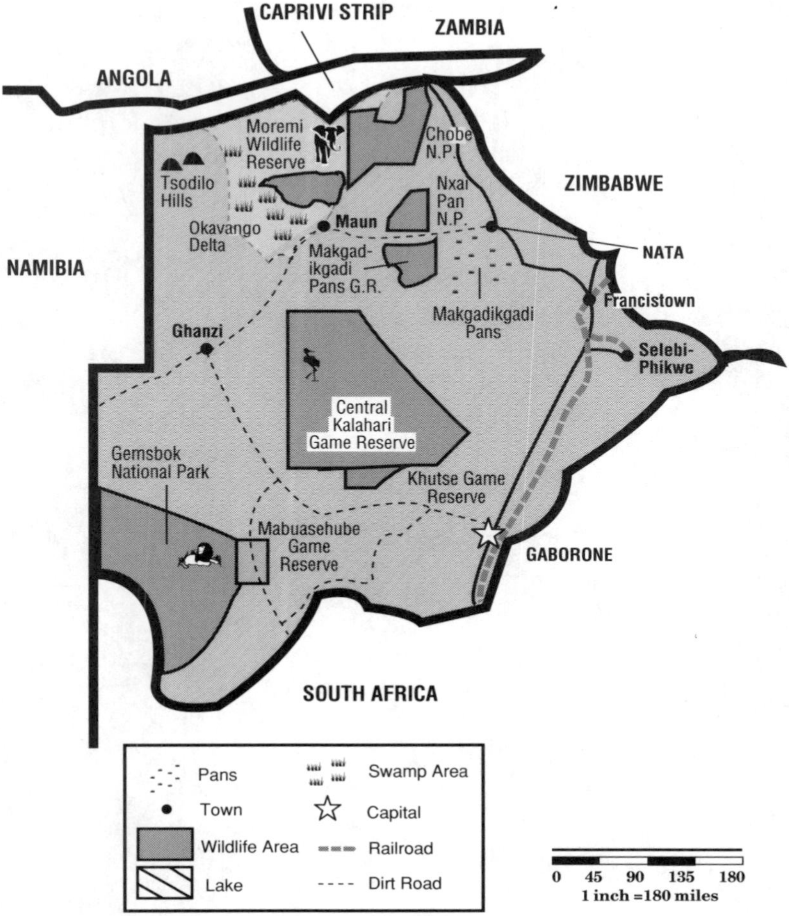


FACTS AT A GLANCE

| | |
|---|---|
| AREA: | 224,606 SQUARE MILES |
| APPROXIMATE SIZE: | TEXAS OR FRANCE |
| POPULATION: | 1.2 MILLION (1992 EST.) |
| CAPITAL: | GABORONE (POP. EST. 125,000) |
| OFFICIAL LANGUAGE: | ENGLISH: SETSWANA IS THE NATIONAL LANGUAGE, ENGLISH IS WIDELY SPOKEN |

# BOTSWANA

The best-selling book, *The Cry Of The Kalahari*, and the hilarious feature films *The Gods Must Be Crazy (I and II)* have assisted Botswana in gaining international recognition as a top safari destination.

More than four-fifths of the country is covered by the Kalahari sands, scrub savannah and grasslands. The land is basically flat with a mean elevation of 3280 feet. Over 85 percent of the population is concentrated near the better water resources in the eastern part of the country.

The Kalahari Desert is not a barren desert of rolling dunes as one might imagine. It has scattered grasslands, bush, shrub and tree savannah, dry river beds, and occasional rocky outcrops.

The "Pula" is Botswana's unit of currency, and also the Setswana word for rain, which is so critical to this country's wealth and survival. The rainy season is December-March, with the heaviest rains in January and February. Winter brings almost cloudless skies. January (summer) temperatures range from an average maximum of 92° F. to an average minimum of 64° F. July (winter) temperatures range from an average maximum of 72° F. to an average minimum of 42° F. Frost occasionally occurs in midwinter.

The San, Basarwa, or Bushmen were the first inhabitants of the area and may have come to southern Africa 30,000 years ago. Most of the estimated 60,000 Bushmen live in what is now Botswana and Namibia. Their language uses "clicking" sounds, distinguishing it from Bantu and most other languages in the world.

Traditionally, Bushmen have been nomadic hunter-gatherers, but today only a few thousand live this kind of existence in the Kalahari. Men hunt with poisoned arrows and spears while women use sticks to dig up roots and gather other food for the group.

Bushmen are unique in that they distribute wealth equally among the members of the group, share in the day-to-day aspects of life, and believe they are not superior to their environment and must live in harmony with it.

The Sotho-Tswana group of people comprise over half of the country's population and speak the Setswana language. The Batswana prefer to live in large, densely populated villages. Cattle are the most important sign of wealth and prestige. Ancestor worship was the chief form of religion until missionaries arrived in 1816 and converted large numbers of Batswana to Christianity.

Bechuanaland became a protectorate of the British Empire on September 30, 1885, and became the independent country of Botswana on September 30, 1966.

Today, very few of the people dress in their traditional costume except for special celebrations. However, for many Batswana, tribal customs are still important in day-to-day life. English is spoken by most of the people, and especially by the youth.

Botswana has a multiparty democracy and is one of the most economically successful and politically stable countries on the continent. Diamonds are Botswana's greatest foreign exchange earner, followed by cattle (there are three times as many cattle in Botswana as people), copper-nickel matte, and tourism.

# WILDLIFE AND WILDLIFE AREAS

As far as wildlife is concerned, Botswana is one of Africa's best-kept secrets. National parks and reserves cover 17 percent of the country's area — one of the highest percentages of any country in the world.

Botswana's combination of very good game, uncrowded reserves, excellent small camps (most cater to 16 or less guests), and the use of open vehicles for game viewing is difficult to beat.

The four main reserve areas most often visited by international tourists are all in northern Botswana. These are the Okavango Delta, Moremi Wildlife Reserve, the Savuti (southwestern part of Chobe National Park), and the Serondela region in the northeastern part of Chobe National Park near Kasane. The latter three are Botswana's best reserves for seeing big game.

As these four regions are distinct in character, a well-rounded wildlife safari to Botswana should include two to three days in each region (if time allows).

Chobe National Park and Moremi Wildlife Reserve rank as two of the best wildlife areas in Africa and fall easily within the top ten. The Okavango Delta is the largest inland delta in the world. This "water in the desert" phenomenon has created a unique and fascinating ecosystem well worth exploring.

Generally speaking, game viewing for the Okavango Delta, Chobe and Moremi is best in the dry winter season (June-October) and poorest December-February during the hot, rainy season.

In the dry season, wildlife is concentrated near the swamps and along the rivers. After the first rains, much of the wildlife ventures far into the interior.

Calving season throughout the country is November-February during the rainy season. Fishing for tigerfish, bream, barbel and pike is very good.

Other northern attractions include Nxai Pan National Park and Makgadikgadi Pans Game Reserve. Game viewing in Nxai Pan is best in the wet summer season (November-April), and Makgadikgadi Pans is best January-April. Reserves in the south are at times excellent but are seldom visited by international travelers.

Most camps are serviced by small aircraft, allowing visitors to minimize time spent on bumpy roads between reserves and maximize time viewing wildlife and a variety of other activities the country has to offer.

Game viewing by air is usually quite fruitful. On one flight from the Savuti to the Okavango Delta, we spotted four large herds of elephant, among numerous other species. Most charter flights have weight limits of 22-30 pounds per person, so bring only what you need.

First-class (full service) and budget (participatory) mobile tented safaris are less expensive per day than flying safaris and are another excellent way to experience the bush. Deluxe mobile tented camp safaris are also available.

The Wildlife Department runs the parks. Driving in the parks is not allowed at night. Camping is allowed at designated spots. Many lodges and camps close January-February.

## THE NORTH

### MAUN

A dusty little town situated at the southeastern tip of the Okavango Delta, Maun is the safari center of the country's most important tourist region. Many travelers fly into Maun to join a safari. Others begin their safari at Victoria Falls (Zimbabwe) and end up in Maun.

The Duck Inn is a favorite meeting place in town. Within walking distance from the airport, this is a good place to have a drink or meal and meet the locals. The bar at Riley's Hotel is another good spot.

Maps of the Okavango Delta/Moremi Wildlife Reserve and Chobe National Park, books and souvenirs are available from shops a short walk from the airport.

ACCOMMODATION - FIRST CLASS: * *Riley's Hotel* is the best place to stay in Maun. The hotel has air-conditioned rooms with ensuite facilities, popular bar and restaurant.

TOURIST CLASS: * *Island Safari Lodge* is located nine miles north of town on the western bank of the Thamalakane River and has brick and thatch bungalows with private facilities, campsites, swimming pool, bar and restaurant. * *Crocodile Camp* is located eight miles north of Maun on a sandy road (four-wheel-drive vehicle recommended) on the banks of the Thamalakane River. Chalets with ensuite facilities and camp sites are available.

## THE OKAVANGO DELTA

The Okavango, the largest inland delta in the world, covers over 4000 square miles and is in itself a unique and fascinating ecosystem. Instead of finding its way to the ocean as most rivers do, the Okavango River fans out into a vast system of thousands of waterways, separated by innumerable islands, to eventually disappear into the Kalahari sands.

The Okavango, an ornithologist's and botanist's dream come true, is beautifully presented in Peter Johnson and Anthony Bannister's book, *Okavango: Sea Of Land, Land Of Water* (Struik Publishers), and *Okavango: Jewel Of The Kalahari* by Karen Ross (Macmillan Publishing Co.).

Game viewing for the larger land mammal species should not be your main reason for visiting the Okavango. Big game exists in the delta, but is less commonly seen than in Chobe. The main reason for visiting the Okavango should be to explore the wonder of this inland delta, to enjoy the primordial silence, the unusual flora, the birdlife, hippo, crocs, and excellent fishing.

However, this is not to say that large land mammals are not encountered in the delta. Large herds of buffalo and a variety of antelope are often seen; lion and other predators are occasionally encountered. Game viewing is actually quite good on Chief's Island and the outlying areas of the delta during the cooler months (June-September) when the water is high.

Crocodiles are most heavily concentrated in the larger waterways and in the northern part of the delta where there is permanent deep water. However, crocs are found throughout the delta.

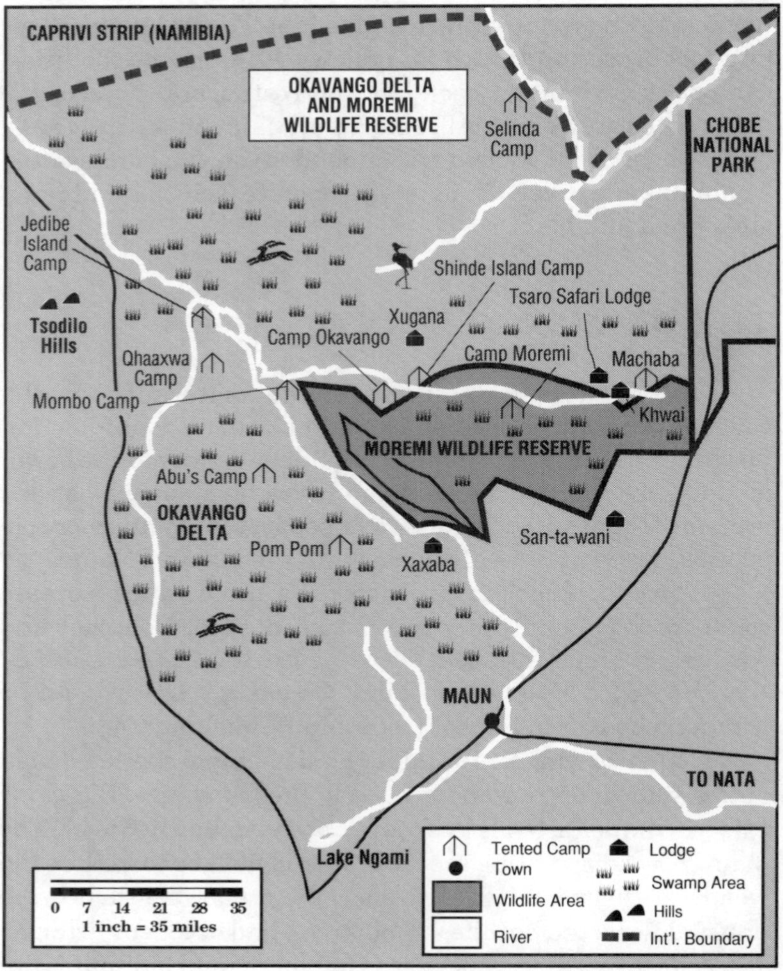


Mother nature must have smiled on this region, for the delta waters are highest during the dry season, since it takes six months for the rainy season flood waters to travel from their source in the Angolan highlands to the delta.

Most visitors reach the camps in the Okavango by small aircraft. Flying into the delta gives one an overall perspective of the swamp and is an adventure in itself. Game can be easily spotted and photographed from the air.

Mokoro Trail through the Okavango Delta.

A 150-mile-long buffalo fence has been constructed to keep cattle from the swamp: therefore, little game is found on the Maun (southern) side of the fence.

Calling the Okavango a "swamp" is a misnomer, since the waters are very clear. This is mainly due to the fact that there is only about a 200-foot drop in altitude over 150 miles from the top to the bottom of the delta. The water flows gradually and therefore carries very little sediment. Many people drink directly from the delta waters. Apparently the desert sands filter out most of the impurities. Little bilharzia exists in the area.

An excellent way to experience the Okavango is by mokoro (dugout canoe). Traveling by mokoro allows you to become a part of the environment. Sitting inches from the waterline, thoughts of angry hippos or hungry crocodiles overturning your boat cross your mind, but soon pass away with assurances from your guide and the peacefulness of this pristine environment.

Patterns of gold are created from the reflection of papyrus on the still waters of the narrow channels at early morning and late afternoon. You sometimes pass through channels that often appear to be narrower than the boat itself. Silence is broken only by the ngashi (boatman's pole) penetrating and leaving the water, by the cries of countless birds, and the movement of mostly unseen game along the delta's banks. Tiny white bell frogs chime to some unknown melody. Sunsets with rosy-pink clouds reflected in the waters are too beautiful for words. Life slows to a regenerative pace. This relaxed form of adventure and exploration is difficult to match anywhere in the world.

On one occasion, I tried poling our canoe across a small lagoon. My guide was right. It's definitely not as easy as it looks!

Guided excursions, using mekoro (plural for mokoro), canoes or small motor boats, that range in length from a few hours to a full day are offered by many camps in the delta. Canoes are larger and therefore a little more comfortable; mekoro harmonize better with the natural surroundings. Mokoro trips for two or more days are available, where you camp on remote islands in the delta. Activities include mokoro excursions, nature walks, bird watching, and fishing on request. Motor boats allow you to visit more distant attractions and must be used where the water is too deep to pole a mokoro or canoe and for fishing.

The Okavango has possibly the highest concentration of fish eagles in the world. On numerous occasions our guide waved a fish in the air and called to a fish eagle perched high in a tree over a half mile away, then tossed the fish into the water about 30 feet from the boat. Like magic, the eagle dived down at full speed and plucked the fish from the water. You must be fast with a camera to catch that on film!

Other bird species we spotted on a recent visit included the coppery-tailed coucal, purple heron, striped kingfisher, Meyer's parrot, black-collared barbet, yellow-fronted tinker barbet, hamerkop, red-billed woodhoopoe, saddle-billed stork, Dickenson's kestrel, little spotted eagle, grey lourie, swallow-tailed bee-eater, carmine bee-eater, slaty egret, little egret, reed cormorant, green-backed heron, goliath heron, blacksmith plover, pied kingfisher, yellow-billed kite, western banded snake eagle, African darter and African jacana.

Speeding along one afternoon in a small motorboat, we

drove right by an eight-foot-long crocodile. We went back for a closer look and discovered it was fast asleep. We maneuvered the boat within five feet of it, and it still didn't wake up — and I'm glad it didn't!

On a canoe trip we spotted an elusive sitatunga running through the reeds. Later on a short walk, we saw impala and red lechwe.

The islands in the delta are thought to have been made over the eons by termite mounds. Because of the cement-like qualities of termite mounds, these mounds are dug up and used to build airstrips and elevated paths in camps. Meanwhile, diamond prospectors inspect termite mounds closely. Since dirt is brought up from quite a depth, it provides them with easily accessible core samples.

Fishing in the Okavango is best in the northwestern part of the delta. The Okavango River above the delta is too heavily fished. The best time of the year for catching tigerfish is October and November. For barbel, the best time is the end of September through October when the barbel are running (migrating). Overall, the best time for fishing is September-March.

In the extreme western part of the delta is a natural floating island which bounces you along as it gives way under your feet. The island, predominantly made of a thick layer of reeds and papyrus, is strong enough to support most humans. Activities in the Okavango include travel by mokoro or canoe, motor boat rides, fishing, walks on islands, and game drives. Where there is access by land, a four-wheel-drive vehicle is necessary.

Elephant-back safaris on African elephants are a new and unique way of experiencing the bush. Guests fly to Abu's Camp to join Abu, the lead elephant, along with his family, Bennie, Kathy and seven babies on safari for six days.

If you wish to visit Tsodilo Hills [see below] to see the Bushmen and rock paintings, consider making reservations in advance so you may fly there from your camp in the Okavango.

ACCOMMODATION - CLASS A: * *Xugana Game Lodge*, situated under large shade trees on the banks of one of the delta's largest lagoons in the northeastern Okavango, has

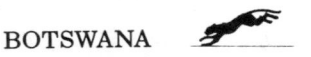

On elephant back -- a unique safari in Botswana.

eight reed chalets built on stilts (16 beds) with ensuite facilities and swimming pool. Xugana offers boat rides, mokoro trips from a few hours to several days in length, walks and excellent fishing.

CLASS A/B: * *Jedibe Island Camp* is located in the heart of the permanent waters of the delta — an excellent area for mokoro excursions and boat trips on the larger waterways and lagoons, walks, fishing and bird watching. Guests are accommodated in eight large tents (16 beds) with private facilities nearby. * *Camp Okavango* is a 12-bed tented camp in the eastern delta. Emphasis is placed on a "luxury in the bush" experience. The tents are plushly decorated with open-roofed private facilities about 20 feet away. Activities include canoe safaris, boat trips, walks and bird watching. * *Shinde Island Camp* is a small camp 45 minutes by boat from the airstrip, with seven deluxe tents (14 beds) with open-roofed shower and toilet facilities placed a few feet behind each tent, and a small swimming pool. Activities include mokoro trips, boat rides, fishing, walks, and game drives. * *Pom Pom* has seven deluxe tents (14 beds) overlooking a lagoon in the central delta and a small swimming pool. Activities include game drives, walks, and mokoro rides. * *Abu's Camp* is a ten-bed deluxe tented camp with private facilities from which the elephant-back safaris are operated. Mokoro rides, walks and game drives by vehicle are also offered. * *Selinda Camp* is a six-bed tented camp with private facilities near the Chobe/ Linyanti River system north of the Okavango Delta.

CLASS B: * *Qhaaxwa Camp* is a tented camp (16 beds) situated on the edge of a large lagoon under shady trees in the extreme western part of the delta. Boat rides, walks, bird watching, fishing and excursions to the "floating island" are offered. * *Xaxaba Camp* is situated in the delta west of Chief's Island and has ten reed and thatch chalets with private facilities. Activities include mokoro rides, walks, bird watching and sundowner cruises.

## TSODILO HILLS

Over 2700 Bushmen paintings are scattered through the rocky outcrops of Tsodilo Hills, one of the last places in Botswana where Bushmen can be readily found. The largest of the four hills rises 1000 feet above the surrounding plain. Archaeological evidence indicates that these hills may have been inhabited as long as 30,000 years ago.

Located west of the Okavango Delta, Tsodilo Hills is accessible by a flight from Maun or from safari camps in northern Botswana, or a very long and rough day's ride from Maun by four-wheel-drive vehicle. There are no facilities, so travelers must be totally self-sufficient. Unfortunately, this site has become a bit touristic, so don't expect to see Bushmen living as they did thousands of years ago. However, the rock paintings are well worth a visit. Please do not drink anything in the presence of Bushmen — water is scarce.

ACCOMMODATION: None.

## MOREMI WILDLIFE RESERVE

Moremi is the most diversified of all the Botswana parks in terms of wildlife and scenery, and many people feel it is the most beautiful. Located in the northeastern part of the Okavango Delta, Moremi contains over 1160 square miles of permanent swamps, islands, floodplains, forests and dry land.

In the floodplains reedbuck, common waterbuck, lechwe, tsessebe, ostrich, sable and roan antelope, crocodile, hippo and otter can be found. In the riparian forest you may spot elephant, greater kudu, Southern giraffe, impala, buffalo, Burchell's zebra, along with such predators as lion, leopard, wild dog, ratel (honey badger), spotted hyena, and very rarely, rhino.

Black-backed and side-striped jackals are often seen in the riparian forest as well as in the floodplain. Seldom-seen species include pangolin, bat-eared fox, porcupine and hedgehog.

On a morning game drive, we saw two herds of sable antelope, elephant, greater kudu, tsessebe, impala and Burchell's zebra. On another game drive we spotted seven lion, cheetah, bat-eared fox, and several species of antelope.

That afternoon we spotted four young tsessebe standing alone under a tree. We approached within about 50 feet of them, but they still held their ground. Shortly afterwards, a herd of adult tsessebe came within about 100 feet of us and stopped. The two groups began communicating, using clicking sounds. A female ran from the adult herd to the juveniles, then ran off into the bush with what we guessed was her calf. A second female did the same thing, followed by two other females which took away the last two juveniles. It was a charming sight of mothers evidently collecting their children.

Elephant and buffalo are the only large animals that migrate. After the rains have begun, they move northward to the area between Moremi and the Kwando-Linyanti River systems. Other wildlife may move to the periphery of, or just outside, the reserve.

In the bush it is not always the larger animal, but more often the more aggressive one that gets his way. While on a game drive in Moremi, we experienced a perfect example of this. A lone hippopotamus chased an entire herd of over 20 elephant out of "its" water hole. Astounding!

Moremi is an ornithologist's delight. Fish eagles, kingfishers and bee-eaters abound. Other bird species include parrots, shrikes, egrets, jacanas, pelicans, hornbills, herons, saddle-billed storks, yellow-billed oxpeckers, wattled cranes, reed cormorant, spur-winged goose, long-tailed shrike and flocks of thousands of red-billed quelea which fly together in a sphere like a great spotted flying ball.

Moremi is open year-round; however, some areas may be temporarily closed due to heavy rains or floods. Four-wheel-drive vehicles are necessary. The South Gate is about 62 miles north of Maun.

ACCOMMODATION - CLASS A: * *Mombo Camp* is situated near the northern tip of Chief's Island where the savannah meets the Okavango. Big game is plentiful, including lion which are often sighted. Accommodation is in seven large tents and one chalet — all with ensuite facilities (16 beds total). Activities include day and night game drives, walking safaris, fishing and bird watching. * *Tsaro Lodge* offers accommodation in eight thatched bungalows (16 beds) with ensuite facilities and swimming pool. Activities include game drives and walks outside the reserve.

CLASS A/B: * *Camp Moremi* is a 12-bed deluxe tented camp located within the reserve, with an elevated bar and dining room overlooking Xakanaxa Lagoon. Private facilities are situated a short walk behind each tent. Game drives are offered. * *Machaba Camp* has seven large tents (14 beds) with ensuite facilities and a small swimming pool. The camp offers day and night game drives, fishing and walks outside the reserve.

CLASS B: * *Xakanaxa Camp* is a 16-bed tented camp with separate facilities located within the park, overlooking the Xakanaxa Lagoon. Game drives and boat trips are offered. * *Khwai River Lodge* has comfortable brick and thatched bandas with ensuite facilities (26 beds) and swimming pool. The camp offers game drives. * *San-Ta-Wani Safari Lodge*, located near Moremi's south gate, has eight brick and thatched chalets (16 beds) with private facilities located in nearby bandas. Day game drives and walks are conducted outside the park.

CAMPING: * *South Gate Campsite* is located just outside the South Gate and has toilet facilities only. * *Third Bridge* is Moremi's most popular campsite and can be very crowded in peak season. This camp has long-drop toilets only. Water is available from the river. Beware of lions. * *Xaxanaka* has no facilities. * *North Gate* campsite is situated just inside the reserve and has shower and toilet facilities, and water.

## SAVUTI

The Savuti is an arid region located in the southern part of Chobe National Park. The landscape ranges from sandveld to mopane forest, acacia savannah, marshlands (usually dry) to rocky outcrops. The Savuti Swamps are dry except when there are heavy rains, which is quite uncommon.

Game viewing opportunities here are usually excellent. Savuti, like the northern part of Chobe National Park, is known for its elephant. The area also contains large populations of zebra, buffalo, eland, kudu, roan antelope, sable antelope, waterbuck, tsessebe, wildebeest, impala, and many other members of the family of ungulates (hoofed mammals).

The predator population is correspondingly tremendous. The Savuti is famous for its lions, which occasionally are seen wearing radio-tracking collars. Within a two month period prior to my recent visit, lions had killed 19 giraffe in the area.

On one game drive, we parked within 15 feet of a pride of nine lion and turned off the engine. I was sitting next to the driver in the open land cruiser. A very large male and a large female lion walked by within five feet of us. They both stood taller than we were sitting, and they could have easily dragged us out of the vehicle had they wanted. I simply held my breath and reminded myself that I was quite safe inside the vehicle!

Other predators include leopard, cheetah, wild dog, spotted hyena, black-backed jackal and bat-eared fox. Hyena have tremendous crushing power with their jaws; they have been known to chew hinges off of refrigerators in camps in the Savuti in order to get at the food inside.

On another game drive we spotted impala, five greater kudu, warthog, elephant, two black-backed jackals, steenbok, about 50 tsessebe, a herd of blue wildebeest, *twelve* bat-eared fox, tawny eagles, yellow-billed hornbills and kori bustards. We followed vultures to a warthog kill where we found only the head remaining and a large male lion in the bush nearby.

Sometimes during the dry season 70 to 90 elephant gather at the water hole (a borehole) at once. They are usually lone males gathering together; females tend to stick close to permanent water.

Game viewing is good to excellent April-September/October and fair in November. Burchell's zebra migrate from the Mababe Depression, which is south of the Savuti Marsh, northward to the Linyanti Swamps in December and January, and return to the Mababe Depression around March. Therefore, game viewing in the Savuti, unlike Moremi or Northern Chobe, is also good March-May.

A few Bushmen paintings may be seen not far from the camps listed below. Four-wheel-drive vehicles are necessary for the Savuti.

ACCOMMODATION - CLASS A/B: * *Lloyd's Camp,* set on the banks of the dry Savuti Channel, is a 12-bed tented camp with facilities located near the tents. The camp offers game drives and a hide overlooking a water hole.

CLASS B: * *Allans Camp* has eight chalets (16 beds) with ensuite facilities. Game drives are offered. * *Savuti South* is a 16-bed tented camp with facilities located a short walk from the tents. Game drives are offered.

CAMPING: A *National Parks Campsite* is located near the camps mentioned above. Toilet and shower facilities are not always operational.

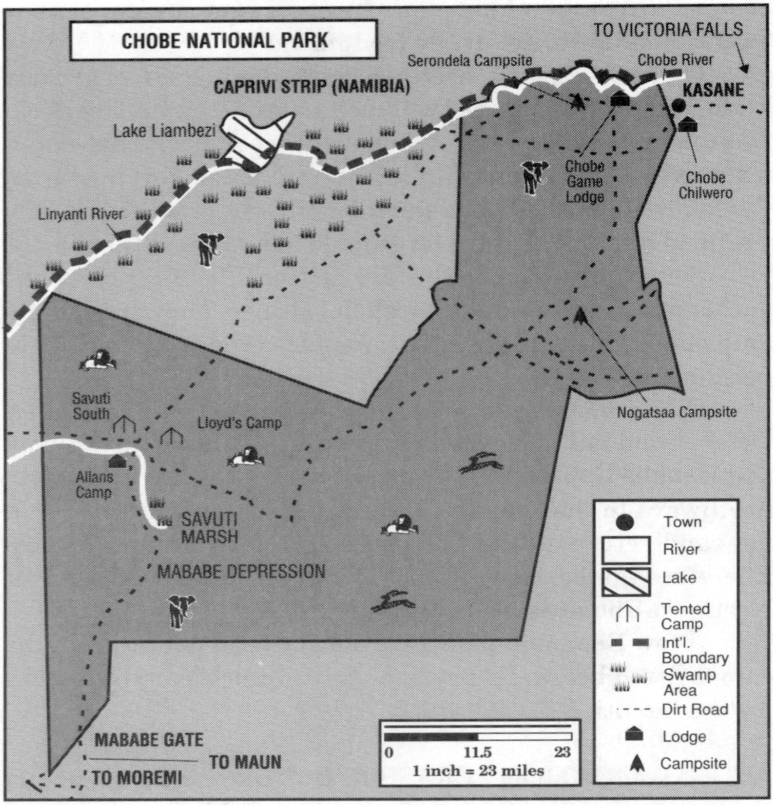


## CHOBE NATIONAL PARK

Famous for its large herds of elephant, Chobe National Park covers about 4200 square miles. The park is situated only about 50 miles from Victoria Falls in Zimbabwe with the Chobe River forming its northern and northwestern boundaries. Across the river is Namibia's Caprivi Strip. Birdlife is prolific, especially in the riverine areas.

The four main regions of the park are Serondela in the northeast near Kasane, the Corridor around Ngwezumba and Nogatsaa, the Linyanti Swamps in the northwest, and the Savuti (discussed above) in the west.

The Serondela region is famous for its huge elephant and buffalo populations numbering in the thousands. The elephant are some of the most vocal and active I've encountered on the continent, constantly trumpeting, making mock charges, and sometimes sparring with each other. Great entertainment!

Game viewing by boat along the Chobe River can be spectacular, especially July-October in the dry season. Often large herds of elephant and a variety of other wildlife come down to the river to drink. By boat you can get within close range of these animals. Large monitor lizards are commonly seen.

Along the Chobe River between the Chobe Game Lodge and the village of Kasane, you are likely to see numerous hippo, red lechwe, common waterbuck, warthog, and guinea fowl. Driving from the lodge towards Serondela Camp you can usually see giraffe, impala, zebra, and occasionally kudu and Chobe bushbuck.

The hot and dry Corridor (Ngwezumba to Nogatsaa) is the only area in the country where oribi is found. Gemsbok, eland, ostrich and steenbok are sometimes seen. Prevalent species include giraffe, elephant, roan and sable antelope.

The Linyanti Swamps, situated north of the Savuti, are predominately papyrus marsh and are home to many crocodiles, hippo, sitatunga, and lechwe, along with some elephant and buffalo.

The Serondela or northern region is accessible by two-wheel-drive vehicles while four-wheel-drive vehicles are necessary for the rest of the park.

ACCOMMODATION - NORTHERN CHOBE - CLASS A: * *Chobe Chilwero Camp* has eight comfortable wooden chalets (doubles) with ensuite facilities situated on an escarpment overlooking Chobe National Park. One of the best views in Botswana is from the upstairs lounge. The food is excellent. Game drives are made by vehicle and by boat. * *Chobe Game Lodge* is a beautifully decorated Moorish-style lodge with 100 beds set on the banks of the Chobe River within the park eight miles from Kasane. The lodge has a large swimming pool and beautifully kept spacious grounds. All rooms have private facilities, and four luxury suites have private swimming pools. Sundowner cruises and game drives are offered.

CAMPING: The public campsites at Serondela, Linyanti, Savuti and Nogatsaa have toilets and showers while the campsite at Tjinga only has a water tank. Serondela is often very crowded; it is accessible by two-wheel-drive vehicles and is close to Kasane.

## KASANE

Kasane is a small town a few miles northeast of Chobe National Park about a one-and-one-half-hour drive from Victoria Falls (Zimbabwe). Many tourists are driven here from Victoria Falls to begin their Botswana safari. Kasane Enterprises has a small shop of quality souvenirs.

ACCOMMODATION - CLASS B: * *Kubu Lodge* is a very comfortable lodge with wood and thatch chalets, private facilities, swimming pool and spacious lawns, and is only a ten-minute drive from the Chobe National Park gate.

CLASS C: * *Chobe Safari Lodge* has rooms and rondavels with private facilities, swimming pool and boats for hire.

CAMPING: Sites are available at *Chobe Safari Lodge*.

## NXAI PAN NATIONAL PARK

Nxai Pan National Park, well known for its huge giraffe population, covers 810 square miles and is located 22 miles north of the Maun-Nata road in Northern Botswana.

The Nxai Pan is a fossil lake bed about 15 square miles in size; it is covered with grass during the rains. The landscape is dotted with trees. Kgama-Kgama Pan is second to Nxai Pan in size.

In addition to Southern giraffe, wildlife includes gemsbok, eland, greater kudu, blue wildebeest, red hartebeest, springbok, steenbok, brown and spotted hyena, cheetah, and other predators. During the rains, elephant and buffalo may also be seen. After the rains have fallen, game viewing can be excellent (i.e., December-April). Birdlife is excellent during the rains.

This park is seldom visited by international travelers as there are no permanent fully catered camps. A four-wheel-drive vehicle is necessary.

ACCOMMODATION: None.

CAMPING: There are two campsites, one of which has an ablution block. Water is usually available at both sites.

Some travelers prefer to camp at *Baines' Baobabs* (no facilities), situated between the park and the Maun-Nata road, instead of camping in the park. Visitors must be totally self-sufficient.

Baines' Baobabs were immortalized by the famous painter Thomas Baines in 1862. His painting, entitled "The Sleeping Five," is of the five baobabs, one of which is growing on its side. Seldom are baobab trees found growing so closely together. Baines' Baobabs were later painted by Prince Charles.

## MAKGADIKGADI PANS GAME RESERVE

Makgadikgadi Pans Game Reserve includes a portion of the 4600-square-mile Makgadikgadi Pans, which are the size of Portugal. The pans are nearly devoid of human habitation and give one a true feeling of isolation.

Once one of the world's largest prehistoric lakes, the Makgadikgadi Pans are salt plains covered with grasslands and isolated "land islands" of vegetation, baobab and palm trees.

The reserve itself covers about 1500 square miles and is located south of the Maun-Nata road in northern Botswana, just south of Nxai Pan National Park. Large herds of blue wildebeest, zebra, springbok, gemsbok and thousands of flamingos can usually be seen December-March. A four-wheel-drive vehicle is highly recommended.

ACCOMMODATION: There are no camping or other facilities, and travelers must be totally self-sufficient.

## CENTRAL KALAHARI GAME RESERVE

This 21,000-square-mile reserve, one of the largest reserves in the world, covers but a portion of the Kalahari Desert. There is an abundance of wildebeest, hartebeest, springbok, gemsbok, ostrich, eland and giraffe — especially in the rainy season December-April. May and June may also be good months for game viewing.

ACCOMMODATION: None.

CAMPING: No facilities. Travelers must be self-sufficient and use four-wheel-drive vehicles.

## KHUTSE GAME RESERVE

The Khutse Game Reserve shares its northern boundary with the Central Kalahari Game Reserve and is the closest reserve to Gaborone. Khutse covers 950 square miles of gently rolling savannah and pans (over 50), and is best known for its birdlife.

Lion, leopard, cheetah, and antelope adapted to an arid environment are present. However, wildlife is seasonal, depending on the rains. If there has been little rain, then game is usually scarce. The best time to visit is after the rainy season has begun, usually December-April.

Khutse is 136 miles (a five-hour drive) from Gaborone via Molepolole. The route is not well sign-posted. Four-wheel-drive vehicles are essential.

ACCOMMODATION: None.

CAMPING: There is one public campsite with toilets. Water is available at the gate.

# THE SOUTH

## GABORONE

Gaborone, phonetically pronounced "Habarony," is the capital of Botswana. In the center of town is the main shopping and commercial center — the Mall. Besides some shopping, there is little of interest for the international traveler except for possibly the National Museum.

ACCOMMODATION - DELUXE: * *Gaborone Sheraton Hotel* has 152 rooms, three restaurants, outdoor heated pool, fitness center, lighted tennis courts and business center.

FIRST CLASS: * The *Gaborone Sun* is located on the outskirts of the city. This 158-room, air-conditioned hotel has a swimming pool, tennis and squash courts, casino, resident band and cabaret. * The *President Hotel* is a very comfortable and attractive air-conditioned hotel centrally located in the Mall.

## MABUASEHUBE GAME RESERVE

Mabuasehube is an extremely remote reserve in southwestern Botswana. Mabuasehube shares its western border with Gemsbok National Park. The park has six large pans and sand dunes over 100 feet high.

The best time to visit is during the rainy season October-April when an abundance of eland, hartebeest, gemsbok, wildebeest, springbok, lion and other predators are present.

Mabuasehube is 330 miles from Gaborone. A four-wheel-drive vehicle is needed, and the drive takes at least 11 hours.

ACCOMMODATION: None.

CAMPING: No facilities. Water may be available at the Game Scouts Camp.

## GEMSBOK NATIONAL PARK

Entry is only possible from the Republic of South Africa. See "Kalahari Gemsbok National Park" in the chapter on South Africa for details.

# BURUNDI

## THE LIKABLE CHIMPANZEE

The chimpanzee resembles the human in many physical as well as behavioral aspects. As humans, we are fascinated by these similarities and love to compare the familiar actions of chimpanzees to our own.

Chimpanzees begin their day with an early morning snack followed by a more selective feeding for a couple of hours. They may use twigs and leaves as tools (like we use knives and forks) to find food, using twigs to locate termites in decaying wood or as wooden hammers to crack nuts, and leaves as spoons to gather water or honey from within tree trunks.

During their parents' midday rest, youngsters utilize this quiet time to display many playful actions using their five-digit hands, including tug of war with plants and roots, tree climbing and playing with ball-shaped objects, e.g., wild fruits.

They beat their chests when excited and often disturb their parents with squabbling, screeches and screams. As they are naturally inquisitive creatures, they show their curiosity and indecisive nature by scratching their heads or pretending not to have noticed by continuing to feed. They will yield a stick to defend themselves and others if attacked.

At dusk they build their nests in the higher branches of trees (19-60 feet) and may go to sleep on their backs, hands behind their heads, or on their sides with their knees drawn up to their bodies.

# BURUNDI

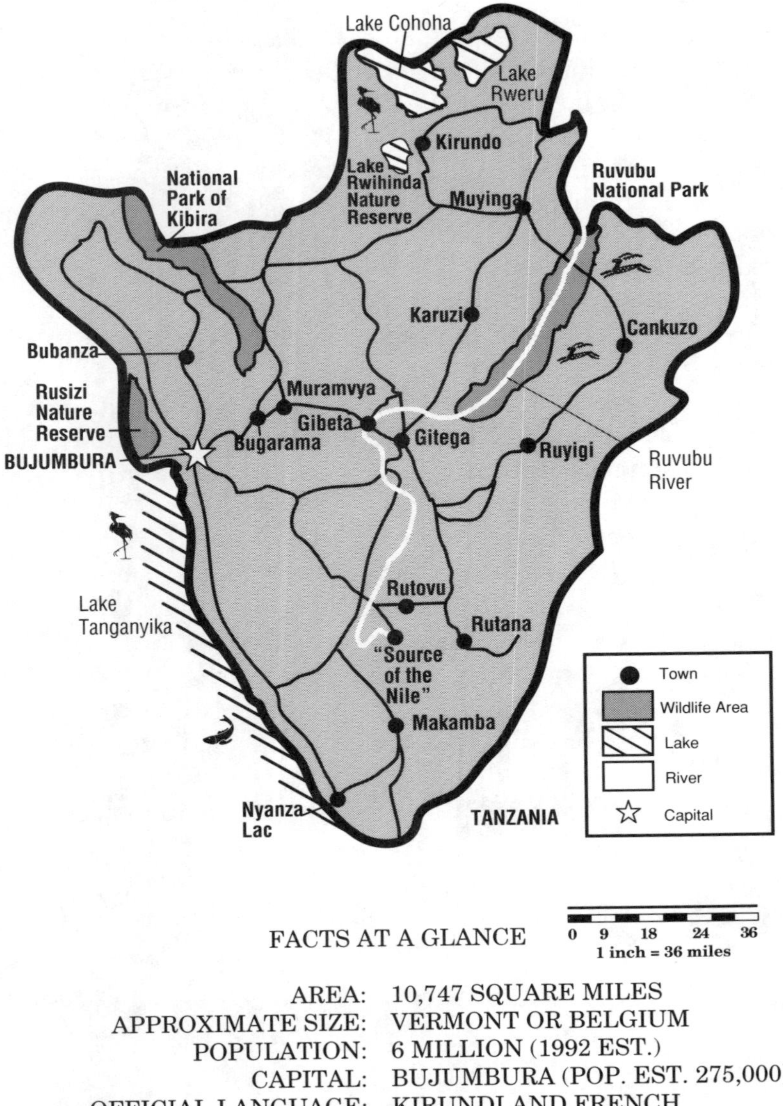


FACTS AT A GLANCE

| | |
|---|---|
| AREA: | 10,747 SQUARE MILES |
| APPROXIMATE SIZE: | VERMONT OR BELGIUM |
| POPULATION: | 6 MILLION (1992 EST.) |
| CAPITAL: | BUJUMBURA (POP. EST. 275,000) |
| OFFICIAL LANGUAGE: | KIRUNDI AND FRENCH |

# BURUNDI

Burundi is one of the poorest and most densely populated countries in Africa. Presently, Burundi is visited more by international tourists in transit than as a destination in itself. However, there are some attractions that warrant a short visit, especially for the prolific birdlife, chimpanzees and other primates.

Burundi is a hilly country with altitudes ranging from 2600-9000 feet. The weather in Bujumbura and along the shores of Lake Tanganyika is warm and humid with average temperatures ranging from 74-86° F.; frost sometimes occurs at night in the highlands. Dry seasons are June-September and December-January; the principal rainy season is February-May.

The three major ethnic groups in the country are the Hutu, Tutsi and Twa (pygmy). Hutus are primarily farmers and comprise more than half the population; their Bantu-speaking ancestors came to Burundi over 800 years ago. The Tutsi are a pastoral tribe and comprise less than a quarter of the population; they came to the region a few hundred years after the Hutus. The pygmy (Twa) were the original inhabitants who presently comprise less than two percent of the population.

For centuries, the region that is now Burundi had a feudal social structure headed by a king. Although Europeans explored the region as early as 1858, Burundi did not come under European administration until it became part of German West Africa in the 1890s.

In 1916, Belgian troops occupied the country and the League of Nations mandated it to Belgium as part of the Territory of Ruanda-Urundi in 1923. Ruanda-Urundi became a U.N. Trust Territory under the administration of Belgium after World War II, and in 1962 became the independent country of Burundi.

French and Kirundi are the official languages, and Swahili is also spoken. At the top hotels, restaurants and shops, some English-speaking staff are usually available to assist travelers; otherwise, very little English is spoken in the country. Most of the people are Catholic.

There are only two large cities in the country — Bujumbura and Gitega. Over 90 percent of the population are subsistence farmers. Burundi's major exports include coffee, tea, cotton and food crops, with coffee providing 80-90 percent of the country's foreign exchange earnings.

## WILDLIFE AND WILDLIFE AREAS

The National Institute for the Conservation of Nature (INCN) has recently created several parks and nature reserves. Most of the parks and reserves lack access roads, camping sites and other facilities. Hunting is forbidden throughout the country.

Burundi's premier wildlife attraction is chimpanzees, along with crested mangabeys and red colobus monkeys. Other wildlife includes buffalo, several species of antelope, hyena, serval, wildcats, monkeys, baboons, a wide variety of birdlife and over 400 species of fish in Lake Tanganyika, more than most any other body of water in the world. Hippo and crocs are present in Lake Tanganyika, the Rusizi and Ruvubu Rivers.

The combination of varying altitude and water create a wide range of microclimates giving rise to a great variety of flora.

## RUSIZI NATURE RESERVE (RESERVE GÉRÉE DE LA RUSIZI)

Rusizi Nature Reserve is the smallest of the national parks: it is located less than ten miles northwest of Bujumbura. The park has hippo, crocs, and a variety of birdlife.

## KIBIRA NATIONAL PARK (PARC NATIONAL DE LA KIBIRA)

Kibira National Park and the Kibira Forest are the best areas in Burundi to look for chimpanzees, red colobus monkeys and crested mangabeys. This 155-square-mile park is situated 30 miles or more to the north and northeast of Bujumbura and has a network of over 100 miles of tracks (poor roads).

## RUVUBU NATIONAL PARK (PARC NATIONAL DE LA RUVUBU)

Ruvubu National Park covers a strip of land from one to six miles wide along both sides of the Ruvubu River in eastern Burundi. Wildlife in the Ruvubu basin and Parc National de la Ruvubu includes hippo, crocs, buffalo, leopard, antelope, monkeys and some lion. The closest road access to the park is 140 miles from Bujumbura. The park has about 60 miles of tracks. Accommodation is available in a newly erected camp.

## LAKE RWIHINDA NATURE RESERVE (RESERVE NATURELLE GÉRÉE DU LAC RWIHINDA)

The Lake Rwihinda Nature Reserve and the other lakes in the northern part of the country, located approximately 120 miles from Bujumbura, are called the "Lakes of the Birds" and include Lakes Cohoha, Rweru, Kanzigiri and Gacamirinda;

Martial eagle

they are a bird watcher's paradise. These lakes can be explored by barge or canoe.

## BUJUMBURA

Founded in 1896 by the Germans, Bujumbura is the capital city, major port and commercial center of Burundi. The city has excellent French and Greek restaurants. A fun restaurant and bar on Lake Tanganyika is Cercle Nautique which also offers sailing, boating, and fishing, and has an abundance of hippos for entertainment. There is a public beach called Kakaga near Club du Lac Tanganyika (beware of crocodiles and hippos).

The ethnological **Musée Vivant** has a traditional Burundian village and daily traditional drum shows. The

**Parc du Reptiles** is next door. The **Musée du Géologie du Burundi** has a good fossil collection.

ACCOMMODATION - DELUXE: * *Novhotel* has 114 air-conditioned rooms with private facilities, swimming pool, video and tennis courts. * *Méridien Source du Nil* has 117 air-conditioned rooms with private facilities, swimming pool and all the usual amenities of Méridien hotels.

FIRST CLASS: * *Club du Lac Tanganyika*, situated a few miles from the center of town on Lake Tanganyika, has a swimming pool and air-conditioned rooms with private facilities.

TOURIST CLASS: * *Hotel Burundi-Palace* has 29 rooms with private facilities.

## INLAND

The people outside Bujumbura seldom see tourists. Try to visit a village on market day to get a feeling of daily life in Burundi.

En route to Gitega, one passes **Muramvya**, the ancient city of the king and royal capital, and an active market at **Bugarama**.

**Gitega**, the former colonial capital, is situated on the central plateau in the middle of the country, and is the second largest city. Sights include the National Museum, fine arts school, and beer market.

The artistic center of **Giheta**, seven miles from Gitega, sells wood carvings, leather goods, baskets and ceramics. The southernmost possible source of the Nile is four miles from the village of **Rutovu** and about 60 miles from Gitega.

# KENYA

## THE HUNTING CHEETAH

As cheetah hunt by day, you may be fortunate enough to watch the action of this important show. They are most active early in the morning and in the late afternoon (some may even hunt at midday when all the tourists are off the plains, having lunch).

As animals of the open grassland, their color markings help with the stalking process. If motionless, the cheetah may be obscured as the underpart of its body is in shadow, making the lighter, lower part as dark as the upper body. This makes it difficult to notice the spots. They will stalk from a few minutes to a couple of hours to be within 100 yards of the prey and then prepare for their attack.

This is when you see the speed of the cheetah. The acceleration from 0-45 mph in a couple of seconds is made possible by their huge strides, which are six times their body length. At three strides per second, the hind feet strike the ground far in front of the head to reach a top speed of 70 mph.

As sprinters, they have up to 15 seconds to catch their prey. Two factors make this difficult. The optimum speed of 70 mph may not be reached as the cheetah slows down to swerve, following the zigzag path of the quarry, using the tail to balance. At this speed cheetahs also have to judge the timing of the strike. Either they do this be swiping the legs from under the prey with the front paw or by hooking the dew claw into the animal's side.

Your patience may be rewarded by witnessing this spectacle — but if you approach too close, you may distract the prey or you may be too far away to witness the kill by the time the cheetah has covered ground in the chase.

# KENYA

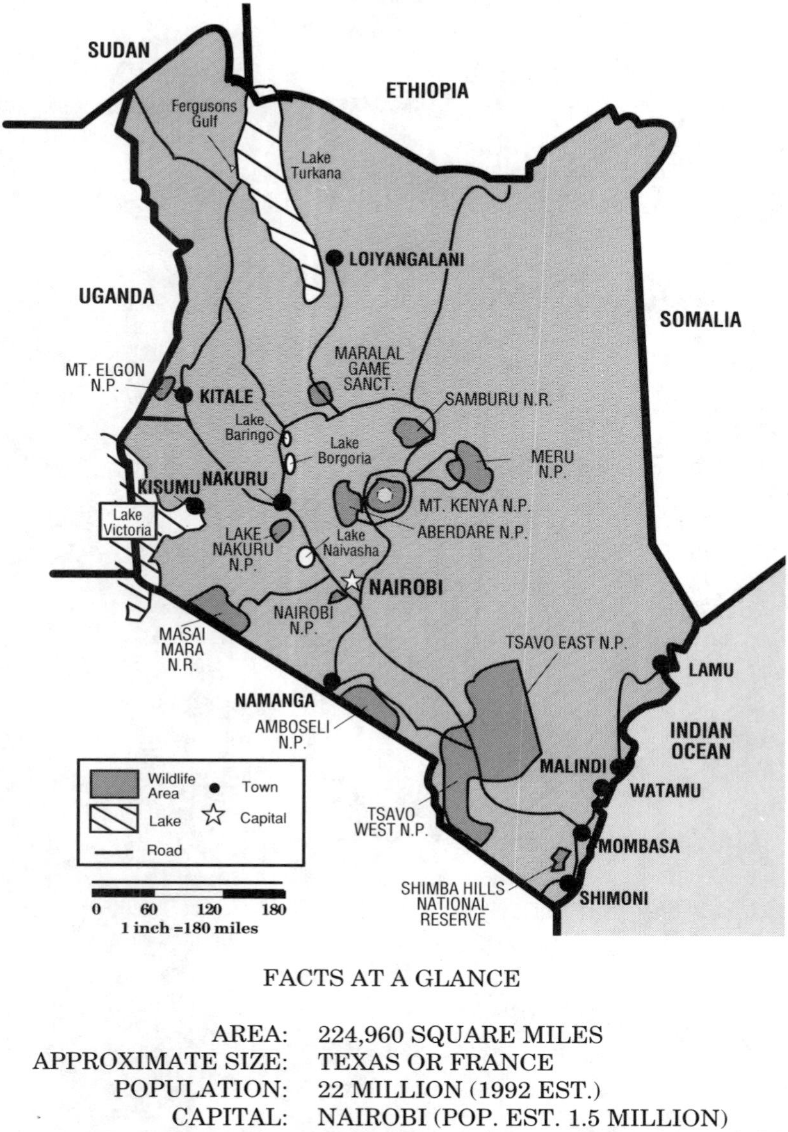


FACTS AT A GLANCE

| | |
|---|---|
| AREA: | 224,960 SQUARE MILES |
| APPROXIMATE SIZE: | TEXAS OR FRANCE |
| POPULATION: | 22 MILLION (1992 EST.) |
| CAPITAL: | NAIROBI (POP. EST. 1.5 MILLION) |
| OFFICIAL LANGUAGE: | OFFICIAL: KISWAHILI AND ENGLISH |

# KENYA

The word safari is Swahili for "travel," and Kenya is where it all began. Great historical figures like Theodore Roosevelt and Ernest Hemingway immortalized this country. Kenya is now the most popular of the safari countries, with over 800,000 visitors per year. Visitors to Kenya can enjoy game viewing, bird watching, hot-air ballooning, mountaineering, SCUBA diving, freshwater and deep sea fishing, and numerous other activities.

Kenya is well known for the magnificent Serengeti migration (shared with Tanzania) of more than one million wildebeest and zebra, and for the colorful Masai, Samburu and other tribes that contribute so much to making this a top safari destination.

Kenya has one of the most diversely majestic landscapes on the continent. The Great Rift Valley, with the steep walled valley floor dropping as much as 2000-3000 feet from the surrounding countryside, is more breathtakingly dramatic here than anywhere else in Africa.

The eastern and northern regions of the country are arid. Most of the population and economic production is in the south which is characterized by a plateau ranging in altitude from 3000-10,000 feet sloping down to Lake Victoria in the west and a coastal strip to the east.

Over half the country is Christian, about 25 percent

Samburu Morani

indigenous beliefs, and six percent Muslim concentrated along the coast. The Masai are found mainly to the west and south of Nairobi, the Kikuyu in the highlands around Nairobi, and the Samburu in the north.

Bantu and Nilotic peoples moved into the area before Arab traders arrived on the Kenyan coast by the first century A.D. The Swahili language was created out of a mixture of Bantu and Arabic and became the universal trading language.

The Portuguese arrived in 1498 and took command of the coast, followed by the Omani in the 1600s and the British in the late nineteenth century. Kenya gained its independence within the Commonwealth from Britain on December 12, 1963. Key foreign exchange earners are tourism, coffee and tea.

## WILDLIFE AND WILDLIFE AREAS

Kenya is one of the best countries on the continent for game viewing. Its only drawback is that it is too popular. Many of the well-known parks are crowded, so don't expect to be out there in the more popular parks on your own.

Unfortunately, several vehicles are commonly seen surrounding a few lion, or even a sole rhino, cheetah or leopard. However, on the positive side, safaris are generally less expensive here than in Tanzania, Botswana or Zimbabwe.

Richard Leaky, Director of National Parks and Wildlife, has instituted many positive changes which are reducing poaching and limiting the building of new lodges and camps in reserves.

The Masai Mara is the best park in Kenya for game viewing, and should, if at all possible, be included in your itinerary unless you will be touring the Serengeti National Park in Tanzania at the times of the year when wildlife is more concentrated there.

In general, game viewing is best during the dry seasons mid-December-March and July-early October. Game is easiest to spot in the Masai Mara, Amboseli and Nairobi National Parks, which have great wide-open plains. Samburu National Reserve is the country's best northern reserve and is also excellent for game viewing.

The country is an ornithologist's paradise with over 1000 species of birds recorded within its borders. Greater and lesser flamingos migrate along the Rift Valley and prefer the alkaline lakes of Magadi, Elmenteita, Nakuru, Bogoria or Turkana. Lakes Naivasha and Baringo are freshwater lakes. Bird watching is good year-round and excellent in the rainy season.

Flying safaris are available to many of the parks and reserves. Camel safaris are operated in the north where guests walk down dry river beds or ride these "ships of the desert."

Visitors to Kenya should also consider visiting Tanzania's northern parks, which include the Serengeti, Ngorongoro Crater, Lake Manyara and Arusha National Parks.

## THE SOUTH

## NAIROBI

Nairobi is situated at about 6000 feet altitude and means "place of cool waters" in the Masai language. The availability of international-class accommodations and most western goods and services makes visiting here an enjoyable adventure.

The **National Museum** of Nairobi features the Leakey family's paleoanthropological discoveries, botanical drawings of Joy Adamson, and taxidermy displays of wild animals that are good to study to help you identify the live game while on safari. Across from the museum is the **Snake Park**, exhibiting over 200 species of the well-loved reptilian family. The **Municipal Market** in the center of town on Market Street sells produce and curios (be sure to bargain). The **Railroad Museum** will be of interest to railroad enthusiasts. The **Nairobi Race Course** has horse racing on Sunday afternoons (in season) and is highly recommended as a place for people watching and meeting a diverse cross section of Nairobians.

One of the more popular dining and disco spots is the Carnivore, famous for its beef and game meat. The Horseman, located in the suburb of Karen, is also excellent. The Tamarind is known for excellent seafood. The Thorn Tree Cafe is a renowned meeting place for travelers on safari who leave messages on a bulletin board; it is one of the best spots in town for people-watching. Other excellent restaurants include Alan Bobbies' Bistro and the Red Bull.

For tips on the best eating establishments in Kenya from the country's leading expert, pick up a copy of *Kathy Eldon's Eating Out Guide To Kenya*. Also look for Kathy's *Specialties Of The House* featuring Kenya's tastiest recipes.

Other attractions include the **Bomas of Kenya** which features daily performances of ethnic dances and 16 varying styles of Kenyan homesteads. At the **Giraffe Manor** guests can feed the Rothschild's giraffes from an elevated platform and learn more about them. The **Karen Blixen Museum** is interesting to visit.

ACCOMMODATION - DELUXE: * *Norfolk Hotel,* a landmark in Nairobi, has traditional safari atmosphere, swimming pool, the fabulous Ibis Grill, and an open-air bar especially popular on Friday nights. All rooms are air-conditioned with ensuite facilities. * *Safari Park Hotel,* located seven miles from the city center in a quiet country setting, has 228 beautifully decorated rooms with ensuite facilities, huge swimming pool, tennis and squash courts, and several excellent restaurants — all in a lush garden setting. * *The Windsor Golf and Country Club,* located several miles outside Nairobi, is a colonial-style hotel with 130 rooms with ensuite facilities, an 18-hole golf course, tennis courts, health club and gymnasium. * *Nairobi Safari Club* is an air-conditioned, all-suite hotel (144 rooms) with private facilities, health club and swimming pool. * *Hilton International* is centrally located and has 329 air-conditioned rooms with facilities ensuite and swimming pool. * *Nairobi Serena Hotel,* located a ten-minute walk from town, has 200 air-conditioned rooms with private facilities and swimming pool.

FIRST CLASS: * *Inter-Continental Hotel,* near the center of town, has a swimming pool, 440 air-conditioned rooms with private facilities and casino. * *New Stanley Hotel,* located in the center of town, has 240 air-conditioned rooms with private facilities.

TOURIST CLASS: * *Boulevard Hotel,* located on the edge of town, has 70 rooms with private facilities and swimming pool. * *Jacaranda Hotel,* located just outside the city center, has 124 rooms with ensuite facilities set in four acres of lovely gardens.

## LUNATIC EXPRESS

Highly recommended is the comfortable overnight train between Nairobi and Mombasa for a taste of old-time colonial Kenya. Dinner and breakfast are served on this journey which passes Mt. Kilimanjaro in the night. There are daily departures from both Nairobi and Mombasa.

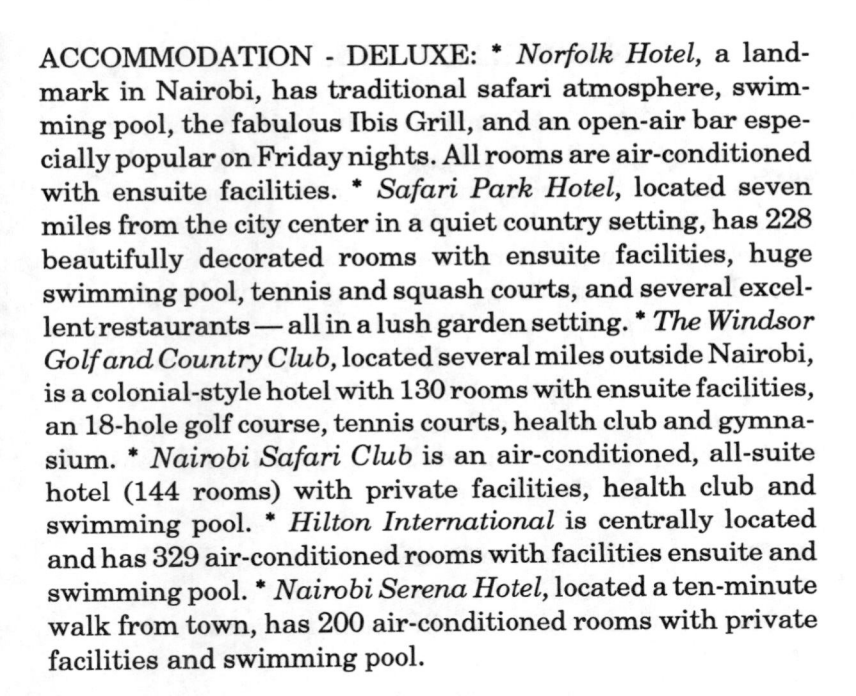

## NAIROBI NATIONAL PARK

Nairobi National Park is only eight miles south of Nairobi and sporadically has an abundance of game (depending on the weather) including rhino (on our first visit we saw three), lion, cheetah, hippo and a variety of antelope — a bit of everything but elephants.

There is something very strange about being in the midst of wild game and still within sight of a city's skyline. Altitudes range from 4950-5850 feet above sea level.

The Animal Orphanage (a small zoo) near the main park entrance cares for hurt, sick or stray animals. The side of the park facing Nairobi is fenced. A four-wheel-drive vehicle is recommended in the rainy season.

ACCOMMODATION: See "Nairobi."

CAMPING: Camping is not allowed in the park.

## AMBOSELI NATIONAL PARK

The real attraction of this park is the spectacular backdrop of Mt. Kilimanjaro. Also, rhino are fairly easy to locate here, and this may be the best park in Kenya to see elephant. *Elephant Memories*, a fascinating book by Cynthia Moss, is based primarily on her research in Amboseli.

This 146-square-mile park is probably the most crowded in the country, and a large portion of it has been turned into a dust bowl. However, elephant, lion and giraffe are easily found, and watching and photographing them as they pass in front of majestic Mt. Kilimanjaro is a sight to behold. The mountain seems so close; actually it is located in Tanzania, more than 30 miles from the park.

Amboseli National Park is surrounded by a game reserve; the park and reserve together cover 1235 square miles and average about 3900 feet in altitude.

From Nairobi travel south across the Athi Plains inhabited by the Masai. One enters the park on a badly corrugated

## AMBOSELI NATIONAL PARK

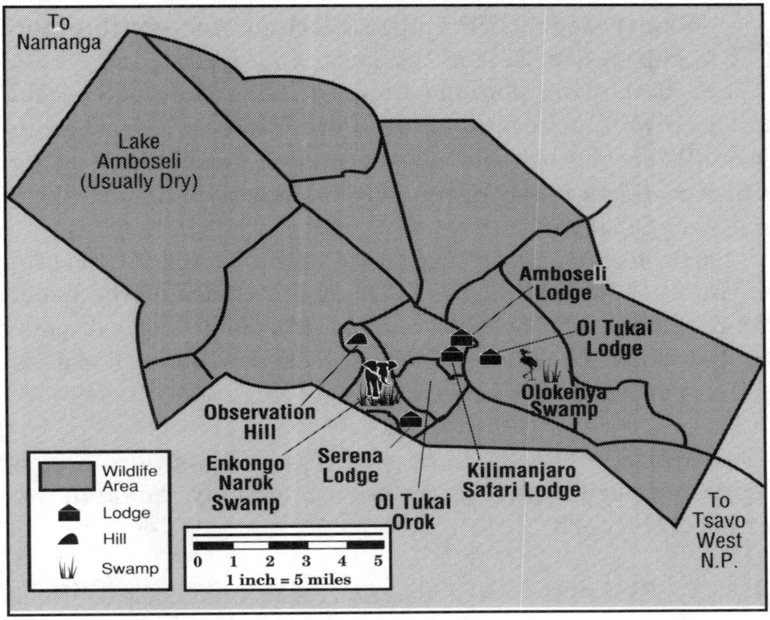


road from Namanga and passes Lake Amboseli (a salt pan), bone dry except in the rainy seasons, eastward across sparsely vegetated chalk flats to Ol Tukai. Mirages are common under the midday sun.

Approaching the center of the park, the barren landscape turns refreshingly green from springs and swamps fed by underground runoff from the overshadowing Mt. Kilimanjaro. These swamps provide water for nearby grasslands and acacia woodlands, attracting an abundance of game and waterfowl, which give life to an otherwise parched land.

Large herds of elephant and buffalo are often seen around the swamps, especially at **Enkongo Narok Swamp** where it is easy to obtain photos of animals (especially elephant) in the foreground and Mt. Kilimanjaro in the background. Early morning is best before Kilimanjaro is covered in clouds; the clouds may partially clear in late afternoon. However, there are days when the mountain remains completely covered in clouds.

**Observation Hill** is a good location for spotting lion and to get an overview of the park. One has a pretty good chance of spotting lion, cheetah, giraffe, and impala. Wild dog, aardwolf, oryx and gerenuk are less likely to be seen. Over 420 species of birds have been recorded. Game viewing is best mid-December-March (also best views of Kilimanjaro) and July-October.

In order to limit destruction to the environment, driving off the roads is forbidden, and heavy fines are being levied against those who break the rules. Please do not ask your driver to leave the road for a closer look at wildlife. The park is about 140 miles from Nairobi.

ACCOMMODATION - *Amboseli Lodge, Kilimanjaro Safari Lodge* and park headquarters are located at Ol Tukai in the center of the park.

CLASS A/B: * *Amboseli Serena Lodge,* located in the south of the park, is a modern lodge with 96 rooms with private facilities and swimming pool.

CLASS B: * *Amboseli Lodge* has 60 rooms with facilities ensuite and swimming pool. * *Kilimanjaro Safari Lodge* has rooms with ensuite facilities and swimming pool.

CLASS D: * *Ol Tukai Lodge* has self-service bandas.

CAMPING: Campsites are located outside the park on Masai land four miles past Observation Hill. No facilities except long-drop (pit) toilets. Bring your own water.

## TSAVO WEST NATIONAL PARK

Halfway between Nairobi and Mombasa lie West and East Tsavo National Parks, which together total 8231 square miles.

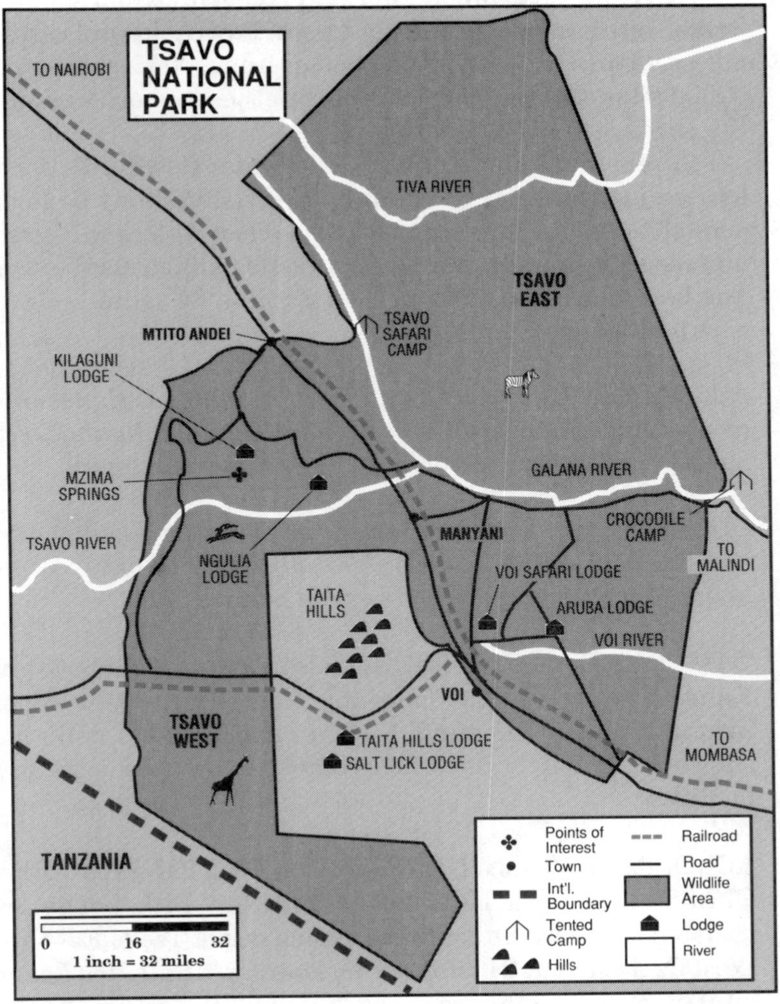


Large herds of over 100 elephant, with a total of over 15,000 in Tsavo West and East combined, over 60 species of mammals and 400 species of birds have been recorded. Also present are lion, caracal, giraffe, zebra, and a variety of antelope.

Less game is usually seen here than in Amboseli National Park. However, the park's rugged terrain is quite impressive in itself.

Tsavo West is predominately extensive semiarid plains broken by occasional granite outcrops. Lava fields are located near Kilaguni Lodge. Altitudes range from 1000 feet to nearly 6000 feet in the Ngulia Mountains in the northern region of the park.

From the Mzima Springs' underwater viewing platform, located just south of Kilaguni Lodge, visitors may be lucky enough to watch hippo swim about the clear waters with grace and ease. Crocs and numerous species of fish can also be seen. The best viewing is early in the morning. Kilaguni Lodge is about 180 miles from Nairobi.

ACCOMMODATION - CLASS B: * *Kilaguni Lodge* has 50 rooms with facilities ensuite and swimming pool. * *Ngulia Lodge* has 52 rooms with ensuite facilities and swimming pool.

CLASS D: * *Ngulia Safari Camp* is located near Ngulia Lodge and has self-service bandas. * *Kitani Lodge* is located near Mzima Springs and has self-service bandas.

CAMPING: Campsites are available at Kitani, Kamboyo and Kangechwa, and at the following park gates: Mtito Andei, Ziwani, Chyulu (Kilaguni), Kasigau and Tsavo. Chyulu has showers and toilets; the other campsites have basic (if any) facilities.

ACCOMMODATION NEAR TSAVO NATIONAL PARK - CLASS A: * Taita Hills Lodge and Salt Lick Lodge are situated between the southern extensions of Tsavo East and West Parks, about 240 miles from Nairobi. * *Salt Lick Lodge,* built on stilts to enhance viewing of wildlife visiting the salt lick, has 64 rooms with facilities ensuite and swimming pool. * *Taita Hills Lodge* has 62 rooms with ensuite facilities and swimming pool.

## TSAVO EAST NATIONAL PARK

Tsavo East is mostly arid bush dotted with rocky outcrops traversed by seasonal rivers lined with riverine forest. Tsavo East is generally hotter, dryer, and lies at a lower altitude (about 1000 feet) than its western counterpart. The 3000 square miles south of the Galana River is the main region open to the public.

East Tsavo's only permanent water hole is at Aruba Dam, and the drive from Voi makes for a good game run. Just north of the dam is an isolated hill, Mudanda Rock, another good spot for game. The scenic drive along the Galana River often produces sightings of hippos and crocs.

Tsavo East receives fewer visitors than Tsavo West; wildlife is generally more heavily concentrated in Tsavo West. Voi is about 210 miles from Nairobi.

ACCOMMODATION - CLASS B/C: * *Voi Safari Lodge,* in the hills above the town of Voi, has 52 rooms with facilities ensuite, swimming pool and photographic hide.

CLASS C: * *Tsavo Safari Camp,* located 15 miles from Mtito Andei Gate on the Athi River, has tents with facilities ensuite. * *Crocodile Tented Camp* has a swimming pool and is located on the Galana River two miles east of Sala Gate on the park's eastern boundary.

CLASS D: * *Aruba Lodge* is a self-service lodge located at Aruba Dam.

CAMPING: Campsites are available at Voi, Sala and Buchuma Gates, and at Aruba Lodge. There are little or no facilities.

## MASAI MARA NATIONAL RESERVE

This is the finest reserve in Kenya. All the big game is here: elephant, lion, leopard, cheetah and buffalo are prevalent, along with black rhino. Other commonly sighted species include zebra, wildebeest, Thomson's gazelle, eland, and Masai giraffe. This is the only place in Kenya where topi are common.

Masai Mara National Reserve, a northern extension of the Serengeti Plains (Tanzania), is located southwest of Nairobi and covers 590 square miles of open plains, acacia woodlands, and riverine forest along the banks on the Mara and Talek Rivers, which are home for many hippos, crocs and waterfowl.

One of the best places to look for game is in the **Mara Triangle** in the western part of the reserve, bounded by the Siria (Esoit Oloololo) Escarpment rising 1000 feet above the plains on the west, the Tanzanian border to the south and the Mara River to the east. A multitude of savannah animals can be found on these open grasslands.

Lion are distributed throughout the park. Cheetah are most often seen on the short grass plains. Black rhino are most highly concentrated in the Olmisigiyoi Region in the center of the park, in the northwest and extreme east parts of the park; there are no rhino in the Mara Triangle.

The best time to visit is during the Serengeti migration from approximately mid/late-July to mid-September when great herds of wildebeest (1.4 million) and zebra (400,000) reside in the Mara and northern Tanzania before returning to Serengeti National Park. At this time prides of 40 or more lion may be seen. From the Serengeti of Tanzania, a major portion of the migration moves northwest toward Lake Victoria, then north across the Mara River into Kenya in search of grass, usually returning to Tanzania in mid-September/early October.

Over a period of three days during a recent visit, we saw wild dog, five rhino, several lion, spotted hyena, a herd of 40 elephant and several smaller herds, buffalo, Masai giraffe, black-backed jackal, wildebeest, zebra, topi, and ostrich, among other species.

In the Mara Triangle and the northwestern part of the park, four-wheel-drive vehicles are recommended. There are two flights a day from Nairobi servicing the park. Keekorok Lodge is located about 170 miles and the Mara Serena about 210 miles from Nairobi.

Fishing safaris by private air charter to **Rusinga Island** on Lake Victoria are available from all the camps (book in advance).

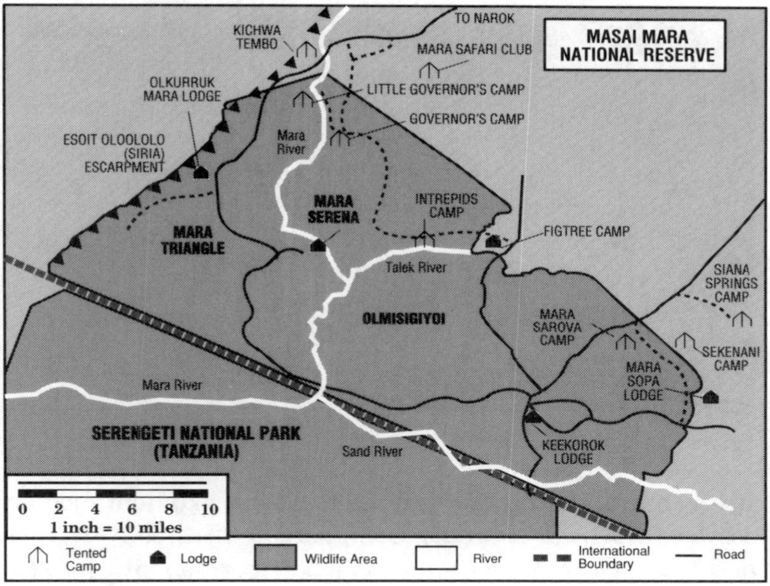


ACCOMMODATION - All lodges and camps listed below either conduct **hot-air balloon safaris** or will take you to where one is being offered. Many guests fly into the Mara (highly recommended) and are taken game viewing in four-wheel-drive vehicles (preferably) or minivans. Most camps and lodges are a five-to-six-hour drive from Nairobi.

ACCOMMODATION IN THE RESERVE - CLASS A: * *Mara Intrepids Club* is situated on the Talek River and has 30 deluxe tents with four-poster beds, ensuite facilities, and swimming pool. Groups of two to four tents share a private mess tent with bar and refrigerator. Walks are offered in the adjacent Masai land. * *Little Governor's Camp,* located in the northwest part of the park on the Mara River, has 17 tents with facilities ensuite. Guests reach the camp from Governor's (Main) Camp by crossing the Mara River. * *Governor's Camp,* located a few miles from Little Governor's Camp on the Mara

Elephant crossing the Mara River.

River, has 40 tents with ensuite facilities, excellent food and service. * *Governor's Paradise Camp,* situated between Governor's and Little Governor's Camps, is a semipermanent camp (the location changes) with 20 tents with facilities ensuite.

CLASS A/B: * *Keekorok Lodge* is an old-style lodge with 72 rooms and 12 tents with private facilities and swimming pool. * *Olkurruk Mara Lodge* has 63 deluxe rondavels with ensuite facilities, overlooking the "Mara Triangle" next to the Esoit Oloololo Escarpment. * *Mara Serena Lodge,* located in the central western part of the park, has 78 rooms with private facilities and swimming pool.

CLASS B: * *Mara Sopa Lodge,* located on the eastern border of the park high on a ridge overlooking the Mara near Ololaimutiek Gate, has 72 rooms with facilities ensuite, swimming pool and excellent food.

CLASS B/C: * *Sarova Mara Camp* has 55 tents with private facilities and swimming pool.

ACCOMMODATION ON THE PERIPHERY OF THE RESERVE - CLASS A: * *Mara Safari Club* is a deluxe tented camp (40 beds) located north of the park and surrounded on three sides by the Mara River at the base of the Aitong Hills.

CLASS A/B: * *Sekenani Camp,* located just outside the park near the Sekenani Gate, has ten luxury tents with private facilities including full-length bathtubs. Walks escorted by Masai are offered in the Sekenani Valley and the surrounding hills. * *Kichwa Tembo Camp* has 51 tents with private facilities and swimming pool. * *Siana Springs Camp* has 38 tents with facilities ensuite. Walks, day and night game drives are offered.

CLASS B/C: * *Fig Tree Camp,* located on the Talek River, has chalets and tents (100 beds total) with facilities ensuite and swimming pool. Walks, day and night game drives are offered.

CAMPING: Sites are located outside the park along the Talek River.

## THE WEST

## MT. ELGON NATIONAL PARK

Seldom visited, this 65-square-mile park is a huge, extinct volcano shared with Uganda, and at 14,178 feet is the second highest mountain in Kenya. Mt. Elgon also has the giant Afro-alpine flora found on Mts. Kenya and Kilimanjaro.

The forests are often so thick that a full-grown elephant could be standing 20 feet from the road and not be seen. Buffalo, waterbuck, and bushbuck are more likely to be spotted.

Kitum and Makingeny Caves are unique in having a good portion of their size created by elephants. Small herds often enter the caves near dusk to spend several hours in complete darkness mining salts with their tusks. Thousands of bats keep the elephants company. Makingeny is the largest, but Kitum is more frequently visited by elephants. During our visit elephant droppings were everywhere, foreshadowing the real possibility of their sources being inside.

To explore the caves be sure to bring two or more strong flashlights. Access to the park is difficult in the rainy season, when four-wheel-drive vehicles are recommended. There are no huts on the mountain; campers must bring their own tents. The park is 255 miles from Nairobi.

ACCOMMODATION - CLASS C: * *Mount Elgon Lodge*, situated less than a mile before the park entrance, has 17 rooms with private facilities.

CAMPING: Several campsites are available in the park.

## KISUMU

Kisumu, located on the shores of **Lake Victoria** about 215 miles from Nairobi, is the third largest city in Kenya with a population over 125,000.

ACCOMMODATION - TOURIST CLASS: * *Sunset Hotel* has 50 air-conditioned rooms with private facilities and swimming pool.

# THE MOUNT KENYA CIRCUIT

## ABERDARE NATIONAL PARK

This 230-square-mile park of luxuriant forest includes much of the Aberdare (renamed Nyandarua) Range of mountains. Guests of two tree hotels, Treetops and the Ark, are entertained by a variety of wildlife visiting their water holes and salt licks.

The park can be divided into two sections by altitude. A high plateau of undulating moorlands with tussock grasses and giant heather lies between Ol Doinyo Lasatima (13,120 feet) and Kinangop (12,816 feet). This region affords excellent views of Mt. Kenya and the Rift Valley. Rhino, lion, hyena, buffalo, elephant, eland, reedbuck, suni, black serval cat, bushpig and, very rarely, the nocturnal bongo can be seen.

On the eastern slopes below lies the forested hills and valleys of the Salient, home to black rhino, leopard, forest elephant, buffalo, waterbuck, bushbuck, giant forest hog, black and white colobus monkey.

Night temperatures range from cool to freezing as most of the park lies above 9800 feet. A four-wheel-drive vehicle is recommended for travel within the park. The Ark and Treetops are about 110 miles from Nairobi.

ACCOMMODATION - CLASS B/C: * The *Ark,* a "tree hotel" overlooking a water hole, has rooms without facilities, suites with private facilities (102 beds total), glass-enclosed main viewing lounge, and outside verandas on each level, floodlit for all-night game viewing, and ground-level photo hide. The area near the Ark is a rhino reserve. Game drives into the Salient are offered. Guests usually have lunch at the Aberdare Country Club before being transferred to the Ark and are transferred back to the Aberdare Country Club by nine o'clock the following morning to depart to their next safari destination. Children under seven are usually not allowed.

CLASS C: * *Treetops,* the first of the "tree hotels" (on stilts), older and more rustic than the Ark, has been recently refurbished. Guests usually have a buffet lunch at the Outspan Hotel before being transferred to Treetops and are transferred back to the Outspan by nine o'clock the following morning to continue their safari. Children under 12 are not allowed.

CAMPING: Only by special permission from the warden. Beware of lions.

Mountain Lodge, Mt. Kenya Circuit.

## MT. KENYA NATIONAL PARK

Kenya's highest mountain and the second highest on the continent, Mount Kenya lies just below the equator, yet has several permanent glaciers.

Mt. Kenya's two highest peaks, **Batian** (17,058 ft./5199 m.) and **Nelion** (17,023 ft./5188 m.), are accessible by about 25 routes and should be attempted only by experienced rock climbers. **Point Lenana** (16,355 ft./4985 m.) is a nontechnical climb accessible to hikers in good condition and is best climbed in the dry seasons. January-February is the best time to go when views are the clearest and temperatures are warmer on top; July-October is also dry but colder. Vegetation changes are similar to those described for the Ruwenzori Mountains (see Zaire) and Mt. Kilimanjaro (see Tanzania).

Rock climbing routes on the south side of the mountain are in best condition from late December-mid-March, while routes on the north side are best climbed from late June-mid-October. Ice routes are best attempted during the same periods but on opposite sides of the mountain. Howell Hut (17,023 ft./5188 m.), located on the summit of Nelion, sleeps two.

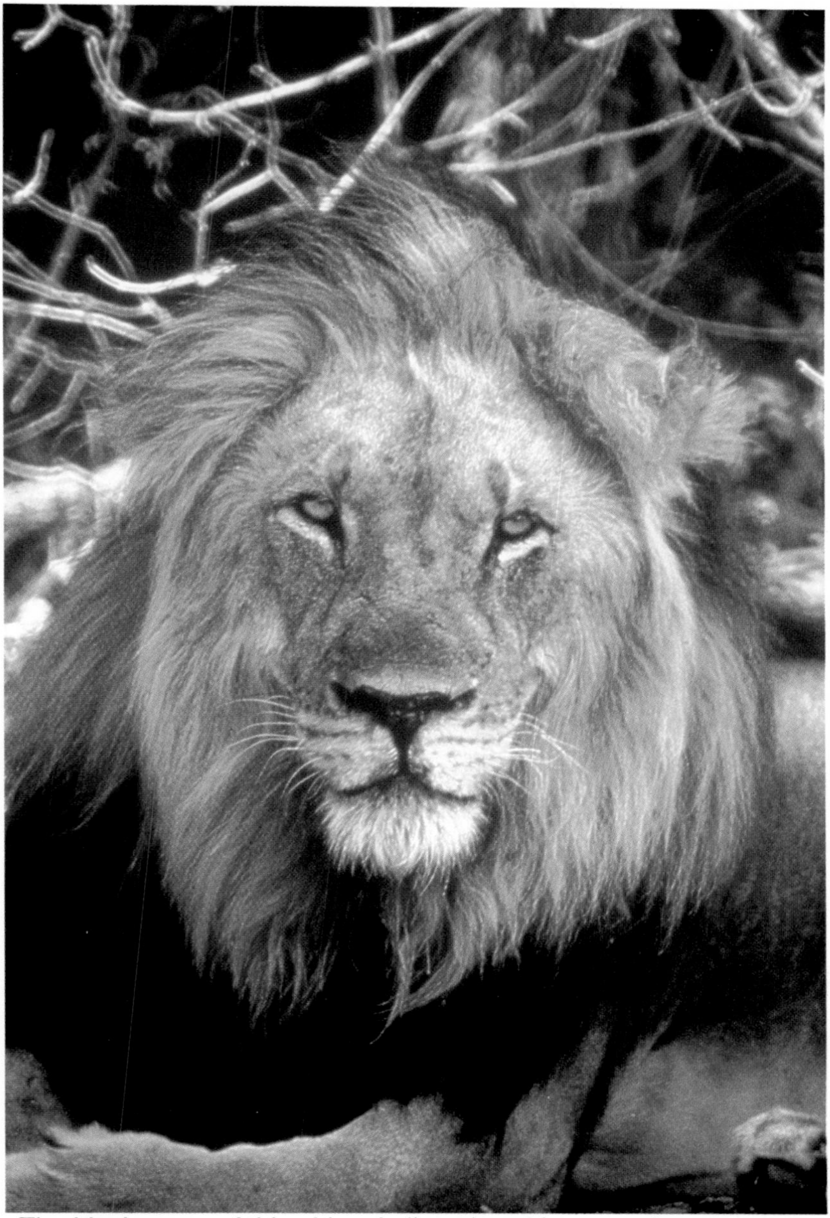

The black mane of this old male lion gives him a regal appearance.

Elephants after a midday drink at Etosha Pan, Namibia.

Fish eagle feeding at sunset in the Okavango Delta, Botswana.

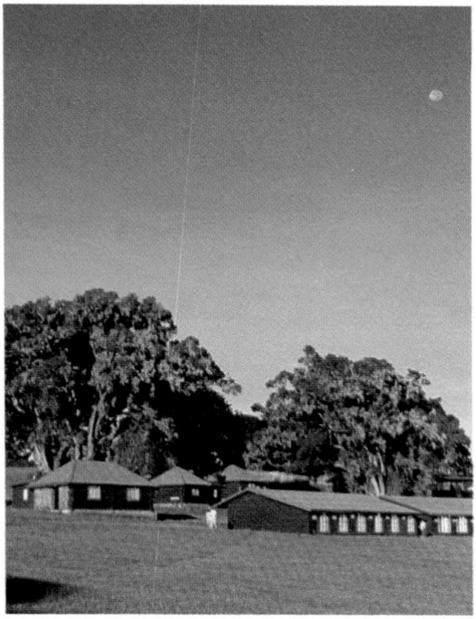

Upper left: Buffet lunch on safari.
Upper right: Ngorongoro Crater Lodge, Tanzania. Typical East African accommodation.
Lower left: Blooming jacaranda in downtown Harare, capital of Zimbabwe.
Lower right: Young Masai teenagers in traditional costume.

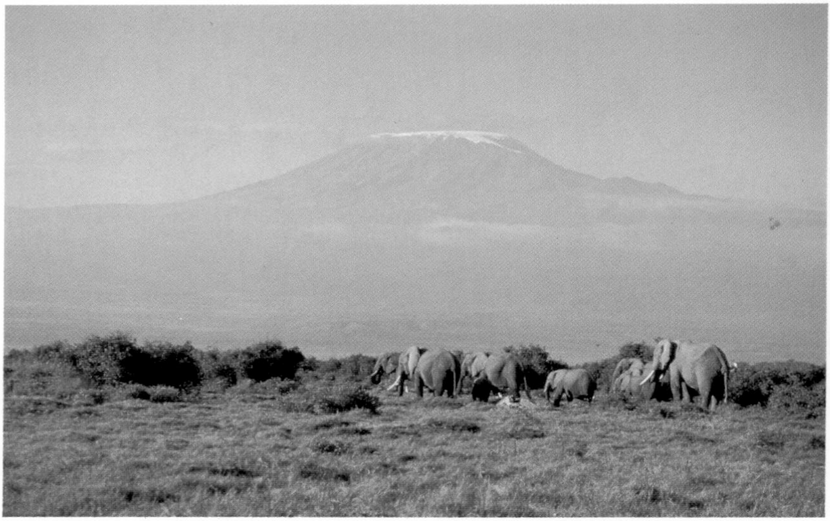

Sunrise at Mt. Kilimanjaro as seen from Amboseli National Park.

Each of these Grevy's zebras has its own distinct stripes — as unique as fingerprints.

A tender moment between mother and child Masai giraffe.

Elephant babies are protected by adult members of the herd.

Himba family, Namibia.

Majestic greater kudu bull with his herd at a water hole.

A pair of grey-hooded kingfishers.

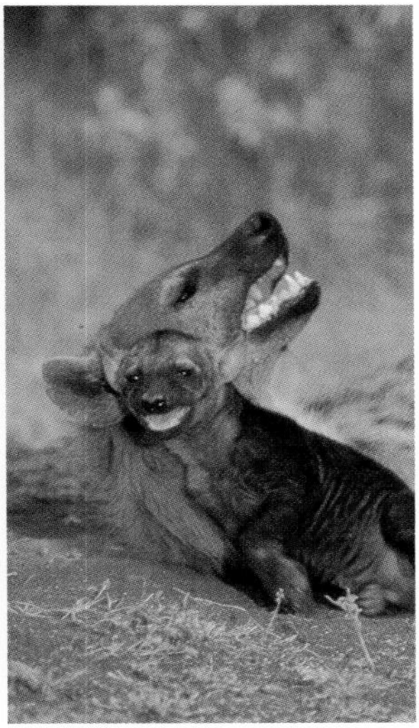

Female spotted hyena playing with her cub.

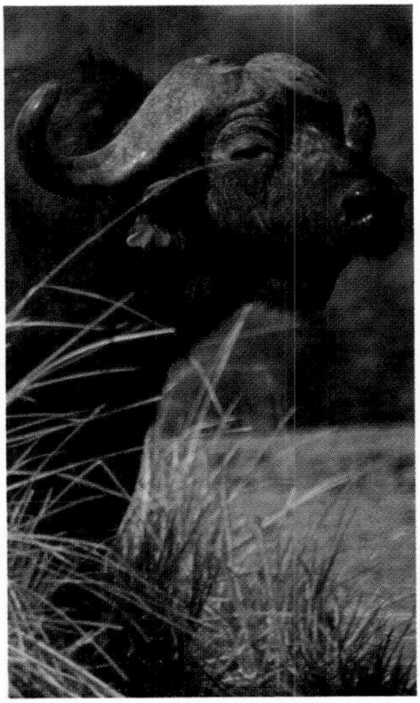

Cape buffalo are found throughout sub-Sahara Africa.

Herd of wildebeest in the Serengeti.

An inquisitive lioness emerges from the bush.

An aerial view of the Okavango Delta.

Although rarely seen, climbers should be on the lookout for buffalo and forest elephant. Other wildlife that may be encountered includes leopard, duiker, bushbuck, giant forest hog, Syke's monkeys, and colobus monkeys.

Because climbers can ascend to high altitudes very quickly, Mount Kenya claims more than half of the world's deaths from pulmonary edema. My climbing partner had symptoms of pulmonary edema after reaching Austrian Hut (15,715 feet), and we had to abandon our attempt of Batian Peak and return to lower altitudes. Therefore, a slow, sensible approach is recommended.

The world's highest altitude SCUBA diving record was shattered at Two Tarn Lake (14,720 feet), one of the more than 30 lakes on the mountain. The previous record of 12,500 feet was set at Lake Titicaca in Bolivia. In addition, climbers are occasionally seen ice skating on the Curling Pond below the Lewis Glacier.

## Naro Moru Route

The climb to Point Lenana normally takes two or three days up and one or two down. The first night is often spent at Naro Moru Lodge, or better yet, at the Met — Meteorological Station—(10,000 ft./3050 m.) to assist altitude acclimatization.

From Nairobi, drive 105 miles to Naro Moru, then ten miles on a dirt road to the park gate (7874 ft./2400 m.). You may be able to drive to the Met Station unless the road has been washed out by the rains. However, walking is better for acclimatizing to the altitude.

From the park gate, hike for about three and one half hours (six miles) through conifer, hardwood and bamboo forests to the *Met Station*. Beware of buffalo en route. The Met Station has self-service bandas with mattresses, cooking facilities, long-drop toilets and water. In order to help you acclimatize, consider hiking for about an hour up to the tree line (10,500 ft./3200 m.) in the afternoon, returning well before dark.

From the Met Station, hike through the muddy **Verti-**

**cal Bog**, a series of muddy hills with patches of tussock grass. In order to keep your boots dry, you may wish to wear tennis shoes through the bog. Cross the Naro Moru River and continue to **Teleki Valley**, where Mt. Kenya's peaks finally come in clear view (if it is not cloudy). Since leaving the tree line, vegetation has changed to tussock grass and heather moorlands with everlasting flowers, giant groundsel, and giant lobelia sometimes exceeding 30 feet in height.

From the Met Station, it takes about six hours to reach *Mackinder's Camp* (1378 ft./4200 m.), which has a brick lodge and campsites. *American Camp* (14,173 ft./4320 m.), a camping spot one hour from Mackinder's Camp, is used by some campers who bring their own tents. Water is available from a nearby stream.

*Austrian Hut* (15,715 ft./4790 m.) is a three-to-four-hour hike from Mackinder's Camp. Another hour is usually required to gain the additional 640 feet (195 meters) in altitude needed to reach Point Lenana, only a half mile away.

Austrian Hut is bitterly cold at night and is most often used by technical rock climbers attempting Nelion or Batian Peaks. Many climbers wishing to conquer Point Lenana begin from their camps in the Teleki Valley (Mackinder's, American) long before sunrise to reach Point Lenana shortly after sunrise and return to Teleki Valley for the night. The view from Point Lenana is the clearest and one of the most magnificent panoramas I've seen from any mountain — and well worth the effort!

## Around The Peaks

From Mackinder's Camp, hike two to three hours to *Two Tarn Hut* (14,731 ft./4490 m.). Stop for the night or continue for another three or four hours over two passes exceeding 15,000 feet to *Kami Hut* (14,564 ft./4439 m.), located on the north side of the peaks. From Kami Hut, it is a five-to-six-hour hike up the north ridge of Point Lenana or directly to Austrian Hut. Return via the Naro Moru Route described above.

## Chogoria Route

This is the most scenic route on the mountain. From the Chogoria Forest Station on the eastern side of Mt. Kenya, hike or drive ten miles to *Bairunyi Clearing* (8858 ft./2700 m.) and camp, or continue for another four miles (four-wheel-drive required) to *Chogoria Lodge* (9898 ft./3017 m.) and stay in their self-catering bandas.

Hike through hagenia forest to *Urumandi Hut* (10,050 ft./3063 m.), owned by the Mountain Club of Kenya. Room for camping is available nearby. *Minto's Hut* (14,075 ft./4290 m.) is about a six-hour hike from Chogoria Lodge. Space for tents is available nearby. *Two Campsites,* situated a mile beyond Minto's Hut, is another good place to camp.

Austrian Hut is a four-hour hike from Minto's Hut. Some climbers descend using the Naro Moru Route.

## Sirimon Route

Ten miles past Nanyuki on the Nanyuki-Timau Road, turn right on a dirt road and drive six miles to the park gate. Sirimon is the least used and most strenuous of the three major routes on Mt. Kenya.

The northern side of the mountain, being much drier than the western side (Naro Moru Route), has no bamboo or hagenia zone. Acacia grasslands cover much of the northern slopes; zebra and a variety of antelope are likely to be seen.

Although the track continues up to the moorlands to about 13,000 feet (3960 meters), it is better to make your first camp around 8000-9000 feet in order to acclimatize. There is another campsite at 10,990 feet (3350 meters), five miles from the park gate. About a mile further is *Judmeier Camp* (operated by Bantu Lodge). *Liki North Hut* (13,090 ft./3990 m.) is about a four-hour hike from Judmeier. Another four-hour hike brings you to *Shipton's Cave Campsite* (13,450 ft./4100 m.). *Shipton's Camp* (operated by Bantu Lodge) is a little further up the mountain. Austrian Hut is a five-hour hike from Shipton's Cave.

Lone climbers are usually not allowed to enter the park. Little equipment is available in Kenya, so bring whatever you need. For climbing tips and equipment checklist, see "Mt. Kilimanjaro" in the chapter on Tanzania. For a map of Mt. Kenya (highly recommended), see page 486 (catalog).

ACCOMMODATION NEAR THE PARK - CLASS A: * *The Mount Kenya Safari Club,* located on the slopes of Mt. Kenya outside the national park near Nanyuki about 140 miles from Nairobi, was built by actor William Holden and is the most famous lodge in all of East Africa. The spacious gardens are frequented by many species of exotic birds. Facilities include swimming pool, nine-hole golf course, very comfortable rooms, suites and luxury cottages with fireplaces (264 beds total). The Animal Orphanage contains a number of rare species such as zebraduiker and bongo. Game drives are not conducted here. * *Mt. Kenya Safari Lodge* has 11 luxury rooms with ensuite facilities.

CLASS B: * *Mountain Lodge,* about 110 miles north of Nairobi, is a "tree hotel" set in a forest outside the park boundary overlooking a water hole and salt lick, similar to Treetops and the Ark. All 42 double rooms have private facilities and face the water hole.

CLASS C & D: * *Naro Moru River Lodge,* located below the entrance to the park, has chalets with private facilities and rustic self-service cabins. Climbers often stay here before and after their attempts at Mt. Kenya's peaks. Trout fishing here is very good.

CAMPING: Camping is allowed at the Naro Moru Lodge and at sites in the park.

## OL PEJETA RANCH

This 110,000-acre private game reserve of savannah and riverine forest has a variety of wildlife, including black rhino, reticulated giraffe, buffalo, zebra, oryx, kongoni, and Thomson's gazelle. As this is private property, night drives may be conducted. Camels are also available for riding. A four-wheel-drive vehicle may be necessary to reach the camp from the main road during the rains.

ACCOMMODATION - CLASS A: * *Ol Pejeta Lodge* is a luxury ranch house surrounded by exquisite cottages with two swimming pools, tennis courts, sauna and jacuzzi. * *Sweetwaters Tented Camp* has 25 huge tents with private facilities facing a water hole and swimming pool. The camp is located 150 miles north of Nairobi.

## MERU NATIONAL PARK

Meru is best known for where Elsa, the lioness of Joy Adamson's *Born Free*, was rehabilitated to the wild. This 300-square-mile park is located east of Mt. Kenya, 220 miles from Nairobi (via Nyeri).

The swamps are host to most of Meru's 5000 buffalo, sometimes seen in herds of more than 200, and a number of elephant. Oryx, eland, reticulated giraffe, and Grevy's zebra are plentiful on the plains where lion are also most likely to be seen. Lesser kudu, gerenuk, and cheetah can be found along with hippos and crocs within the Tana River. Leopard are also present, and over 300 species of birds have been recorded.

ACCOMMODATION - CLASS C: * *Meru Mulika Lodge* has 66 chalets with private facilities and swimming pool.

CAMPING: Sites are available at Murera Gate and Park Headquarters.

# UP THE RIFT VALLEY

## LAKE NAIVASHA

Lake Naivasha, about an hour's drive (55 miles) northwest of Nairobi, is a freshwater lake prolific in birdlife and a favorite spot for picnics and water sports for Nairobi residents.

Take a boat ride to **Crescent Island** and walk around this game and bird sanctuary, which is host to zebra, giraffe, several antelope species, and a few camels.

ACCOMMODATION - CLASS B: * *Lake Naivasha Hotel* is a beautifully landscaped hotel with 48 rooms with private facilities, swimming pool and golf course. A special Sunday afternoon tea is served.

CLASS C: * *Safariland Lodge* has 56 rooms with ensuite facilities and swimming pool. Horseback riding is available.

CAMPING: Campsites are available at The Safariland Lodge and Fisherman's Camp.

## NAKURU NATIONAL PARK

Nakuru National Park encompasses the alkaline lake of the same name and is frequently visited by hundreds of thousands (sometimes more than a million) of greater and lesser flamingos — more than 400 bird species in all. Located 100 miles northwest of Nairobi on a fair road, the park covers 78 square miles — most of which is the lake itself.

Nakuru has been declared a black rhino sanctuary and has a number of these endangered animals under guard. Other wildlife includes leopard, Rothschild's giraffe (introduced), waterbuck, reedbuck, hippo, baboon, pelican, and cormorant.

ACCOMMODATION - CLASS C: * *Sarova Lion Hill Lodge* is located in the park and has 60 air-conditioned cottages with ensuite facilities and swimming pool.

CAMPING: Camping sites with running water are available in the park.

## NYAHURURU FALLS (THOMPSON'S FALLS)

Thompson's Falls, located at 7800 feet altitude about 115 miles above the Rift Valley between Nanyuki and Nakuru, is a refreshing place to relax.

ACCOMMODATION - CLASS C: * *Thompson's Falls Lodge* is a rustic country hotel; rooms have private facilities.

## LAKE BOGORIA NATIONAL RESERVE

Lake Bogoria National Reserve, located north of Nakuru, has numerous hot springs and geysers along the lake shore. Thousands of flamingos frequent this alkaline lake, as do greater kudu on the steep slopes of the lake's eastern and southern shores.

CAMPING: Campsites are available with little or no facilities.

## LAKE BARINGO

Lake Baringo, a freshwater lake located 20 miles north of Lake Bogoria, is a haven for a colorful and mixed variety of birdlife (over 400 species recorded) and a sporting center for water skiing, fishing and boating.

The early morning boat ride along the lake shore is one of the finest bird watching excursions I've experienced. Hippo, crocodile, fishermen and villages along the shore may also be seen.

ACCOMMODATION - CLASS A/B: * *Island Camp* is a very peaceful tented camp located in the center of Lake Baringo on

Ol Kokwa Island. All tents have private facilities. Take a walk and you may see a few waterbuck and meet the Njemps tribespeople who also inhabit the island. Boat safaris and water sports (beware of hippo and crocs) are available. * *Lake Baringo Club* has rooms (100 beds) with ensuite facilities and swimming pool. Boat and fishing trips are offered.

CLASS F: * *Betty Robert's Campsite,* situated on the lake shore, has bandas.

CAMPING: * *Betty Robert's Campsite.*

## THE NORTH

### LEWA DOWNS

Located between Mt. Kenya and Samburu National Reserve, Lewa Downs is a privately owned ranch with over 5000 head of cattle and a variety of wildlife. Horseback riding, hiking, day and night game drives and visits to a nearby rhino sanctuary are offered.

ACCOMMODATION - CLASS A/B: * *Lewa Downs* has cottages (8 beds total) located near the ranch house.

### SAMBURU NATIONAL RESERVE

This relatively small (40 square miles) but excellent park of scrub desert, thornbush, riverine forest, and swamps along the Ewaso Ngiro River is situated north of Mt. Kenya.

Elephant and lion are plentiful as are Beisa oryx, Somali ostrich, reticulated giraffe, gerenuk, Grevy's zebra, and other species adapted to an arid environment.

Samburu, probably the best park in northern Kenya, is located about 220 miles north of Nairobi. Under special arrangement, walking may be offered just outside the reserve.

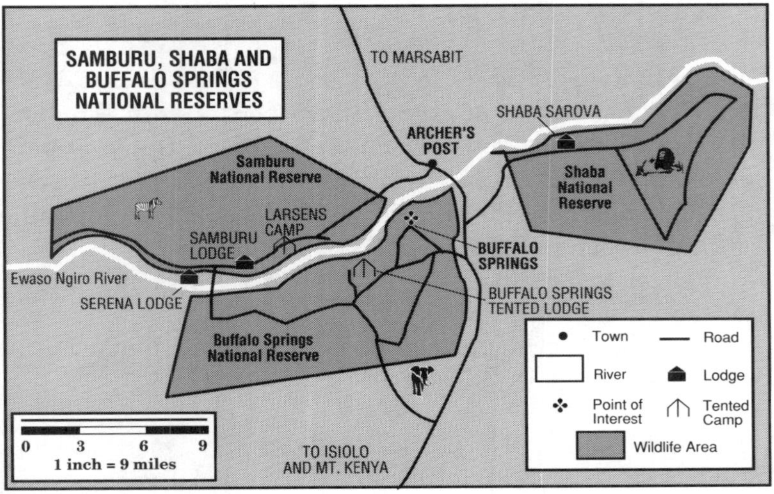


ACCOMMODATION - CLASS A: * *Larsen's Tented Camp,* situated on the banks of the Ewaso Ngiro River, has 13 double and four huge suite tents, all with facilities ensuite (34 beds total). * *Samburu Intrepids Camp* has 25 luxury tents, each with a private terrace and facilities ensuite.

CLASS B: * *Samburu Serena Lodge,* also situated on the banks of the Ewaso Ngiro River, has 52 rooms with facilities ensuite and swimming pool. The lodge baits for croc and leopard. * *Samburu Lodge,* located on the banks of the Ewaso Ngiro River, has rooms, cottages and tents (75 units) with private facilities and swimming pool. This lodge also baits for croc and leopard.

CAMPING: Campsites are located along the Ewaso Ngiro River between the West Gate and Samburu Lodge. Most sites have long-drop toilets only.

## BUFFALO SPRINGS NATIONAL RESERVE

Buffalo Springs is located south of the Ewaso Ngiro River, which serves as its northern border with Samburu National Reserve. The unusual doum palm, the only palm tree species whose trunk divides into branches, grows to over 60 feet in height in this arid park. Wildlife seen here is similar to what is seen in Samburu National Park.

On a two-hour game drive during a recent visit, we encountered oryx, gerenuk, Grant's gazelle, waterbuck, and two large herds of elephant. Baboon are often found drinking at the springs.

ACCOMMODATION - CLASS C: * *Buffalo Springs Tented Lodge* has basic tents and bandas (76 beds) with private facilities and swimming pool. The camp baits for crocodile.

CAMPING: Campsites have no facilities.

## SHABA NATIONAL RESERVE

The turnoff to the entrance to Shaba National Reserve is located east of Samburu National Reserve, two miles south of Archer's Post. The Ewaso Ngiro River forms the reserve's northwestern border and flows through the western part of the reserve.

The park is characterized by rocky hills and scattered thornbush. Volcanic rock is present in many areas. Mt. Shaba, a 5300-foot-high volcanic cone after which the park was named, lies to the south of the park.

A marsh in the center of the park is a good spot to look for game. During my most recent visit to this rugged, rocky park, we spotted oryx, gerenuk, common waterbuck, Thomson's and Grant's gazelle, dikdik, and ostrich.

Wildlife is less abundant and cannot be approached as closely as in the Samburu and Buffalo Springs National Reserves. However, there is much less traffic in this reserve.

The gerenuk or "giraffe antelope."

ACCOMMODATION - CLASS A: * *Shaba Sarova Lodge*, situated on the Ewaso Ngiro River, is a magnificent resort-style lodge with 85 rooms with facilities ensuite and a huge swimming pool.

CAMPING: Ask at the gate.

## MARALAL NATIONAL SANCTUARY

Maralal National Sanctuary, located northwest of Samburu and 95 miles north of Nyahururu (205 miles from Nairobi) near the town of Maralal, has zebra, buffalo, eland, impala and hyena which come to drink at the water hole adjacent to the Maralal Safari Lodge.

Leopard are baited and can often be seen just before sunset from the blind near the lodge. We fortunately saw two of these fascinating creatures during our visit.

ACCOMMODATION - CLASS B: * *Maralal Safari Lodge* has 24 cabins with fireplaces, private facilities, and swimming pool.

CLASS F & CAMPING: * *Yare Safaris Hostel and Campsite* located two miles south of Maralal, has bandas, dormitories and campsites.

## MATHEWS RANGE

Located northwest of Samburu National Park, this remote wilderness area with lush green vegetation rises, above the surrounding semidesert lowlands. Nature walks, fishing and game drives are offered. Four-wheel-drive vehicles are necessary in this region.

ACCOMMODATION - CLASS B: * *Kitich Camp* has ten comfortable tents with ensuite facilities.

## LAKE TURKANA

Called the Jade Sea because of its deep green color, Lake Turkana is a huge inland sea surrounded by semidesert near the Ethiopian border, three days of hard driving over rough terrain from Nairobi.

Formerly named Lake Rudolf, this huge lake is over 175 miles long and 10 to 30 miles wide, set in a lunar-like landscape of lava rocks, dried up river beds and scattered oases.

The brown Omo River flows from the Ethiopian highlands into the northern part of the lake where the water is fairly fresh, but becomes increasingly saline further south due to intense evaporation. The presence of puffer fish implies that the lake was at one time connected to the Mediterranean Sea by the River Nile.

One of the continent's largest populations of crocodiles is found here. Because the bitter alkaline waters render their skins useless for commercial trade, crocodiles are not hunted and grow to abnormally large sizes. Although the water is very tempting in such a hot, dry climate, swim only at your own risk!

Fishing is a major attraction. Nile perch, the world's largest freshwater fish, can exceed 400 pounds. Tigerfish, however, put up a more exciting fight. The El Molo tribe, the smallest tribe in Kenya (about 500 members), can be found near Loiyangalani.

**Central Island National Park**, a two-square-mile island containing three volcanic cones, is the most highly concentrated breeding ground of crocodiles in Africa. Half-day excursions are available from Lake Turkana Lodge. Excursions to **South Island National Park**, also volcanic and full of crocodiles, are available from the Oasis Lodge.

Easiest access to the park is by small aircraft. Four-wheel-drive vehicles are necessary. Loiyangalani is about 415 miles and Ferguson's Gulf about 500 miles north of Nairobi.

ACCOMMODATION - CLASS C: * *Lake Turkana Lodge,* situated on the western shore of the lake on Ferguson's Gulf, has thatched roof, double bandas with private facilities, and swimming pool. Fishing boats and equipment are available for hire. * *Oasis Lodge,* located on the southeastern shore of the lake at Loiyangalani, has rooms with facilities ensuite, two swimming pools, fishing boats and equipment for hire.

CLASS D: * *El Molo Lodge* has bandas.

CAMPING: At El Molo Lodge, Sunset Strip Campsite and El Molo Bay.

# THE COAST

## MOMBASA

Mombasa is the second largest city in Kenya with a population of over 600,000. This island, 307 miles from Nairobi on a paved road, is a blend of the Middle East, Asia and Africa.

The **Old Harbor** is haven for dhows carrying goods for trade between Arabia and the Indian subcontinent and Africa, especially December-April. **Kilindini** ("place of deep water") is the modern harbor and largest port on the east coast of Africa.

Built by the Portuguese in 1593, **Fort Jesus** now serves as a museum. The **Old Town** is Muslim and Indian in flavor with winding, narrow streets and alleys too narrow for cars, tall nineteenth century buildings with handcarved doors and overhanging balconies, and small shops. Old Town and Fort Jesus are best seen on foot.

Mombasa is the best place in Kenya for excellent Swahili food. The Tamarind Restaurant, located just north of Mombasa, and the Nomad Restaurant, located in Diani Beach, serve excellent seafood.

The city of Mombasa has no beaches so most international visitors stay on the beautiful white sand beaches to the south or north of the island. Nyali Beach, Mombasa Beach, Kenyatta Beach and Shanzu Beach lie just to the north of Mombasa, while Diani Beach lies about 20 miles to the south.

Most beach hotels on the coast offer a variety of water sports for their guests, including sailing, wind surfing, water skiing, SCUBA diving and snorkeling on beautiful coral reefs.

ACCOMMODATION IN MOMBASA - TOURIST CLASS: * *Castle Hotel*, located on Mombasa Island, has 59 rooms with facilities ensuite.

ACCOMMODATION JUST NORTH OF MOMBASA - DELUXE: * *Nyali Beach Hotel* has 235 air-conditioned rooms with ensuite facilities and minibars, disco, nightclub and swimming pool. * *Serena Beach Hotel* has 150 air-conditioned rooms with facilities ensuite, swimming pool and tennis. * *Mombasa Beach Hotel* has 150 air-conditioned rooms with ensuite facilities, swimming pool, and tennis courts. * *Hotel Inter-Continental* is a five-star hotel with 192 air-conditioned rooms with facilities ensuite, swimming pool, health club, squash and tennis.

FIRST CLASS: * *White Sands Hotel* has 346 air-conditioned rooms with private facilities, swimming pool and tennis.

ACCOMMODATION JUST SOUTH OF MOMBASA - DELUXE: * *Diana Reef Hotel* has 304 air-conditioned rooms with facilities ensuite, swimming pool, dive school, and tennis courts. * *Pinewood Village* has 20 private villas with ensuite facilities and private chefs.

FIRST CLASS: * *Jadini Beach Hotel* has 152 air-conditioned rooms with private facilities and swimming pool. * *Africana Sea Lodge* has 152 air-conditioned rooms with ensuite facilities and swimming pool.

CAMPING: Campsites available at *Twiga Lodge* (Tiwi Beach) and *Dan's Trench* (Diani Beach).

## SOUTH OF MOMBASA

## SHIMBA HILLS NATIONAL RESERVE

This 74-square-mile reserve of rolling hills and forests is located an hour's drive south of Mombasa and ten miles inland. At 1500 feet above sea level, this is a good place to cool off from the heat of the coast. From the park one has magnificent views of the Indian Ocean, and Mt. Kilimanjaro can even be seen on exceptionally clear days.

Wildlife includes elephant, buffalo and leopard. This is the only park in Kenya with sable antelope.

ACCOMMODATION - CLASS B: * *Shimba Hills Lodge* is a three-story "tree hotel" overlooking a floodlit water hole with 64 beds.

## KISITE MPUNGUTI MARINE RESERVE

Kisite Mpunguti Marine Reserve is situated near the small fishing village of **Shimoni** ("place of the caves") where slaves were held before shipment, near the Tanzanian border far from the mainstream of tourism. Delightful boat excursions to **Wasini Island**, an ancient Arab settlement across a channel from Shimoni, and snorkeling excursions are available.

The **Pemba Channel**, just off of Shimoni, is one of the world's finest marlin fishing grounds. Rugged five-day SCUBA diving expeditions on a live-aboard dhow to Pemba Island (Tanzania) are another way to enjoy East Africa's underwater treasures.

ACCOMMODATION - TOURIST CLASS: * *Shimoni Reef Fishing Lodge* has thatched cottages with private facilities and swimming pool.

# NORTH OF MOMBASA

## MALINDI-WATAMU MARINE NATIONAL RESERVE

Malindi-Watamu Marine National Reserve encompasses the area south of Malindi to south of Watamu, from 100 feet to three nautical miles offshore, and has very good diving and snorkeling.

ACCOMMODATION IN WATAMU - FIRST CLASS: * *Hemingway's* has 51 rooms with private facilities, swimming pool, and charter boats for deep sea fishing and diving. * *Turtle Bay* has air-conditioned rooms with ensuite facilities.

## MALINDI

Malindi, located 75 miles north of Mombasa (two hours by car) has numerous beach hotels, nightclubs and shops. The International Bill Fishing Competition is held here every January.

ACCOMMODATION - DELUXE: * *Kingfisher Lodge* is an exclusive, isolated lodge with only four air-conditioned rooms with facilities ensuite.

TOURIST CLASS: * *Driftwood Beach Club* has 27 air-conditioned rooms with private facilities and swimming pool. * *Silversands Villas* has 27 air-conditioned rooms and suites with private facilities.

CAMPING: * *Silversands Campsite* is one mile north of town.

## LAMU

Swahili culture has changed little in the past few hundred years on the island of Lamu. The only motorized vehicle on the island is owned by a government official, but plenty of donkey carts provide substitutes. Narrow, winding streets and a maze of alleyways add to the timeless atmosphere. Many travelers have compared Lamu to a mini-Katmandu.

The **Lamu Museum** has exhibits of Swahili craftwork. Of the more than 30 mosques on Lamu, only a few are open to visitors. The best beaches are at **Shela**, a 45-minute walk or short boat ride from the town of Lamu to the Peponi Beach Hotel. **Matondoni** is a fishing village where dhows, fishing nets and traps are made. Numerous attractions also lie on nearby islands.

The best way to reach the island is to fly; day and overnight excursions from Mombasa and Malindi are available. The road from Malindi is very rough and may be impassable in the rainy season.

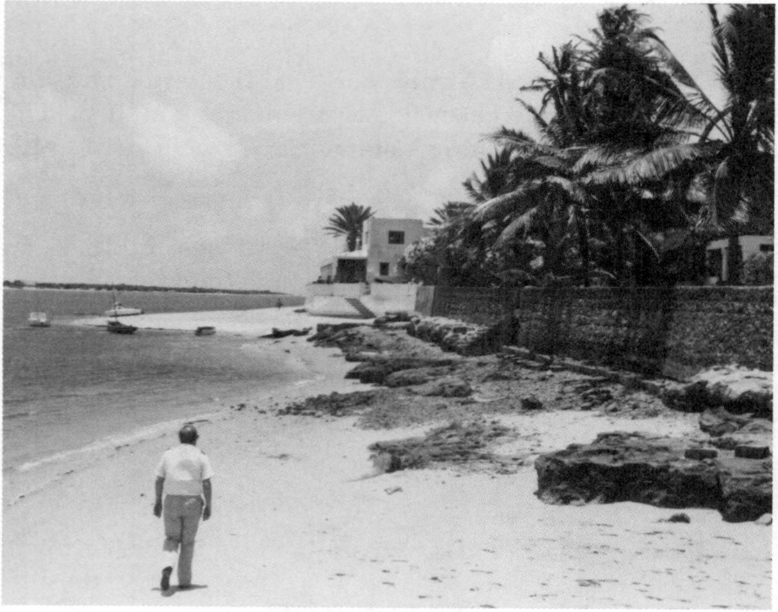

Exploring Lamu Island.

ACCOMMODATION - FIRST CLASS: * *Peponi Beach Hotel*, a pleasant beach resort, is located about one mile from the town of Lamu. All rooms have facilities ensuite. * *Lamu Palace Hotel* has air-conditioned rooms (50 beds) with ensuite facilities and is located 200 yards from the Jetty.

TOURIST CLASS: * *Petley's Inn* has been a landmark since the nineteenth century with the only bar in town, rustic atmosphere, and rooms with private facilities and ceiling fans.

# LESOTHO

## THE WANDERING ELAND

The cow-like eland are very mobile animals within their chosen environment and have adapted their feeding habits accordingly.

Food availability dictates where they move within their local area, either nomadically or migrating between areas. For their size (5.5-feet shoulder height) and weight (many over 1500 pounds), they are staggeringly good jumpers and will clear seven feet if a fence or obstacle is in the way of their feeding path.

They browse during the winter months and have been known to eat 60 types of food plants, including 11 grasses. Feeding includes chewing twigs and branches (*mopane, combretum, and lonchocarpus*) up to two inches thick, using their horns extensively to break the higher branches. They will reach leaves (*grewia, mopane, syringa*), berries, flowering bushes (*tagestes* and *bidens*), and tasty fruit pods with their lips.

In the summer months they will graze the new shoots of grass to sustain their high-protein diet. In the drier regions they feed on the succulent branches, acacia leaves and roots to take in enough moisture if water is not readily available. They will also feed at night when the grasses are laden with dew.

As they walk from feeding ground to feeding ground, they make a distinct clicking sound caused either by their knees or tendons or by the two toes of each hoof coming together as they pick the hoof up.

# LESOTHO

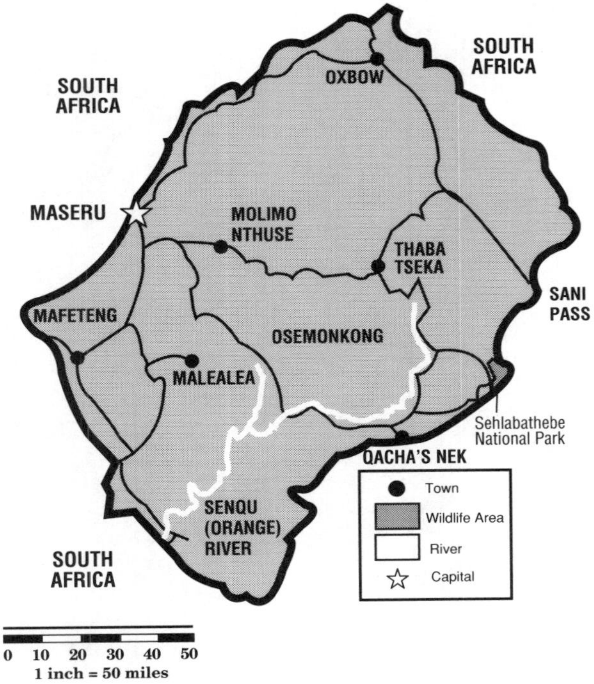


FACTS AT A GLANCE

| | |
|---|---|
| AREA: | 11,700 SQUARE MILES |
| APPROXIMATE SIZE: | MARYLAND OR BELGIUM |
| POPULATION: | 1.7 MILLION (1992 EST.) |
| CAPITAL: | MASERU (POP. EST. 110,000) |
| OFFICIAL LANGUAGE: | ENGLISH AND SESOTHO<br>ENGLISH IS WIDELY SPOKEN |

# LESOTHO

Lesotho is a rugged country with spectacular mountain scenery which can best be explored on pony treks, hiking and camping in the remote regions of the country.

Called the "Kingdom in the Sky," Lesotho has the highest lowest altitude of any country in the world. In other words, Lesotho's lowest point (4530 feet above sea level) is higher than the lowest point of any other country. Most of the country lies above 6000 feet.

Lesotho is an "island" surrounded by the Republic of South Africa which makes it one of only three countries in the world (including the Vatican and the Republic of San Marino) surrounded entirely by one other country.

The country is called Lesotho (pronounced *Lesutu*), an individual is called Mosotho, and the people Basotho. Many men wear multicolored traditional blankets to keep them warm in the cool and often freezing air; they also wear the traditional conical basket hats.

The Basotho are the only Africans to adapt to below-freezing temperatures that can drop to -8° F. Snow can fall in the mountains any time of the year and in the lowlands between May and August. Summer temperatures seldom rise over 90° F. The rainy season is during the summer with 85 percent of the annual rainfall (about 28 inches) occurring October-April, making many roads impassable.

The western part of the country is lowland with altitudes of 5000-6000 feet. The eastern three-quarters of the country is highland rising to 11,000 feet in the Drakensberg Mountain Range, bordering the Natal Province of South Africa.

Bushmen (Qhuaique) inhabited Basutoland (now Lesotho) until the end of the sixteenth century. For the following 300 years, the area was inhabited by refugees from numerous tribal wars in the region; these refugees formed the Basotho tribal group.

Moshoeshoe I reigned from 1823-1870, and his kingdom was powerful enough to keep the warring Zulus at bay. Wars with South Africa from 1823-1868 resulted in the loss of much land, called "The Lost Territory." Lesotho asked to become a British Protectorate to gain assistance in halting the encroachment of its lands by the Orange Free State (South Africa). Lesotho was a British Protectorate for 96 years from 1868 until its independence on October 4, 1966.

Lesotho has the highest literacy rate in Africa. Its economy is based on agriculture and earnings from laborers working in mines in South Africa. Light manufacturing and tourism are also important foreign exchange earners.

The mountains of Lesotho are Southern Africa's most important watershed. The Highlands Water Project, a large project that involves selling water to South Africa, is underway and promises to provide Lesotho with much needed income.

The two best ways of seeing what this country has to offer are by pony trekking or a four-wheel-drive safari into its most remote regions.

## WILDLIFE AND WILDLIFE AREAS

Sehlabathebe National Park, small by African standards, is Lesotho's premier wildlife reserve. The country is more often visited for its scenic beauty than wildlife, which should be considered a bonus.

Stopping at a village during a pony trek.

## PONY TREKKING

Lesotho is one of the best countries in the world for pony trekking. The Basotho pony is the chief means of transportation in the mountainous two-thirds of this country and the best way to explore this land of new roads. Bridle paths crisscross the pristine landscape from one village or family settlement to the next.

The Basotho pony is the best pony in the world for mountain travel and was highly prized during wartime. It can climb and descend steep, rocky paths with ease which other breeds of horses would not attempt. The riding style in Lesotho, as in most countries in Africa, is *English.*

## PONY TREKKING FROM MOLIMO NTHUSE

**Molimo Nthuse,** located about an hour drive (34 miles) on a good tarred road from Maseru, is the center for pony trekking in this region. Escorted day trips to the refreshing rock pools of **Qiloane Falls** and other rides of up to seven days in length are offered. The ponies are well trained and a pleasure to ride.

Pony treks are conducted year-round — in "swimsuit" weather in the summer as well as in cold, snowy weather in winter. Remember, the seasons are reversed from the northern hemisphere!

Accommodation on overnight treks is in Basotho huts or camping (bring your own tent).

ACCOMMODATION - CLASS C: * *The Molimo Nthuse Lodge* offers 16 rooms with veranda and private facilities in a beautiful mountain setting.

## PONY TREKKING FROM MALEALEA TO SEMONKONG

One of the most interesting pony treks in Lesotho (offered from September-April) is a four-day ride from Malealea in southwestern Lesotho to Semonkong and Maletsunyane Falls — the highest single-drop waterfall in southern Africa.

The pony trek begins after examining some interesting Bushmen rock paintings and rock pools located near **Malealea,** about 50 miles from Maseru. Riding east, the dark-blue skies are broken by high mountains in the distance. Basotho, wrapped in their traditional blankets and traveling on foot and by pony, offer friendly greetings and warm smiles. Riding in a cool breeze on a moonlit night in these remote mountains calms the soul and brings peace and harmony to one's spirit.

The nights are spent in traditional huts usually owned by the headman of the village, providing a firsthand knowledge of how the people live. Hikes to view **Ribaneng Falls** and **Ketane Falls** (495 feet) are made along the way.

The final destination is **Maletsunyane Falls**, a few miles and less than a half-hour ride from Semonkong. These impressive falls drop over 620 feet in a majestic setting.

**Semonkong** is a dusty little town resembling America's "Wild, Wild West" with a general store, hitching posts, stables and horses providing the main means of transportation. Scheduled flights on Air Lesotho back to Maseru are available.

ACCOMMODATION - CLASS F: MALEALEA: * *Malealea Lodge* is a small self-service lodge with five bedrooms and six rondavels. Day pony treks are available. SEMONKONG: * *Mountain Delight Lodge* is a small self-service lodge with ten beds.

CAMPING: Campsites available at Fraser Lodge (Semonkong).

## THE MOUNTAIN ROAD

This route cuts through the center of Lesotho from west to east through spectacular mountain scenery to "The Roof of Africa." From Maseru the road ascends over **Bushmen Pass** (Lekhalong la Baroa) to **Molimo Nthuse** ("God Help Me Pass"). Between December and March colorful scarlet and yellow red-hot pokers (flowers) may be seen in this area.

Continue to **Thaba Tseka** where the good road ends and four-wheel drive is necessary to negotiate the tracks that pass small villages and isolated herd-boys. After **Sehonghong** the route descends into the **Orange (Senqu) River Canyon** dotted with unusual rock formations, then climbs over **Matebeng Pass** (9670 feet) which had snow, sleet and ice cycles during my visit in April, and onward to Sehlabathebe National Park.

## SEHLABATHEBE NATIONAL PARK

Sehlabathebe has the highest sandstone formations (including arches) in southern Africa. This park is situated on a high plateau with small lakes offering tremendous views of the Drakensberg Mountains and Natal. Sehlabathebe means "Plateau of the Shield" and has an average altitude of over 8000 feet. Three peaks, called "The Three Bushmen" (Baroa-ba-Bararo), dominate the skyline.

This small 26-square-mile fenced park has oribi, eland, reedbuck, wildebeest, baboons, and abundant birdlife, including the rare lammergeyer.

The best time to visit Sehlabathebe for game viewing, hiking and for some of the best freshwater fishing in southern Africa is November-March. Quickest access is by charter flight. Land access is by a 185-mile drive across Lesotho from Maseru or from South Africa via Qacha's Nek, Sani Pass, or a five-to-six-hour hike (or three-to-four-hour pony trek) of 15 miles from Bushman's Nek Lodge.

ACCOMMODATION - CLASS D: * *Sehlabathebe Park Lodge* is a self-service lodge with four double rooms. CLASS F: Dormitory accommodation is available.

CAMPING: Campsites are available near the lodge.

## MASERU

This is the capital and largest city and is located in the western lowlands. Sights include the Cathedral and the Royal Lesotho Carpet Factory. The tourist office is next to the Victoria Hotel.

Some interesting day excursions from Maseru include **Thaba-Bosiu** (The Mountain at Night), the table mountain fortress 19 miles from Maseru where the Basotho fought off the Boers, and the **Ha Khotso** rock paintings, considered to be some of the finest in southern Africa, located 28 miles from Maseru off the mountain road.

ACCOMMODATION - DELUXE: * *The Lesotho Sun* is situated on a hill overlooking Maseru, with 238 rooms with ensuite facilities, swimming pool, tennis courts, health club and casino.

FIRST CLASS: * *Maseru Sun Cabanas* has 216 rooms with ensuite facilities, tennis courts, swimming pool and horseback riding stables.

# MAURITIUS

## THE EXTINCT DODO

"Dead as a dodo" is a popular saying in memory of this island bird. The name stems from the Portuguese meaning "foolish" or "simple."

Mistakenly thought to be related to the swan family, it belonged to the family of pigeons. Though it had small wings, it had no flight feathers and a large fat body. The crop under the chin was used to hold stones which broke up the nuts and grains which constituted its diet.

As it could not fly, it was doomed as game meat for the visiting sailors to give them a change of diet. And sadly, the Dutch settlers' domestic animals and the ships' rats soon plundered the dodos' one-egg nests, making this bird a legend.

# MAURITIUS

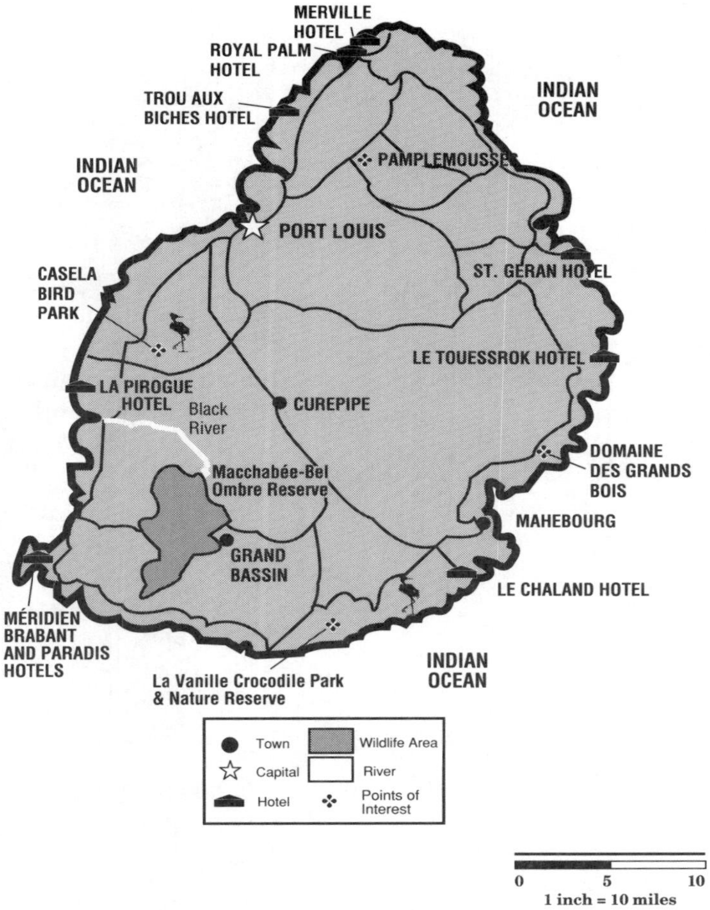


FACTS AT A GLANCE

| | |
|---|---|
| AREA: | 720 SQUARE MILES |
| APPROXIMATE SIZE: | RHODE ISLAND OR LUXEMBOURG |
| POPULATION: | 1.1 MILLION (1992 EST.) |
| CAPITAL: | PORT LOUIS (POP. EST. 142,000) |
| OFFICIAL LANGUAGE: | ENGLISH, FRENCH AND CREOLE PREDOMINATE. |

# MAURITIUS

If you have come part way around the world to visit Africa, you'll want to think about visiting Mauritius which lies east of the coast of Southern Africa.

Mauritius is a favorite destination for jet-setters, celebrities and royalty from around the world, many of whom rate this as one of the best getaways on earth. The combination of a cosmopolitan atmosphere, virgin-white beaches, crystal-clear waters, exquisite Creole, Indian, Chinese and European cuisine, chic hotels and service to match is difficult to beat.

This mountainous island paradise lies in the middle of the Indian Ocean in the tropics about 1200 miles east of Durban (South Africa), 1100 miles southeast of Mombasa (Kenya), 2900 miles southwest of Bombay (India) and 3700 miles west of Perth (Australia). Incorporating a visit to this remote island with a tour on the African mainland or an around-the-world vacation should be considered.

The most appropriate and frequently heard phrase on this island is "No Problem in Paradise." Unlike many "paradises", most of the people here have maintained their genuine and refreshing friendliness in the face of tourism.

This 720-square-mile island has a central plateau with the south being more mountainous than the north. Much of the lush vegetation has been converted into sugar cane and banana fields.

The population of just over one million consists of Indians, Creoles, French and Chinese. Hindu, Muslim, Christian and Chinese festivals occur with uncanny frequency. English is the official language and French is widely spoken, while most of the people prefer to speak Creole.

The island is known for the awkward dodo bird which, it is believed, lost its ability to fly because there were no predators from which it needed to escape. This evolutionary trait ironically contributed to its demise; the dodo was easily hunted to extinction during Dutch rule in the 1800s.

Creole cooking, emphasizing the use of curries, fresh seafood and tropical fruits, is often served. Mauritian beer and rum are popular.

Mauritius has a tropical oceanic climate. The best time to visit this island paradise for a beach holiday is from September-mid-December and April-June, when the days are sunny and temperatures warm. From mid-December-March is the cyclone season, bringing occasional tropical rains. June-August (winter) nights are cool and the temperatures along the coastline pleasant.

The average daily maximum temperature in January is 86° F. and in July is 75° F. Surf temperatures inside the reefs near shore are around 74° F. in winter and 81° F. in summer.

The first known discovery of Mauritius was by colonizers from Iran in 975 A.D., but they chose not to settle. They moved on to what is now Mombasa and Pemba Island. Later, in the sixteenth century, the Portuguese used the island as a staging post along their trade route to India.

The Dutch came in 1598 led by Wybrandt van Warwyck who named the island Mauritius after Prince Maurice of Nassau. However, the Dutch did not settle on the island until 1638. In 1710 they left the island to be replaced by the French in 1715; the French renamed it *Ile de France*. The island then became a "legal" haven for pirates who preyed on British cargo ships in time of war between Britain and France. In fact, this type of pirating was viewed by many as a respectable business.

After 95 years of French control and influence, the British took over in 1810. Slavery was abolished in 1835. As

La Pirogue Sun Hotel at Flic-en-Flac.

the emancipated slaves no longer wished to work on the sugar plantations, thousands of indentured Chinese and Indian workers were brought in to fill their places.

Mauritius became an independent member of the British Commonwealth in 1968. Mauritius has a parliamentary democracy, holding elections every five years.

Industrial products and sugar are the country's major exports. Tea and tobacco are also exported.

## WILDLIFE AND WILDLIFE AREAS

Mauritius' major wildlife attractions are found both on land and below the surface of the Indian Ocean.

### BIRDLIFE

Mauritius has a number of endemic species of birds — birds which are found nowhere else in the world. Many ornithologists or keen birders wishing to add unique species to their lists will find the long journey to this island paradise well worthwhile.

The pic-pic is the only one of the nine known remaining endemic species on the island commonly seen. The pink pigeon is thought to be the rarest pigeon in the world. The Mauritius kestrel is one of the rarest birds in the world; only four were known to exist in 1974. Fortunately, due to conservation efforts, populations are increasing. The other endemic species include the fly catcher, parakeet, Mauritius fody, olive white-eye, the Merle, and the cuckoo shrike.

About 45 species in total are found on the island. *Birds Of Mauritius*, a book by Claude Michel, is available in Mauritius.

## CASELA BIRD PARK

This peaceful 20-acre park harbors over 140 varieties of birds from five continents, including the Mauritian Pink Pigeon.

## MACCHABÉE-BEL OMBRE RESERVE

There are a number of small nature reserves on Mauritius. The best for hiking and spotting the endemic bird species mentioned is the Macchabée-Bel Ombre Reserve, located in the southwest. The reserve's upland and lowland forests provide a variety of habitats for birdlife.

## DOMAINE DES GRAND BOIS

In this 2000-acre forested park, located north of Mahebourg on the east coast, roam stags, deer, wild boar and monkeys.

## LA VANILLE CROCODILE PARK AND NATURE RESERVE

Located in the south, this farm breeds Nile crocodiles brought from Madagascar. There is also a small zoo with wild animals found on Mauritius and a nature walk.

## SCUBA DIVING/SNORKELING

The 100-mile coastline of Mauritius is almost completely surrounded by coral reefs, making this an excellent destination for snorkeling and SCUBA diving. You can dive on the colorful coral reefs and over 50 wrecks which harbor a great variety of sea life.

The best conditions for SCUBA diving and sailing are October-March. Most of the larger beach hotels offer dive excursions, dive lessons and rent equipment.

Spearfishing while diving with an Aqua-lung is prohibited; spearfishing while snorkeling is allowed, but the catch cannot exceed ten fish per day.

## BIG GAME FISHING

Big game fish, including blue marlin (plentiful), black marlin, yellow fin and skipjack tuna, jackfish, wahoo, barracuda, sea bass and many species of sharks can be caught. Fishing is excellent only a few miles off shore; the ocean drops to over 2300 feet in depth just one mile out!

The best fishing is from December-March and is sometimes good as late as May. An international fishing tournament is held every year in December.

The largest fleets of deep sea fishing boats are based at the Centre de Pêche at Rivière Noire (Black River) and at the Organization de Pêche du Nord at Trou-aux-Biches. Boats can be hired through your hotel or travel agencies and should be booked well in advance during this season. Fishing in the lagoons during this same period is also very good.

## PORT LOUIS

Port Louis, the chief harbor and capital city, is partially surrounded by mountains and is multifaceted in character. The city has a large market selling indigenous fruits and vegetables, pareos (colorful cloth wraps) and other clothing and souvenirs. Just off the main square along Place d'Armes are some eighteenth century buildings including the Government House and Municipal Theatre.

Chinatown is also worth a visit. The Chinese casino, L'Amicale de Port Louis, located on Royal Street, is popular. The season for horse racing at the Champ de Mars is from May-November.

## CUREPIPE

Curepipe is a large town located on the central plateau and is a good place to cool off from the warm coast and to shop. The extinct volcano, Trou aux Cerfs, may be visited nearby.

## PAMPLEMOUSSES

The world-renowned botanical gardens of Pamplemousses have dozens of bizarre plants and trees including the talipot palm — at 60 years of age, it blooms for the first time then dies. Giant water lilies imported from Brazil are also found here.

## TERRES DE COULEURS

The land takes on the colors of the rainbow (on sunny days) at Terres de Couleurs (the colored earth), located in the southwest in the mountains near Chamarel.

## GRAND BASSIN

Grand Bassin is a lake in an extinct volcano: it is the holy lake of the Hindus who celebrate the Maha Shivaratree, an exotic festival held yearly in February or March.

## GORGES DE LA RIVIÈRE NOIRE

Gorges de la Rivière Noire (Black River Gorges) are gorges located in the highest mountain chain on the island and offer splendid views of the countryside.

## ACCOMMODATION - BEACH HOTELS

The beaches, water sports, fabulous holiday hotels and exquisite dining are by far the major attractions of the island.

Hotels are spread out, so visitors spend most of their time enjoying the many activities and sports their particular hotel has to offer. In many of the top hotels, most water and land sports, with the exception of SCUBA diving, horseback riding and big game fishing, are free, including wind-surfing, water-skiing, sailing, snorkeling, volleyball, golf and tennis. Small sailboats are available at most resorts. Casinos are operated at the Saint Géran, La Pirogue, Méridien Brabant and Paradis and Trou aux Biches.

If you wish to visit the island during the high season, December-February and July-August, I suggest you book your trip several months in advance. Demand for accommodation in the top hotels is high year-round.

DELUXE: * *Royal Palm Hotel* is an elegant 84-room deluxe hotel located on Grand Bay on the northwest tip of the island. This is a good hotel for couples looking for a quiet hotel with nightly entertainment. * *Saint Géran* is a hotel resort of the highest standard with an international flair unmatched on the island. If you are going to see anyone famous while on this island, it will probably be here. Located on Pointe de Flacq on

Le Touessrok Sun Hotel, located at Trou d'Eau Douce.

the east coast of the island, facilities include a casino, 9-hole golf course, sailing and SCUBA diving. All 177 rooms are air-conditioned with private facilities. * *Le Touessrok* is a splendid holiday hotel, situated on the east coast south of the Saint Géran at Trou d'Eau Douce. Facilities include two swimming pools, two superb restaurants, disco, shops, and beauty parlor. What truly sets this resort apart from the rest is the pristine Ile-aux-Cerfs (Isle of Stags). Guests have complimentary transfers by boat to this nearby island. Ile-aux-Cerfs has miles and miles of the most beautiful beaches you will ever see. The hotel has 162 air-conditioned rooms, each with private facilities, refrigerator and minibar. * *Méridien Paradis* is located in the southwest of the island on a lagoon at the foot of the dramatic Le Morne Mountain. The hotel has air-conditioned rooms with facilities ensuite, swimming pool, casino, disco, nightly entertainment, and a fleet of deep sea fishing boats.

FIRST CLASS: * *La Pirogue* is located on a fine white beach at Flic-en-Flac on the island's west coast. Thatched cottages are spread out from the main building with its distinctive sail-like roof. There is a casino, and all 244 rooms are air-conditioned with private facilities. * *Méridien Brabant* has air-conditioned rooms with private facilities and is situated next to Méridien Paradis. Guests of the Méridien Brabant may use the facilities of Méridien Paradis.

TOURIST CLASS: * The *Merville Beach Hotel* is a comfortable hotel situated on Grand Bay near the northern tip of the island, with 170 air-conditioned rooms with private facilities, swimming pool, and the usual water sports. * *Shandrani Hotel* is conveniently located four miles from the international airport on Blue Bay at the southeastern coast. This 186-room hotel has a fine beach, all the usual water sports and tennis. All rooms are air-conditioned with private facilities.

# NAMIBIA

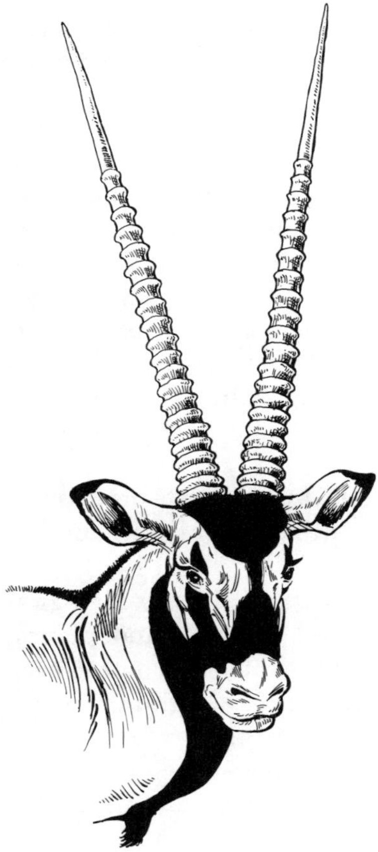

## THE HEAT-ADAPTED GEMSBOK

As the gemsbok are located in arid areas, they have splendid colorations and other heat-resistant methods to avoid the dry environment.

Their black face markings act to reflect heat and light away from their faces. The dark leg and underpart markings reflect away from the body.

During the heat of the day, they have a few unique ways of cooling. When subjected to high temperatures, they will increase their body temperature as much as ten degrees and will lose heat by radiation (and not evaporation), even if standing out in the midday sun. They will lower their temperature several more degrees during the cooler desert nights.

They will also increase their breathing up to five times as much, for the blood flowing through the vessels close to the surface of the nose is cooled by the air blowing in and out of the nose, maintaining lower blood temperatures that are returning to the brain.

They are able to conserve moisture by their highly efficient kidneys which pass waste product as only a few drops of concentrated urine.

They have also adapted amazing digging techniques to find bulbs, roots and underground plants, including the cucumber and Tsamma melon, to obtain much-needed moisture. Their stomachs have a high moisture content (80 percent), and Bushmen are known to squeeze and strain the stomach contents for the water.

In extremely hot areas, they will try to use any form of shade and will also dig a small area in the sand with their hooves to lie down to reduce their surface area.

# NAMIBIA

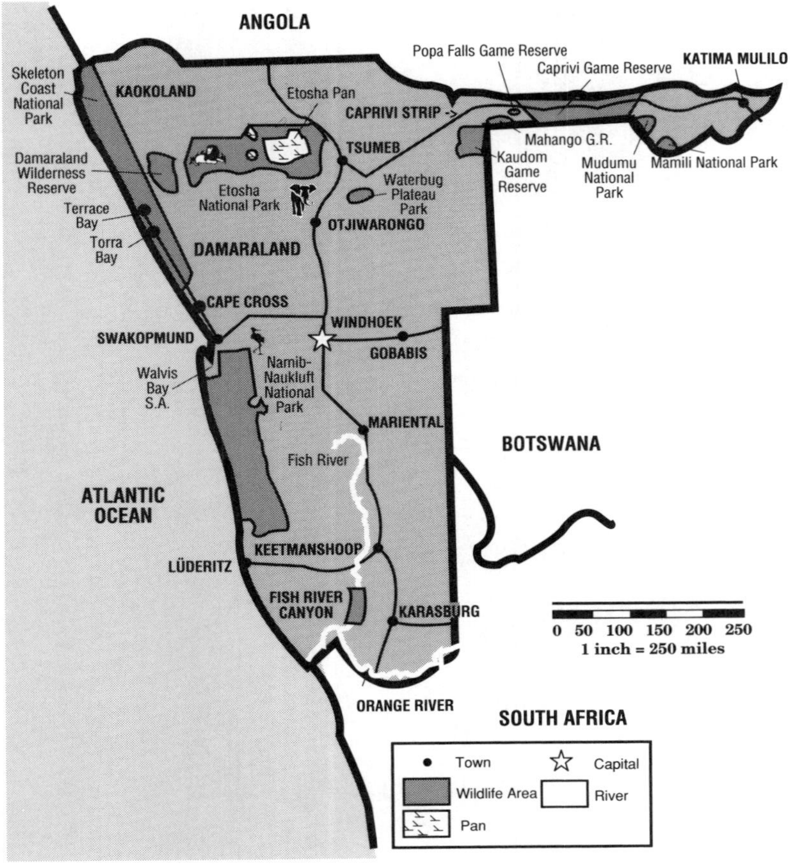


FACTS AT A GLANCE

| | |
|---|---|
| AREA: | 321,000 SQUARE MILES |
| APPROXIMATE SIZE: | TEXAS + OKLAHOMA OR ONE AND A HALF TIMES THE SIZE OF FRANCE |
| POPULATION: | 1.3 MILLION (1992 EST.) |
| CAPITAL: | WINDHOEK (POP. EST. 130,000) |
| OFFICIAL LANGUAGE: | ENGLISH |

# NAMIBIA

In addition to wildlife, Namibia has some of the most spectacular desert ecosystems in the world. It is famous for its stark beauty, diversity of tribes, and is a geologist's and naturalist's paradise.

Namibia has a subtropical climate. Inland summer (October-April) days are warm to hot with cool nights. Summer is the rainy season, with most rainfall occurring in the north and northeast.

Namibia is one of the world's most sparsely populated countries. Its population is 86 percent black, seven percent white and seven percent colored (of mixed descent). Most people live in the northern part of the country where there is more water. Herero women, colorfully dressed in red and black, continue to wear conservative, impractical and extremely hot attire fashioned for them by puritanical nineteenth century missionaries who wished to cover the savage breast.

In 1884 much of the coast became German Southwest Africa until 1915 when South Africa took control during World War I. The Union of South Africa received a mandate by the League of Nations over the region in 1920; the United Nations retracted the mandate in 1966 and renamed the country Namibia. The country became independent on March 21, 1990.

Namibia is the world's largest producer of diamonds,

and has the world's largest uranium mine. Tsumeb is the only known mine which has produced over 200 different minerals.

## WILDLIFE AND WILDLIFE AREAS

Etosha National Park is Namibia's premier reserve for wildlife and is one of the best reserves in Africa. Skeleton Coast and Namib-Naukluft National Parks have small concentrations of wildlife in fascinating desert environments with spectacular scenery. Several new reserves have been created in the Caprivi Strip "panhandle."

Winter (May-September) is the best time to visit the game parks and the central and northern regions when days are warm with clear skies and nights are cold.

Closed game viewing vehicles are required for most of Namibia's national parks. However, in the Damaraland Wilderness Reserve, Caprivi Game Reserve, Mudumu and Mamili National Parks, open vehicles are allowed. The parks are well-organized and the facilities clean.

## THE NORTH

### WINDHOEK

Windhoek is the capital, administrative, commercial and educational center of Namibia, situated in the center of the country at 5600 feet above sea level.

Sights include the three Windhoek castles (Schwerinsburg, Sanderburg and Heinitzburg) built between 1913-1918 and the State Museum at the Alte Feste (Old Fort).

ACCOMMODATION - FIRST CLASS: * *Hotel Safari* and *Safari Court,* located two miles out of town, has 452 air-conditioned luxury rooms with ensuite facilities, swimming pool and free transport to and from Windhoek.

DELUXE: * *Kalahari Sands* has 187 air-conditioned rooms and suites with private facilities, disco, swimming pool, and fitness center. The Presidential Suite was used by H.M. Queen Elizabeth II for Namibia's Independence celebrations.

TOURIST CLASS: * *Hotel Thüringerhof* has 42 air-conditioned rooms with ensuite facilities and beer garden. * *Continental Hotel* has 70 air-conditioned rooms, most with ensuite facilities, a popular nightclub and disco.

CAMPING: * *Daan Viljoen Game Park,* 17 miles from Windhoek, has campsites available.

## ETOSHA NATIONAL PARK

Etosha is one of Africa's greatest parks in both size and variety of wildlife species. The park covers 8600 square miles in the northern part of the country and lies 3300-4900 feet above sea level.

The park is mainly mixed scrub, mopane savannah and dry woodland surrounding the huge Etosha Pan. The pan is a silvery-white shallow depression, dry except during the rainy season. Mirages and dust-devils play across what was once a lake fed by a river that long ago changed course. Along the edge of the pan are springs that attract wildlife during the dry winter season.

The eastern areas of the park experience the most rainfall and have denser bush than the northwestern region which is mainly open grasslands. About 40 water holes spread out along 500 miles of roads provide many vantage points from which to watch game.

Etosha is famous for its huge elephant population which is most visible August-September in the center of the park. When the rains begin in October-November, elephants migrate north to Angola and west to Kaokoland and begin returning in March. Large populations of zebra, blue wildebeest, springbok and gemsbok migrate westward from the Namutoni area in October-November to the west and north-

Gemsbok can survive for long periods of time without drinking.

west of Okaukuejo Camp where they stay until around March-May. From June-August they migrate eastward again past Okaukuejo and Halali Camps to the Namutoni plains where there is water year-round. The park is totally fenced although this does not always stop the elephants from going where they please.

Lion are commonly seen, and zebra are often sighted way out on the barren pan where lions have no cover from which to launch an attack. Black-faced impala and Damara dikdik are two distinctive species of this area. Rhino prefer the western regions.

During my most recent visit, we spotted black rhino, elephant, lion, red hartebeest, greater kudu, giraffe, gemsbok, zebra, blue wildebeest, springbok, black-faced impala, black-backed jackal, honey badger, warthog and mongoose. Other wildlife in the park includes brown hyena, spotted hyena, caracal, African wildcat, leopard, cheetah, aardwolf, silver fox, bat-eared fox, eland, roan antelope and grey duiker.

Birdlife is prolific with over 325 species recorded, particularly on the Etosha Pan during the summer rainy season from mid-January to March. However, a diverse range of bird species can be seen year-round. Kites, pelicans, greater and lesser flamingos, and marabou storks migrate seasonally.

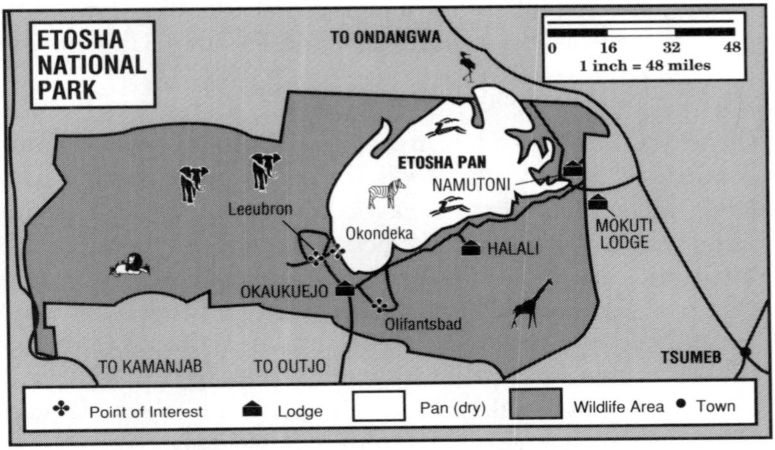


Other species commonly sighted include kori bustards, guinea fowl, francolins, ostrich, turtle doves, lilac-breasted roller, Namaqua sandgrouse and crimson-breasted shrike.

Roads run along the eastern, southern and western borders of the Etosha pan. The area around Namutoni Camp in the eastern part of the park receives more rain than the other region of the park. Eland, kudu and the Damara dikdik, Africa's smallest antelope, are often seen in this area. A good spot to see elephants is at Olifantsbad, a water hole between Halali and Okaukuejo Camps.

At the floodlit water hole at Okaukuejo Camp, we witnessed a stand-off between a black rhino and two elephants over control of the water hole that lasted for more than an hour. A lioness also came for a drink. The flatulence of the elephants was almost deafening!

From Okaukuejo one can drive along the southwestern edge of the pan to Okondeka and west to the Haunted Forest, a dense concentration of eerie-looking African moringa trees. I wouldn't want to walk through this forest at night! On the road from Okaukuejo to Leeubron, one passes under a social weaver's nest (bird's nest) the size of a car.

ACCOMMODATION - CLASS A/B: * *Mokuti Lodge,* located

500 yards from the Van Lindequist Gate (near Namutoni Camp), has 96 air-conditioned thatched bungalows with ensuite facilities, swimming pool and air strip. Game drives into the park are offered.

CLASS C & D: There are three National Park camps: *Namutoni, Halali,* and *Okaukuejo*. All three camps have lodge accommodations, caravan and camping sites, swimming pool, restaurant, store, petrol station and landing strip. The camps are fenced for the visitor's protection. * *Namutoni Camp,* situated seven miles from the Van Lindequist Gate, features a very attractive fortress built in 1903 and converted to hotel rooms, many of which have private facilities. * *Halali Camp,* the most modern of the camps, lies halfway between Namutoni and Okaukuejo Camps at the foot of a dolomite hill. Some rooms have private facilities. * *Okaukuejo Camp,* situated 11 miles from the Anderson Gate entrance, has a floodlit water hole and all rooms have private facilities.

## DAMARALAND

Damaraland is a large region with many attractions and is located east of Skeleton Coast National Park. Damara herders can be seen throughout this region.

The **Brandberg** is a massive mountain covering an area 19 by 14 miles and rises 6500 feet above the surrounding plains to 8440 feet above sea level. Its special attraction is that it harbors thousands of rock paintings, including one of the most famous in the region — "The White Lady."

**Twyfelfontein** has rock engravings of wildlife, including rhino, elephant and giraffe, which are considered to be some of the best on the continent. The **Petrified Forest** has many broken petrified tree trunks up to about 100 feet in length. Welwitschia plants may also be seen here. **Burnt Mountain**, a colorful mountain composed of many shades of purple and red, glows as if on fire when it is struck by the rays of the setting sun.

The best time to visit is May-December.

ACCOMMODATION - CLASS D: * *Khorixas Rest Camp* has rondavels with ensuite facilities. * *Palmwag Rest Camp* has rondavels.

CAMPING: * *Khorixas Rest Camp* and *Palmwag Rest Camp* have campsites with an ablution block.

## DAMARALAND WILDERNESS RESERVE

This privately operated, 1620-square-mile reserve is situated between Etosha National Park and Skeleton Coast National Park in northwestern Damaraland. This is an arid mountainous region of spectacular rugged scenery.

Wildlife is sparse and should be considered a bonus. However, many consider the search for wildlife which has adapted to a near-waterless environment well worth the effort. Wildlife includes desert elephant, black rhino, lion, desert-dwelling giraffe and Hartmann's mountain zebra. Wildlife migrates east and west along the dry river beds in search of food and water.

ACCOMMODATION - CLASS C: * *Etendeka Mountain Camp* is a tented camp (14 beds) with bucket shower and bush toilets. Exploring the region by open four-wheel-drive vehicle and walks are offered.

## KAOKOLAND

This is a region of rugged mountain ranges interspersed with wide valleys bordered on the west by Skeleton Coast National Park. Wildlife is sparse but includes elephant, giraffe, oryx, ostrich and some black rhino and lion. Himba tribes are often seen in the region.

The best time to visit is May-December. A minimum of two fully self-contained four-wheel-drive vehicles per party are required, and a professional guide is highly recommended. There is no fuel in the region.

## WATERBERG PLATEAU PARK

This 156-square-mile park is the home of several scarce and endangered species, including black rhino, white rhino, roan antelope and sable antelope. Other species include brown hyena, eland, tsessebe, kudu, oryx, giraffe, impala, klipspringer and dikdik. Leopard are sometimes seen on the top of the plateau.

Waterberg Plateau Park also contains unique flora along with rock paintings and engravings. Three trails lead up to the top of the plateau, which rises over 300 feet above the surrounding plains, and one across the top.

ACCOMMODATION - CLASS C & D: * *Bernarbe de la Bat Rest Camp* has bungalows with and without ensuite facilities, restaurant and a swimming pool.

CAMPING: Campsites with an ablution block are available.

ACCOMMODATION NEAR WATERBERG - CLASS B: * *Okonjima Guest Farm* is family-run and located on a private game reserve. Accommodations are in a farmhouse and separate units. Activities include bird watching, walks, and watching orphaned wild animals taken in by the family roam freely about the farm.

## KAUDOM GAME RESERVE

Situated in the extreme northeast section of the country on the Botswana border, this 1480-square-mile park, composed primarily of Kalahari sand dunes and dry woodland savannah, is one of the most remote reserves in Namibia.

Mammal species include elephant, lion, leopard, side-striped jackal, African wild dog, giraffe, wildebeest, eland, kudu, roan antelope and sable antelope.

During the dry season (June-October), game viewing can be good, especially at springs and water holes lying along dry river beds which serve as "roads." However, wildlife is not nearly as concentrated as in Etosha National Park. Kaudom should primarily be visited by those seeking a wilderness experience in a reserve which they will most likely have to themselves. Bushmen are sometimes found in the region.

Access to the park is from Tsumkwe in the south or Katere in the north. A minimum of two four-wheel-drive vehicles is required per party visiting the reserve.

ACCOMMODATION - CLASS D: * *Sigaretti* is located in the south of the reserve with three thatched huts. * *Kaudom* is situated in the north of the park with two huts.

CAMPING: Campsites are available at *Sigaretti* and *Kaudom*.

## THE CAPRIVI STRIP

The Caprivi Strip is the "panhandle" of Namibia, bordered by Angola and Zambia to the north and Botswana on the south.

Much of the wildlife in this region has been poached, especially during the conflict with Angola. However, wildlife populations are increasing, and the Caprivi is well worth a visit for anyone looking for a wilderness experience first, with wildlife as a bonus. A real plus of this region is that one seldom meets other tourists.

Unlike the parks in "mainland" Namibia, reserves in the Caprivi (Mudumu, Mamili and Caprivi) allow walking and game viewing in open vehicles. Mudumu National Park and Mamili National Park are similar to Botswana's Okavango Delta.

## MAHANGO GAME RESERVE

Mahango is a 96-square-mile reserve of floodplain and lush vegetated savannah with baobab trees. The park is situated along the banks of the Kavango River and bordered by the Caprivi Game Reserve on the east.

Wildlife includes elephant, hippo, crocs, waterbuck, lechwe, reedbuck, bushbuck, kudu, tsessebe, impala, and the rare sitatunga. Bird life includes fish eagles, wattled crane, crowned crane and African skimmers. Two four-wheel-drive vehicles are required to explore the most remote regions of the park.

ACCOMMODATION AND CAMPING: None.

ACCOMMODATION AND CAMPING NEAR MAHANGO: See "Popa Falls" below.

## POPA FALLS GAME RESERVE

This small park features rapids (more so than "falls") of the Kavango River, which has numerous hippo and crocs. This is a good base from which to explore the Mahango Game Reserve and Caprivi Game Reserve.

ACCOMMODATION - CLASS D: * *Popa Falls Government Camp,* located about ten miles north of the Mahango Game Reserve entrance, has thatched bungalows and ablution facilities.

CAMPING: Campsites with ablution facilities are available.

## CAPRIVI GAME RESERVE

Wildlife in this park includes elephant, buffalo, hippo, crocs, roan antelope, sable antelope, lechwe and plenty of waterfowl. An all-weather gravel road runs through the park.

ACCOMMODATION: None.

ACCOMMODATION NEAR THE PARK - CLASS C: * *Sitwe Camp* is located on the Kwando River southeast of West Caprivi Game Reserve and has five bungalows (ten beds) with separate facilities. Game drives in open vehicles, day and night game drives by boat, kayak safaris and walks are offered.

CLASS D: See "Popa Falls" above.

CAMPING: Campsites with no facilities are available.

## MUDUMU NATIONAL PARK

This newly proclaimed park of floodplains, islands and bush is similar to the Okavango Delta (Botswana), but with not quite as much game. The Kwando River runs along the park's western border. On a recent visit we encountered elephant, impala and a number of other species on walks. Other wildlife includes lion, hippo, crocs, roan antelope and sitatunga.

Game viewing by open vehicle and walks are allowed. Four-wheel-drive vehicles are recommended.

ACCOMMODATION - CLASS B: * *Lianshulu Lodge* is located on the banks of the Kwando River and has eight thatched chalets (doubles) with ensuite facilities. Activities include game drives, walks, game viewing by boat, sunset cruises on a double-decker barge, and excursions to Mamili National Park. Access is by air charter and by road.

CLASS C: * *Mvubu Camp* is situated on the banks of the Kwando River and has five tents (doubles) with separate facilities. Game viewing by open vehicles and by boat and walks are offered.

## MAMILI NATIONAL PARK

This newly proclaimed park is predominately floodplain and has similar wildlife as Mudumu National Park. The Linyanti River flows along its southeastern border which it shares with Botswana. Wildlife is increasing in this park quite rapidly, and plenty of game is seen on the Botswana side of the river.

ACCOMMODATION: None. See "Mudumu Reserve" above.

CAMPING: Campsites with no facilities are available.

## THE COAST

The freezing Benguela Current of the Atlantic flows from Antarctica northward along the Namibian coastline and meets the hot, dry air of the Namib Desert, forming a thick fog bank which often penetrates inland up to 60 miles. The best time to visit the coast for sunbathing, fishing, and surfing is from December-February; June-July is cold and rainy.

## SKELETON COAST NATIONAL PARK

Skeletons of shipwrecks and whales dot the treacherous coast of this park which stretches along the seashore and covers over 2000 square miles of wind-shaped dunes, canyons and jagged peaks of the Namib.

*Skeleton Coast* by Amy Schoeman (Macmillan Publishers) is a superb pictorial and factual representation of this fascinating region.

Fog penetrates inland for over 20 miles almost every day and often lingers until the desert sun burns it off at 9:00-10:00 a.m. When the wind blows from the east, there is instant sunshine.

The park is divided into southern and northern sections. The southern section is more accessible and lies between the Ugab and Hoanib Rivers. Permits and reservations (paid in advance) must be made with the Directorate of Tourism and Resorts for stays at either Torra Bay or Terrace Bay.

The northern part of the park has been designated as a wilderness area and can only be visited with fly-in safaris.

This exclusive northern region has many unusual and

Flying into camp on the Khumib River, Skeleton Coast.

fascinating attractions. One such attraction is the **Cape Frio Seal Colony**, which has grown to about 40,000 seals.

A walk down the **roaring dunes** will give you the surprise of your life. Suddenly everyone is looking up to spot the B-52 bomber that must be overhead. Apparently the sand is just the right diameter and consistency to create a loud noise when millions of its granules slide down the steep dune. Incredible!

Driving through Hoarusib Canyon, one witnesses striking contrasts of dark-green grasses against verdite canyon walls and near-vertical white dunes. Elephant and lion spoor (prints) are numerous. Small fish dart about in shallow ponds as lizards make their way along the rocky walls. One then passes a fairy-tale land of castles and other dynamic water-sculptured figures of sand created over eons by this stream. A rising moon, though, places a soft loving spell over this merciless landscape. From February-April, many colorful desert flowers are in bloom.

Large game is sparse. However, many small, but just as fascinating creatures have uniquely adapted to this environment and help make this one of the most interesting deserts in the world. Larger wildlife includes black rhino, desert elephant, lion, leopard, and baboon. Brown hyena are plentiful but rarely seen. Black-backed jackal, springbok and gemsbok are often sighted.

Lion living along the coast have become especially adapted to living off seals, fish and birds. Lion spoor are sometimes seen in or around camp.

The east wind brings detrite (small bits of plant matter) providing much needed compost for plants and food for lizards and beetles. The west wind brings moisture on which most life depends in this desert, which is almost completely devoid of water. The ancient "fossil" plant, *Welwitschia mirabilis,* is also found in the region.

ACCOMMODATION - NORTHERN SKELETON COAST (FLY-IN SAFARIS) - CLASS C: * *False Cape Frio Camp* is composed of wooden igloos set on the beach about three miles from the seal colony. In addition, there are three fixed tented camps with chemical toilets in the region: two within the park and one in Damaraland.

ACCOMMODATION - SOUTHERN SKELETON COAST - CLASS D: * *Terrace Bay* is open year-round and offers full board and lodging in basic bungalows with private facilities. There is a landing strip for light aircraft.

CAMPING: * *Torra Bay* has campsites and caravan sites and is open only over the holidays December 1-January 31.

## SWAKOPMUND

The resort town of Swakopmund, located on the coast and surrounded by the Namib Desert, has many fine examples of German colonial architecture.

ACCOMMODATION - TOURIST CLASS: * The *Hansa Hotel* is an attractive hotel with 34 rooms with private facilities. * The *Strand Hotel* is located on the beach front and has 42 rooms with private facilities.

## CAPE CROSS SEAL RESERVE

Cape Cross Seal Reserve, home of over 200,000 seals, is open daily except Fridays from 10:00 a.m. to 5:00 p.m.

# THE SOUTH

## NAMIB-NAUKLUFT NATIONAL PARK

The consolidation of the Namib Desert Park and the Naukluft Mountain Zebra Park and incorporation of other lands, including most of what was called "Diamond Area #2", created the largest park in Namibia and one of the largest in the world. Namib-Naukluft National Park covers 19,215 square miles of desert savannah grasslands, gypsum and quartz plains, granite mountains, an estuarine lagoon, a canyon and huge drifting apricot-colored dunes.

The Kuiseb River runs through the center of the park from east to west and acts as a natural boundary separating the northern grayish-white gravel plains from the southern deserts.

Herds of mountain zebra, gemsbok, springbok and flocks of ostrich roam the region. The dunes are home to numerous unique creatures such as the translucent Palmato gecko, the shovel-nosed lizard and the golden mole.

The five main regions of the park are the Namib, Sandvis, Naukluft, Sesriem and Sossusvlei areas.

The **Namib** may well be the world's oldest desert. The welwitschia flats region lies on a dirt road about 22 miles north of the Swakopmund-Windhoek road and is the best area to see the prehistoric *Welwitschia mirabilis* plants. Actually

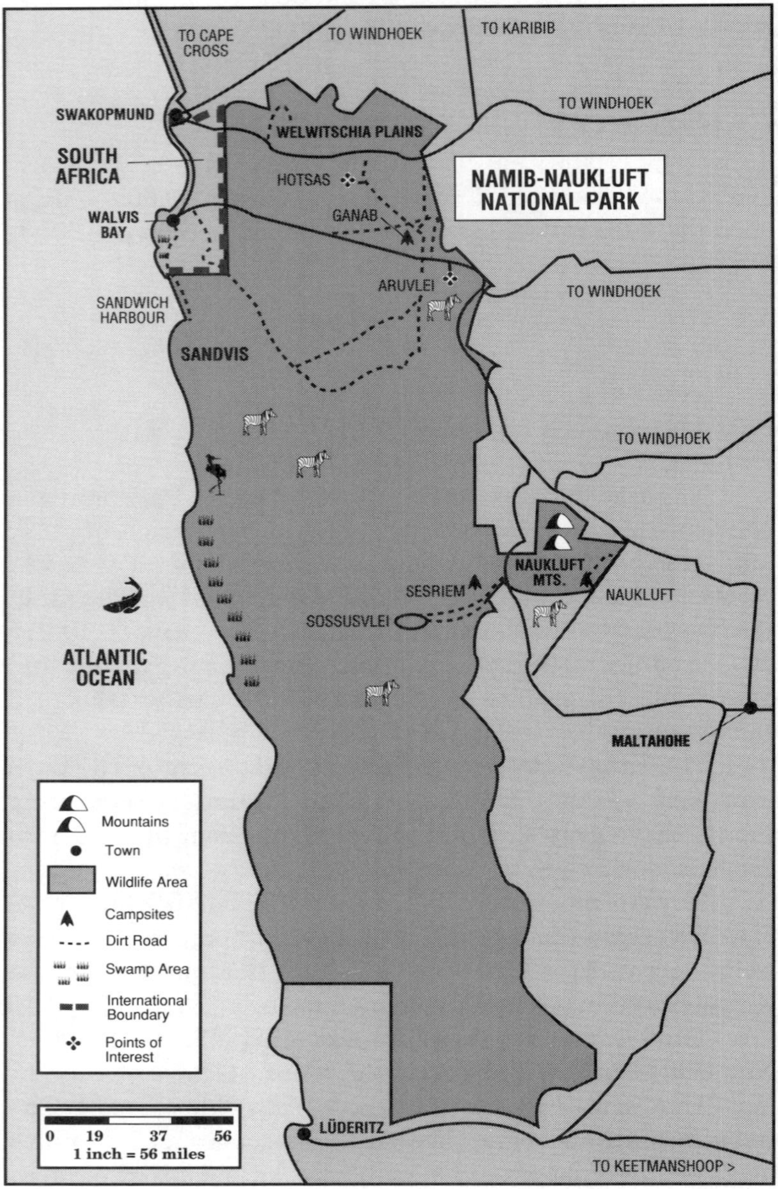

TO CAPE CROSS
TO WINDHOEK
TO KARIBIB
TO WINDHOEK
SWAKOPMUND
WELWITSCHIA PLAINS
SOUTH AFRICA
HOTSAS
NAMIB-NAUKLUFT NATIONAL PARK
GANAB
WALVIS BAY
ARUVLEI
TO WINDHOEK
SANDWICH HARBOUR
SANDVIS
TO WINDHOEK
NAUKLUFT MTS.
SESRIEM
NAUKLUFT
SOSSUSVLEI
ATLANTIC OCEAN
MALTAHOHE
Mountains
Town
Wildlife Area
Campsites
Dirt Road
Swamp Area
International Boundary
Points of Interest
0 19 37 56
1 inch = 56 miles
LÜDERITZ
TO KEETMANSHOOP >

Many *Welwitschia mirabilis* trees common in Namib-Naukluft National Park are more than 2,000 years old.

classified as trees, many welwitschia are thousands of years old and are perfect examples of adaptation to an extremely hostile environment. The water holes at Hotsas and Ganab are good locations to spot game; Ganab and Aruvlei are known for mountain zebra.

If you plan to deviate from the main road through the park, a permit is required and is obtainable weekdays only at the Nature Conservation Office in Swakopmund or the Nature Conservation Reservation Office Windhoek.

The **Sandvis** area includes Sandwich Harbour, 26 miles south of Walvis Bay, and is accessible only by four-wheel-drive vehicles. Fresh water seeps from under the dunes into the salt-water lagoon, resulting in a unique environment. Bird watching is excellent September-March, and at times over half a million birds are present. Only day trips are allowed to the harbor and the area is closed on Sundays. Permits are required and may be obtained from Department of Nature Conservation or from Service Stations in Walvis Bay.

The **Naukluft** region is an important watershed characterized by dolomitic mountains over 6300 feet in height with massive picturesque rock formations and thickly foliated river beds. Large numbers of mountain zebra, along with springbok, kudu, klipspringer, rock rabbits, baboons and black eagles, are frequently sighted. Also present are cheetah and leopard.

There are several hiking trails from which to choose. One of the more interesting trails is the Naukluft Trail, 10 ½ miles in length, requiring six to seven hours of hiking.

**Sesriem Canyon** is about 0.6 of a mile long and is as narrow as six feet wide with walls about 100 feet high. When the river is high, one can swim upstream where the canyon takes on a cave or tunnel-like appearance. The canyon is only a few minutes drive from Sesriem Camp.

**Sossusvlei** is located in the extreme southern part of the park and has the highest sand dunes in the world, exceeding 1000 feet. The base of the second highest sand dune in the world can be fairly closely approached by vehicle.

The hike along the knife-edge rim to the top is strenuous, requiring 1-1 ½ hours of taking two steps up and sliding one step down. The view from the top into other valleys and of the mountains beyond is marvelous. Even up here, colorful beetles, ants, and other desert critters roam about.

Driving back to camp from Sossusvlei, a gemsbok ran full speed beside our vehicle for several minutes, proving the strength and resiliency of these majestic animals.

Plan on leaving camp at Sesriem early to see a spectacular sunrise on these magnificent and colorful dunes. At Sossusvlei, camping is not allowed and there is no accommodation.

ACCOMMODATION - CAMPING: Campsites with ablution facilities are available in the Namib, Naukluft and Sesriem regions of the park. * *Namib Campsites* have no firewood or

This sand dune, the second highest in the world (about 1,000 feet), is located at Sossuvslei.

water. * *Naukluft Campsites* have water, firewood and ablution facilities. * *Sesriem Campsite* has two ablution blocks with hot and cold water; firewood and fuel are available.

ACCOMMODATION NEAR SESRIEM - CLASS C: * *Namib Rest Camp* has rooms with ensuite facilities and is located about 37 miles from Sesriem.

## FISH RIVER CANYON

Second in size only to the Grand Canyon, Fish River Canyon is 100 miles in length, up to 17 miles in width, and up to 1800 feet deep. The Fish River cuts its way through the canyon to the Orange River, which empties into the Atlantic Ocean.

The vegetation and wildlife are very interesting. Many red aloes make the area appear like one imagines the planet Mars. Baboons, mountain zebra, rock rabbits, ground squirrels and klipspringer are often seen, while kudu and leopard remain elusive. The river water is cold and deep enough in areas to swim.

There is a well-marked path into the canyon in the north of the park where the four-day hike begins. For those hiking into the canyon for the day, allow 45-60 minutes down, and 1½ hours back up. Permission to walk down to the canyon floor must first be obtained from the ranger at Hobas.

The main hiking trail is 53 miles in length and is open May-August. The going is tough since much of the walking is on the sandy, rock-strewn floor. No facilities exist en route, so this hike is not for the tenderfoot. Water is readily available from the many pools that join to become a river during the rainy summers. Hot sulphur springs are located about halfway through the hike.

A maximum group of 40 people is allowed per day. Permits must be obtained in advance from the Directorate of Tourism and Resorts. A medical certificate of fitness is also required.

ACCOMMODATION - CLASS C: * *Ai-Ais Hot Springs,* located at the southern end of the canyon at the end of the hiking trail, has rooms with private facilities, refrigerators and hot plates, large thermally heated swimming pool and mineral baths. Ai-Ais is open from the second Friday in March until the 31st of October.

CAMPING: * *Ai-Ais* campsites have hot showers. * *Hobas* campsite, located at the trailhead in the north of the park, has hot showers and a swimming pool.

# RWANDA

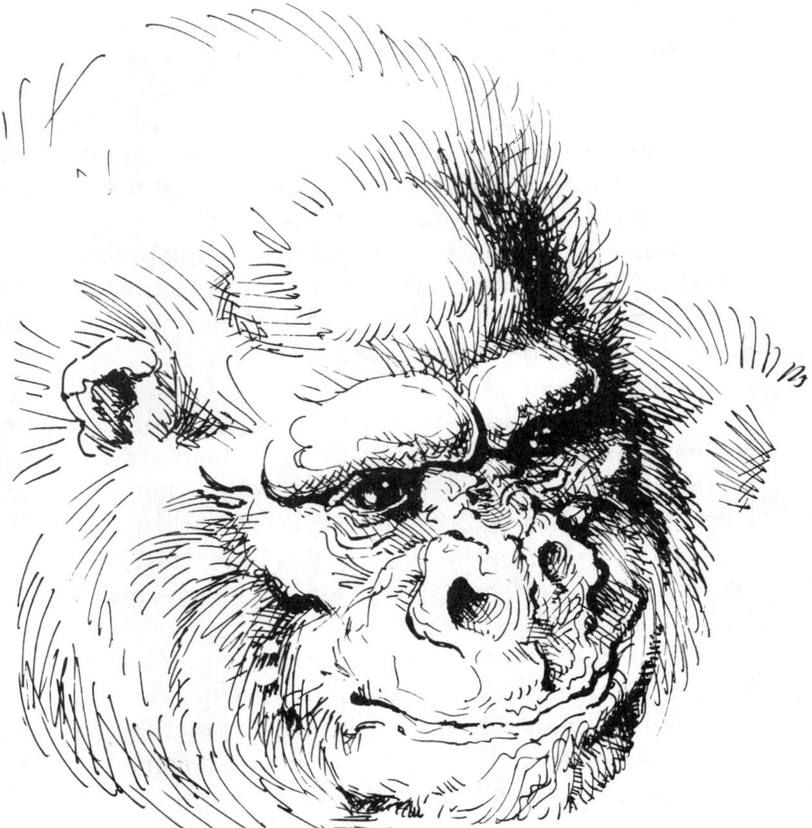

## THE NESTING GORILLA

As gorillas are diurnal and on the move constantly, they find themselves at a different location each night, where they meticulously build their beds (nests) and go to sleep.

As the nests do not appear to offer any decent protection from the rain or cold, building them seems to be more an activity that has continued from the past when they were more arboreal than a necessary part of life.

Females take time and care in the construction of their nests and more often will build their nests on the ground instead of in trees. That they are heavy animals is a factor as the youngsters may form their nests in trees. Signs of tree nests last longer than those on the ground and can be found up to five months to a year after being built.

Males, who are not as careful in building their nests as females, have been observed trying to snuggle into the nest of a female and child to get out of the rain. Hollow tree trunks are good protection from the rain, and they use them when they can and may line the nest with moss.

An average nest built by females takes between three to five minutes to construct. They begin to break the tips of non-food vegetation, like *lobelia,* and weave them in a semi-circle around their bodies like the rim of a bathtub, using the leaves as a lining on the bottom. The tasty nettles, thistles, celery and bamboo shoots they like to eat do not make a comfortable mattress.

Youngsters make a great pretense at nest building. They begin at about 18 months and have up to the time they are between three and four years old to practice. They will bend and break the pliable stems into their laps, stand up and then quickly try to sit down on them, holding on with their hands. Their small light bodies cannot keep the springy stems down. Signs of frustration are numerous as they learn to master the art of building the rim and using the leafy portion for a mattress. The babies will try to mimic, but their beds are usually a flimsy pile of leaves.

# RWANDA

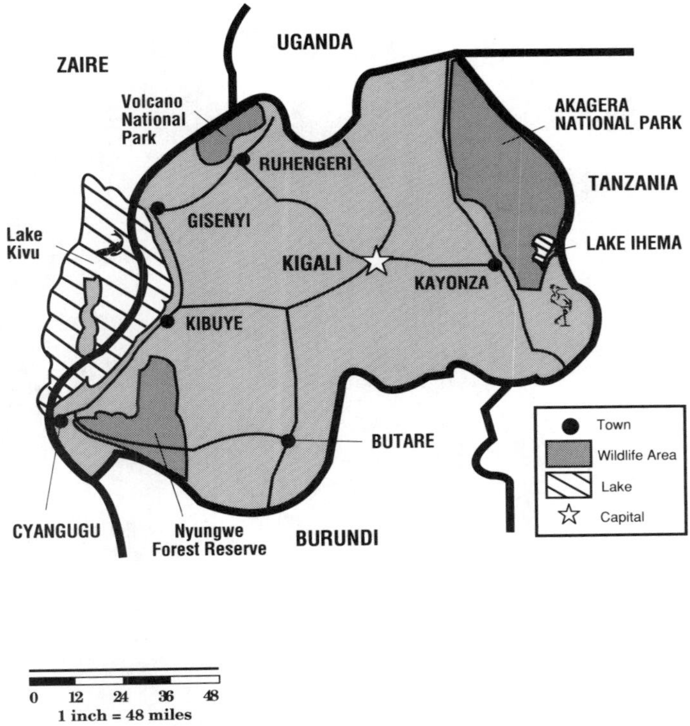


FACTS AT A GLANCE

| | |
|---|---|
| AREA: | 10,169 SQUARE MILES |
| APPROXIMATE SIZE: | MARYLAND OR BELGIUM |
| POPULATION: | 7 MILLION (1992 EST.) |
| CAPITAL: | KIGALI (POP. EST. 270,000) |
| OFFICIAL LANGUAGE: | KINYARWANDA AND FRENCH |

# RWANDA

Mountain gorillas are by far Rwanda's major international attraction. After the release of the feature film *Gorillas In The Mist* about the late Dian Fossey's pioneering work habituating the gorillas, interest in gorilla trekking reached new heights.

Travelers from all over the world venture to this remote country to experience these magnificent animals in their native environment. Watching these fascinating creatures on television is exciting enough but nothing in comparison to the thrill of visiting them firsthand.

Appropriately called "The Country of a Thousand Hills," Rwanda is predominantly grassy uplands and hills, with altitudes above sea level varying from a low of 3960 feet to Mt. Karisimbi, the highest of a range of extinct volcanoes in the northwest which reach almost 14,800 feet. Lake Kivu forms part of the border with Zaire and is one of the most beautiful lakes in Africa.

Also called "The Country of Perpetual Spring," Rwanda's comfortable climate is temperate and mild with an average daytime temperature of 77° F. The main rainy season is from mid-February to mid-May, and the shorter one is from mid-October to mid-December.

Ninety-seven percent of the people live in self-contained compounds and work the adjacent land. Sixty percent of the population is Christian (80 percent of which are Catholic), though many people follow traditional African beliefs. About 90 percent of the population is Hutu (Bahutu), nine percent Tutsi (Batusi) and one percent Twa (Batwa) pygmies.

The Tutsi dominated the Hutu farmers with a feudal system analogous to that of medieval England. The system was based on cattle and was surpassed in Africa only by Ethiopia.

Because of its physical isolation and fearsome reputation, Rwanda was not affected by the slave and ivory trade from Zanzibar in the 1800s. The area peacefully became a German protectorate in 1899, and in 1916 was occupied by the Belgians.

Following World War One, Rwanda and Burundi were mandated by the League of Nations to Belgium as the territory of Ruanda-Urundi. Full independence for Rwanda and Burundi was achieved on July 1, 1962.

High population density is at the root of Rwanda's economic problems. Almost all arable land is under cultivation. Coffee is the country's major export. French and Kinyarwanda are widely spoken while Kiswahili is spoken in the major towns and regions close to the borders. English is spoken in the deluxe hotels and exclusive shops, but very little English is spoken in the countryside.

## WILDLIFE AND WILDLIFE AREAS

In addition to Volcano National Park, Rwanda has two other important reserves — Akagera National Park and the Nyungwe Forest Reserve. Many tourists combine a trip to Rwanda with the parks of eastern Zaire, Kenya and/or Tanzania.

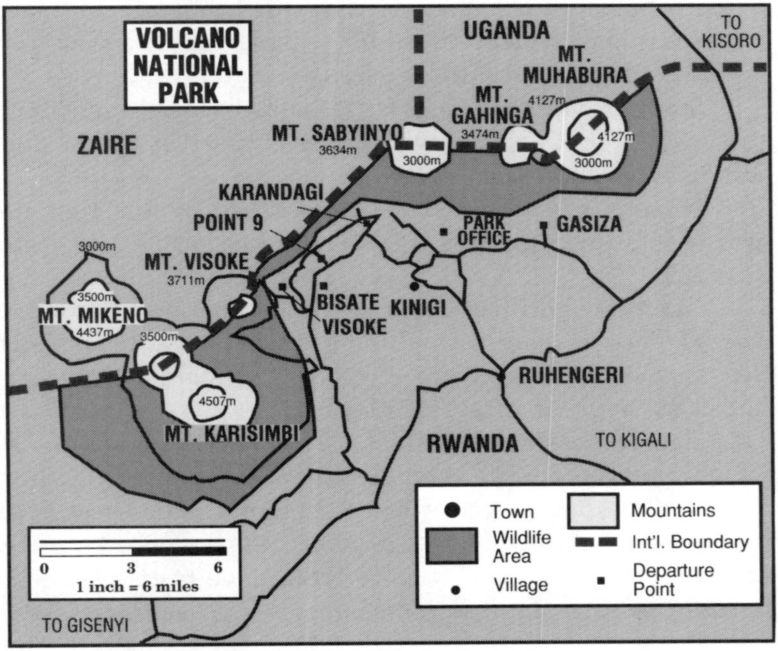


## THE WEST

# VOLCANO NATIONAL PARK (PARC NATIONAL DES VOLCANS)

Volcano National Park is home to the mountain gorilla, discovered by Europeans in the early 1900s. The peaks of the Virunga Mountains, heavily forested extinct volcanoes, serve as a border with Zaire and Uganda and are part of the watershed between the Zaire and Nile river systems.

This 46-square-mile park supports several vegetation zones from lowland forest to luxuriant mountain forest to Afro-alpine. From 8500-11,000 feet primary forest is dominated by hagenia trees growing 30-60 feet in height. Hagenia have twisted trunks with low branches covered with lichen out of which parasitic orchids often grow.

Volcano National Park borders Virunga National Park in Zaire and the Gorilla Sanctuary in Uganda. The park receives a high amount of rainfall, averaging 40 inches per year. Daytime temperatures average about 50° F.

The mountain gorilla is larger and has longer hair than the lowland gorilla. It grows to over six feet in height and weighs more than 440 pounds.

Mountain gorillas form themselves into fairly stable groups of three to 30. They are active by day and sleep in nests at night.

Mountain gorillas eat leaves, buds and tubers (like wild celery). They are continuously on the move, looking for their favorite foods. They eat morning and afternoon, their dining habits interspaced with a midday nap.

Fourteen species of primates are found in these forests, including the red colobus and the crested mangabey. Other wildlife in the park includes forest elephants, giant forest hog, black-fronted duiker (very common), yellow-backed duiker and buffalo. Over 90 species of birds have been recorded, including spectacular mountain touracos and black partridges.

Forest elephants are smaller than those found on the savannah and are most often found in the lower forest zone. Forest elephants do not hesitate to climb the steep slopes of the volcanoes and are known to climb to the bamboo zone where they eat the young bamboo shoots.

## Gorilla Trekking

Searching for gorillas in the misty mountain air of volcanoes can be likened to an adventurous game of "hide and seek" in which the guides know where they were yesterday but must find their trail again today and follow it. Finding gorillas can almost be guaranteed for those willing to hike one to four hours in search of them.

Each group of visitors is led by a park guide. Porters may be hired (their services are included in most package tours) to carry lunch, drinks, etc., and to assist anyone who may wish to return early.

The search often involves climbing down into gullies, then pulling yourself up steep hills by holding onto vines and bamboo. Even though the pace is slow, you must be in good condition to keep up; the search may take you to altitudes from 7500 to 9800 feet. While this sounds difficult, almost anyone in good physical condition without a heart problem can do it.

Once the gorilla group has been located, the guide communicates with them by making low grunting sounds and imitates them by picking and chewing bits of foliage. Juvenile gorillas are often found playing and tend to approach within a few feet of their human guests. Occasionally our guides had to keep them from jumping into our laps!

Adult females are a little more cautious but may still approach within several feet of you. The dominant male, called a silverback because of the silvery-grey hair on his back, usually keeps more than 20 feet from his human visitors.

Gorilla-viewing "etiquette" is important. Do not make eye contact with a silverback. If a silverback begins to act aggressively, look down immediately and take a submissive posture by squatting or sitting, or he may take your staring as aggression and charge. The key is to follow the directions of your well-trained guide. Gorillas are herbivores (vegetarians) and will not attack a human unless provoked. Please do not touch the gorillas as they are very susceptible to catching human colds and diseases.

After spending up to 60 minutes visiting with these magnificent animals, visitors descend to a more open area for a picnic lunch.

The groups visited by tourists have been numbered or named by the researchers studying them. Gorilla Groups 9 and 11 may be visited by up to six tourists each day, and Groups 13 and Susa may be visited by up to eight. However, conservation groups are exerting pressure to keep the maximum number of visitors for all the gorilla groups limited to six persons per day.

Visitors to Group 11 meet at the Visoke departure point. Muside has two departure points for visitors to Group 13, Karandagi or Kanuma, so be sure to learn which is your departure point at Park Headquarters.

Group 9 divides its time between Rwanda and Zaire and therefore permits are sold only at the Park Headquarters at Kinigi up to one day in advance. Groups 11, 13 and Susa must be booked in advance of arrival to the park. Children under 15 years of age are not allowed to visit the gorillas.

Visitors must check in at Park Headquarters near Kinigi village, about a 45-minute drive from Ruhengeri, between 7:00-8:00 a.m. Be sure to have your voucher before making the 30-40 minute (up to ten-mile) drive to departure points where the searches begin. Visitors must meet their guides at designated departure points no later than 9:00 a.m.

The most popular time to visit the gorillas is during the dry seasons, mid-June-September and December-March.

The park was temporarily closed due to unrest in the country. However, as of this writing, the park is open to international visitors. Check with an Africa travel specialist (see page 481) for current information.

Use 400 ASA film or higher as gorillas are often found in the shadow of the forest. You will probably want to "push" 400 ASA to 800 ASA to get enough light. 1000 and 1600 ASA films are used by many trekkers. Bring several rolls of film on the trek — you very well may need it!

Mornings are almost always cool and misty; even if it doesn't rain, you will undoubtedly get wet from hiking and crawling around wet vegetation. Wear a waterproof jacket (or poncho) and pants (preferably gortex), leather gloves to protect your hands from stinging nettles, waterproof light or medium weight hiking boots to give you traction on muddy slopes and to keep your feet dry, wool socks and wool hat. Bring a waterproof pouch for your camera and plenty of film, water bottle and snacks. Do not wear bright clothes, perfumes, colognes or jewelry as these distractions may excite the gorillas.

Visiting the gorillas is one of the most expensive yet most rewarding safaris in Africa. However, the park fees, which are among the highest in Africa, go toward the preservation of these magnificent, endangered creatures. It is very difficult get to the park and departure points unless you join a tour (the best option) or rent your own vehicle (expensive). There is no public transportation from Ruhengeri to the Park Headquarters or to the trek departure points.

## Mountain Climbing

Hiking in the beautiful Virunga Mountains is in itself an adventure. Trails lead to the craters or peaks of the park's five volcanoes, upwards through the unique high-vegetation zones of bamboo, hagenia-hypericum forests, giant lobelia and senecio, and finally to alpine meadows. Views from the top, which overlook the lush Rwandan valleys and into Zaire and Uganda, are spectacular.

Some travelers spend a day or two searching for gorillas interspaced with hikes to one or more of the volcanoes.

**Karisimbi** (14,786 ft./4507 m.) is Rwanda's highest and occasionally snowcapped mountain. It is the most arduous ascent, requiring two days from the Visoke departure point. The night may be spent in a metal hut at about 12,000 feet (3660 meters).

**Visoke** (12,175 ft./3711 m.) has a beautiful crater lake and requires four hours of hiking up a steep trail to reach the summit from the Visoke departure point. The walk around the crater rim is highly recommended. Allow seven hours for the entire trip.

**Lake Ngezi** (9843 ft./3000 m.), a small, shallow crater lake, is the easiest hike in the park, taking only three to four hours round-trip from the Visoke departure point.

**Sabyinyo** (11,922 ft./3834 m.) can be climbed in five to six hours starting at Park Headquarters near Kinigi. A metal hut is located just before you reach the lava beds. The final section is along a narrow rocky ridge with steep drops on both sides.

**Gahinga** (11,398 ft./3474 m.) and **Muhabura** (13,540 ft./4127 m.) are both reached from the departure point at Gasiza. The trail rises to a hut in poor condition on the saddle between the two mountains. Gahinga's summit can be reached in four hours, while two days are recommended to reach the summit of Muhabura.

A park guide must accompany each group. Porters are optional. Should you encounter gorillas on your hikes, you may not leave the path to follow them. You may only track gorillas if you have previously purchased the proper permits.

ACCOMMODATION - DELUXE: See Gisenyi.

TOURIST CLASS: * *Hotel Muhabura* is a very rustic hotel (the best in Ruhengeri) with the most convenient access to Volcano National Park. It is about a ten-mile/45-minute drive to Park Headquarters. Ten simple double rooms and two pavilions with bathrooms ensuite, plus popular local bar, disco and dining room are available.

CLASS F: Very basic bungalows located at Park Headquarters may be available.

CAMPING: Campsites at Park Headquarters near Kinigi with cold shower and toilet facilities may be available. Beware of thieves.

## GISENYI

Gisenyi is a picturesque resort on beautiful Lake Kivu with sandy white beaches believed to have little or no bilharzia. Crocodiles are absent from the lake due to volcanic action eons ago which wiped them out, making swimming safer.

ACCOMMODATION - DELUXE: * *Hotel Izuba Méridien* is an excellent hotel with 68 double rooms and four suites with private facilities: it is located 1¾ -hours, drive from Volcano National Park. Situated on Lake Kivu, the hotel has a swimming pool, tennis courts and solarium.

TOURIST CLASS: * *Hotel Palm Beach* has rooms with private facilities and is located on the lakeshore drive.

## KIBUYE

Kibuye, located on Lake Kivu midway between Gisenyi and Cyangugu, is a small town with an attractive beach. Be sure not to miss the over 330-foot-high **Ndaba Waterfall** (Les Chutes des Ndaba), not far from Kibuye.

ACCOMMODATION - TOURIST CLASS: * *Kibuye Guest House* is located on Lake Kivu and has 18 double rooms with private facilities, tennis courts and sports activities on the lake.

## NYUNGWE FOREST RESERVE (LA FORÊT DE NYUNGWE)

The Nyungwe Forest is one of the most biologically diverse high-altitude rain forests in Africa. Located in southwestern Rwanda bordering the country of Burundi, this 375-square-mile reserve is home for 12 species of primates including a rare subspecies of black and white colobus monkey, the rare golden monkey, blue monkeys and mangabeys.

In addition to a variety of butterflies and orchids, over 200 species of birds have been recorded.

Although Nyungwe Forest Reserve is situated at a lower altitude and is dryer (receives less rain) than Volcano National Park, hiking is more difficult in Nyungwe. The vegetation at Nyungwe is much thicker and many slopes are steeper, if not impossible to ascend. Colobus and the other primates are often difficult to approach closely. However, this will hopefully change with time.

ACCOMMODATIONS: Day trips to Nyungwe Forest Reserve can be made from Butare. See "Accommodations" under "Butare" below.

CAMPING: Campsites have no facilities.

## BUTARE

Located in southern Rwanda not far from the border with Burundi, Butare is the intellectual capital of Rwanda. Here you find the National Museum (good archaeology and ethnology exhibits), and the National University and National Institute of Scientific Research (ask about folklore dances). Several craft centers are located in villages within ten miles of Butare.

ACCOMMODATION - TOURIST CLASS: * *Hotel Faucon* and *Hotel Ibis* have rooms with facilities ensuite.

# CENTRAL AND EAST

## KIGALI

The capital of Rwanda, Kigali is the commercial center of the country. A number of very good restaurants are located in the deluxe hotels.

ACCOMMODATION - DELUXE: * *Hotel des Diplomats* has 24 double rooms and 16 apartments, all with ensuite facilities, video and private terraces, and tennis. * *Hotel des Mille Collines* has 112 rooms with private facilities, and video and swimming pool. * *Umubano Méridien* is located a few miles outside the city center.

TOURIST CLASS: * *Hotel Kiyovu* has rooms with facilities ensuite. * *Chez Lando* has rooms with private facilities.

## AKAGERA NATIONAL PARK (LE PARC NATIONAL DE L'AKAGERA)

Akagera National Park is located in northeastern Rwanda along the Akagera River (a Nile affluent) bordering

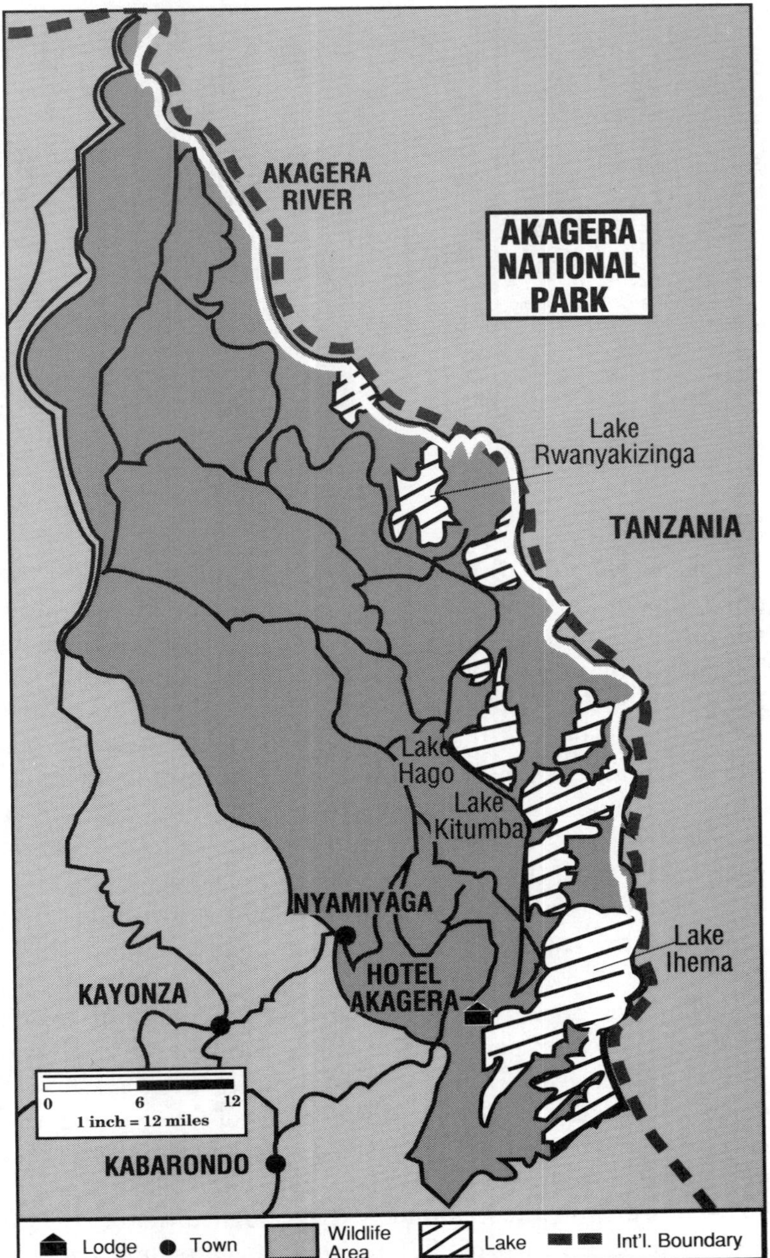
AKAGERA RIVER
AKAGERA NATIONAL PARK
Lake Rwanyakizinga
TANZANIA
Lake Hago
Lake Kitumba
NYAMIYAGA
Lake Ihema
HOTEL AKAGERA
KAYONZA
0 6 12
1 inch = 12 miles
KABARONDO
Lodge
Town
Wildlife Area
Lake
Int'l. Boundary

Impala.

Tanzania. Over 400,000 animals of great variety inhabit the park, including some of the largest buffalo in Africa, along with zebra, giraffe (recently introduced), hippo, crocodile, lion, leopard, impala, Defassa waterbuck, eland, sable antelope, bushbuck, oribi, roan antelope and black-backed jackal.

Akagera is one of the best places in Africa to see sitatunga, which are often seen from towers overlooking the swamps. Rhino, elephant and leopard are rarely seen. Birdlife is excellent with 525 species of birds recorded — a record for any park or region of this size.

Akagera National Park covers 980 square miles (ten percent of the country's area) and can be divided into three regions.

The northern part of the park is predominantly low, treeless hills interspaced with both dry and marshy valleys. Buffalo, zebra, waterbuck, topi, and many other species of herbivore prefer this region. However, as of this writing, the northern part of the park is closed due to unrest in the area.

Interestingly enough, buffalo, zebra and topi are much larger here than those found in East Africa. Some buffalo males weigh in excess of 2200 pounds with shoulder heights of six feet and horn widths of 3.5 feet. In addition, isolation from other populations in East Africa has caused inbreeding, which has resulted in some buffalo with horns twisted and turned in an ungainly fashion and some zebra trading in their stripes for spots — blotches of black and white.

The second region is the most unique and is possibly the best preserved and most diverse swamp in terms of both flora and fauna in East and East-Central Africa. It is composed of three large swamps separated by lakes along the eastern border of the park. Papyrus dominates the swamps. Large numbers of waterfowl, including herons, ducks, storks, waders and plovers can be seen in areas with floating ferns, swamp grasses and water lilies.

At the fishing station (Pêcherie) on Lake Ihema, the largest of the lakes, boats can be rented, or you may join irregularly scheduled group departures to the islands and far shores of the lake. Plage aux Hippos (Hippo Beach) on Mihindi Lake has picnic facilities and is a great spot for watching hippos, crocodiles and waterfowl.

The third region covers the central and southern areas lying west of the swamps and is characterized by more trees and thicker vegetation than the northern region.

Two hundred and eighty miles of relatively good all-weather tracks run through the park; these tracks are marked with numbered crossroads. Stay in your vehicle, except at marked picnic spots, camping or hotel grounds.

The best time to visit the park is during the dry season, July-September, while February, June and October are also good. Tsetse flies can be a nuisance, but without them the land would probably be used for farming.

ACCOMMODATION - CLASS A/B: * *Hotel Akagera* is a modern lodge overlooking Lake Ihema with 54 double rooms and six apartments with private facilities and private terraces, video and swimming pool.

CAMPING: Several sites are within the park. Permits have to be obtained in advance from the Rwanda Tourist Office in Kigali.

# SOUTH AFRICA

## THE TERRITORIAL WHITE RHINO

The male species of the white rhino maintains a territory while the cow travels from territory to territory. As the territorial bull is the only bull who will mate with a female within a marked territory, they have devised several ways of marking and maintaining these distinct boundaries.

They will paw the ground and scuffle the dust with their feet or scrape the bushes or bark of a tree with their horns. They will then spray urine backwards between their legs on these marks, curling their tails back over the rump. Their own smell impregnates the mark, and other bulls moving within the area will use the spot to urinate, but will not spray-urinate as a respect to the area already being reserved.

The territorial male also uses the same spots for defecating. These dung latrines are known as middens, and rhinos will scrape their dung over the midden pile in a backward motion with their feet, similar to their spraying.

As territories do overlap, a bull may be challenged by another bull looking for a new territory or following a female in oestrus. If the territorial bull loses, he will become a subordinate bull and move out of the marked area to find a new one.

If a female in heat moves into a territory, the bull will try to keep her in his territory using squeals, horn clashing and actively preventing her from leaving.

While on conducted walks tracking rhino footprints, territorial markings are signs of a bull's presence, and these markings can indicate how recently a rhino has moved through the area, helping the guide interpret how long ago they may have passed.

# SOUTH AFRICA

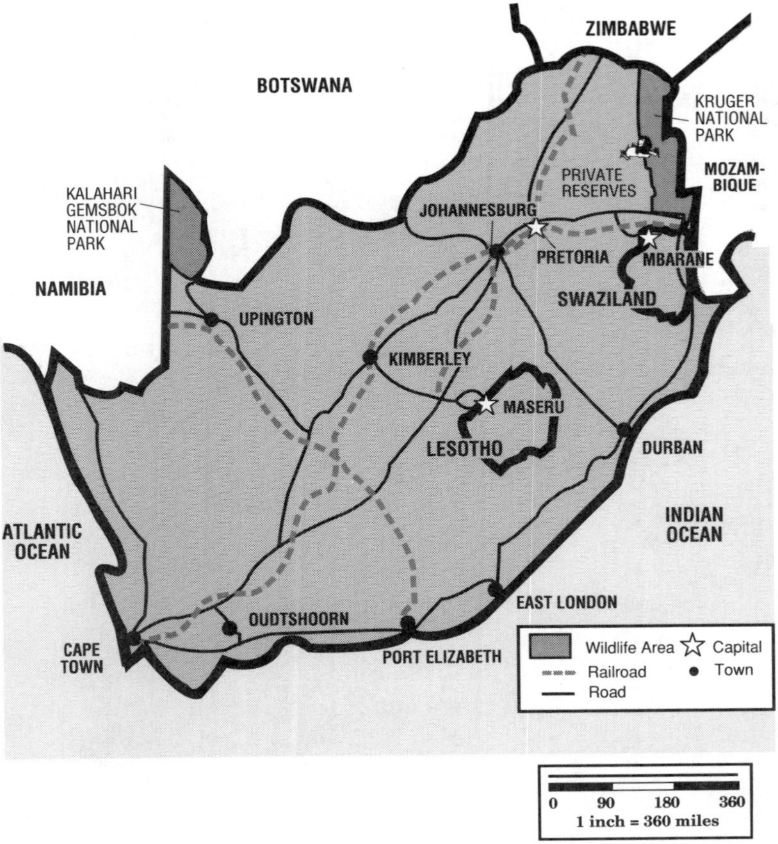


FACTS AT A GLANCE

| | |
|---|---|
| AREA: | 437,900 SQUARE MILES |
| APPROXIMATE SIZE: | THREE TIMES THE SIZE OF TEXAS OR FIVE TIMES THE SIZE OF GREAT BRITAIN |
| POPULATION: | 32 MILLION (1992 EST.) |
| CAPITAL: | PRETORIA (POP. EST. 850,000) |
| OFFICIAL LANGUAGE: | ENGLISH AND AFRIKAANS |

# SOUTH AFRICA

South Africa is a large country rich in natural beauty and wildlife whose actual size has been made much larger by the news. Actually, it covers less than 3.8 percent of the continent.

Seventy percent of the total population belongs to four ethnic groups: Zulu (the largest), Xhosa, Tswana and Bapedi. Fifteen percent of the population is white, of which 60 percent are Afrikaners. English and Afrikaans are spoken throughout the country.

In 1488 the Portuguese navigator Bartholomew Dias discovered the Cape of Good Hope. The first Dutch settlers arrived in 1652 and the first British settlers in 1820. To escape British rule, Boer (meaning farmer) Voortrekkers (meaning forward marchers) moved to the north and east, establishing the independent republic of Transvaal and Orange Free State.

Two very big economic breakthroughs were the discovery of diamonds in 1869, and even more importantly, the discovery of gold in Transvaal shortly thereafter. Conflict between the British and Boers resulted in the Anglo-Boer War from 1899 until British victory in 1902.

In 1910 the Union of South Africa was formed and remained a member of the British Commonwealth until May 31, 1961, when the Republic of South Africa was formed out–

side the British Commonwealth. The relaxing of sanctions against South Africa in 1991 has resulted in increased tourism to this country.

## WILDLIFE AND WILDLIFE AREAS

Kruger National Park and Kalahari Gemsbok National Park are the premier reserves of South Africa. Several private reserves adjacent to Kruger National Park offer the best options for international visitors, providing excellent accommodations, day and night game drives in open vehicles, and walks.

The parks, reserves and sanctuaries in South Africa are very well organized and maintained, and in many ways are similar to those in North America. Most campsites have ablution blocks with running hot and cold water, and many sites have laundromats.

Generally speaking, the major roads in the parks are tarred with the minor ones constructed of good quality gravel, allowing for comfortable riding. Tourists must stay in their vehicles, except where specifically permitted, and cannot leave the roads in search of game. Open vehicles are not allowed in the parks, and roof hatches on vehicles must remain closed.

## THE TRANSVAAL

### JOHANNESBURG

Johannesburg began as a mining town when the largest deposits of gold in the world were discovered in the Witwatersrand in 1886. One-third of the gold mined in the world since the Middle Ages has come from the Witwatersrand field.

This "City of Gold" is now the country's largest commercial center and city (pop. two million) and is the main gateway

Table Mountain, Cape Town.

for overseas visitors. Attractions include the Africana Museum, the Gold Mine Museum, and Gold Reef City — a reconstruction of Johannesburg at the turn of the century.

ACCOMMODATION - DELUXE: * *Johannesburg Sun,* the largest hotel in Africa, has 792 air-conditioned rooms with private facilities, swimming pool, gym, squash courts and jogging track. * *Sandton Sun* is located ten miles from Johannesburg in one of the country's finest shopping malls. The hotel has 334 spacious air-conditioned rooms with private facilities and refrigerator; there is also a health club, swimming pool, and five restaurants, including the exquisite "Chapters." * *Carlton Hotel* is located in a large mall (Carlton Center) and has 463 air-conditioned rooms with facilities ensuite, swimming pool and health club.

FIRST CLASS: * *Balalaika Hotel,* located in the suburb of Sandton, has 60 rooms with ensuite facilities. * *Sandton Holiday Inn* has 249 rooms with private facilities. * *Airport Sun Hotel,* located less than a mile from Jan Smuts International Airport, has 238 air-conditioned rooms with facilities ensuite, swimming pool and sauna.

TOURIST CLASS * *City Lodges* have simple rooms with private facilities.

## THE BLUE TRAIN

The world-renowned luxurious Blue Train offers an experience that has all but disappeared in modern times. The train is promoted as "A Five-Star Hotel on Wheels," and that it is.

Two identical Blue Trains were built in South Africa and put into service in 1972. Each train has 16 permanently coupled passenger couches accommodating a maximum of 107 guests. The trains are air-conditioned and carpeted, with individually controlled music and radio channels as well as hot, cold and iced water taps in all compartments. Five-star meals are served in the beautifully appointed dining car with its exquisite table settings. Most passengers dress elegantly for dinner, although this is not required.

The train runs from Cape Town to Johannesburg and Pretoria, and vice-versa, year-round. Four types of compartments are available, ranging from small rooms to luxury suites. All compartments have private baths except D-Class, whose guests may use showers at the end of their car. Book well in advance as reservations are often difficult to obtain.

## ROVOS RAIL

Rovos Rail is a restored luxury steam train with eight coaches, dining car and observation car. A three-night/four-day train safari runs from Pretoria to Graskop in the Eastern Transvaal and back to Pretoria. Two nights are spent on the train and one night at a private game reserve near Kruger National Park, where visitors have day and night game drives in open vehicles. Blyde River Canyon, Pilgrim's Rest and Bourke's Luck Potholes are also visited.

Rovos Rail also runs from Johannesburg to Durban and return, and Pretoria-Johannesburg-Cape Town and return.

## BOPHUTHATSWANA

Bophuthatswana is a homeland in the southwestern Transvaal, north and northwest of Johannesburg.

## PILANESBERG NATURE RESERVE

This relatively small 212-square-mile reserve is located within a 17-mile-wide volcanic bowl which rises over the surrounding plains. Pilanesberg has a variety of wildlife including black rhino, white rhino, elephant, giraffe, hippo, eland, gemsbok, sable antelope, tsessebe, red hartebeest, leopard and cheetah. Over 300 species of birds have been recorded.

ACCOMMODATION - CLASS A: * *Kwa Maritane* has comfortable cabanas with ensuite facilities and swimming pool.

CLASS B/C: * *Tshukudu Rest Camp* has chalets with ensuite facilities.

CLASS C & D: * *Kololo*, * *Mankwe*, * *Manyane* and * *Metswedi* camps provide basic tented accommodation.

CAMPING: * *Manyane Caravan* and *Camping Site* has campsites and ablution facilities.

## SUN CITY

Sun City is a premier entertainment vacation complex with Las Vegas-style floor shows, casino, golf, tennis, and water sports. Sun City is a two-hour drive by car or a short flight from Johannesburg.

ACCOMMODATION - DELUXE: * *The Cascades* is a luxurious hotel with 245 rooms with facilities ensuite, spectacularly designed and landscaped with lush gardens, waterfalls, and

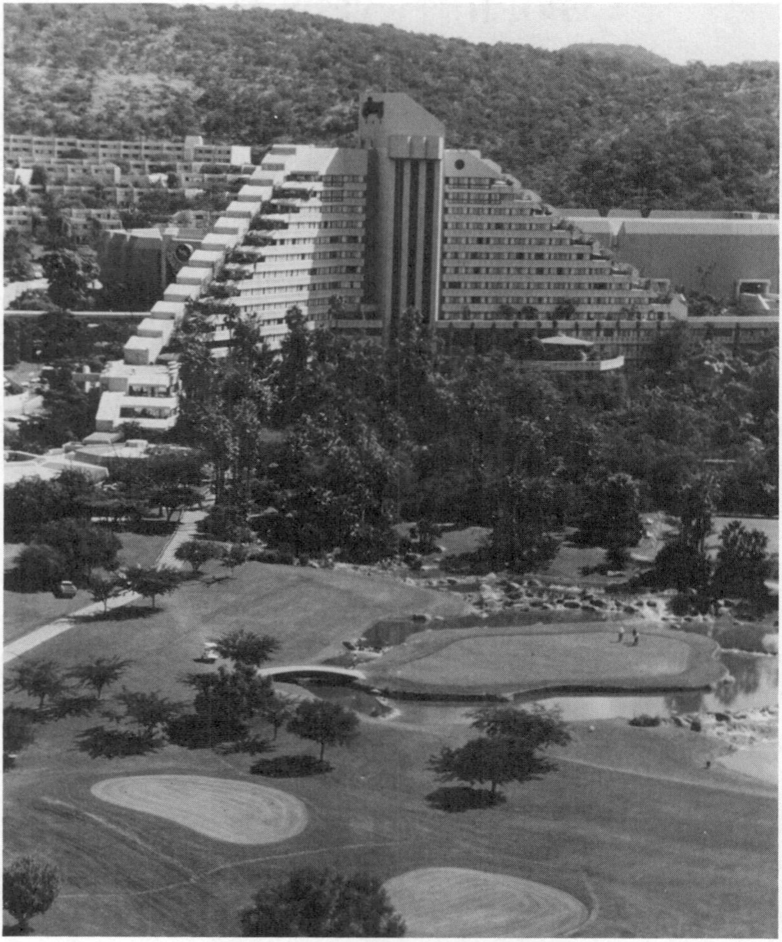

The Cascades Hotel, Sun City.

swimming pool; the cuisine is fit for a king. All rooms have ensuite facilities.

FIRST CLASS: * *Sun City Hotel* has 340 rooms with private facilities and swimming pool. * *Sun City Cabanas* has 284 cabanas with facilities ensuite.

## PRETORIA

Pretoria is an attractive city and the administrative capital of South Africa. Points of interest include Paul Kruger's house, Voortrekker Monument, Union Buildings, the State Opera House and Church Square.

ACCOMMODATION - DELUXE: * *Hotel Burgerspark* has 238 rooms and suites with private facilities and swimming pool.

## THE EASTERN TRANSVAAL

## KRUGER AND THE PRIVATE RESERVES

The most popular area of the country for wildlife safaris for international visitors is Kruger National Park and the private reserves that lie along its western border.

There is a tremendous difference in the variety and quality of experience between visiting Kruger National Park versus visiting the adjacent private reserves. In Kruger, which has over 500,000 tourists each year, only closed vehicles are allowed, and night game drives and off-road driving are not allowed. Facilities are fair.

In the adjacent private reserves, day and night game viewing is conducted in open vehicles, walking is allowed, and facilities are excellent. In other words, visitors have a greater opportunity to experience the bush than in Kruger. However, a safari to Kruger National Park using national park camps is less expensive than one of the same length in the private reserves.

The best game viewing for this region is June-September during the sunny, dry winter season when the grass has been grazed down and the deciduous plants have lost their leaves. Calving season is in early spring (September-October) for most game species.

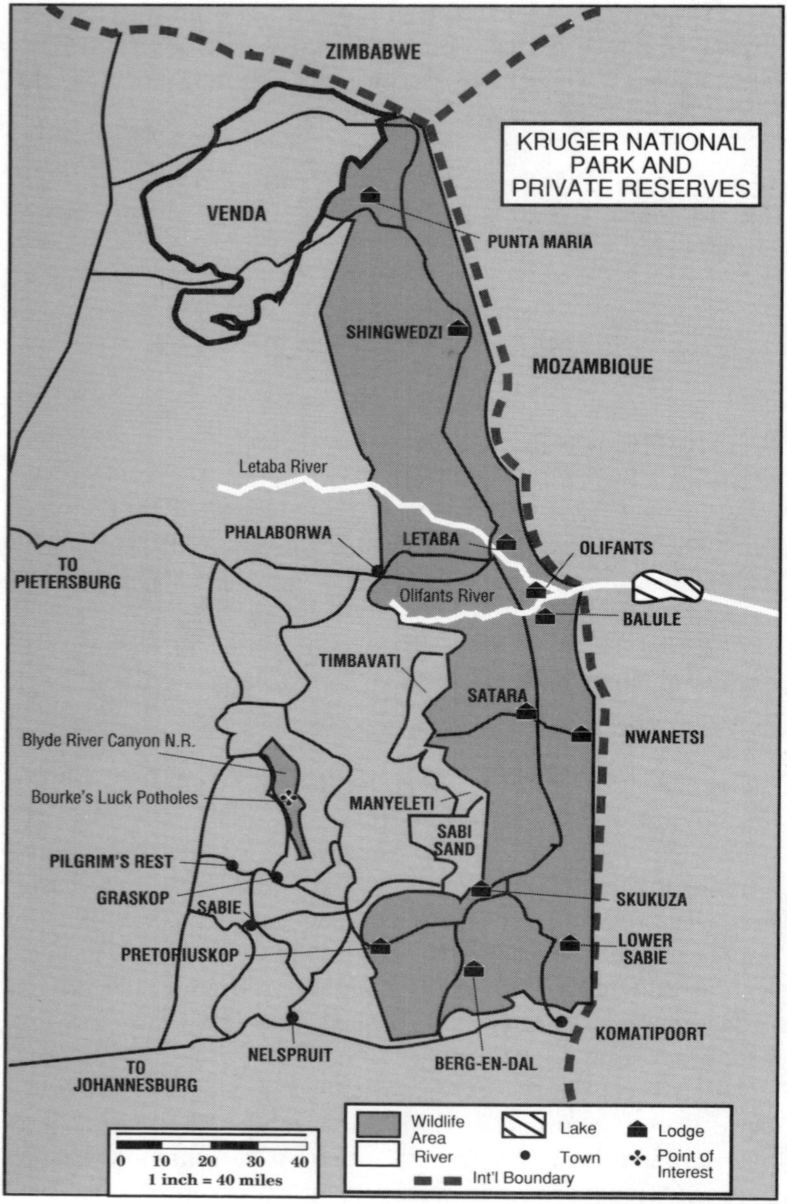
KRUGER NATIONAL PARK AND PRIVATE RESERVES
ZIMBABWE
VENDA
PUNTA MARIA
SHINGWEDZI
MOZAMBIQUE
Letaba River
PHALABORWA
LETABA
OLIFANTS
TO PIETERSBURG
Olifants River
BALULE
TIMBAVATI
SATARA
NWANETSI
Blyde River Canyon N.R.
Bourke's Luck Potholes
MANYELETI
SABI SAND
PILGRIM'S REST
GRASKOP
SABIE
SKUKUZA
PRETORIUSKOP
LOWER SABIE
KOMATIPOORT
NELSPRUIT
BERG-EN-DAL
TO JOHANNESBURG
0 10 20 30 40
1 inch = 40 miles
Wildlife Area
River
Lake
Town
Lodge
Point of Interest
Int'l Boundary

Winter days are usually warm with an average maximum of 73° F. and clear skies. Late afternoons are cool, while temperatures at night and early morning sometimes drop below freezing. From October to February there are light rains, with December, January and February receiving the heaviest downpours with temperatures sometimes rising to 104° F. March and April are cooler as the rains begin to diminish.

The best time to look for over 450 bird species in this region is October-March — just the opposite from the best game viewing periods. However, bird watching is good year-round since less than half the bird population is composed of seasonal migrants.

To get to the area, many people take about a one-hour flight to Skukuza, Phalaborwa or air charter directly to their camp. Alternatively, the drive from Johannesburg to Kruger (Skukuza) is about 250 miles northeast on tarred roads and takes five to six hours.

## KRUGER NATIONAL PARK

Kruger is the largest South African park and has more species of wildlife than any other game sanctuary in Africa; 130 species of mammals, 114 species of reptiles, 48 species of fish, 33 species of amphibians, and 468 species of birds.

The park is home to large populations of elephant (over 8000), buffalo (over 25,000), Burchell's zebra (over 25,000), greater kudu, giraffe, impala, white rhino, black rhino, hippopotamus, lion, leopard, cheetah, wild or cape hunting dog, and spotted hyena, among others.

Kruger's 7700 square miles make it nearly the size of the state of Massachusetts. The park is 55 miles wide at its widest point and 220 miles long. It is totally fenced, cutting off the annual winter migration routes of antelope, zebra and various other species in search of water and better grazing. Several hundred windmills and artificial water holes have been constructed to provide the water so desperately needed in the dry season.

The park can be divided into three major regions: northern, central/southeastern, and southwestern. Altitude varies from 650 feet in the east to 2950 feet at Pretoriuskop in the southwest. Summer temperatures may exceed 105° F. while winter temperatures seldom drop below freezing.

The northern region from the Letaba River to the Limpopo River is the driest. Mopane trees dominate the landscape with the unique baobab (upside-down) trees becoming increasingly numerous toward Pafuri and the Limpopo River. From Letaba to Punda Maria is the best region for spotting elephant, tsessebe, sable and roan antelope. Elephant prefer this area since it is less developed than the other regions, making it easier to congregate away from roads and traffic, and mopane trees (their preferred source of food) are prevalent.

The central/southeastern region is situated south of Letaba to Orpen Gate and also includes the eastern part of the park from Satara southward covering Nwanedzi, Lower Sabie and Crocodile Bridge. Grassy plains and scattered knobthorn, leadwood, and marula trees dominate the landscape. Lion inhabit most areas of the park but are most prevalent in this region where there is also an abundance of zebra and wildebeest — their favorite prey. Cheetah and black-backed jackal are best spotted on the plains. Wild or cape hunting dogs are mainly scattered through flatter areas, with possibly a better chance of finding them in the Letaba-Malopene River area and northwest of Malelane.

The southwestern part of the park, including a wide strip along the western boundary from Skukuza to Orpen Gate, is more densely forested with thorny thickets, knobthorn, marula and red bush-willow. This is the most difficult region in which to spot game — especially during the rainy season. Many of the park's 600 white rhino prefer this area.

Black rhino are scattered throughout the southern and central areas, often feeding on low-lying acacia trees. Leopard are rarely seen. Buffalo roam throughout the park while hippo prefer to inhabit the deeper parts of Kruger's many rivers by day.

During school holidays and long weekends, the number

White rhinos are predominantly grazers. Their square-shaped lips facilitate this feeding habit.

of day visitors to the park is limited and accommodation almost impossible to obtain, so be sure to reserve in advance.

ACCOMMODATION - CLASS C, D & CAMPING: There are 16 *National Park Rest Camps* offering a wide range of accommodations including cottages with private bath, thatched huts with or without private facilities, and campsites. The larger rest camps have licensed restaurants. Many of the cottages and huts have cooking facilities and refrigerators.

ACCOMMODATION NEAR KRUGER NATIONAL PARK - DELUXE: * *Malelane Lodge*, located near Kruger's southernmost gate, has 102 chalets and suites with ensuite facilities, overlooking several water holes.

FIRST CLASS: * *Pine Lake Inn*, located in White River, a short drive from Kruger, has comfortable rooms with private facilities.

## THE PRIVATE RESERVES

Along the western border of Kruger lie a number of privately owned wildlife reserves. These reserves are associations of ranchers who have fenced around the reserves but have not placed fences between their individual properties, allowing game to roam throughout the reserves. The private reserves, in general, have exceptionally high standards of accommodation, food and service.

A very important advantage private reserves have over national parks is that private reserves use open vehicles which give not only a better view but also a much better feel of the bush. At most reserves, a game tracker sits on the hood or the back of each vehicle. Drivers are in radio contact with each other, greatly increasing the chances of finding those species that guests want to see most.

Vehicles may leave the road to pursue game through the bush. Night drives, which are not allowed in Kruger, provide an opportunity to spot game rarely seen during the day. Walking is also allowed.

ACCOMMODATION - SABI-SAND PRIVATE GAME RESERVE: Sabi-Sand Private Game Reserve is situated to the north and northwest of Skukuza and includes Sabi Sabi Game Reserve (Bush Lodge and River Lodge), Mala Mala Game Reserve (Mala Mala, Kirkman's and Harry's Camps), Londolozi (Main Camp, Treehouse and Bush Camp) and Inyati.

Almost all camps offer day and night game drives and walks. Many guests fly to Skukuza and are transferred to their respective camps, while some guests drive to the camp of their choice or travel by tour bus.

CLASS A: * *Mala Mala* is a very expensive camp (50 beds) with a swimming pool and with air-conditioned thatched rondavels — each with two bathrooms. * *Londolozi* Game Reserve has three camps, Tree Camp, Bush Camp, and Main Camp. * *Tree Camp*, the most exclusive of the three properties, is built around a giant ebony tree and has four rooms (doubles). * *Bush Camp* has four rock bungalows. Rooms in all three camps have ensuite facilities. * *Main Camp* accommodates 24 guests in rondavels and luxury suites. * *Sabi Sabi* offers deluxe air-conditioned rooms with private facilities and a swimming pool at both of their camps — Bush Lodge and River Lodge. *Bush Lodge* (25 doubles) overlooks a water hole while *River Lodge* (20 doubles) is set on a riverbank. * *Inyati Game Lodge* has nine thatched chalets (doubles) with ensuite facilities and swimming pool.

CLASS A/B: * *Kirkman's Camp* has air-conditioned cottages with ensuite facilities and swimming pool. * *Harry's Camp* has seven air-conditioned thatched rondavels with private facilities and swimming pool.

ACCOMMODATION - TIMBAVATI AND MANYELETI GAME RESERVES: Guests of Tanda Tula (Timbavati Private Nature Preserve), Khoka Moya and Honeyguide (Manyeleti Game Reserve) fly to Phalaborwa or by charter aircraft directly to Tanda Tula; some guests drive to their respective camps. Each camp has a splash pool (small swimming pool) in which to cool off on hot days. Day game drives and walks are offered.

CLASS A/B: * *Tanda Tula,* on the Timbavati Game Reserve, has seven air-conditioned thatched brick bungalows (14 beds) with ensuite facilities. * *Khoka Moya Trails Camp* is situated on the Manyeleti Game Reserve and caters to only eight guests in four rustic wood and thatch bandas with facilities ensuite. Daily walking trails and night game drives are offered. * *Honeyguide Safari Camp* is also located on the Manyeleti Game Reserve and caters to a maximum of 12 guests in luxury tents with private facilities. Daily walking trails and night game drives are offered.

## BLYDE RIVER CANYON, PILGRIM'S REST, AND BOURKE'S LUCK POTHOLES

West of Kruger National Park and the private reserves, in the Drakensberg Mountains, lie a number of areas of natural beauty.

**Blyde River Canyon** is an impressive red sandstone gorge rising over half a mile above the river below. The "Three Rondavels" — peaks shaped like traditional African huts — may be seen from here.

**Pilgrim's Rest** is an attractively restored gold mining town where you can try your luck at panning gold.

**Bourke's Luck Potholes**, situated at the confluence of the Treur and Blyde Rivers, are deep colorful cylindrical holes naturally formed by erosion.

ACCOMMODATION IN THE REGION - DELUXE: * *The Coach House* (Tzaneen), possibly the country's best country hotel, has 35 rooms with ensuite facilities and swimming pool.

FIRST CLASS: * *Mount Sheba* (Pilgrim's Rest) has rooms with private facilities and swimming pool. * *Cybele Forest Lodge* (White River) is a lovely lodge with rooms with facilities ensuite, excellent cuisine and swimming pool.

# THE CAPE PROVINCE

## KALAHARI GEMSBOK NATIONAL PARK

Located in the northwest corner of South Africa and sharing borders with Namibia and with Gemsbok National Park in Botswana, this 3700-square-mile park is predominantly semidesert and part desert. Scattered thorn trees and grasses lie between red Kalahari sand dunes. Bushmen inhabited the area as much as 25,000 years ago.

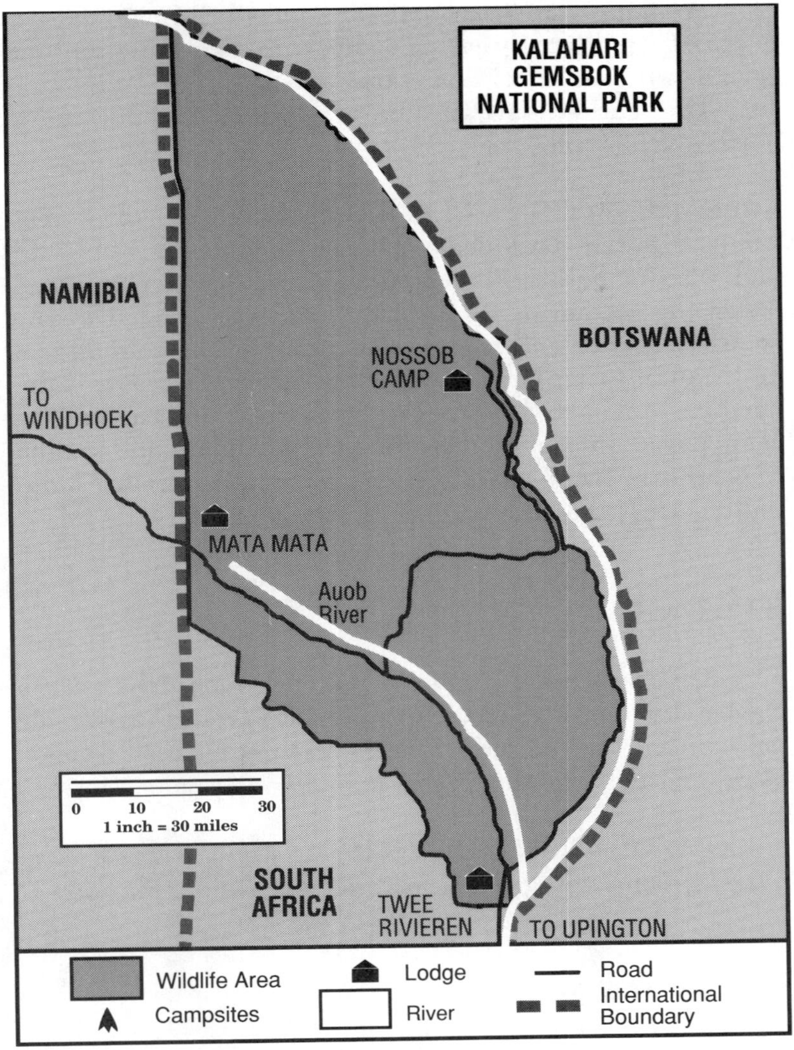


The park features large herds of blue wildebeest, eland, springbok, and the stately gemsbok with their long, straight spear-like horns. Also present are red hartebeest, duiker, steenbok, Kalahari lion, cheetah, brown hyena, and wild dog.

Summer temperatures can exceed 104° F. Winter days

are pleasant but temperatures can drop below freezing at night. Wells provide water for the animals which have adapted to desert conditions by eating plants with high water content such as wild cucumber and tsamma melon.

The southern entrance to the park is about 215 miles north of Upington.

ACCOMMODATION - CLASS C/D: There are three rest camps with self-contained cottages with kitchens, huts with and without bathrooms, camping sites, stores, petrol and diesel (no restaurants). * *Twee Revieren* is located at the southern entrance of the park. The camp has a swimming pool and a landing strip for small aircraft. * *Nossob* is located in the northeastern part of the park near the Botswana border. The camp has an information center about the plant and animal life of the park and a landing strip for small aircraft. * *Mata Mata* is located on the western border of the park.

## KIMBERLEY

Kimberley is the "diamond city" where one of the world's biggest diamond strikes occurred in 1868. Visit the open air museum and the "Big Hole" where over three tons of diamonds were removed from the largest man-dug hole on earth.

ACCOMMODATION - FIRST CLASS: * *Kimberley Sun Hotel* has 114 rooms with private facilities and swimming pool.

## CAPE TOWN

Sir Francis Drake once said of the Cape Town area: "The fairest cape we saw in the whole circumference of the globe." Today Cape Town is thought to be by many well-traveled people one of the most beautiful settings in the world. The Cape reminds me of the California coast — stark, natural beauty and a laid-back atmosphere.

The cable ride (or three-hour hike) up **Table Mountain**

The big hole at Kimberley.

with breathtaking views is a must. Bring warm clothing since it is usually much cooler and windier on top. An afternoon **Champagne Cruise** past islands with hundreds of seals, rocky cliffs and sandy beaches allows a delightful perspective of the area.

The one-day drive down the Cape Peninsula to the **Cape of Good Hope Nature Reserve** and **Cape Point** is one of the finest drives on the continent. The reserve has a population of bontebok, as well as other species, and a variety of beautiful wild flowers. Some people say this is where the Atlantic meets the Indian Ocean, while others say it is at Cape Agulhas, the southernmost point of Africa.

**Sea Point** is bustling with nightlife, with many distinctive restaurants, bistros and bars. **Kirstenbosch National Botanical Gardens**, one of the finest gardens in the world, has 9000 of the 21,000 flowering plants of Southern Africa.

February-March is the best time to visit the Cape when there is very little wind; October-January is warm and windy; May-August rainy.

There are four popular wine routes through the beautiful wine country northeast of Cape Town. The Stellenbosch Route covers 23 private cellars and cooperative wineries, including the Bergkelder, Blaauwklippen and Delheim, and the Van Ryn Brandy Cellar. The Paarl Route covers seven cooperative wineries and estates, including Nederburg Estate and KWV Cooperative. The Franschoek Route includes private wine estates, including Bellingham and Boschendal. The Worcester Route has 25 cooperative wineries and estates.

Some of the finer restaurants include Belvedere House, La Vita, and La Perla (in Sea Point). The Wooden Bridge, situated across Table Bay, is exceptionally nice in summer; guests may watch the sun set behind Table Mountain.

ACCOMMODATION - DELUXE: * *Cape Sun* is a modern hotel with a great view of the harbor; it has 362 rooms with facilities ensuite, pool, health club and gym. * *Mount Nelson* is an old-world British hotel set on seven landscaped acres. The hotel has rooms with facilities ensuite and swimming pool. * *St. George's,* a sophisticated British-style hotel located in the center of the business district, has 137 rooms with private facilities and swimming pool.

FIRST CLASS: * *Inn on the Square,* located on the eighteenth century Greenmarket Square, has 170 air-conditioned rooms with facilities ensuite. * *Townhouse Hotel* has 104 rooms with private facilities, swimming pool, and gym.

ACCOMMODATION IN THE CAPE AREA - DELUXE: * *Bay Hotel,* located on the beach at Camps Bay, a ten-minute drive out of Cape Town, has 70 rooms and suites with ensuite facilities and swimming pool. * *Peninsula Hotel,* located in Sea Point facing the Atlantic Ocean, has 112 suites comprised of one to three bedrooms and two swimming pools. * *D'Ouwe Werf,* located in Stellenbosch (the wine region), is a beautiful old inn with 28 rooms with ensuite facilities and swimming pool. * *Mountain Shadows,* a lovely Cape Dutch manor house situated near Paarl, caters to a few guests.

Cable car ride to the top of Table Mountain.

## SCUBA DIVING

The world's two great oceans, the cold south Atlantic and the warm Indio-Pacific, rub brawny shoulders along the southernmost curve of Africa. This contrast of temperatures produces two extremes in underwater habitats and at least three unique opportunities for the adventurous diver: the Southern Cape, Southern Natal Coast (Durban area), and Northern Natal Coast (near Sodwana Bay).

For those seeking the ultimate underwater thrill, the Southern Cape offers the magnificent cold water predator — the *great white shark*. South Africa is one of the few places in the world where divers can encounter these formidable fish from the safety of a shark cage. The great white shark is a protected species in South Africa and reaches heroic proportions in these rich waters.

Great white shark dives are a specialized activity. These trips are sole-purpose adventures and are only conducted when individuals or small groups request them. The dives are boat-based, and the sharks are lured into range by chumming and baiting the area.

The best time of the year to dive with them is December-March. Visibility ranges from 10-100 feet, and water temperatures range from 50-70° F.

Diving facilities, equipment and training in South Africa have been modeled after the American system and modified to suit local conditions and are excellent.

## GARDEN ROUTE

One of the most beautiful drives on the continent, the Garden Route is lined with Indian Ocean coastal scenery, beautiful beaches, lakes, forests, and mountains with small country hotel accommodations.

The Garden Route runs between Mossel Bay (east of Cape Town) and Storms River (west of Port Elizabeth).

There are a number of tours and self-drive programs available from Cape Town to Port Elizabeth/Durban (or vice versa) for a minimum of two nights/three days. These programs visit a variety of areas and attractions. The southern route from Cape Town passes through the winelands, Hermanus, Mossel Bay, Oudtshoorn, and the coastal areas of Wilderness, Knysna, Plettenberg Bay to Port Elizabeth. The northern route from Cape Town passes through the winelands, Matjiesfontein, and Prince Albert to Oudtshoorn, and then joins the southern route to Port Elizabeth.

Departing Cape Town on the southern route, you travel over Sir Lowry's Pass. Soon you come to the turnoff to **Hermanus**. The road down to the coast yields fine views of the rugged coastline. The southernmost vineyards in Africa are located nearby.

Continue to the town of **Mossel Bay** and then drive north to **Oudtshoorn** where you can ride an ostrich — or at least watch them race — and tour an ostrich farm. Located about 16 miles north of Oudtshoorn are the **Kango Caves,** the largest limestone caves in Africa, with colorful stalactites and stalagmites.

Return to the coast via George, an old-world town with oak tree-lined streets set at the foot of the Outeniqua Moun-

Ride an ostrich at Oudtshoorn.

tains. A narrow-gauge steam train may be taken in the morning from George across the Knysna Lagoon to Knysna, and back to George that same afternoon.

Continue east to the **Wilderness Area**, which encompasses a number of interlinking lakes, onward to **Knysna**, a small coastal town with a beautiful lagoon excellent for boating. The Knysna Forest and the Tsitsikamma Forest together form South Africa's largest indigenous high forest.

Further east lies **Plettenberg Bay**, the Garden Route's most sophisticated resort area. Nearby is **Tsitsikamma National Park** — a lushly vegetated 50-mile strip along the coast. Wildlife includes the Cape clawless otter, grysbok, bushbuck, and blue duiker. Over 275 species of birds have been recorded. The park has hiking trails, including the famous Otter Trail, and underwater trails for both snorkelers and SCUBA divers.

The northern route passes Paarl winelands area through a portion of the Great Karoo (semidesert) to **Matjiesfontein,** a charming little town where the buildings and railway station have been preserved in their original Victorian style. From here the route runs southeast through Prince Albert to Oudtshoorn where it meets the southern route.

ACCOMMODATION ON THE GARDEN ROUTE - DELUXE: * *Wilderness Hotel* (Wilderness) is situated close to the ocean and the lagoon and has 160 rooms with ensuite facilities. * *The Plettenberg* (Plettenberg Bay), formerly a magnificent nineteenth century mansion, has elegant rooms and suites with ensuite facilities. * *Beacon Island* (Plettenberg Bay), dramatically surrounded on three sides by the Indian Ocean, has 197 rooms and suites with ensuite facilities.

FIRST CLASS: * *Beach House* (near Hermanus) has 23 beachfront rooms with ensuite facilities. * *The Lord Milner* (Matjiesfontein) is one of South Africa's finest country inns. * *The Swartberg Hotel* (Prince Albert) is a charming 20-room hotel with private facilities. * *The Fancourt* (George) is an elegant hotel (a national monument) with 37 rooms and suites with ensuite facilities. * *Belvidere House* (Knysna) has guest cottages with ensuite facilities. * *Tsitsikamma Forest Inn* (Storms River) has 34 Swiss-style chalets with facilities ensuite. * *Hunter's Country House* (Plettenberg Bay) has ten elegantly decorated thatched cottages with ensuite facilities. * *Formosa Inn* (Plettenberg Bay), an old established coach house, has 38 garden chalets with ensuite facilities.

## NATAL

Natal, the smallest of South Africa's provinces, is located in eastern South Africa along the Indian Ocean. The Drakensberg Mountains rise to over 11,000 feet and run roughly north and south along its western border, which it

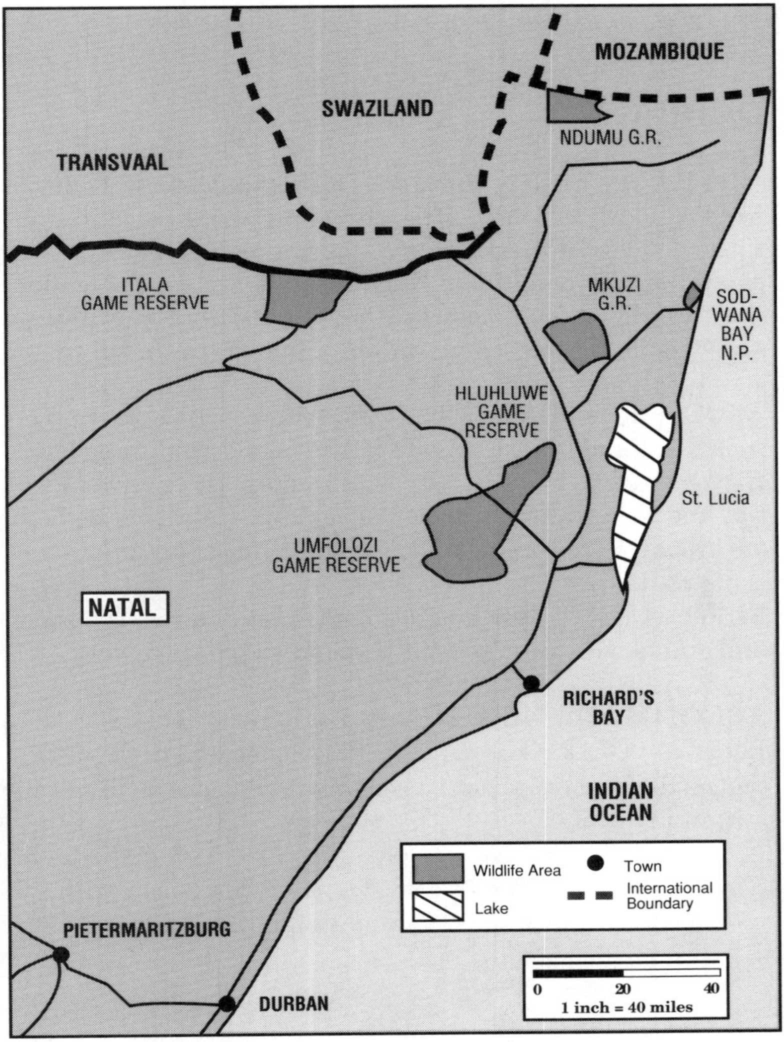
MOZAMBIQUE
SWAZILAND
TRANSVAAL
NDUMU G.R.
ITALA GAME RESERVE
MKUZI G.R.
SOD-WANA BAY N.P.
HLUHLUWE GAME RESERVE
St. Lucia
UMFOLOZI GAME RESERVE
NATAL
RICHARD'S BAY
INDIAN OCEAN
Wildlife Area
Town
Lake
International Boundary
PIETERMARITZBURG
DURBAN
0 20 40
1 inch = 40 miles

shares with Lesotho.

Natal is the home of the Zulu and a large variety of wildlife concentrated in several small yet interesting reserves.

## DURBAN

The largest city in Natal, Durban has beautiful beach front called *The Golden Mile* with amusement parks, amphitheater, colorful markets, and aquarium (Sea World). Ricksha pullers in traditional Zulu costume are available along the beach front. The Victoria Market and Grey Street Mosque are evidence of the strong Indian influence in this area.

ACCOMMODATION - DELUXE: * *Maharani Hotel* has 270 rooms and suites with private facilities and swimming pool. * *Elangeni Hotel* has 450 rooms and suites with private facilities and two swimming pools. * *The Royal Hotel* overlooks the yacht basin, has rooms with ensuite facilities and swimming pool.
FIRST CLASS: * *Marine Parade Holiday Inn* has 336 rooms and suites with ensuite facilities and swimming pool.

ACCOMMODATION NEAR DURBAN (UMHLANGA ROCKS) - DELUXE: * *Beverly Hills* is located north of Durban on the beach and has 91 rooms with ensuite facilities and swimming pool.

FIRST CLASS: * *The Oyster Box* is on the beach with 206 rooms with facilities ensuite and swimming pool.

## ZULULAND

This is a land of scenic hills and valleys dotted with KwaZulu homesteads — many with traditional beehive huts. Zululand has the largest concentration of wildlife conservation areas and game ranches in the country.

ACCOMMODATION - FIRST CLASS: * *Shakaland* has traditional beehive huts with ensuite facilities.

## UMFOLOZI

Located about 165 miles north of Durban, this 185-square-mile reserve of open grassland and savannah woodland is one of the two oldest reserves (the other is Hluhluwe) in South Africa and most well known for having the world's largest concentration of white rhino — approximately 900.

Other species include black rhino, elephant, nyala, kudu, waterbuck, zebra, wildebeest, buffalo, giraffe, black-back jackal, lion and cheetah. Over 400 species of birds have been recorded. Walking is allowed with national park guides. The best time to visit is during the dry winter months (May-September).

ACCOMMODATION - FIRST CLASS: See "Hluhluwe Game Reserve" below.
CLASS D: * *National Park* self-service huts with ablution blocks.

CAMPING: None.

## HLUHLUWE GAME RESERVE

This 90-square-mile reserve of grassland, forest, and woodland is host to a variety of wildlife including large numbers of white rhino, along with black rhino, elephant, buffalo, giraffe, nyala, wildebeest, Burchell's zebra, kudu, lion, cheetah, Samango monkeys, hippo and crocs. Over 425 bird species have been recorded.

The reserve shares its southwestern border with Umfolozi Game Reserve and is located about 18 miles from St. Lucia and 175 miles from Durban. The park contains walking trails. The best time to visit is May-September.

ACCOMMODATION - FIRST CLASS: * *Zululand Safari Lodge* has 41 rondavels with ensuite facilities and swimming pool. Game drives to Umfolozi, Hluhluwe and Lake St. Lucia are offered.

CLASS C/D & D: * *National Park* has cottages with private facilities and self-service huts with ablution blocks.

## MKUZI GAME RESERVE

This 134-square-mile park has a diversity of vegetation including riverine forest, savannah woodland, and forests of large sycamore fig trees. Wildlife includes leopard, side-striped jackal, white rhino, black rhino, eland, kudu, nyala, bushbuck, reedbuck, klipspringer, hippo, crocs and a variety of aquatic birds.

ACCOMMODATION - CLASS A/B: * *Phinda Lodge* has 20 thatched chalets with ensuite facilities and swimming pool. CLASS D: * *National Park* bungalows with facilities ensuite and huts with ablution blocks.

## ST. LUCIA AND MAPUTALAND MARINE RESERVES

These two reserves combined form Africa's largest marine reserve, covering 340 square miles. The reserve runs along the coastline to the Mozambique border and 3.5 miles out to sea.

Species of turtles, including loggerhead turtles and the endangered leatherback turtle, lay their eggs on the northern beaches. St. Lucia includes the southernmost coral reefs in the world and is the only breeding spot for pink-backed pelicans in South Africa. Flamingos migrate to the reserve.

ACCOMMODATION - CLASS B: * *Rocktail Bay Lodge* has five attractive double-room wooden chalets (20 beds) with private facilities.

CLASS D: * *National Parks* huts and log cabins with ablution blocks are available.

CAMPING: Campsites are available.

## NDUMU GAME RESERVE

Located in northeastern Natal on the Mozambique border, this reserve is comprised of riverine floodplains and is called "the Little Okavango" (referring to the Okavango Delta, Botswana).

In spite of its small size (39 square miles), it is considered to be one of the finest reserves in Natal. There are no large herds of mammals here; however, riverine wildlife is superb. Wildlife includes hippo, crocs, nyala, bushbuck, red duiker, black rhino and white rhino.

ACCOMMODATION - CLASS D: * *National Parks* cottages with ablution facilities.

CAMPING: None.

## SODWANA BAY NATIONAL PARK

Fishing (especially for marlin) and SCUBA diving are the main attractions of this 1.6-square-mile reserve.

ACCOMMODATION - CLASS B/C: * *Sodwana Bay Lodge* has chalets with ensuite facilities, offers SCUBA diving and big game fishing.

CAMPING: Campsites are available.

## SCUBA DIVING

In the transition zone between Sodwana's coral and the Cape's kelp forests lie the city of Durban and the Southern Natal Coast. Aliwal Shoal, Lander's Reef and the *Produce* Wreck are the diving focal points of the region.

Escorted boat dives to these rocky reefs gives one an opportunity to view a wide variety of southern Africa's marine animals, including potato bass (a large grouper), eels, rays, turtles and reef fish.

The best time to see Aliwal's famed "raggies" is June-July. A group of huge resident bridle bass (jewfish) and schools of dagger salmon make the nearby wreck of the *Produce* their home.

Diving is possible year-round, with the best conditions March-May. Water temperatures range from 65-72° F. Diving depths range from 30-120 feet.

Zululand's semitropical coast has South Africa's warmest and clearest waters — ideal for SCUBA diving. Escorted boat dives are offered from Sodwana Bay (see above) to Africa's most southern coral reefs. Quarter-mile, two-, three-, four-, seven, and nine-mile reefs (distances from the Sodwana launch site) are composed of hard and soft reefs. The reefs are home to many species of colorful Indian Ocean tropi-cal fish, rock cods (groupers), kingfish (a large jack), barracudas and moray eels. Dolphins are sometimes sighted on the way to dive sites, and humpback whales migrate through the area in February and September. "Raggies" (grey nurse sharks/sand tiger sharks) and whale sharks are sometimes seen by divers January-February. Manta rays and pelagics are also part of the fish mix. Loggerhead, green and leatherback sea turtles use the undeveloped coastline for nesting December-March. Night drives and walks to see turtles nesting can be arranged.

Diving is possible year-round, with the best conditions being February-June. Visibility ranges 20-100+ feet, depending on sea conditions, with an average of 65 feet. Water temperature ranges from 70-80° F. Most diving is conducted from 25-125 feet below the surface.

## ITALA GAME RESERVE

This scenic 115-square-mile reserve consists of open savannah, deep valleys, granite outcrops and rivers.

The reserve has a high concentration of a variety of wildlife, including black rhino, white rhino, giraffe, eland, kudu, tsessebe, waterbuck and cheetah. Over 300 bird species have been recorded, including birds of prey such as martial eagles, black eagles, Wahlberg's eagles, and snake eagles.

Wilderness trails and guided day walks are available. The park is located in northern Natal just south of the Pongola River.

ACCOMMODATION - CLASS B: * *Ntshondwe Camp* has 39 thatched chalets with ensuite facilities, overlooking a water hole.

ACCOMMODATION - NEAR ITALA - CLASS B: * *Fugitives' Drift Lodge* consists of five "colonial-style" cottages with ensuite facilities.

# SWAZILAND

## THE MIGRATING ZEBRA

The zebras' regal black-and-white striped coats are a spectacle when they are assembled in herds during the annual migration in the dry season. As they go in search of a new water source, the gregarious behavior of male and female animals is interesting to observe.

The rich and polished stripes give us the impression of a healthy animal, plump with plenty of fat reserves. As they do not have ruminant stomachs, they need to eat nearly double the amount of grass as say, the wildebeest, to give them enough protein. Zebras are odd-toed ungulates, similar to the rhino, and play an important role in the migratory herbivorous trail, as they graze the taller, upper parts of the new grasses while the wildebeest and other antelope eat the shortened grasses.

The breeding season is stimulated by the coming rains. Stallions test the breeding female zebras for oestrus by exhibiting flehmen. This is a characteristic act where they raise their heads high, sniff the female's urine, and curl back their lips assessing the reproductive status. The oestrus filly is also cause for fight as they rear, bare their teeth and bite each other, kicking and thumping their hooves around.

The young foals will usually be born as the migration is starting to move, their brown furry faces and wobbly legs a gorgeous sight to view as they keep up with their mothers. This calving season is timed to coincide with the new growth of food.

# SWAZILAND

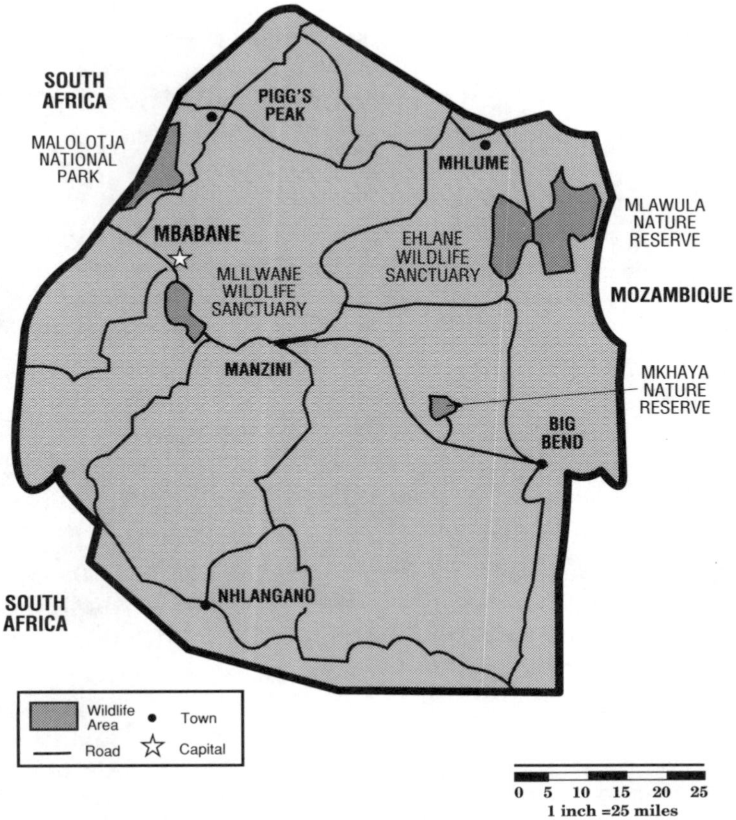


FACTS AT A GLANCE

| | |
|---|---|
| AREA: | 6704 SQUARE MILES |
| APPROXIMATE SIZE: | TEXAS OR FRANCE |
| POPULATION: | 712,000 (1992 EST.) |
| CAPITAL: | MBABANE (POP. EST. 60,000) |
| OFFICIAL LANGUAGE: | ENGLISH AND SISWATI |
| | ENGLISH IS WIDELY SPOKEN |

# SWAZILAND

The combination of friendly people, interesting culture, beautiful countryside, and small game reserves make Swaziland an attractive country to visit.

Swaziland, along with Lesotho and Morocco, is one of the last three remaining kingdoms in Africa. The country is deeply rooted in tradition — an important part of present-day life.

Although Swaziland is the second smallest country in Africa, within its boundaries lie every type of African terrain except desert. Swaziland has several small wildlife reserves, bushmen paintings, international-class resorts, and superb scenery.

Unlike most African countries, Swaziland has never been a totally subject nation. Although the British administered the country for 66 years, the people have always been governed by their own rulers according to their own traditions.

Swaziland has an excellent climate; the higher altitudes have a near temperate climate while the rest of the country has a subtropical climate. Summers (November-January) are rainy, hot and humid. Winters (May-July) are crisp and clear, with occasional frosts in the highveld (higher altitudes). July is usually windy and dusty.

Geographically, the country is divided into four belts of about the same width, running roughly north to south: the mountainous highveld in the west, the hilly middleveld, the Lubombo Plateau along the eastern border, and the lowveld bush.

Swaziland may have been inhabited by Bushmen between the early Stone Age and fifteenth century. In the fifteenth century, descendants of the Nguni migrated to what is now Maputo, Mozambique, from the great lakes of Central Africa. About 1700 the Nkosi Dlamini settled within the present-day borders of Swaziland.

Mswati the Second was proclaimed king of the people of the Mswati in 1840, forming the seed of a Swazi nation. By this time the kingdom had grown to twice its present size, and whites began to obtain valuable commercial and agricultural concessions.

Dual administration of the country by British and Boer (Transvaal) governments failed. The Boers took over from 1895 until the Anglo-Boer War broke out in 1899. Swaziland became a High Commission Territory under the British after the war in 1903.

In 1921, Sobhuza the Second became king and remained on the throne until his death in 1982, making him the longest ruling monarch in the world. This long reign gave his country a higher level of political stability than experienced by most of the world.

Only four rulers in modern times have reigned over 60 years: Queen Victoria of Great Britain, Louis the Fourteenth of France, Karl Friedrich the Grand Duke of Badan, and Sobhuza the Second.

Swaziland gained its independence on September 6, 1968, making it the last directly administered British colony in Africa. The Queen Regent, Indlovukazi, ruled after the death of Sobhuza, until Prince Makhosetive was crowned king in 1986. The mining of the highland's (Ngwenya's) iron ore deposits began as early as 26,000 B.C., until 1980, when supplies were exhausted. In the late 1800s, the Swazi gold rush centered around Pigg's Peak and Jeppe's Reef and lasted for 60 years.

The people are called Swazi(s), most of whom are subsistence farmers, following a mixture of Christian and indigenous beliefs. About 95 percent are of Swazi descent, with the rest of the population composed of Zulu, European, Mozambiquean and mulatto. Most live in scattered homesteads instead of concentrating themselves in villages and cities.

More than 15,000 Swazis work outside the country, primarily in South African gold and platinum mines. Much of Swazi tradition revolves around the raising of cattle.

The country's main crops are maize, sugar, citrus, cotton, pineapples, and tobacco. Seventy-five percent of the population works in agriculture.

## WILDLIFE AND WILDLIFE AREAS

Less than 100 years ago, Swaziland was abundant in most forms of wildlife. But much wildlife was exterminated by hunters in the years to follow. Hunting is now illegal, and conservation programs have partially revived this nation's wildlife heritage.

Swazi reserves are among the smallest on the continent, but for their size contain a great variety of species. The parks are ideal for horseback or walking safaris, providing close contact with nature. Open vehicles are most often used.

The country is prolific in birdlife, hosting more than 450 different species; these include such rarities as the bald ibis and blue crane. Other more common species include the glossy starling, lilac-breasted roller, hamerkop, sunbirds, kingfishers, geese and guinea fowl.

In the country's wide range of altitude grow over 6000 different species of flora, including 25 varieties of aloes and six species of cycads.

Cycads, often called "living fossils", are the oldest known seed-bearing plants in the world. According to carbon dating, these plants have changed very little during the last 50 million years, and are presently protected by law.

## THE NORTH

## MALOLOTJA NATIONAL PARK

This is the country's largest park, covering 70 square miles of mountains and gorges harboring unique highveld flora and fauna. Rock faces, rapids, waterfalls, grasslands, impenetrable riverine forests, and mountains rising to an altitude of 5900 feet provide scenic backdrops for game. Tree cycads over 20 feet may be found in the valleys.

**Malolotja Falls** with a 300-foot drop are the highest in the country. Wildlife includes oribi, vaal rhebok, klipspringer, impala, red duiker, reedbuck, white rhino, wildebeest, aardwolf, black-backed jackal, honey badger, serval and zebra. Over 150 species of birds have been sighted. There are bald ibis colonies and blue cranes in the park November-February. Flora, characteristic only of this region of Southern Africa, include barberton, kaapsehoop and woolly cycads.

**Ngwenya Mine** may be the site of the world's earliest known mine, thought to have been worked as early as 26,000 B.C.

With limited roads, the park is best suited for walkers and backpackers. Wilderness trails one to seven days in length are well marked and require a permit; day trails may be used without permit. Camping along the trail is only allowed at official sites; these sites have water but no facilities. Permits must be obtained for backpacking and for fishing at the Forbes Reef Dam and Upper Malolotja River from the tourist office.

The best time to visit is August-April; June-July is cold and windy. The main gate is located 22 miles northwest of Mbabane on the road to Pigg's Peak.

ACCOMMODATION - CLASS C & D: * *National Park Cabins* have six fully furnished cabins, each with six beds, private facilities, crockery and cutlery. Bring your own food, bedclothes and towels.

CAMPING: Campsites with ablution blocks are available.

## EHLANE WILDLIFE SANCTUARY

Located in the northwestern corner of the country about 44 miles from Manzini, this 55-square-mile sanctuary is composed of unspoiled acacia bushveld. Over 10,000 animals congregate here during the dry months, but move south with the coming of spring rains.

Wildlife includes black-backed jackal, spotted hyena, giraffe, kudu, blue wildebeest, waterbuck, steenbok, and zebra.

ACCOMMODATION - CLASS D: * *Bhubesi Rest Camp* has three self-service lodges.

CLASS F: * *Ndlovu Rest Camp* has rustic huts (ten beds) and ablution block. * Basic huts are available.

CAMPING: Camping is allowed.

## MLAWULA NATURE RESERVE

Situated east of Ehlane Wildlife Sanctuary, Mlawula is composed of lowveld and Lubombo mountainside which support oribi, white rhino, leopard, ostrich, and red hartebeest, among other species.

ACCOMMODATION: None.

CAMPING: Campsites are available.

## MLILWANE WILDLIFE SANCTUARY

Located in the Ezulwini Valley, Mlilwane means "little fire" from the lightning which often strikes a nearby hill where large deposits of iron ore exist. This 17-square-mile game sanctuary has a variety of wildlife including white rhino, giraffe, hippo, buffalo, zebra, crocodile, jackal, caracal cat, serval cat, civet, nyala, blue wildebeest, eland, sable antelope, kudu, waterbuck, blesbok, reedbuck, bushbuck, oribi, springbok, duiker, and klipspringer.

The sanctuary is composed of middleveld and highveld with altitudes ranging from 2200-4750 feet. It is located on an escarpment that was a meeting point of westerly and easterly migrations of animals, which resulted in the congregation of a large number of wildlife species.

The northern limits of Mlilwane are marked by the twin peaks of "Sheba's Breasts." "Execution Rock" is another legendary peak where common criminals were supposedly pushed to their deaths.

Over 60 miles of gravel roads run throughout the sanctuary. Visitors are not allowed out of their vehicles unless accompanied by a guide. Guided tours in open vehicles, on foot, or on horseback can be arranged in advance at the Rest Camp. Horseback-riding safaris are conducted along bridle trails through the park. The best time to visit is the dry season, May-September.

ACCOMMODATION - DELUXE/FIRST AND TOURIST CLASS: See "Ezulwini Valley" below.

CLASS D: * *Mlilwane Rest Camp* has thatched wooden huts and traditional "beehive" huts and an ablution block.

CAMPING: Campsites are available.

## EZULWINI VALLEY

The Ezulwini Valley, or "Place of Heaven", is the entertainment center of the country and is the most convenient area in which to stay when visiting the Mlilwane Wildlife Sanctuary.

ACCOMMODATION - DELUXE: * The *Royal Swazi Sun Hotel,*

*Casino and Country Club*, situated on 100 acres, has 145 rooms with ensuite facilities, swimming pool, sauna, hot tub, casino, adult cinema, 72-par golf course, horseback riding, tennis, squash, mini-golf, lawn-bowling, casino, a disco, nightclub and cabaret. Guests of the Ezulwini Sun Cabanas and the Lugogo Sun Cabanas may use the facilities of the more exclusive Royal Swazi; complimentary hotel bus transfer service is provided.

FIRST CLASS: * *Ezulwini Sun Cabanas* has 120 air-conditioned rooms with private facilities and swimming pool. * *Lugogo Sun Cabanas* has 202 air-conditioned rooms with ensuite facilities and swimming pool.

## LOBAMBA

Lobamba is the spiritual and legislative capital of the country. The Queen Mother's village is situated here. The National Museum, concentrating on Swazi culture and traditions, and the House of Parliament may be visited.

The country's two most important ceremonies are the Ncwala and Umhlanga, both of which take place at the Ludzidzini Royal Residence.

The most important of the two ceremonies is the **Ncwala** or First Fruit Ceremony, usually held in December and January; its exact date depends on the phases of the moon as analyzed by Swazi astrologers. The Ncwala symbolizes the religious spirit identifying the Swazi people with their King. The Ncwala is spread over about a three-week period, and involves the entire Swazi nation.

The famous week-long Umhlanga (**Reed Dance**), is a colorful ceremony in which hundreds of Swazi maidens gather reeds and march with them to the Royal Residence at Ludzidzini where the reeds are used to repair the windbreakers around the residence of the Queen Mother, Indlovukazi. The Umhlanga occurs in late August/early September.

Photographs of these two ceremonies can be taken only with permission from the Swaziland Information Services (P.O. Box 338, Mbabane, Swaziland, tel: 4-2761).

## PIGG'S PEAK

Pigg's Peak, located in one of the most scenic areas of the country, was named after William Pigg who discovered gold there in January of 1884. Nearby is the country's most famous Bushmen painting, located at the **Nsangwini Shelter**. Ask the District Officer at Pigg's Peak to find a guide to take you there.

ACCOMMODATION - FIRST CLASS: * *Protea Pigg's Peak Hotel & Casino*, located six miles north of Pigg's Peak, has 106 rooms with facilities ensuite, swimming pool, gym, tennis and squash courts, cinema and casino.

# THE SOUTH

## MBABANE

Mbabane, the capital of Swaziland, is located in the mountainous highveld overlooking the Ezulwini Valley. Mbabane has a number of shops selling local crafts. Most international visitors stay in Ezulwini Valley instead of Mbabane. The international airport (Matsapha) is located about 15 miles from Mbabane, between Mbabane and the industrial city of Manzini.

## NHLANGANO

Nhlangano means "The Meeting Place of the Kings" and commemorates the meeting between King Sobhuza the Second and King George the Sixth in 1947. Nhlangano is located in the southwestern part of the country in an unspoiled mountainous area and is the burial place of many Swazi kings.

ACCOMMODATION - FIRST CLASS: * The *Nhlangano Sun* is the best hotel in the area, with casino, disco bar, swimming

Witch doctor's shop in Nhlangano.

pool, squash, tennis, and 48 comfortable chalet-type rooms with ensuite facilities.

## MKHAYA NATURE RESERVE

The newest reserve in Swaziland, Mkhaya covers 24 square miles with sandveld savannah in the north and acacia-dominated savannah in the south. Altitude ranges from 600-1150 feet. Winters are warm by day and cold at night; summers are hot with temperatures exceeding 100° F.

Wildlife includes elephant, hippo, black and white rhino, zebra, roan antelope, wildebeest, waterbuck, kudu, tsessebe, reedbuck, red duiker, grey duiker, steenbok, ostrich, spotted hyena, black-backed and side-striped jackal and crocodile.

ACCOMMODATION - CLASS C: * *Stone Camp* has tents with private bush toilets. Game drives in open land rovers and walks are offered.

# TANZANIA

## THE LION'S FEAST

On a game drive you will either see lion lying in the shade, too sleepy to raise their heads, or grouped around a recent kill eating their "share."

It may seem that since the female does most of the hunting — for the male simply helps drive the prey to the waiting females — she may be the first to gorge. However, this is not the lions' pecking order. The male will select his preferred contents, usually the lungs, liver and kidneys, followed by the rump and moving up toward the head. Skin and hair are also eaten, giving the lions the roughage they need. When food is plentiful, the females and cubs will feed next.

However, there is usually lots of cat fighting, snarls, hisses and arguments during feeding, with the males expressing their appreciation with roars. They will retire, satisfied (of course), and the females survive on the remains, with the cubs frequently going hungry or being killed in the scramble.

If a small pride is feeding on the kill together, the dominant male will control who eats where and what. If any female or cub oversteps this order, they will be disciplined by a snarl or a slap of a paw. Inevitably, the younger cubs will try all sorts of tricks to distract the male, who will usually tolerate these antics as he is not as fierce as he appears.

When they have finished their feast and either wander off for a drink or commence grooming themselves, all is peaceful in the lion pride.

# TANZANIA

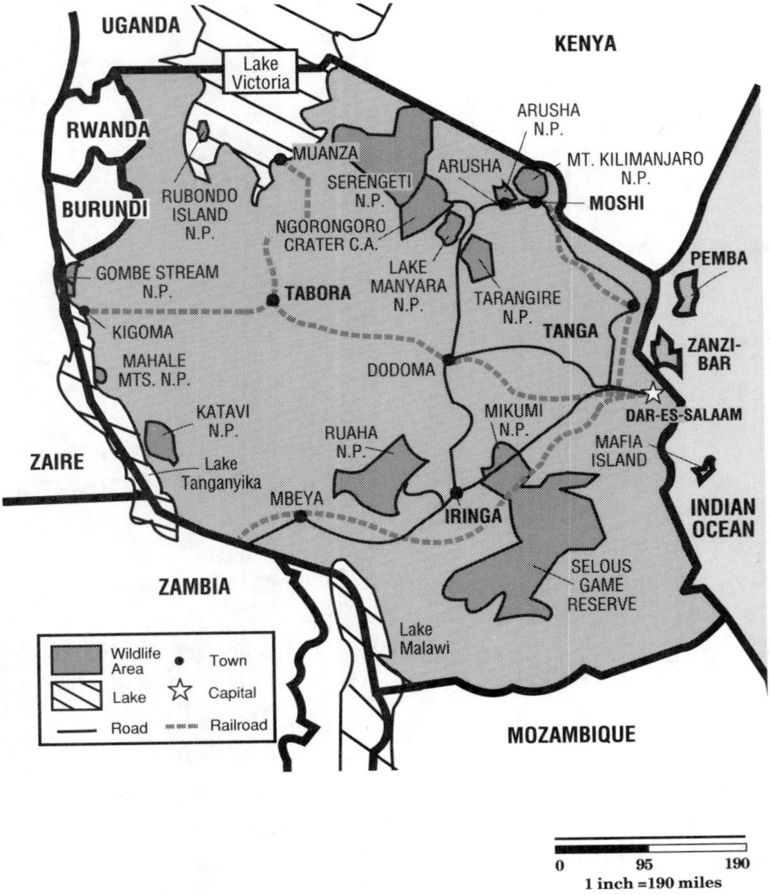


FACTS AT A GLANCE

| | |
|---|---|
| AREA: | 363,708 SQUARE MILES |
| APPROXIMATE SIZE: | TEXAS PLUS OKLAHOMA OR FRANCE |
| POPULATION: | 24 MILLION (1992 EST.) |
| CAPITAL: | NOMINAL: DODOMA |
| FUNCTIONAL: | DAR ES SALAAM (POP. EST. 1,500,000) |
| OFFICIAL LANGUAGE: | SWAHILI; ENGLISH WIDELY SPOKEN |

# TANZANIA

Between Africa's highest mountain (Kilimanjaro) and Africa's largest lake (Victoria) lies one of the best game-viewing areas on the continent. This region also includes the world's largest unflooded intact volcanic caldera or crater (Ngorongoro) and the most famous wildlife park (the Serengeti). To the south lies one of the world's largest game reserves — the Selous.

Volcanic highlands dominate the north, giving way southward to a plateau, then semidesert in the center of the country and highlands in the south. The coastal lowlands are hot and humid with lush vegetation. One branch of the Great Rift Valley passes through Lakes Manyara and Natron in northern Tanzania to Lake Malawi (Lake Nyasa) in the south while the other branch passes through Lakes Rukwa and Tanganyika in the west.

Heavy rains usually occur in April and May, and lighter rains in late October and November. Altitude has a great effect on temperature. At Arusha (4600 feet) and the top of Ngorongoro Crater (7500 feet) nights and early mornings are especially cool. Tanzania's highest temperatures occur in December-March and lowest in July.

Evidence suggests East Africa was the cradle of mankind. The earliest known humanoid footprints, estimated to be 3.5 million years old, were discovered at Laetoli by Dr.

Mary Leakey in 1979. Dr. Leakey also found the estimated 1.7 million-year-old skull *Zinjanthropus boisei* at Olduvai Gorge in 1957.

By the thirteenth century Arabs, Persians, Egyptians, Indians and Chinese were involved in heavy trading on the coast. Slave trade began in the mid-1700s and was abolished in 1873.

British Explorers Richard Burton and John Speke crossed Tanzania in 1857 to Lake Tanganyika. Speke later discovered Lake Victoria which he felt was the source of the Nile.

The German East Africa Company gained control of the mainland (then called German East Africa) in 1885, and the German government held it from 1891 until World War I when it was mandated to Britain by the League of Nations. Tanganyika gained its independence from Britain in 1961, and Zanzibar gained its independence in 1963. Zanzibar, once the center of the East African slave trade, was ruled by sultans until its union with Tanganyika in 1964, forming the United Republic of Tanzania.

There are 120 tribes in Tanzania. Bantu languages and dialects are spoken by 95 percent of the population, with Kiswahili the official and national language. Over 75 percent of the people are peasant farmers. The export of coffee, cotton, sisal, tea, cloves, and cashews bring 70 percent of the country's foreign exchange.

## WILDLIFE AND WILDLIFE AREAS

Reserves cover over 95,000 square miles of area — possibly more than any other country on earth. There are 11 national parks, 17 game reserves and one conservation area comprising over 15 percent of the country's land area. Tanzania's great variety of wildlife can be at least partially attributed to its great diversity of landscapes, with altitudes ranging from sea level to almost 20,000 feet.

Tanzania is one of the best wildlife countries in Africa for mobile tented camp safaris. Vehicles with roof hatches or pop-tops are used on safari. Walking is not allowed in most of the national parks except Arusha, Gombe Stream, Mahale Mountains and Rubondo Island National Parks and the Selous Game Reserve where visitors must be accompanied by a national park guide.

The best weather for viewing game is July-September and December-March. January, February and August are the busiest months. Heavy rains falling in April and May hamper travel and game viewing. Light rains usually fall October-November.

The country contains 35 species of antelope and over 1.5 million wildebeest — over 80 percent of the population of this species in Africa. The calving season for wildebeest is from mid-January to mid-March.

## THE NORTH

This region from Mt. Kilimanjaro in the east to Serengeti National Park in the west is the area most visited by tourists and contains the country's most famous parks.

Many visitors reach Arusha on a four-hour drive from Nairobi (Kenya) via Namanga or fly into Kilimanjaro International Airport and then are transferred to Arusha. Kilimanjaro International Airport, located 34 miles east of Arusha and 22 miles west of Moshi, has a bank, bar and restaurant.

The "Northern Circuit" includes Lake Manyara National Park, Ngorongoro Conservation Area, Olduvai Gorge, Serengeti National Park and Tarangire National Park.

From Arusha, the Northern Circuit runs 45 miles west on a good, newly constructed tarmac road across the gently rolling Masai Plains with scattered acacia trees to Makuyuni. You may then either continue on the main road toward Dodoma for another 20 miles to Tarangire National Park or turn right (northwest) on an all-weather dirt road to Mto wa Mbu (Mosquito Creek).

En route you pass many Masai bomas (villages), Masai in their colorful traditional dress walking on the roadside, riding bicycles, herding their cattle, and driving overloaded

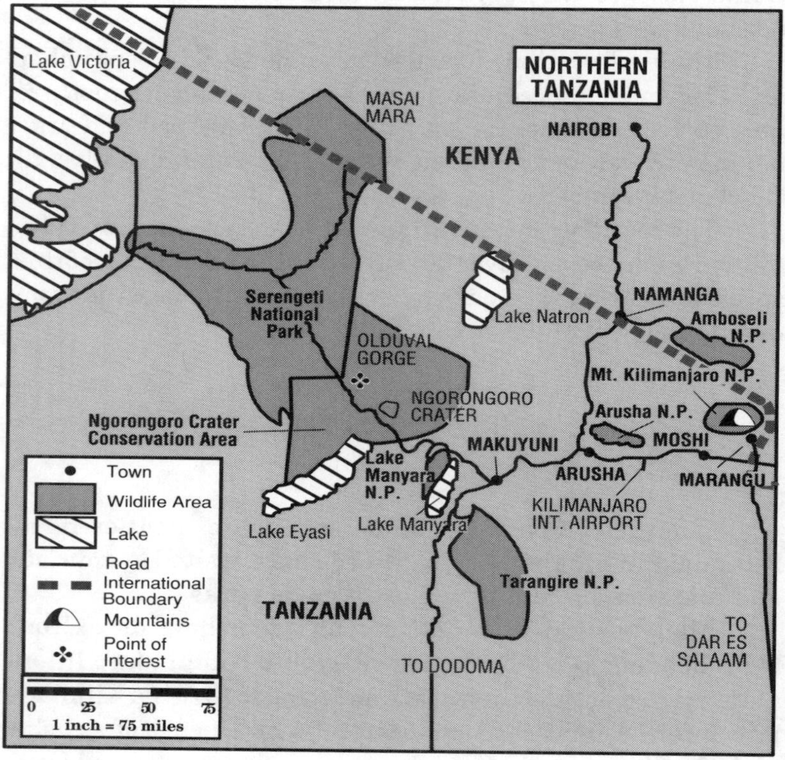


donkey carts.

Masai Morani completing the circumcision ritual are sometimes seen clad in black with white paint on their faces. They leave the village as a child for a period for training and instruction by elders and return as men.

Mto wa Mbu is a village with many roadside stands filled with wood carvings and other local crafts for sale. Be sure to bargain. If you take a few minutes to walk into the village behind the stands, you will get a more realistic (and less touristic) view of village life.

Continuing west you soon pass the entrance to Lake

Masai herding cattle.

Manyara National Park. The road becomes quite rough as it climbs up the Rift Valley escarpment past huge baobab trees and numerous baboons looking for handouts. Fabulous views of the valley and Lake Manyara Park below can be seen. You then pass through beautiful cultivated uplands and small villages past the turnoff to Gibb's Farm and on up the slopes of the Crater Highlands to Ngorongoro Crater. The road then follows the rim of the crater past the Wildlife Lodge, Rhino Lodge and Crater Lodge, and finally descends the western side of the crater to Olduvai Gorge and Serengeti National Park.

## ARUSHA

This town is the center of tourism for northern Tanzania and is situated in the foothills of rugged Mt. Meru. Named after one of the Arusha tribes, it is located on the Great North Road midway between Cairo and Cape Town. *Makonde* carvings and other souvenirs are available in the numerous craft shops at the center of town. Walking around the Arusha Market, located behind the bus station, is an interesting way to spend a few hours.

ACCOMMODATION: - Also see "Accommodation" under "Arusha National Park."

FIRST CLASS: * *Mountain Village* has 40 bungalows (doubles) and three triples with ensuite facilities set in lovely gardens and is six miles outside Arusha overlooking Lake Duluti. Horseback riding and fishing are available. * *Mt. Meru Hotel* is a 200-room hotel with ensuite facilities and swimming pool.

TOURIST CLASS: * *New Arusha Hotel,* located in the center of town, has 72 rooms and attractive gardens. * *Hotel 77* is Tanzania's largest hotel, with 400 double rooms with private facilities.

## LAKE MANYARA NATIONAL PARK

Once one of the most popular hunting areas of Tanzania, this 123-square-mile park has the Great Rift Valley escarpment for a dramatic backdrop. Two-thirds of the park is covered by alkaline Lake Manyara, which is situated at an altitude of 3150 feet.

The turnoff to Lake Manyara is past Mto wa Mbu on the road from Makuyuni to Ngorongoro Crater, about 75 miles west of Arusha.

Five different vegetation zones are found in the park. The first zone reached from the park entrance is groundwater forest fed by water seeping from the Great Rift Wall, with wild fig, sausage, tamarind and mahogany trees. Elephants prefer these dense forests as well as marshy glades. The other zones include the marshlands along the edge of the lake, scrub on the Rift Valley Wall, open areas with scattered acacia, and open grasslands.

Manyara, like Ishasha in the Ruwenzori National Park in Uganda, is well known for its tree-climbing lions found lazing on branches of acacia trees. Some people believe that lions climb trees in Manyara to avoid tsetse flies and the dense undergrowth while remaining in the cool shade, while lions of the Ruwenzori National Park in Uganda climb trees

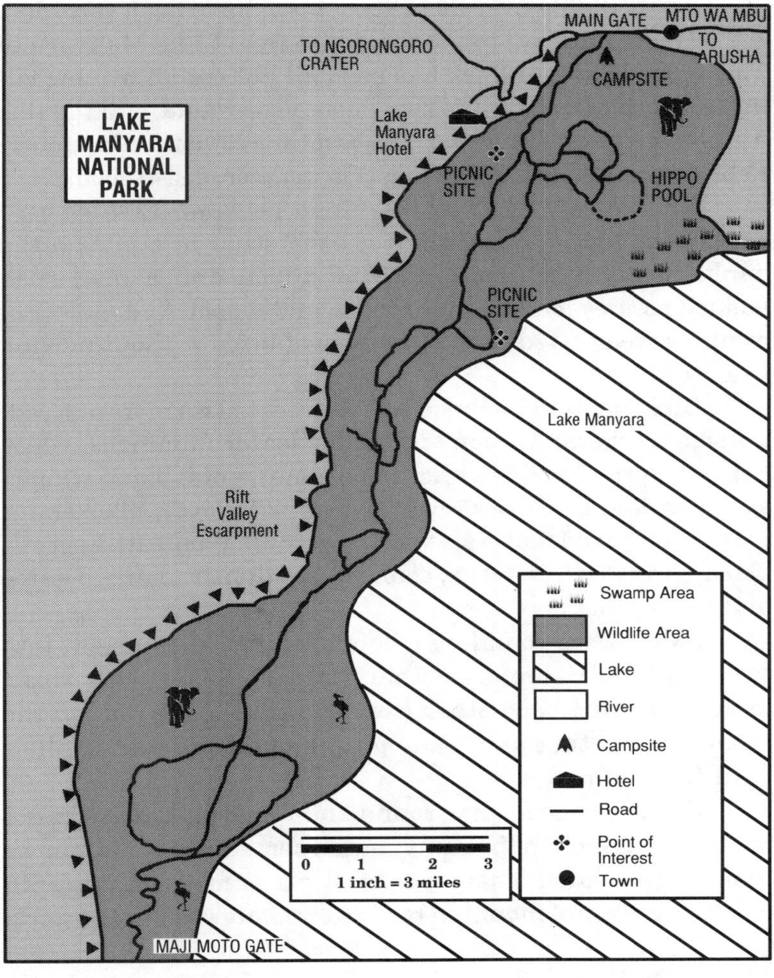


to gain a hunting advantage. Finding lion in the trees is very rare, so don't set your heart on it — look at it as an unexpected bonus.

Manyara features large concentrations of elephant and buffalo. Black rhino and leopard are rare. Other wildlife includes common waterbuck, Masai giraffe, zebra, impala, baboons, blue monkeys and Syke's monkeys. Over 380 species of birds, including over 30 birds of prey, have been recorded.

The traditional migration route from Lake Manyara to Tarangire National Park has been all but cut off by new villages. Much of the wildlife is resident year-round, making this a good park to visit anytime. The best time to visit is December-February and May-July; August-September is also good.

On a recent visit to the hippo pool, we saw over 20 gregarious hippos lying all over each other in a pile on the bank. Something finally spooked them, and a mad rush ensued as they joined other hippos in the pool. In a matter of minutes we spotted over 20 species of birds without moving from that spot.

Birds spotted included white-breasted cormorants, red-billed oxpeckers, African spoonbills, lesser flamingos, white pelicans, grey-headed gulls, wood sandpipers, black-winged stilts, white-faced ducks, white-crowned plover, blacksmith plover, long-toed plovers, avocet, water dikkops, cattle egrets, black-winged white terns, common sandpiper, painted snipe and sacred ibis.

As we were rounding a bend, we almost ran right into two huge bull elephants that were sparring with tusks locked, pushing each other from one side of the road to the other, trumpeting and kicking up mounds of dust in their fight for dominance.

Roads are good year-round and four-wheel drive is not needed, although in the rainy season some side tracks may be temporarily closed. There is a small museum at the gate with a large number of mounted birds commonly seen in the park.

ACCOMMODATION - CLASS B: * *Lake Manyara Hotel*, magnificently set on the Rift Valley Escarpment overlooking the park and the Rift Valley 1000 feet below, has 212 rooms with private facilities, swimming pool and airstrip.

CLASSES D & F: * *National Park Self-Service Bandas* (ten doubles) are located near the park entrance. Some bandas have private facilities and everyone shares a communal kitchen.

CAMPING: Two campsites are located near the park entrance, both with toilet and shower facilities. One campsite is situated within the park with no facilities; this site requires a special permit.

ACCOMMODATION BETWEEN LAKE MANYARA AND NGORONGORO CRATER - CLASS A/B: * *Gibb's Farm* has attractively decorated cottages (30 beds), a spacious colonial house with sitting rooms, and restaurant serving excellent food. Walks to nearby waterfalls can be arranged. * *Flycatchers Farmhouse* is a small guesthouse set in lovely gardens.

## NGORONGORO CRATER CONSERVATION AREA

**Ngorongoro Crater** is the largest unflooded, intact caldera (collapsed cone of a volcano) in the world. Known as the eighth wonder of the world, its vastness and beauty is truly overwhelming and is believed by some to have been the proverbial Garden of Eden. Many scientists suggest that before its eruption, this volcano was larger than Mt. Kilimanjaro.

Ngorongoro contains possibly the largest permanent concentration of wildlife in Africa with an estimated average of 30,000 large mammals. In addition, this is probably the best park in Africa to see black rhino.

Large concentrations of wildlife make Ngorongoro Crater their permanent home. Game viewing is good year-round. Because there is a permanent source of fresh water, there's no reason for the wildlife to migrate as they must do in the Serengeti.

The 102-square-mile crater itself is but a small portion of the 3200-square-mile Ngorongoro Conservation Area, which is characterized by a highland plateau with volcanic mountains as well as several craters, extensive savannah and forests. Altitudes range from 4430-11,800 feet.

Ngorongoro Crater is about 12 miles wide and its rim rises 1200-1600 feet off its expansive 102-square-mile floor. From the crater rim, elephant appear as small dark specks on

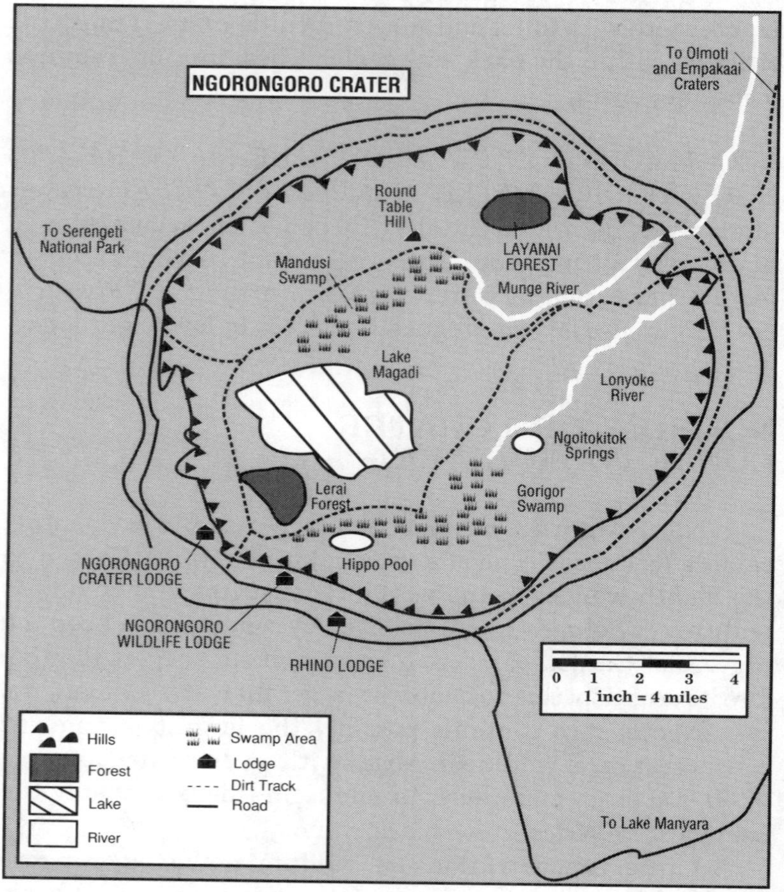


the grasslands. The steep descent into the crater along a narrow rough, winding road takes 25-35 minutes from the crater rim. The crater floor is predominantly grasslands (making game easy to spot) with two swamps fed by streams and the Lerai Forest. The walls of the crater are lightly forested.

Once on the floor, your driver will more than likely turn left on a dirt road and travel clockwise around the crater floor. Lake Magadi, also called Crater Lake and Lake Makat, is a shallow soda lake near the entry point of the crater which attracts thousands of flamingos and other water birds.

The dirt road continues past Mandusi Swamp. Game viewing is especially good in this area during the dry season (July-October) as some wildlife migrates to this permanent source of fresh water. Hippo, elephant, and reedbuck, among many other species, can usually be found here.

You then come to Round Table Hill which provides a good view and excellent vantage point to get one's bearings. The circular route continues over the Munge River, whose source is in the Olmoti Crater north of Ngorongoro Crater, to Ngoitokitok Springs. From there, you journey past Gorigor Swamp, fed by the Lonyokie River, to the Hippo Pool, which is probably the best place to see hippo.

The Lerai Forest, primarily composed of fever trees (a type of acacia) is a good place to spot elephant, and, if you are very lucky, leopard. There are two picnic areas and campsites here with long-drop toilets and running water. The exit road climbing the wall of the crater is behind the forest.

On a full-day's game drive during a recent visit, we saw seven black rhino, including one mother with her baby, 27 lion, several golden jackal and spotted hyena, and numerous elephant, buffalo, zebra, wildebeest, an ostrich guarding the eggs in her nest, flamingos, baboons, monkeys, bat-eared fox at their den, kori bustards and a host of other species. Elephant are also found in the wooded areas and on the slopes of the crater. Cheetah are present, but there are no giraffe or topi.

Over 350 species of birds have been recorded. Birds commonly sighted include ostrich, crowned cranes, Egyptian geese, and pelicans.

At the picnic site vervet monkeys are very aggressive in getting at your food. Kites (a species of bird) made many swooping attempts at our lunches. You may wish to eat inside your vehicle. As of March 1, 1992, overnight camping is no longer allowed on the crater floor.

One important thing to remember: game is not confined to the crater; wildlife is present throughout the conservation area including near hotels and lodges. This I learned the hard way on my first visit to Ngorongoro many years ago. One evening just outside the Ngorongoro Wildlife Lodge, I walked blindly to within 20 feet of three large buffalo. One buffalo

Two fine male species (looking for females . . . ?)

appeared as if it was going to charge, then fortunately it ran off. Welcome to Africa! I thought, relieved beyond words.

Game viewing in the Ngorongoro Conservation Area west of the crater bordering the Serengeti is best between November and May when the Serengeti migration is in the area.

Ngorongoro Crater is about 118 miles west of Arusha. An airstrip is located further along the crater rim, but it is often fogged in. Four-wheel-drive vehicles are required for game drives into the crater.

The Serengeti Plains cover the western part of the conservation area. Since this is classified as a conservation area and not a national park, wildlife, human beings and livestock exist together. Ground cultivation is not allowed. The Masai are allowed to bring in their cattle for the salts and permanent water available on the crater floor, but must leave the crater at night.

The 10,700-foot-high **Empakaai Crater**, situated 20 miles northwest of Ngorongoro Crater on a road that is difficult to impossible to negotiate even with four-wheel-drive vehicles, is known for its scenic beauty. The drive through Masailand offers great views. Hiking is allowed if accompanied by an armed wildlife guard.

About 30 miles west of Ngorongoro Crater and a few

miles off the road to the Serengeti is **Olduvai Gorge**, site of many archeological discoveries including the estimated 1.7-million-year-old *Zinjanthropus boisei* fossil. The fossil is housed in the National Museum in Dar es Salaam.

A small museum overlooks the gorge itself, and a guide there will tell you the story of the Leakeys' research and findings. For a small tip, the guide will take you down into the gorge and show you where the *Zinjanthropus boisei* fossil was found.

ACCOMMODATION - CLASS B: * *Ngorongoro Sopa Lodge* is a new lodge with 100 rooms with private facilities located on the eastern rim of the crater. * *Camp Ngorongoro* is a tented camp (20 beds) on the southeastern rim of the crater. Each tent has its own bucket shower and toilet. Access is by air charter. As this is a semipermanent camp, its location on the crater rim may vary.

CLASS B/C: * *Ngorongoro Crater Lodge*, a rustic lodge with panoramic views of the crater, has individual cottages and blocks of cottages with ensuite facilities (134 beds). There is a large double fireplace between the bar and dining room. * *Ngorongoro Wildlife Lodge*, an attractive 78-room hotel with spectacular views of the crater, has a large lounge and dining area and veranda with telescopes.

CLASS C: * *Ngorongoro Rhino Lodge* is a small lodge with no view of the crater. Two rooms share one toilet and bathroom.

CAMPING: Campsites are located on the crater rim.

## SERENGETI NATIONAL PARK

This is Tanzania's largest and most famous park and has the largest concentration of migratory game animals in the world. It is also famous for its huge lion population and is one of the best places on the continent to see them. The park has received additional notoriety through Professor Bernard Grzimek's book, *Serengeti Shall Not Die*.

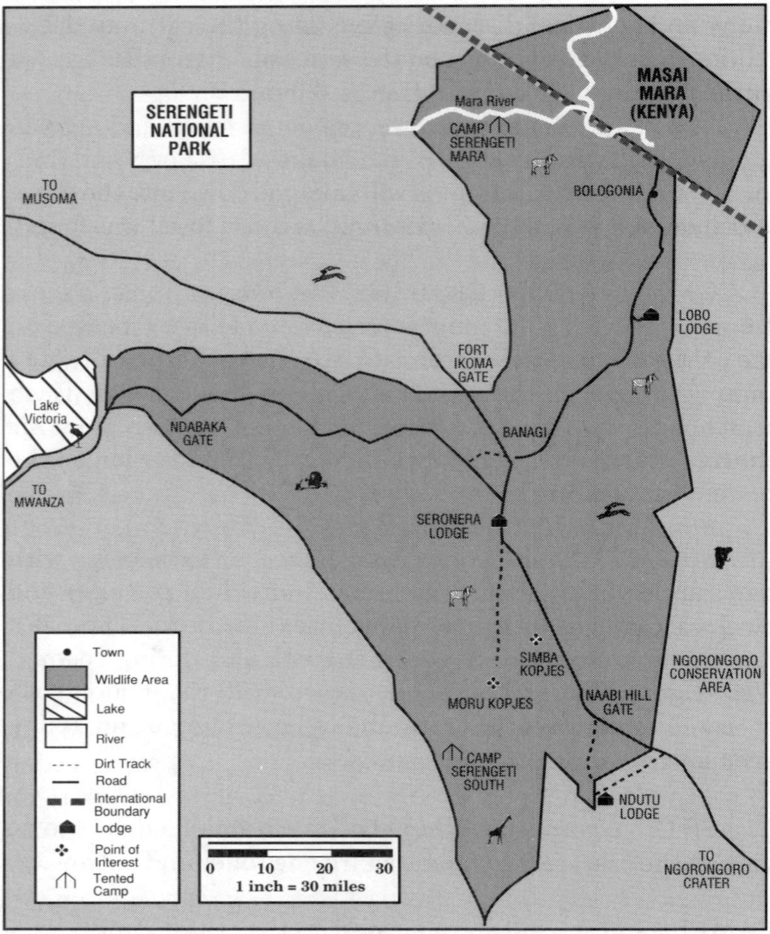


*Serengeti* is derived from the Masai language and appropriately means "endless plain." The park's 5700 square miles make it larger than the state of Connecticut. Altitude varies from 3000-6000 feet.

The park comprises most of the Serengeti ecosystem, which is the primary migration route of the wildebeest. The Serengeti ecosystem also includes Kenya's Masai Mara National Reserve, bordering on the north, the Loliondo Controlled Area, bordering on the northeast, the Ngorongoro Conservation Area, bordering on the southeast, the Maswa Game Reserve, bordering on the southwest, and the Grumeti and Ikorongo Controlled Areas, bordering on the northwest. The "western corridor" of the park comes within a few miles of Lake Victoria.

Nearly 500 species of birds and 35 species of large plains animals can be found in the Serengeti. The park may contain as many as 1.3 million wildebeest, 250,000 Thomson's gazelle, 200,000 zebra, 70,000 topi, 30,000 Grant's gazelle, 20,000 buffalo, 9000 eland, 8000 giraffe, 1500 lion and 800 elephant.

Most of the Serengeti is a vast open plain broken by rocky outcrops (kopjes). There is also acacia savannah, savannah woodland, riverine forests, some swamps and small lakes.

The north is more hilly with thick scrub and forests lining the Mara River, where leopards are sometimes spotted sleeping in the trees. Acacia savannah dominates the central region, with short and long grass open plains in the southeast, and woodland plains and hills in the western corridor.

It is impossible to predict the exact time of the famous **Serengeti Migration**, which covers a circuit of about 500 miles. From December-May wildebeest, zebra, eland and Thomson's gazelle usually concentrate on the treeless short grass plains in the extreme southeastern Serengeti and western Ngorongoro Conservation Area near Lake Ndutu in search of short grass which they prefer over the longer dry-stemmed variety. This is the best time to visit the Serengeti. In April and May, the height of the rainy season, a four-wheel-drive vehicle is highly recommended.

Other species common to the area during this period are Grant's gazelle, eland, hartebeest, topi and a host of predators including lion, cheetah, spotted hyena, honey badger and black-backed jackal. Kori bustards and yellow-throated sandgrouse are also common.

During the long rainy season (April-May), nomadic lions and hyena move to the eastern part of the Serengeti. The migration, mainly of wildebeest and zebra, begins in May or June. Once the dry season begins wildebeest and zebra must

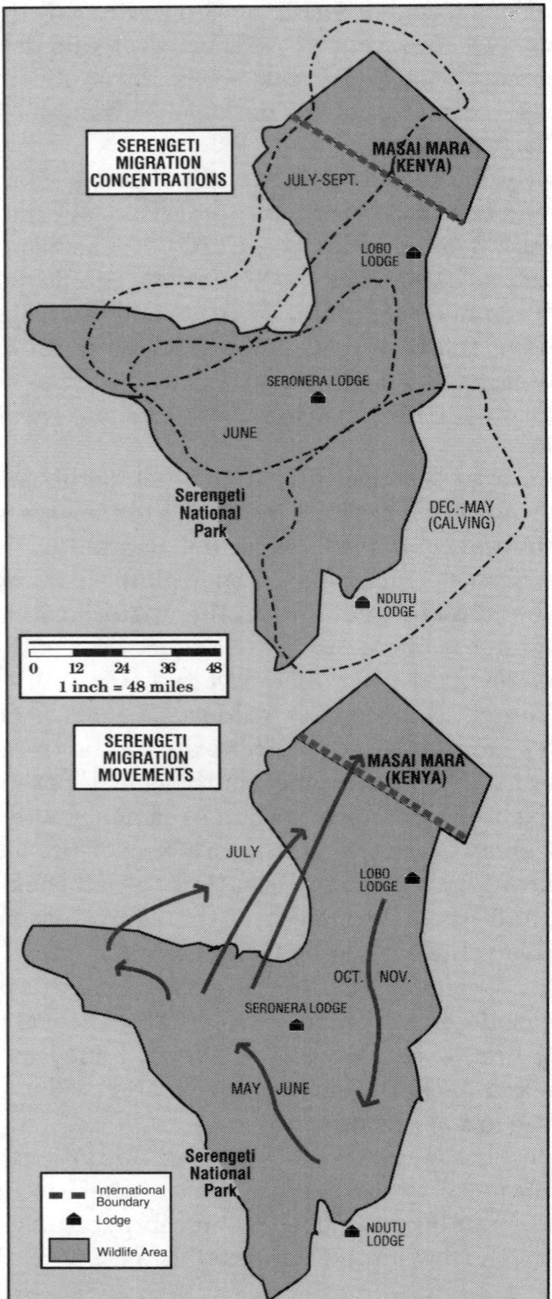
SERENGETI MIGRATION CONCENTRATIONS
MASAI MARA (KENYA)
JULY-SEPT.
LOBO LODGE
SERONERA LODGE
JUNE
Serengeti National Park
DEC.-MAY (CALVING)
NDUTU LODGE
0 12 24 36 48
1 inch = 48 miles
SERENGETI MIGRATION MOVEMENTS
MASAI MARA (KENYA)
JULY
LOBO LODGE
OCT. NOV.
SERONERA LODGE
MAY JUNE
Serengeti National Park
NDUTU LODGE
International Boundary
Lodge
Wildlife Area

migrate from the area. There is no permanent water, and both of these species must drink on a regular basis.

The mating season for wildebeest is concentrated over a three-week period and generally occurs in May or June. After a gestation period of eight and one-half months the calves are born, usually on the short grass plains.

Wildebeest move about six to ten abreast in columns several miles long toward the western corridor. Zebra do not move in columns but in family units.

As a general rule, by June or July the migration has progressed west of Seronera. The migration then splits into three separate migrations: one west through the corridor toward permanent water and Lake Victoria, then northeast; the second one due north, reaching the Masai Mara of Kenya around mid-July; and the third northward between the other two to a region west of Lobo Lodge where the group disperses. At present, there are few roads in the region where the third group disperses; however, this may soon change.

During July-September, the Serengeti's highest concentration of wildlife is in the extreme north. The first and second groups meet and begin returning to the Serengeti National Park around mid-September/early October; the migration then reaches the southern Serengeti by December.

Short grass plains dominate the part of the Ngorongoro Conservation Area bordering the Serengeti. As one moves northwest into the park, the plains change to medium grass plains and then into long grass plains around Simba Kopjes north of Naabi Hill Gate. Topi, elephant, Thomson's and Grant's gazelles, bat-eared fox and warthogs are often seen here.

### Seronera

Seronera Lodge, Park Headquarters and the park village are located together in the center of the park. Game is plentiful in the Seronera Valley, which is famous for lion and

The great Serengeti Migration.

leopard. Other wildlife includes hyena, jackal, topi, Masai giraffe, and Thomson's gazelle. This is the best part of the park to find cheetah, especially in the dry season. In the wet season, many cheetah are found in the short grass plains. They are, however, found throughout the park.

Research on African wild dogs is being conducted in the region. Exciting balloon safaris over the Serengeti Plains are now operated from Seronera Lodge.

Banagi Hill, eleven miles north of Seronera on the road to Lobo, is a good area for Masai giraffe, buffalo and impala. Four miles from Banagi on the Orangi River is a hippo pool.

### Lobo

From Banagi northward to Lobo and the Bologonja Gate are rolling uplands with open plains, bush, woodlands and magnificent kopjes. This is the best area of the park to see elephant. Forests of large mahogany and fig trees are found along the rivers where Patas monkeys, kingfishers, fish eagles and turacos may be seen. Other wildlife found in the Lobo area includes grey bush duikers, Cotton's oribi and mountain reedbuck. Large numbers of Masai giraffe are permanent residents.

Large herds of wildebeest are often in the region from August till the rains begin, usually in November. During this period many wildebeest drown while attempting to cross the Mara River.

On our last visit, we watched a pride of lion with five cubs play for hours. Later we came upon a fire in the park where hundreds of storks were feeding on the insects fleeing the flames.

### Western Corridor

Beginning three miles north of Seronera, the western corridor road passes over the Grumeti River and beyond to a central range of hills. Eighteen miles before Ndabaka Gate is an extensive area of black cotton soil which makes rainy season travel difficult. This area is best visited June-October during the dry season. Colobus monkeys may be found in the riverine areas. Other wildlife includes roan antelope, Patterson's eland, topi, impala and crocodile.

The granite kopjes or rocky outcrops that dot the plains are home to rock hyrax, Kirk's dikdik and klipspringer. Banded, dwarf and slender mongoose are occasionally seen nearby. Verreaux's eagle and black rhino are sometimes sighted near the Moru Kopjes.

There are two saline lakes in the south of the park, **Lake Magadi** and **Lake Lagaja**, known mainly for their populations of lesser and greater flamingos.

Three species of jackal occur in the Serengeti: black-backed, side-striped and golden. Side-striped jackal are rare; golden jackal are usually found in the short grass plains; and black-backed jackal are quite common. The six species of

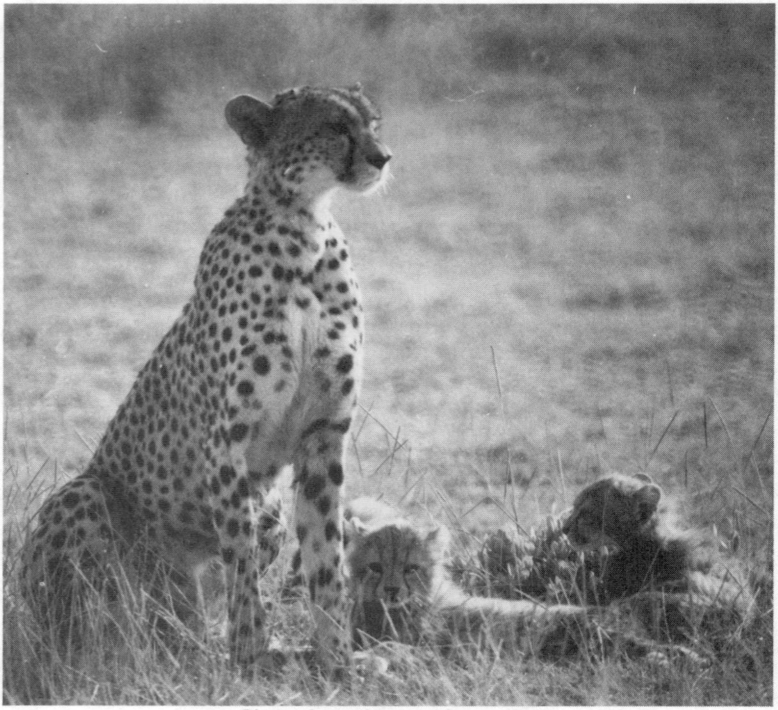

Cheetah mother and her cubs.

vultures occurring in the park are white-backed, white-headed, hooded, lappet-faced, Ruppell's and Egyptian.

At the time of this writing, the border with Kenya between Serengeti National Park and the Masai Mara is officially closed. However, with the proper arrangements, a border transfer may be made. There is a dry weather road (often impassable in the rainy season) from Mwanza and Musoma (Lake Victoria) to the west through Ndabaka Gate. The main road from the Ngorongoro Conservation Area via Naabi Hill Gate is open year-round.

Vehicles must stay on the roads within a ten-mile radius of Seronera. Travel in the park is only allowed from 6:00 a.m. till 7:00 p.m. Visitors may get out of the vehicle in open areas if there are no animals present. Do stay close to the vehicle and keep a careful lookout.

From July-October, when the migration is usually in Kenya, you may want to pass up the Serengeti and spend your time in Tarangire National Park, which is excellent that time of year.

ACCOMMODATION - CLASS B: * *Ndutu Safari Lodge* is a rustic lodge with rooms with private facilities, located on the edge of the park in Ngorongoro Conservation Area. * *Lobo Wildlife Lodge*, a dramatically beautiful lodge in the north of the park 43 miles north of Seronera, is uniquely designed around huge boulders and has a swimming pool carved out of solid rock. All 75 double rooms have private facilities. * *Camp Serengeti South* is a fixed tented camp (20 beds); each sleeping tent has a bucket shower and toilet. Game drives in the Serengeti and walks in the nearby Maswa Game Reserve are offered. * *Camp Serengeti Mara* is a fixed tented camp with ten tents (20 beds), each with a bucket shower and toilet, set on the banks of the Mara River in the northern Serengeti. Game drives are offered. Access is by air charter.

CLASS B/C: * *Seronera Wildlife Lodge*, situated in the center of the park 90 miles from Ngorongoro Crater, has 75 double rooms with private facilities, swimming pool (often empty of water) and airstrip. The lodge sometimes experiences water shortages for bathing.

CAMPING: Campsites are available at Seronera, Ndutu, Naabi Hill Gate, Moru Kopjes, Kirawira and Lobo. Camping in other areas requires permission from the warden and higher fees. It is best to book well in advance.

## TARANGIRE NATIONAL PARK

Large numbers of baobab trees dotting the landscape give the park a prehistoric look the likes of which I have never seen before. This park has a different feel to it than any other northern park — and an eerie feeling at that, making it one of my favorites.

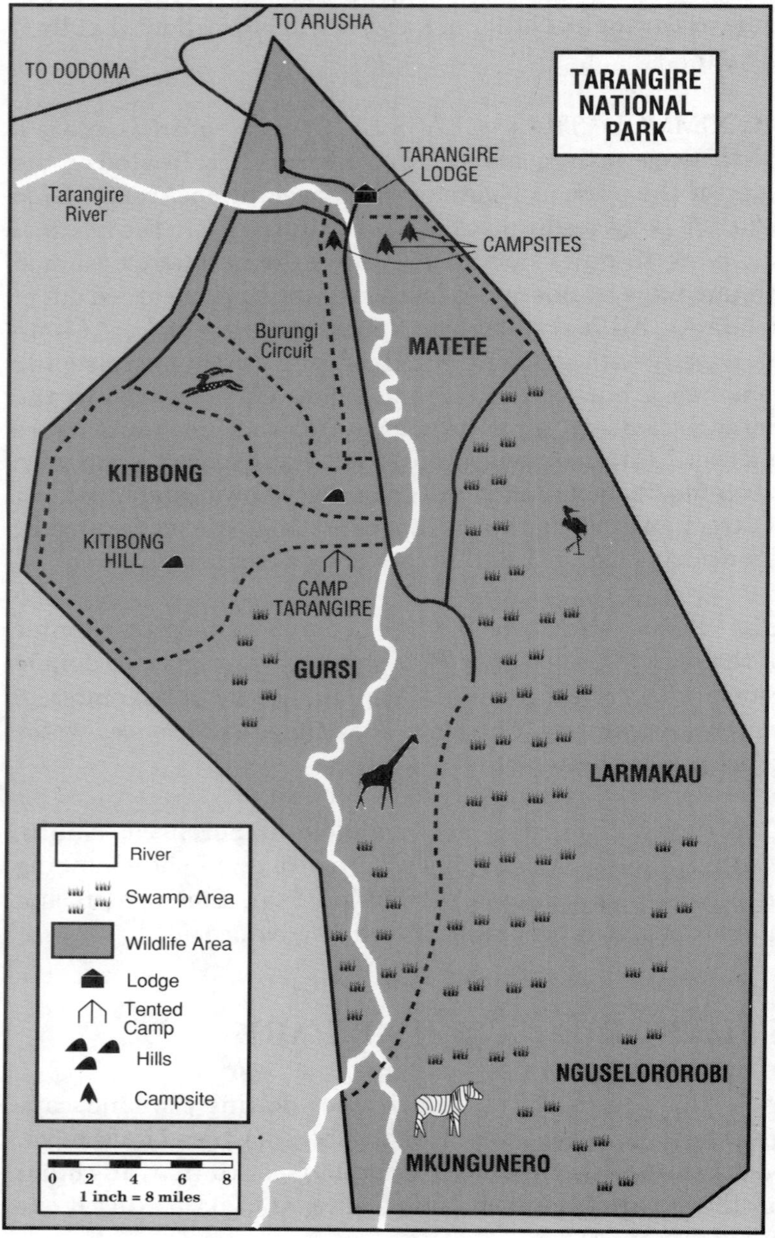
TO ARUSHA
TO DODOMA
TARANGIRE NATIONAL PARK
TARANGIRE LODGE
Tarangire River
CAMPSITES
Burungi Circuit
MATETE
KITIBONG
KITIBONG HILL
CAMP TARANGIRE
GURSI
LARMAKAU
NGUSELOROROBI
MKUNGUNERO
River
Swamp Area
Wildlife Area
Lodge
Tented Camp
Hills
Campsite
0 2 4 6 8
1 inch = 8 miles

Tarangire is the best park on the northern circuit to see elephant. On my last visit Cynthia Moss, author of *Elephant Memories* and *Portraits In The Wild,* identified over 500 individual elephants within the park in a week!

Fewer tourists visit this park than Manyara, Ngorongoro and Serengeti, allowing a better opportunity to experience it as the early explorers did — alone. This park should not be missed; wildlife viewing is excellent, especially from July-October when many migratory animals return to the only permanent water source in the area: the Tarangire River and its tributaries.

At the beginning of October/November during the short rainy season, migratory species including wildebeest and zebra, soon followed by elephant, buffalo, Grant's gazelle, Thomson's gazelle and oryx begin migrating out of the park. However, as more and more migration routes are cut off from the expansion of man's presence, more and more animals are remaining in the park. Giraffe, waterbuck, lesser kudu and other resident species tend to remain in Tarangire. At the end of the long rains in June, the migratory species return to the park.

Tarangire wildlife populations include approximately 30,000 zebra, 25,000 wildebeest, 5000 buffalo, 5000 eland, 3000 elephant, 2500 Masai giraffe and 1000 oryx. Other prominent species include Grant's and Thomson's gazelle, hartebeest, impala, lesser and greater kudu, reedbuck and gerenuk. Lion are often seen. Cheetah, spotted hyena and leopard are also present, as are the banded, black-tipped, dwarf, and marsh mongoose.

The **Lemiyon region**, the northernmost region of the park which includes Tarangire Safari Lodge, is characterized by a high concentration of baobab trees unmatched in any park I've seen. This unique landscape is also dotted by umbrella acacia trees with some open grasslands and wooded areas. Elephant, wildebeest and zebra are often seen. On my last visit a zebra was killed by lion less than 200 yards from the lodge. Visitors with little time for game viewing may want to concentrate on the Matete and the Lemiyon areas including the Tarangire River.

Wildebeest among baobab trees in Tarangire National Park.

The **Matete region** covers the northeastern part of the park and is characterized by open grasslands with scattered umbrella acacia and baobab trees and the Tarangire River. Lion, fringe-eared oryx and klipspringer are seen quite often. Bat-eared fox are also present.

On the 50-mile **Burungi Circuit**, you pass through acacia parklands and woodlands. You are likely to see a number of species including elephant, eland and bushbuck.

The eastern side of the **Kitibong area** is a good place to find large herds of buffalo. The eastern side is mainly acacia parklands and the western side, thicker woodlands.

The **Gursi section** is similar to the Kitibong area with the addition of rainy season wetlands, which are home to large populations of water birds. African wild dogs are sometimes seen.

Hippo are found in the extensive swamps of the **Larmakau region** located in the central eastern part of the park. **Nguselororobi**, in the south of the park, is predominantly swamp with some woodlands and plains. The **Mkungunero section** has a few freshwater pools and a variety of birdlife.

On my most recent visit, we spotted eland, giraffe, buffalo, a few lion, oryx, elephant, impala, Grant's gazelle, zebra, hartebeest, warthog, baboon, and ostrich. We met one group of game viewers who kept their fires burning all night to keep three lions they had heard near the camp at bay!

Elephants have destroyed many baobab trees. A baobab tree with a huge hole through the center of its trunk can be seen near Tarangire Lodge.

Game viewing is excellent in this 1000-square-mile park during the dry season from July-September/October, which happens to be the worst months for viewing game in the Serengeti. Consequently, visitors to Tanzania during those months might consider substituting Tarangire for the Serengeti should there not be time for both, or at least try to add Tarangire to their itinerary. Over 300 species of birds have been recorded in the park. Bird watching is best December-May. During the rainy seasons many roads become impassable.

ACCOMMODATION - CLASS B: * *Tarangire Safari Lodge* has 35 tents and six bungalows (doubles) with private facilities and a large swimming pool. Wildlife viewing can be excellent in the late afternoon from the veranda. * *Camp Tarangire* is a fixed tented camp with ten tents (20 beds), each with bucket shower and toilet. Game drives are offered. Access is by air charter.

CAMPING: There are campsites with no facilities.

## ARUSHA NATIONAL PARK

This highly underrated park is predominately inhabited by forest animals while in the other northern parks savannah animals are the most prevalent. Arusha National Park is the best place in northern Tanzania to spot black and white colobus monkeys and bushbuck, and to photograph larger species with Mt. Kilimanjaro or Mt. Meru in the background. Early mornings are best for this since Mt. Kilimanjaro is less likely to be covered with clouds.

Wildlife is more difficult to spot here than in the other

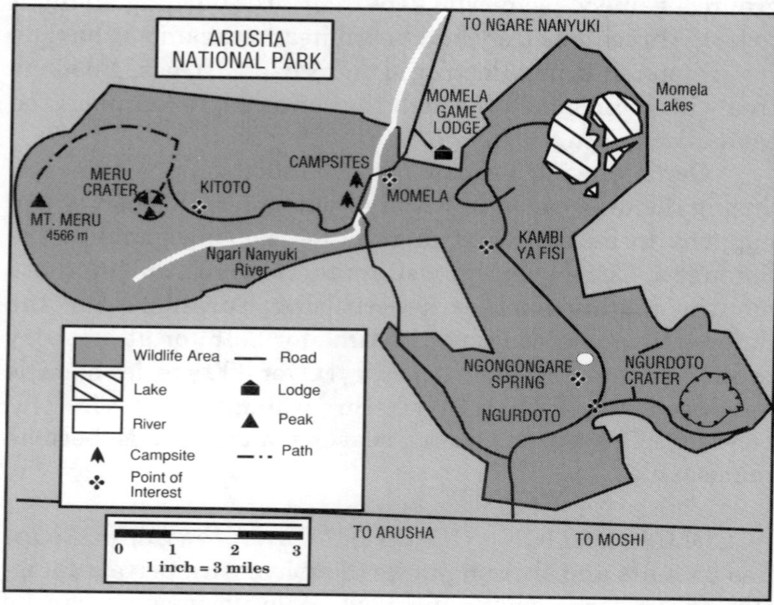


northern parks; do not expect to see large herds of game. However, you are allowed to walk in the western park of this park when accompanied by a park ranger, and there are a number of hikes and picnic sites to enjoy. The best time to visit is July-March.

This 53-square-mile park is actually the merger of three regions: Meru Crater National Park, Momela Lakes, and Ngurdoto Crater National Park. The wide range of habitats from highland rain forest to acacia woodlands and crater lakes host a variety of wildlife. Armed park guides are required to accompany you for walks in the park or for climbing Mt. Meru; guides are available at Park Headquarters at Momela Gate.

The turnoff to the park entrance is 13 miles east of Arusha and 36 miles west of Moshi.

On the open grassland near the entrance to the park, Burchell's zebra are often seen. High in the forest canopy of the Ngurdoto Forest is a good place to find blue monkeys and black and white colobus monkeys. Olive baboons are common and red duiker is sometimes seen.

Walking is not allowed in the two-mile-wide Ngurdoto Crater, which is in essence a reserve within a reserve. However, there are good views of the crater, Momela Lakes and Mt. Kilimanjaro (on clear days).

Driving north from Ngurdoto, you pass Ngongongare Spring, the Senato Pools (sometimes dry) and Lokie Swamp and are likely to see common waterbuck and maybe Bohor reedbuck. Buffalo are often seen around Lake Longil.

As you continue past Kambi Ya Fisi (hyena's camp), the landscape becomes more open, and elephant and giraffe may be seen. Hippo and a variety of waterfowl may be seen at the shallow, alkaline Momela Lakes.

From Kitoto a four-wheel-drive vehicle is needed to reach Meru Crater. The sheer cliff rises almost 5000 feet and is one of the highest in the world.

At the base of Mt. Meru, you may encounter elephant and buffalo. Kirk's dikdik, banded mongoose and klipspringer may also be seen in the park. On our last visit we saw giraffe lying down — very unusual indeed! Over 400 species of birds have been recorded.

**Mt. Meru** (14,980 ft./4566 m.) is an impressive mountain classified as a dormant volcano; its last eruption was just over 100 years ago. The mountain can be climbed in two days, but it is more enjoyable to take three days, allowing more time for exploration.

On the morning of the first day of a three-day climb, walk for about three hours from Momela Gate (about 5000 ft./1500 m.) to Miriakamba Hut. In the afternoon, hike to Meru Crater. On the second day, hike three hours to the Saddle Hut and in the afternoon walk for about one and one-half hours to Little Meru (12,533 ft./3820 m.). On Day Three, reach the summit and return to Momela Gate.

The best months to climb are October and December-February. Bring all your own gear and make your reservations in advance.

ACCOMMODATION - CLASS A/B: * *Oldoinyorok Lodge* —

A small lodge with six bungalows (doubles) and ensuite facilities located on the edge of Arusha National Park.

CLASS C/D: * *Momela Game Lodge* has rondavels (40 beds) with ensuite facilities just outside Arusha National Park.

CLASS F: One self-service resthouse (five beds) is located near Momela Gate.

CAMPING: One campsite is located near Ngurdoto Gate in the forest and three are at the foot of Tululusia Hill. All have water, toilet facilities and firewood.

## MT. KILIMANJARO

Known to many through Ernest Hemingway's book, *The Snows Of Kilimanjaro,* Mt. Kilimanjaro is the highest mountain in the world that is not part of a mountain range and is definitely one of the world's most impressive mountains. Kilimanjaro means "shining mountain;" it rises from an average altitude of about 3300 feet on the dry plains to 19,340 feet, truly a world-class mountain. On clear days the mountain can be seen from over 200 miles away.

The mountain consists of three major volcanic centers: Kibo (19,340 feet), Shira (13,650 feet) to the west, and Mawenzi (16,893 feet) to the east. The base of the mountain is 37 miles long and 25 miles wide. The park covers 292 square miles of the mountain above 8856 feet (2700 meters). The park also has six corridors that climbers may use through the Forest Reserve.

Hikers pass through zones of forest, alpine, and semi-desert to its snowcapped peak, situated only three degrees south of the equator. It was once thought to be an extinct volcano; but due to recent rumblings, it is now classified as dormant.

Climbing Mt. Kilimanjaro was definitely a highlight of my travels. For the struggle to reach its highest peak I was handsomely rewarded with a feeling of accomplishment and many exciting memories of the climb.

Kilimanjaro may in fact be the easiest mountain in the world for a climber to ascend to such heights. But it is still a struggle for even fit adventurers. On the other hand, it can be climbed by people from all walks of life who are in good condition and have a strong will. Mind you, reaching the top is by no means necessary; the flora, fauna and magnificent views seen en route are fabulous.

The first written record of Kilimanjaro was by Ptolemy 18 centuries ago. A Christian missionary, Johann Rebmann, reported his discovery of this snowcapped mountain, but the Europeans didn't believe him. Hans Meyer was the first European to climb Kilimanjaro, doing so in 1889.

The most unique animal in this park is the Abbot's duiker, which is found in only a few mountain forests in northern Tanzania. Other wildlife includes elephant, buffalo, eland, leopard, hyrax, and black and white colobus monkeys. However, very little large game is seen.

The best time to climb is January-March, August and October during the dryer seasons when the skies are fairly clear. January and February are warmer while October is cooler.

July, November and December are also good, while April and May should be avoided because of heavy rains and overcast skies. I, of course, happened to be in Tanzania in April, but I still made the climb and thoroughly enjoyed it.

From April-May, during the long rainy season, the summit is often covered in clouds with snow falling at higher altitudes and rain at lower altitudes. The short rains (October-November) bring afternoon thunderstorms, but evenings and mornings are often clear.

Many routes to the summit require no mountaineering skills. Mountaineers wishing to ascend by technical routes may wish to get a copy of *Guide to Mt. Kenya and Kilimanjaro*, edited by Iain Allan.

The Park Headquarters are located in Marangu, about a seven-hour drive from Nairobi, 2½ hours from Arusha. Children under ten years of age are not allowed over 9843 feet (3000 meters).

Travelers wishing to see Mt. Kilimanjaro but not climb it may do so (provided the weather is clear) from Arusha National Park or Amboseli National Park (Kenya).

## Zones

Mt. Kilimanjaro can be divided into five zones by altitude: 1) Cultivated lower slopes, 2) Forest, 3) Heath and Moorland/Lower Alpine; 4) Highland Desert/Alpine; and 5) Summit. Each zone spans approximately 3300 feet (1000 meters) in altitude. As the altitude increases, rainfall and temperatures decrease; this has a direct effect on the vegetation each zone supports.

The rich volcanic soils of the **lower slopes** of the mountain around Moshi and Marangu up to the park gate (6000 ft./1830 m.) are intensely cultivated, mostly with coffee and bananas.

The **forest zone** (5900-9185 ft./1800-2800 m.) receives the highest rainfall of the zones, with about 80 inches (2000 mm.) on the southern slopes and about half that amount on the northern and western slopes. The upper half of this zone is often covered with clouds, and humidity is high with day temperatures ranging from 60-70° F. Don't be surprised if it rains while walking through this zone; in fact, expect it.

In the lower forest there are palms, sycamore figs, bearded lichen and mosses hanging from tree limbs, tree ferns growing to 20 feet in height, and giant lobelia, which grow to over 30 feet. In the upper forest zone, giant groundsels appear. Unlike many East African volcanic mountains, no bamboo belt surrounds Kilimanjaro.

Black and white colobus and blue monkeys, olive baboons and bushbuck may be seen. Elephant, eland, giraffe, buffalo and suni may be seen on the northern and western slopes. Also present but seldom seen are bushpig, civet, genet, bush duiker, Abbot's duiker and red duiker.

Zone three is a lower alpine zone ranging from 9185-13,125 feet (2800-4000 meters), and is predominantly **heath** followed by **moorlands**. Rainfall decreases with altitude from about 50 inches to 20 inches per year. Giant heather (10-30 feet high), grasslands with scattered bushes and beautiful flowers, including "everlasting" flowers, protea and colorful red-hot pokers, characterize the lower part of this zone.

You then enter the moorlands with tussock grasses and groups of giant senecios and lobelias — weird prehistoric-looking Afro-alpine vegetation that would provide a great setting for a science fiction movie. With a lot of luck, you may spot eland, elephant, buffalo or klipspringer.

The **highland desert/alpine zone** is from around 13,125-16,400 feet (4000-5000 meters) and receives only about ten inches of rain per year. Vegetation is very thin and includes tussock grasses, "everlasting" flowers, moss balls and lichens. The thin air makes flying too difficult for most birds, and the very few larger mammals that may be seen do not make this region their home. What this zone lacks in wildlife is compensated by the fabulous views. Temperatures can range from below freezing to very hot, so be prepared.

The **summit** experiences arctic conditions and receives less than four inches of rain per year, usually in the form of snow. It is almost completely void of vegetation.

Kibo's northern summit is covered by the Great Northern Glacier. On Kibo there is an outer caldera about one and one-half miles in diameter. Uhuru peak is the highest point on the outer caldera and also the highest point on the mountain.

Within the outer caldera is an inner cone which contains the Inner or Reusch Crater, which is about one-half mile in diameter. Vents (fumaroles) spewing steam and sulfurous gasses are located at the Terrace and the base of the crater. Within the Inner Crater is an ash cone with an ash pit about 1100 feet across and about 400 feet deep.

## ROUTES

Climbing Kibo via the routes described below requires no mountaineering skills. A guide for each climbing party is required. Porters are highly recommended. The Marangu, Machame, and Shira Plateau Routes are the most popular. It

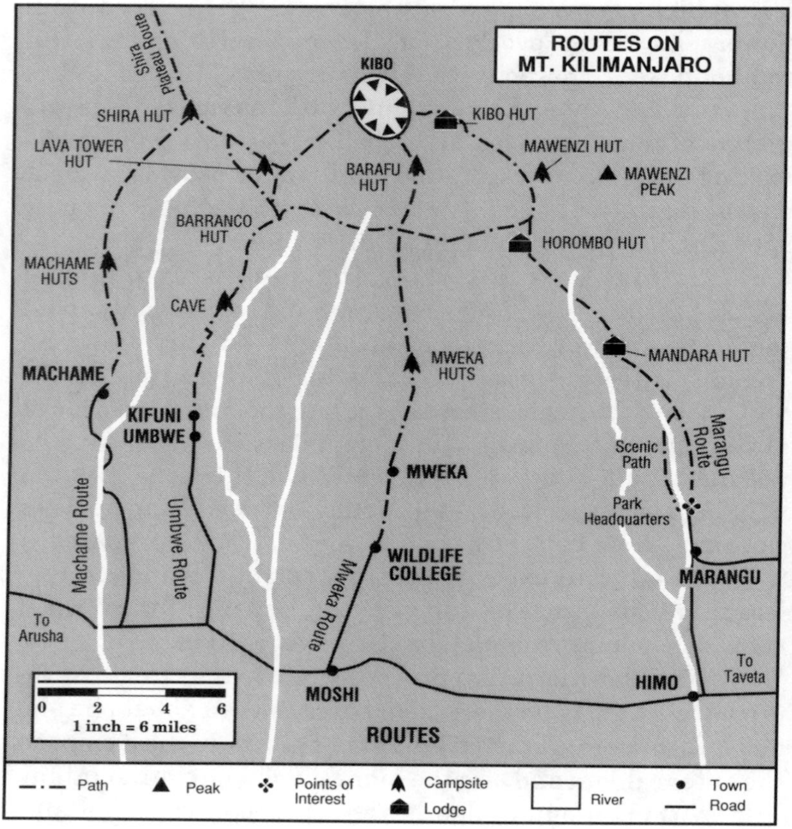


is more interesting (and more expensive) to take other routes up and return via the Marangu Route, offering additional variety to the climb.

Little firewood is available. Do bring fuel (kerosene) for cooking and heating; this will help minimize deforestation. The national park guides are not qualified to lead glacier or ice climbing routes. The services of a professional guide must be arranged in advance.

The Park has a rescue team based at the Park Headquarters with immediate response to emergencies on the Marangu Route. If using another route, descend the mountain and contact Park Headquarters (tel: Marangu 50), and they will send a rescue team to assist.

## Marangu Route

The Marangu Route is the route most often used; it has the best accommodations and is the easiest (most gradual) route to the summit.

This route may be completed in five days, but it's best to take six days, spending an extra day at Horombo hut to allow more time to acclimatize to the altitude. The huts are dormitory-style with common areas for cooking and eating.

Most climbing tours originate in Nairobi, Arusha or Kilimanjaro Airport and are for seven or eight days. The night before and the night after the climb are usually spent in the village of Marangu or in Arusha.

DAY ONE: MARANGU (6004 ft./1830 m.) to MANDARA HUT (8856 ft./2700 m.) REGULAR ROUTE: THREE-FOUR HOURS; FOREST ROUTE: FOUR-FIVE HOURS. ALTITUDE GAIN: 2854 feet (870 meters).

An hour or so is spent at Park Headquarters at Marangu Gate handling registration and arranging the loads for the porters. Try to leave in the morning to allow a leisurely pace and to avoid afternoon showers.

The fastest route and the one most often taken is along an old vehicle track. The forest trail takes longer but has much less traffic than the main trail; this trail veers off to the left a short way past the gate and runs along a stream. You have a choice of rejoining the main trail about halfway to (about one hour before) arriving at Mandara Hut. Both paths are often muddy.

Mandara has a number of small wooden A-frame huts sleeping eight persons each, four to a room, and a main cabin with a dormitory upstairs and dining room downstairs, for a total of 200 beds. Kerosene lamps, stoves and mattresses are provided.

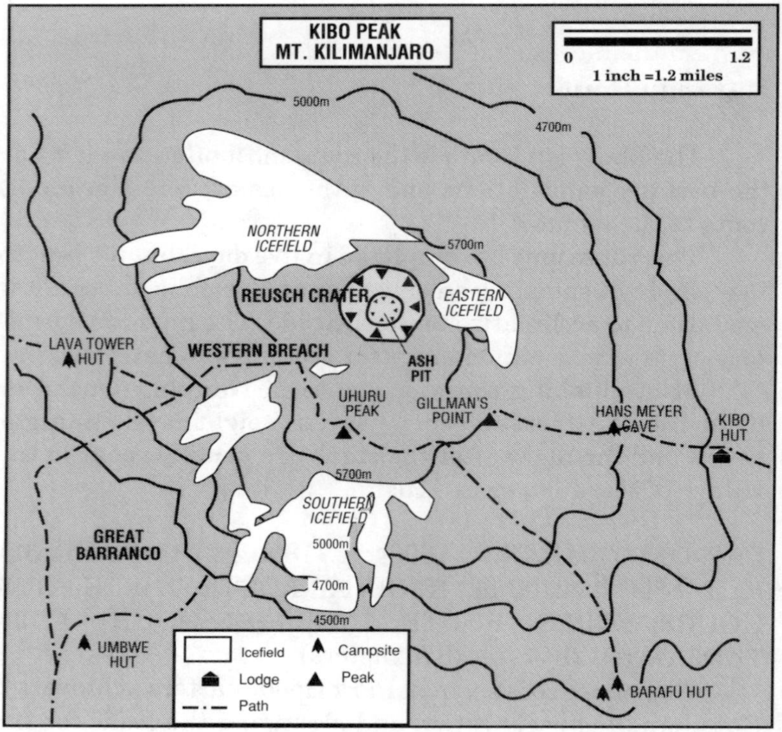


DAY TWO: MANDARA to HOROMBO HUT (12,205 ft./ 3720 m.): FIVE-SEVEN HOURS. ALTITUDE GAIN: 3346 feet (1020 meters).

On Day Two you pass through the upper part of the rain forest to tussock grassland and fascinating Afro-alpine vegetation of giant groundsels and giant lobelias to the moorlands. Once out of the forest, you begin to get great views of the town of Moshi and Mawenzi Peak (16,893 ft./5149 m.). If you can spare an extra day for acclimatizing, Horombo is the best hut for this. There are some nice day hikes that will help you further acclimatize. Kibo is too high to allow a good night's sleep. Horombo also has 200 beds and is similar to Mandara.

DAY THREE: HOROMBO HUT to KIBO HUT (15,430 ft./ 4703 m.): FIVE-SIX HOURS. ALTITUDE GAIN: 3225 feet (983 meters).

On the morning of Day Three, the vegetation begins to thin out to open grasslands. You pass "Last Water" (be sure to fill your water bottles as this is last source of water). The landscape becomes more barren as you reach "the saddle," a wide desert between Kibo and Mawenzi Peak. Kibo Hut does not come in view until just before you reach it. Kibo Hut has 120 beds and is located on the east side of Kibo Peak.

With the wind-chill factor, it can be very cold, so dress warmly. This is the day many hikers feel the effects of the altitude and may begin to experience some altitude sickness. Most people find it impossible to sleep at this height because of the lack of oxygen and the bitter cold, not to mention the possibility of altitude sickness. Get as much rest as you can.

DAY FOUR: KIBO HUT to GILLMAN'S POINT (18,635 ft./ 5680 m.) and UHURU PEAK (19,340 feet/5895 meters) AND DOWN TO HOROMBO HUT. TEN TO TWELVE HOURS.

Your guide will wake you shortly after midnight for your ascent, which should begin around 1:00 a.m. Be sure not to delay the start; it is vital that you reach the summit by sunrise. The sun quickly melts the frozen scree, making the ascent all the more difficult.

The steep ascent to Gillman's Point on the edge of the caldera is a grueling four-to-five-hour slog up scree. Hans Meyer Cave is a good place to rest before climbing seemingly unending switchbacks past Johannes Notch to Gillman's Point.

From Gillman's Point, Uhuru Peak is a fairly gradual climb of 705 feet (215 meters) in altitude. It will take another hour to hour and a half. Uhuru Peak is well-marked and there is a book in which you may sign your name.

If you are still feeling strong, ask your guide to take you down into the caldera to the inner crater which has some steam vents. You return to Gillman's Point by a different route.

On my climb our guide woke us late, and we didn't start the climb until after 2:00 a.m. We made it all right to

Gillman's Point, but the final hike to Uhuru (Freedom) Peak was a killer. Instead of walking across the frozen crust, I fell through knee-deep snow on every step. Had we arrived an hour earlier, this may not have been a problem.

The feeling of accomplishment upon reaching the summit is one of the highlights of my life. I was amazed at the tremendous size of the glaciers so close to the equator. Standing over 16,000 feet above the surrounding plains, the views were breathtaking in every direction. Sunrise over Mawenzi is a beautiful sight. You truly feel you're on the top of the world!

Shortly after sunrise you begin the long walk down the mountain to Kibo Hut for a short rest, then continue onward to Horombo Hut. Provided you are not completely exhausted, the walk down is long but pretty easy going. From Gillman's Point to Horombo takes about four hours and from Uhuru Peak about five.

The entire descent is made in two days, and one's knees take a hard pounding; you may want to wrap your knees with elastic bandages or use elastic knee supports.

DAY FIVE: HOROMBO HUT TO MARANGU

Another long day of hiking as you descend past Mandara Hut to Park Headquarters where you receive a diploma certifying your accomplishment. Most climbers spend the night at Kibo or Marangu Hotel and have the pleasure of sharing their experiences with unwary visitors planning to begin their Kilimanjaro adventure the following day.

## Mweka Route

This is the steepest and most direct route to Uhuru Peak. It starts at Mweka village near the College of Wildlife Management (4593 ft./1400 m.) and runs along an old logging road through banana and coffee plantations for about three miles, then along a seldom-used path for another three and one-half miles to Mweka Hut at 9515 feet (2900 meters). This hike takes six to eight hours. There is water nearby.

After a five-to-six-hour climb the following day through

The author at Uhuru Peak, Mt. Kilimanjaro.

heathlands and alpine desert, you reach Barafu Hut (14,435 ft./4400 m.). The third day is a steep climb between Ratzel and Rebmann Glaciers to Kibo Rim (six to seven hours) and Uhuru Peak (one more hour).

### Umbwe Route

The Umbwe Route is very steep and strenuous. The route begins at Umbwe (about 4600 ft./1400 m.), a village ten miles from Moshi. Walk two miles to Kifuni village and into the forest. Follow the path for another three and one-half miles and then branch left into a mist-covered forest until you reach the forest cave (Bivouac #1) at 9515 feet (2900 meters), six to seven hours from Umbwe. Overhanging ledges extending about five feet from the cliff provide reasonable protection for about six people; however, it is recommended you use your own tents. The wood is usually very damp and water is available, but not close by.

Continue through moorlands and along a narrow ridge with deep valleys on either side. The thick mist and vegetation covered with "Old Man's Beard" moss creates an eerie atmosphere. The second caves at 11,483 feet (3500 meters) are still another two- to three-hour hike from Bivouac #1. The vegetation thins out, and you branch right shortly before arriving at Barranco Hut (12,795 ft./3900 m.) about two hours later.

From Barranco you can backtrack to the fork and turn right (north) and hike for three hours to where Lava Tower Hut (15,092 ft./4600 m.) used to stand. From there the climb is up steep scree and blocks of rock to the floor of the crater and Uhuru Peak via the Great Western Breach. The climb from Lava Tower Hut to the caldera takes about nine hours. An alternative from Barranco Hut is to traverse the mountain eastward and join the Mweka Route.

### Shira Plateau Route

This is a very scenic and yet seldom-used route, providing great views of Kilimanjaro and the Rift Valley and probably the best wildlife viewing on the mountain. A four-wheel-drive vehicle is needed, and the roads may be impassable in the rainy seasons. The route is hard to find. Be sure to have a guide who knows the way.

Drive north from the Moshi-Arusha road at Boma la Ng'ombe to Londorossi Gate, located on the western side of Kilimanjaro. Continue on to a campsite. The track ends shortly thereafter, at 12,270 feet (3720 meters). The defunct Shira Hut (12,467 ft./3800 m.) is only a one-and-one-half-hour's walk away. You may want to take two days to acclimatize before continuing on.

From Shira Hut it is about a four-hour hike to the remains of Lava Tower Hut. The vegetation changes on the Shira Plateau are fabulous as you walk through open grasslands and moorlands dotted with giant senecios over 30 feet high and past the impressive Shira Cone, Cathedral and Needle Peaks. From Lava Tower Hut follow the directions from the Umbwe Route to the summit.

### Machame Route

This is possibly the most beautiful route up the mountain. The park gate is located a few miles above Machame village. Hike four to six hours through rain forest to Machame Huts (9843 ft./3000 m.).

The following day hike five to seven hours to the defunct Shira Hut (12,467 ft./3800 m.) on the Shira Plateau (see Shira Plateau Route for description of the area). Continue hiking about four hours to Lava Tower Hut. From Lava Tower Hut follow the directions from the Umbwe Route to the summit.

### Summit Circuit

There is a circuit between 12,139-15,092 feet (3700-4600 meters) completely around the base of Kibo Peak. Horombo, Barranco and Moir Huts are on the circuit, while Lava Tower, Shira, Kibo and Mawenzi Huts are on side trails not far from the circuit. A tent is needed since there is no hut on the northern side of Kibo. Be sure to bring a well-insulated pad for your sleeping bag.

### Huts

Mandara, Horombo and Kibo Huts are described under the Marangu Route above. The other huts are prefab metal huts, either 10 or 15 feet in diameter in varying states of disrepair; some are basically uninhabitable. Many of the wooden floors have been ripped up and used for firewood. It is best to bring your own tents and let the guides and porters use the huts. Drinking water should be filtered, treated and/or boiled as some sources on the mountain are polluted.

MAWENZI HUT (15,092 ft./4600 m.): From "The Saddle" on the Marangu Route just after passing East Lava Hill, hike one and one quarter miles east-northeast (050 degrees) to the hut at the base of the West Corrie. Mawenzi Hut sleeps five and is about a three-hour hike from Horombo or Kibo Huts. There are no toilets. Mawenzi Peak should only be attempted by well-equipped, experienced mountaineers.

MAWENZI TARN HUT (14,206 ft./4330 m.): This hut is situated northeast of Mawenzi Hut; it is an easy hike around the foot of the peak. The hut sleeps six.

MWEKA HUTS (9515 ft./2900 m.): There are two large huts sleeping 12 persons each. There is a stream nearby.

BARAFU HUT (15,092 ft./4600 m.): The hut sleeps twelve and there is no wood or water.

BARRANCO HUT (12,795 ft./3900 m.): The hut sleeps eight and there is a bivouac site about a 600-foot walk above the hut under a rock overhang. Some wood may be available in the vicinity, and a stream is nearby.

MOIR HUT (13,780 ft./4200 m.): This hut is located on the northwest side of Kibo north of the Shira: it sleeps ten and there is water nearby.

**Climbing Tips**

Here are a number of ways of increasing your chances of making it to the top. One of the most important things to remember is to *take your time. Polepole* is Swahili for "slowly" which is definitely the way to go. There is no prize for being the first to the hut or first to the top.

Pace yourself so that you are never completely out of breath. Exaggerate your breathing, taking deeper and more frequent breaths than you feel you actually need. This will help you acclimatize and keep you from exhausting yourself prematurely or developing pulmonary or cerebral edema.

Ski poles make good walking sticks, can be rented at Park Headquarters, and are highly recommended. Bring a small backpack to carry the items you wish to have quick access to along the trail, such as a water bottle, snacks and camera. Most importantly, listen to what your body is telling you. Don't overdo it! Many people die each year on the mountain because they don't listen or pay attention to the signs and keep pushing themselves.

On steep portions of the hike, use the "lock step" method to conserve energy. Take a step and lock the knee of the uphill leg. This puts your weight on leg bone, using less muscle strength. Pause for a few seconds, letting your other leg rest without any weight on it, and breath deeply. Then repeat. This technique will save vital energy that you may very well need in your quest for the top.

Some climbers take the prescription drug diamox, a diuretic which usually reduces the symptoms of altitude sickness, but there are side effects from taking the drug, including increased urination. You should discuss the use of diamox with your doctor prior to leaving home.

Drink a lot more water than you feel you need. High-altitude hiking is very dehydrating, and a dehydrated body weakens quickly. Climbers should drink three to four liters (quarts) of liquids daily.

Most hikers find it difficult to sleep at high altitude. Once you reach the hut each afternoon, rest a bit, then hike to a spot a few hundred feet in altitude above the hut and relax for awhile. Acclimatizing even for a short time at a higher altitude will help you get a more restful night's sleep. Remember, "Climb high, sleep low!"

Consume at least 4000 calories per day on the climb. This can be a problem. Most climbers loose their appetite at high altitude. Bring along trail mix (mixed nuts and dried fruit), chocolate and other goodies that you enjoy to supplement the meals prepared for you.

Forget about drinking alcoholic beverages on the climb. Altitude greatly enhances the effects of alcohol. Meanwhile, alcohol causes dehydration. Headaches caused by altitude sickness can be bad enough without having a hangover on top of them.

## Equipment Checklist

The better equipped you are for the climb, the higher your chances of making the summit. When it comes to clothing, the "layered effect" works best. Bring a duffle bag to pack your gear in for the climb. Wrap your clothes in heavy garbage bags to keep them dry. Keep the weight under the porter's maximum load of 33 pounds (15 kilograms).

Here's a checklist of items to consider bringing:

CLOTHING —

- Gortex jacket (with hood) and pants
- polypropylene long underwear - tops and bottoms, medium and heavyweight
- wool sweater (one or two)
- Gortex gaiters (to keep the scree out of your boots at higher altitudes)
- tennis shoes or ultralight hiking boots (for lower altitudes)
- medium-weight insulated hiking boots for warmth and to help dig into the scree during the final ascent
- heavy wool or down mittens with Gortex outer shell and glove liners
- several pairs of wool socks and polypropylene liner socks
- several pairs of underwear
- track or warm-up suit (to relax and sleep in)
- long trousers or knickers (wool or synthetic)
- light, loose-fitting cotton trousers
- shorts (with pockets)
- wool long-sleeve and cotton long-sleeve shirts
- T-shirts or short-sleeve shirts
- turtleneck shirt
- down vest
- balaclava (wool or synthetic)
- wide-brimmed hat or cap for protection from the sun
- bandana
- wool hat
- sleeping pad (for all routes except the Marangu Route)

MISCELLANEOUS —

day pack large enough to carry extra clothing, rain gear, plastic water bottle (1 litre/quart), camera and lunch.
sleeping bag (rated at least to zero degrees F.)
pocket flask for summit climb
flashlight with extra bulb and batteries. Some prefer head lamps.
light towel
sunglasses and mountaineering glasses
camera and film
strong sunblock
chapstick
body lotion (otherwise skin may get dry and itchy)
water purifiers
duffle bag
half-dozen heavy garbage bags in which to wrap clothes
toilet paper
Wash-n-Drys
pocket knife with scissors
granola bars, trail mix and sweets that travel well
powdered drink mix

FIRST AID KIT —

malaria pills
moleskin
Band-Aids (plasters)
Ace (elastic) bandages
gauze pads (4" X 4")
diuretics (diamox) - by prescription from your doctor
broad-spectrum antibiotics (pills)
laxative
antihistamine tablets
antibiotic cream
antidiarrhoea - Imodium or Lomotil
iodine
headache pills, i.e., Tylenol
throat and cough lozenges
decongestant

analgesic

Ibuprofen tablets (such as "Motrin") for muscle cramps and sore joints

Park Headquarters are located in Marangu, 29 miles from Moshi, 63 miles from Kilimanjaro Airport and 75 miles from Arusha.

Equipment is available for rent from Park Headquarters, Kibo and Marangu Hotels, but it is often heavily worn or of low quality. I recommend that you bring your own gear.

ACCOMMODATION - CLASS C: * *Kibo Hotel* - Situated less than a mile from Marangu village, this lodge has rooms with private facilities (150 beds). * *Marangu Hotel* - Located a mile and one half from Marangu village, this rustic lodge has 29 double rooms with private facilities.

## RUBONDO ISLAND NATIONAL PARK

Located in the southwestern part of Lake Victoria, the main attraction of this 93-square-mile island is sitatunga, which is indigenous to Rubondo. In addition, walking is allowed and the wildlife may be approached very closely.

Also indigenous to the park are hippo, bushbuck, crocodile, marsh mongoose and python. Chimpanzee, black and white colobus monkey, black rhino, giraffe and roan antelope have been introduced. There are no large predators. Bird watching, especially for waterfowl, is very good here.

In addition to the main island, there are about a dozen small islands that make up the park. Habitats include papyrus swamps, savannah, open woodlands and dense evergreen forests. Visitors accompanied by a guide who is usually armed may walk along forested trails in search of wildlife or wait patiently at a number of hides. The best time to visit is November-February. A few boats are available for hire.

Flying is the only easy way to get to the park. An airstrip is located at Park Headquarters. By vehicle it is a seven-hour drive and two-hour boat ride by one route and a ten-hour drive and half-hour boat ride by another route. Visitors are not

allowed to bring their vehicles to the island.
ACCOMMODATION - CLASS F: A few self-service bandas are available; bring your own food.

CAMPING: Sites are available, but bring your own supplies.

# THE SOUTH

The "Southern Circuit" of wildlife reserves includes the Selous Game Reserve, Ruaha National Park and Mikumi National Park. The Selous and Ruaha are seldom visited and offer a great opportunity to explore wild and unspoiled bush.

## SELOUS GAME RESERVE

This little-known reserve happens to be the largest game reserve in Africa. Over 21,000 square miles in area, the Selous is more than half the size of the state of Ohio, twice the area of Denmark and three and three-fourths times larger than Serengeti National Park. Unexploited and largely unexplored, no human habitation is allowed in this virgin bush except for limited tourist facilities.

The Selous is a stronghold for over 50,000 elephant (recently down from 100,000 due to rampant poaching), 150,000 buffalo (herds often exceed 1000), and large populations of lion, leopard, sable antelope, Lichtenstein's hartebeest, greater kudu, hippo, crocodiles, and numerous other species including giraffe, zebra, wildebeest, waterbuck, African wild dog, impala, and a small number of black rhino. Over one million large animals live within its borders. Over 350 species of birds and 2000 plant species have been recorded.

More patience is required to spot game here than in the northern parks. The wildlife is truly wild (unaccustomed to humans); as a result, it is more difficult to approach closely.

Almost 75 percent of this low-lying reserve (360-4100 feet) is composed of miombo woodlands with the balance being grasslands, floodplains, marshes and dense forests.

The extensive miombo woodlands are a favorite habitat for tsetse flies, which are more prevalent here than in the northern parks. The Selous has been spared encroachment by man because the presence of tsetse flies prevent grazing of domestic animals and because the soil is too poor to farm.

Walking safaris accompanied by an armed ranger are popular and are conducted by all the camps. This reserve will give you the feeling of exploring the bush for the first time as you will encounter few, if any, other visitors during your safari.

The Rufiji River, the largest river in East Africa, roughly bisects the park as it flows from the southwest to the northeast. The Rufiji and its tributaries, including Great Ruaha and Luwego, have high concentrations of hippos and crocs. Fish eagles are numerous.

Exploring the Rufiji River, its channels, swamps and lakes by raft or boat and running the rapids of Stiegler's Gorge by raft are other adventurous ways of exploring the reserve. Fishing is also popular.

All tourist activities are restricted to the northern region. The best time to visit the park is during the dry season, June-October. During the two rainy seasons, November-January (short rains) and February-May (long rains), many of the roads are impassable and wildlife is scattered. The reserve is usually closed March-May.

Most visitors fly to camps in the Selous from Dar es Salaam by charter aircraft. Access by road is difficult and only possible in the dry season. The **Tazara Railway** (Dar es Salaam to Zambia) passes through the northern part of the Selous about four hours after departing Dar es Salaam, and an abundance of game is usually seen. This railway also serves as the border between the Selous and Mikumi National Parks. Some travelers disembark at Fuga Halt where they are taken (by prior arrangement) to the camps.

ACCOMMODATION: — The camps are located from about 160-235 miles from Dar es Salaam, requiring a six-to-ten-hour drive in a four-wheel-drive vehicle. All camps have private airstrips and flying is highly recommended.

CLASS B/C: * *Mbuyu Safari Camp* — This comfortable tented camp on the banks of the Rufiji River has 15 tents with private facilities. Game drives, walking and boat safaris are offered. * *Selous Safari Camp,* also called *Beho Beho Camp,* is located north of the Rufiji River. The camp has bandas with private facilities and offers game drives and walking. * *Stiegler's Gorge Lodge* has chalets with private facilities overlooking the gorge.

CLASS C: * *Rufiji River Camp,* a basic tented camp with ten tents (doubles), offers game drives, fishing, walking and boat safaris.

CAMPING: Sites are available.

## RUAHA NATIONAL PARK

Ruaha, known for its great populations of elephant, greater and lesser kudu, hippo, crocs and magnificent scenery is one of the country's newest and best national parks, and because of its location, it is one of the least visited.

Ruaha's scenery is spectacular and its 5000-square-mile area makes it almost as large as Serengeti National Park. The landscape is characterized by miombo woodland with rocky hills on a plateau over 3300 feet in altitude. Park elevation ranges from 2460 feet in the Ruaha Valley to 6230-foot Ikingu Mountain in the west of the park.

The Great Ruaha River with its impressive gorges, deep pools and rapids runs for 100 miles close to the park's eastern boundary and is home to many hippos and crocodiles. The best place in the park to see elephant is from the track that runs along the Ruaha River downstream from Msembe.

The dry season, June-November, is the best time to visit the park when game is concentrated along the Ruaha River. Large numbers of greater and lesser kudu, elephant, wildebeest and impala can be seen along with eland, sable antelope, roan antelope, buffalo, Defassa waterbuck, ostrich and giraffe. Lion, leopard, spotted and striped hyena, black-backed jackal, bat-eared fox and African wild dog are also present in significant numbers. Black rhino are present but seldom seen. Over 370 species of birds have been recorded.

Many tracks become impassable during the wet months January-March and the wildlife is scattered. Game viewing, February-June, is difficult due to high grass. Tsetse flies are present, especially in the miombo woodlands.

There are a number of photographic hides (blinds) and tree-houses overlooking watering areas allowing close views of wildlife undisturbed by the presence of man.

The park is about a four-hour drive from Iringa through the villages of Mloa and Idodi and across the Ruaha River via the Ibuguziwa Ferry. Park Headquarters and an airstrip are located at Msembe, 70 miles from Iringa and 385 miles from Dar es Salaam.

ACCOMMODATION - CLASS C: * *Ruaha River Camp,* located in the park six miles south of Msembe, has rondavels and tents.

CLASS D: Several basic hotels are located at Iringa, 70 miles east of the park.

CLASS F: * *National Park Rondavels* (self-service) are situated at Msembe.

CAMPING: Campsites are available.

## MIKUMI NATIONAL PARK

Mikumi is the closest park to Dar es Salaam (180 miles) and takes four hours to drive on tarmac from Dar es Salaam via Morongoro.

The park covers 1266 square miles and borders the Selous Game Reserve to the south along the Tazara Railroad line. There is a hippo pool on the main highway which runs to Zambia and divides the park.

The park is dominated by the Mkata River floodplain with swamps and grasslands dotted with baobab trees and miombo woodlands at an average altitude of 1800 feet above sea level. Elephant, buffalo, lion, hippo, zebra, wildebeest and Masai giraffe are prevalent. Sable antelope, common water-buck, Lichtenstein's hartebeest, eland, Bohor reedbuck and impala may also be seen. Black and white colobus monkeys are frequently seen in the south of the park.

During our two-day stay, we saw elephant, zebra, six lion, giraffe, buffalo, impala, ground hornbill and guinea fowl, among other species. There is a variety of birdlife as Mikumi is in the transition zone between north and south.

The long rains are March-May and the short rains from November-December. Rainfall within the park ranges from 20-40 inches yearly.

It is difficult to say what is the best time to visit Mikumi. Unlike most parks, wildlife is concentrated in this park in the wet season when the vegetation is the thickest, making game viewing more difficult. Fewer animals are present in the dry season, but the ones present are easier to spot. Considering this, the best time to visit is June-February.

This park is open all year although some roads are closed during the rainy season. There is an airstrip, petrol station and garage at Park Headquarters.

ACCOMMODATION - CLASS B/C: * *Mikumi Wildlife Lodge* has 50 double rooms with private facilities and a swimming pool.

CLASS D: * *Mikumi Wildlife Camp* has self-contained bandas, restaurant and bar.

CAMPING: Campsites are available.

# THE WEST

## LAKE TANGANYIKA

Lake Tanganyika forms much of the western border of Tanzania and is indeed an "inland sea." This is the world's longest lake (446 miles) and the world's second deepest lake (over 4700 feet). Only Lake Baikal in Russia is deeper, at over 5700 feet. More than 400 species of fish inhabit Lake Tanganyika's clear waters — more than any other body of water in the world. Easiest access to the lake in Tanzania is by flying to Kigoma.

## KIGOMA

Kigoma is the country's major port on huge Lake Tanganyika. From here you can catch a steamer to Burundi or Zambia. Kigoma is the closest town to Gombe Stream National Park and many travelers stay here while in transit to and from the park. Kigoma can be reached by air, by road or by a pleasant two-and-one-half-day train ride from Dar es Salaam.

**Ujiji**, a small town six miles south of Kigoma, is where the line, "Dr. Livingstone, I presume" was spoken by Stanley in 1872. Buses run there regularly from the Kigoma Rail Station.

ACCOMMODATION - CLASS D: * *New Kigoma Railway Hotel* overlooks the lake and has rooms with private facilities. * *Lake View Hotel* has no view of the lake and is second choice to Railway Hotel.

## GOMBE STREAM NATIONAL PARK

Gombe Stream is the setting for Jane Goodall's chimpanzee studies, her films and books, including *In The Shadow Of Man*. This remote 20-square-mile park is situated along the eastern shores of Lake Tanganyika ten miles north of Kigoma in remote northwestern Tanzania.

This tiny park covers a thin strip of land three miles wide and stretches for ten miles along Lake Tanganyika. A mountain range ascends steeply from the lake at an altitude of 2235 feet to form part of the eastern wall of the western branch of the Great Rift Valley, rising to 5000 feet.

Thick gallery forests are found along Gombe Stream and many other permanent steams in the valley and lower slopes of the mountains. Higher up the slopes are woodlands with some grasslands near the upper ridges.

The experience of seeing chimpanzees in the wild is by far the major attraction of this park. Other primates include red colobus monkey, blue monkey and baboon. Other wildlife of note includes buffalo, Defassa waterbuck and leopard.

Chimpanzees can usually be found around the research station and are quite habituated to humans. Two-hour morning and afternoon hikes into the forest searching for chimps can be arranged. The Kakombe Waterfall is worth a visit. There is also a nice walk along the lake shore northward from the guesthouse.

You may reach the park by water taxi (three hours) which departs Ujiji in the morning every day except Sunday.

ACCOMMODATION - CLASS F: There is a basic self-service guesthouse with rooms with separate facilities. Book well in advance or bring a tent as the guesthouse may be full. Only basic supplies are available in Kigoma.

CAMPING: Allowed on special request.

## MAHALE MOUNTAINS NATIONAL PARK

Like Gombe Stream, the main attraction of this remote park, which was only recently gazetted in 1985, is being able to walk among large populations of chimpanzees. The chimps have been studied by Japanese researchers for the last 20 years, and over 100 of them have been habituated to humans.

Located about 95 miles south of Kigoma, this 609-square-mile park is situated on the eastern shores of Lake Tanganyika. The Mahale Mountains with deep ravines, permanent streams and waterfalls run through the center of the park, forming the eastern wall of the Great Rift Valley with altitudes up to 8075 feet above sea level.

The area surrounding Park Headquarters is predominantly acacia woodland, changing to lowland forest and then montane forest as one progresses inland and gains altitude.

In addition to over 1000 chimpanzees, the park is also home to the red colobus monkey, Angolan black and white colobus monkey, banded mongoose, Sharpe's grysbok and blue duiker. Bushbuck and warthog are commonly seen around Park Headquarters.

Seasons are relatively unpredictable. The dry season usually runs from May-October while rainy seasons are usually November-January and March-May. Nights are often cool and rainfall ranges within the park from 60-100 inches per year. The best time to visit is May-October.

There is no easy way to reach this seldom-visited park. Easiest access to the park is by charter flight from Bujumbura, Burundi. The park can also be reached by boat from Kigoma. Take the weekly steamer *MV Liemba* for six hours to the village of Lagosa (Mugambo). You usually arrive in the middle of the night and must be transferred ashore. From here charter a boat for a three-hour ride to Kasoge (Kasiha village) in the park. Small boats from Kigoma make this journey in 12-16 hours. The park may also be reached by four-wheel-drive vehicle on a dirt track from Mpanda via Mwesi, but this route is not advised.

ACCOMMODATION - CLASS B: * *Mahale Mountains Tented Camp* is a small tented camp on the shores of Lake Tanganyika. Hikes to see chimpanzees, sailing by dhow, dugout canoeing, snorkeling and fishing are offered.

CLASS F: There is a basic guesthouse, but you will need to bring your own food, crockery and cutlery, bed linens and

stove. No supplies are available in the park.
CAMPING: Camping sites are available.

## KATAVI NATIONAL PARK

This undeveloped 870-square-mile park is located between the towns of Mpanda and Sumbawanga on the main road running through western Tanzania from north to south.

Lake Katavi and its extensive floodplains are in the north of this park that is about 2950 feet above sea level. To the southeast is Lake Chada, which is connected with Lake Katavi by the Katuma River and its extensive swampland. Miombo woodlands dominate most of the dry areas except for acacia woodlands near Lake Chada.

Wildlife includes hippo, croc, elephant, zebra, lion, leopard, eland, puku, buffalo, roan and sable antelope. Over 400 species of birds have been recorded.

The long rains are March-May. The best time to visit is July-October.

ACCOMMODATIONS: There are only a few huts for shelter. Very basic hotel accommodation is available in Mpanda and Sumbawanga.

CAMPING: Sites are available in the park. Campers must be self-sufficient as there are no facilities.

# THE COAST

## DAR ES SALAAM

Dar es Salaam, meaning "haven of peace" in Arabic, is the functional capital, largest city, and commercial center of Tanzania. Many safaris to the southern parks begin here. Among the more interesting sights are the harbor, National Museum, Village Museum and the Kariakoo Market. Ask at your hotel about traditional dancing troops that may be performing during your stay.

Once the German capital, hub of the slave trade and end-point of the slave route from the interior, **Bagamoyo** is an old seaport 46 miles north of Dar es Salaam. Fourteenth century ruins, stone pens and shackles that held the slaves may be seen.

ACCOMMODATION - FIRST CLASS: * The *Kilimanjaro Hotel* is a large air-conditioned hotel with ensuite facilities, swimming pool and fabulous view of the harbor.

TOURIST CLASS: * The *New Africa Hotel* is air-conditioned and has rooms with ensuite facilities and has popular terrace coffee shop. * *Oyster Bay Hotel* is four miles from town on the coast.

## ZANZIBAR

Zanzibar and its sister island, Pemba, grow 75 percent of the world's cloves. A beautiful island unspoiled by tourism, Zanzibar is only 22 miles from the mainland — a twenty-minute flight from Dar es Salaam or a five-to-seven-hour ride by motorboat. A more traditional, yet difficult-to-arrange way to reach the island is sailing by dhow from Dar es Salaam, usually with a return to Bagamoyo.

The narrow streets and Arabic architecture of historical Zanzibar City are exceptionally mystical and beautiful on a moonlit night. Main attractions include the Zanzibar Museum, the former British Consulate, Arab Fort, Anglican Cathedral built on the site of the old slave market, Sultan's Palace, clove market and Indian bazaar. Livingstone's and Burton's houses are near the picturesque Dhow Harbour. Visitors can take a short boat ride to Slave Island to see the slave trading ruins.

Be aware that visitors to Zanzibar are required to pay for services in foreign currency, regardless of how much they may have previously changed on the mainland.

ACCOMMODATION - DELUXE: * *Mnemba Club* has ten thatched beach cottages with ensuite facilities. Wind surfing, snorkeling and SCUBA diving are available.

FIRST CLASS: * *Hotel Ya Bwawani* is a large hotel with private facilities, saltwater pool and disco.

TOURIST CLASS: * *Africa House,* an old hotel with traditional Arabic design, has rooms with private facilities.

## MAFIA ISLAND

A forty-minute flight south from Dar es Salaam, this island offers some of the best big game fishing in the world. Species caught include marlin, sailfish, tuna and shark.

ACCOMMODATION - CLASS C: *Mafia Island Lodge* has rooms with private facilities.

# UGANDA

## THE NILE CROCODILE

Crocodiles are opportunistic feeders and have adapted techniques for acquiring their staple diet consisting of fish, water birds, terrapins, water monitors and smaller animals.

They will attack and drag smaller animals from the shoreline into deeper water to drown them before feeding. A valve at the back of the throat closes when they have the animal within their jaws and prevents them from swallowing water and drowning themselves.

As they are cold-blooded animals, time is spent regulating their body temperatures by basking in the sun in the early mornings and afternoons, lying in the water during midday to cool off, and at night returning to the warmer water to maintain their body temperature. Interestingly enough, they lay their eggs in the sand along the river banks, and the difference of a few degrees in temperature within the incubated nest under the sand will determine whether the hatchlings are male or female.

Crocodiles spend their time either underwater or floating low in the water, with only nostrils and eyes showing, waiting for their prey. While underwater, they can slow their heart rates to one beat per minute, thereby conserving oxygen. While afloat, they are known to digest stones, which act as ballast to counteract the buoyancy of the lungs.

During a night safari, you may see the red reflected eyes of the crocodile on the top of the water . . . waiting.

# UGANDA

FACTS AT A GLANCE

| | |
|---|---|
| AREA: | 93,981 SQUARE MILES |
| APPROXIMATE SIZE: | OREGON OR GREAT BRITAIN |
| POPULATION: | 17 MILLION (1992 EST.) |
| CAPITAL: | KAMPALA (POP. EST. 1,000,000) |
| OFFICIAL LANGUAGE: | ENGLISH, SWAHILI, LUGANDA AND ENGLISH ARE WIDELY SPOKEN |

# UGANDA

Uganda, once the "Pearl of the British Empire" in East Africa, is one of the most beautiful countries on the continent. One-sixth of its area is covered by water. Along its western boundary lies Africa's highest mountain range, Ptolemy's fabled "Mountains of the Moon." The Ugandans claim the source of the Nile is at Jinja where it leaves Lake Victoria.

The weather in Uganda is similar to Kenya's except that Uganda's is wetter. The driest times of the year are December-February and June-July, and the wettest is from mid-March to mid-May with lighter rains in October-November.

English is spoken as widely here as in Kenya or Tanzania. The main religions are Christianity and Islam.

In the eighteenth century, the Kingdom of Buganda became the most powerful in the region. Together with three other kingdoms and several native communities, it was made a British Protectorate in 1893 and achieved independence in 1962.

Over 90 percent of the population is employed in agriculture. Coffee is the major export.

Uganda has had more than its fair share of turmoil. In spite of this, the people are among the friendliest on the continent. Conditions have greatly improved over the last several years, and security is better than it has been in the last two decades. Adventurous travelers are venturing there and seem to be enjoying their "pioneer" status.

## WILDLIFE AND WILDLIFE AREAS

This country was once very rich in wildlife, but much of the larger game was killed during Idi Amin's rule and in the war to oust him in the late 1970s. However, wildlife populations are returning. A real plus is that you seldom meet another vehicle on game drives — in essence having the park to yourself.

Uganda has five national parks and 15 reserves. The calving seasons for hartebeest and Uganda kob are January-February and for oribi, February-March.

## NORTHERN AND WESTERN

### MURCHISON (KABALEGA) FALLS NATIONAL PARK

This park is named after the famous falls where the Victoria Nile rushes through a narrow, 20-foot-wide rock gorge with tremendous force to crash on the rocks 150 feet below. Fish dazed by this fall are easy prey to one of the largest concentrations of crocodile on the continent.

Located in northwestern Uganda, this park covers approximately 1500 square miles of predominantly grassy plains and savannah woodlands with altitudes ranging from 1650-4240 feet. Riverine forest lines some parts of the Victoria Nile, which traverses the park from east to west. The Rabongo Forest has a population of chimpanzees.

In addition to Murchison Falls, a highlight of the park is the three-hour, seven-mile launch trip from the Paraa Lodge to the foot of the falls. Numerous crocodiles and hippos in the river and along its banks, as well as buffalo, elephant, and prolific birdlife (over 400 species), can be approached closely. Even if the launch is in operation, you may still need to provide 30 liters of diesel, as fuel is often in short supply.

The park is also home to giraffe, waterbuck, oribi, and Uganda kob. Record Nile perch over 200 pounds have been caught in the Nile. Some of the best fishing is just below Karuma Falls and just below Murchison Falls.

The easiest time to spot animals is January-February; the short dry season from June-July is also good. From March-May the landscape is more attractive but the wildlife is less concentrated.

Park headquarters and the most extensive road system for game viewing are near the Paraa Lodge. The Buligi Circuit takes one to the confluence of the Albert and Victoria Niles. Waterfowl are especially abundant, along with a variety of game. Fuel is often not available.

ACCOMMODATION — CLASS C: * *Rabongo Cottage* has rooms with separate facilities and a communal kitchen. At the time of this writing, neither *Chobe Lodge* nor *Paraa Lodge* are operational and are in a state of disrepair.

CAMPING: Several sites available.

## QUEEN ELIZABETH (RUWENZORI) NATIONAL PARK

The park contains about 770 square miles of tremendous scenic variety, including volcanic craters and crater lakes, grassy plains, swamps, rivers, lakes and tropical forest. The snowcapped Ruwenzori Mountains lie to the north and are not part of the park itself. The park is being extended to give migratory species more protection while moving to and from Virunga National Park in Zaire.

The launch trip on the **Kazinga Channel**, which joins Lakes Edward (Lake Rutanzige) and George, affords excellent opportunities for viewing hippos and a great variety of waterfowl at close range; this is a trip that should not be missed.

The Katwe-Korongo area in the north of the park has

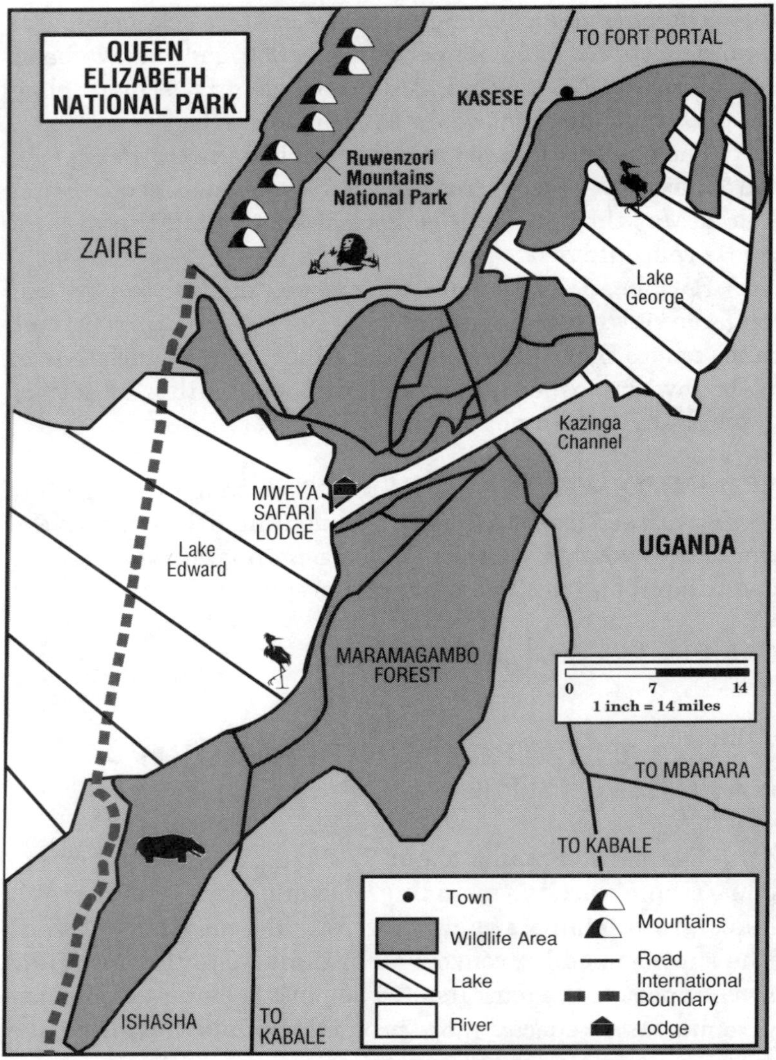


several saline lakes. South of the Kazinga Channel, the **Maramagambo Forest** is home for large numbers of chimpanzees, black and white colobus monkeys, the rare red colobus monkeys, blue monkeys, red-tailed monkeys and baboons. The Ishasha region in the south of the park is famous for its tree-climbing lions.

Elephant were heavily poached but are recovering. Other wildlife includes buffalo, leopard, sitatunga, Uganda kob, topi, and Defassa waterbuck. Over 540 sspecies of birds have been recorded, including the rare prehistoric-looking whale-headed stork, which may be sighted along the shores of Lake George.

Interestingly enough there are no giraffe, zebra, impala, rhino, or crocodiles in the Kazinga Channel or Lakes Edward and George. The crocodiles are believed to have been killed long ago by volcanic activity.

From Kampala the park is 260 miles via Mbarara and 285 miles via Fort Portal. A landing strip is located at Mweya for light aircraft; larger planes can land at Kasese.

ACCOMMODATION - CLASS C: * *Mweya Safari Lodge* is situated on a high bluff overlooking the Kazinga Channel and Lake Edward. All rooms have private facilities.

CLASS F: * *Institute of Ecology Hostel.*

CAMPING: Sites are available near Mweya Lodge and along the Kazinga Channel.

## RUWENZORI MOUNTAINS NATIONAL PARK

This is the highest mountain range in Africa and home for the legendary "Mountains of the Moon." They rise 13,000 feet above the western arm of the Rift Valley to 16,762 feet (5109 meters) above sea level just north of the equator and are usually covered in mist. See "Ruwenzori Mountains" in the chapter on Zaire for a general description.

Hikers in good condition can enjoy walking strenuous trails rising to over 13,000 feet in altitude through some of the most amazing vegetation in the world. There is a circuit with huts that takes a minimum of five days to hike — preferably six or seven.

The main trailhead begins near Ibanda. Drive six miles north from Kasese on the Fort Portal road, then turn left (west) for eight miles. Bring all your own equipment.

### The Bujuku Circuit

On Day One follow a dirt road from Ibanda three miles to Nyakalengija (5250 ft./1600 m.), then take the path to the Nyabitaba Hut (8700 ft./2651 m.). Many climbers prefer staying in a nearby rock shelter instead of the aluminum hut which can sleep up to 12 persons. Water and firewood are not available near the hut. Tent spaces are located nearby.

Day Two is the most grueling of the circuit. Climbers pass heather and groundsel before reaching Nyamiliju Hut (10,900 ft./3322 m.). Again, the rock shelter is often preferred over the hut. Water is available nearby; there is no room for tents. On a clear day you can see Mt. Stanley, Mt. Speak and numerous glaciers.

On Day Three, hike through giant heather and groundsel forest with colorful mosses and through a muddy bog to Bigo Hut (11,300 ft./3444 m.). The hut sleeps up to 12, and it is in good condition. A good rock shelter is nearby. Water and firewood are available. From Bigo Hut, you may hike northeast to Bukurungu Pass, north to Roccati Pass, or southwest to Lake Bujuku.

On Day Four, cross the Kibatsi Bog to Cooking Pot Cave. The left fork of the path leads to Scott Elliot Pass. Take the right fork and hike northwest to Bujuku Hut (13,000 ft./4281 m.), near Lake Bujuku, offering great views of Mt. Baker and Mt. Stanley. Two huts in fair condition can hold up to 14 people. Water is available. A rock shelter for the porters is not far from the hut.

On Day Five, return to Cooking Pot Cave, take the fork to Scott Elliot Pass and continue past Mt. Baker to Lake Kitandara and Kitandara Hut (13,200 ft./4023 m.). Continue on to Kabamba Rock Shelter (12,400 ft./3779 m.).

On Day Six, descend to Kichuchu (a rock shelter) and onwards through a bog and across the Mubuku River to

Nyabitaba Hut and back to Ibanda.

The best time to climb is December-early February and June-July during the dry season. However, no matter when you climb, you will still get wet. Wood found on the mountain is usually wet, so a camp stove and fuel are highly recommended.

For information on climbing the summits and glaciers, I recommend the books *East Africa International Mountain Guide* by Andrew Wielochowski (1986) and *Guide to the Ruwenzori* by Osmaston and Pasteur (1972), both published by West Col Productions in England. The best maps of the area are "The Central Ruwenzoris" with a scale of 1:250,000, and "Margherita" with a scale of 1:50,000.

ACCOMMODATION - CLASS C/D: See "Kasese" below.

CLASS F: A few huts with dirt floors are available for rent at Ibanda. All the huts on the hiking trails are in poor condition. Bring a ground sheet and insulated pad for your sleeping bag. It is best to bring your own tent.

## KASESE

Kasese is the largest town situated near Ruwenzori National Park and the Ruwenzori Mountains and is a good place to purchase supplies. Kasese can be reached by train or by road from Kampala.

ACCOMMODATION - CLASS C/D: * *Margherita Hotel* has rooms with private facilities and is located two miles out of town.

# CENTRAL AND SOUTHERN

## KAMPALA

Kampala, the capital of Uganda, is built on seven hills.

Points of interest include the Uganda Museum and the Kasubi Tombs of the Kabakas — a shrine to the former Baganda kings and a fine example of Baganda craftsmanship.

The international airport is at Entebbe, about a 20-minute drive from Kampala.

ACCOMMODATION - DELUXE: * *Kampala Sheraton Hotel*, situated in an attractive park setting, has 279 air-conditioned rooms with private facilities, health club, several restaurants and swimming pool.

FIRST CLASS: * *Nile Hotel* contains the International Conference Center and has air-conditioned rooms with private facilities. * *Hotel Diplomate*, located on Tank Hill, has air-conditioned rooms with private facilities.

TOURIST CLASS: * *Fairway Hotel* is a basic hotel with private facilities overlooking the Kampala Golf Course.

## LAKE MBURO NATIONAL PARK

Formerly a game reserve, Lake Mburo National Park is located in southwestern Uganda between Masaka and Mbarara. This approximately 200-square-mile park is named after Lake Mburo, the largest of the park's fourteen lakes.

The park is characterized by open plains in the north, acacia grassland in the center and lakes and marshes in the south, and is bounded by the Kampala-Mbarara road on the north, Lake Kachera on the east and the Ruizi River on the west.

Wildlife includes hippo, buffalo, zebra, eland, roan antelope, reedbuck, topi, bushbuck, and klipspringer. Impala, which do not exist in any other park in Uganda, are numerous. There are some lion and leopard.

ACCOMMODATION: None. The closest accommodation is the Katatumba Resort Hotel in Mbarara.

CAMPING: Campsites are available in the park.

## KABALE

Kabale is Uganda's highest town, situated in a beautiful area called "The Little Switzerland of Africa" in southwestern Uganda.

ACCOMMODATION - CLASS D: * *White Horse Inn* has rooms with private facilities.

## BWINDI IMPENETRABLE FOREST NATIONAL PARK

The major attraction of the 127-square-mile Bwindi Impenetrable Forest, which has recently been granted national park status, is the mountain gorilla (*Gorilla gorilla berengei*). Between 150 and 300 mountain gorillas are known to inhabit the park, which is expected to be open for tourism in 1993.

Other primates include chimpanzee, black and white colobus monkey, red colobus monkey, grey-cheeked mangabey, L'Hoest's monkey and blue monkey. Other wildlife includes elephant, giant forest hog and duiker. Access is by road from Kabale.

ACCOMMODATION - CLASS D: See "Kabale" above.

ACCOMMODATION - CLASS F: * *Ruhizha Gorilla Research Center* has a few rooms with separate facilities.

## KIGEZI MOUNTAIN GORILLA GAME RESERVE

The Kigezi Mountain Gorilla Game Reserve is situated on the slopes of Mts. Muhabura and Gahinga in the southwestern corner of Uganda, bordering Rwanda and Zaire.

A joint commission has been set up by Uganda, Rwanda and Zaire to protect the mountain gorilla in the Virunga Mountains where the borders of the three countries meet.

Gorillas are much less likely to be sighted here than in the Volcano National Park in Rwanda or in Kahuzi-Biega National Park or Djomba Gorilla Sanctuary in Zaire. The Ugandan side of the mountains is dryer, providing less moisture to grow the vegetation gorillas prefer eating. However, the clearer skies provide breathtaking views of this, the most beautiful part of Uganda.

Gorillas are usually not spotted in one day; you must allow three days of searching to better insure success. If gorillas are found, it is difficult to approach closely or to spend much time with them; they are not habituated to humans as are gorillas in Rwanda and Zaire. Even if gorillas are not encountered, the hike through this peaceful scenic region of friendly people is well worth the effort.

From Kisoro, hike to the village of Giterderi, about a two-hour walk from Kisoro. Most people camp there for the night. The following morning, hike for about two hours to the area where the gorillas may be found. Return to camp just before dark.

This trek is recommended for only the hardiest of travelers. The hike from base camp can take up to ten hours and all participants must be in good shape. However, the cost of the treks is a fraction of that charged in Rwanda and Zaire.

Other wildlife in this 17-square-mile reserve includes blue monkey, black and white colobus monkey, buffalo and bushbuck.

ACCOMMODATION - CLASS D: * *Traveller's Rest* is the best hotel in the area, providing basic rooms with private facilities.

CAMPING: By permission of the land owner. There are no facilities.

# ZAIRE

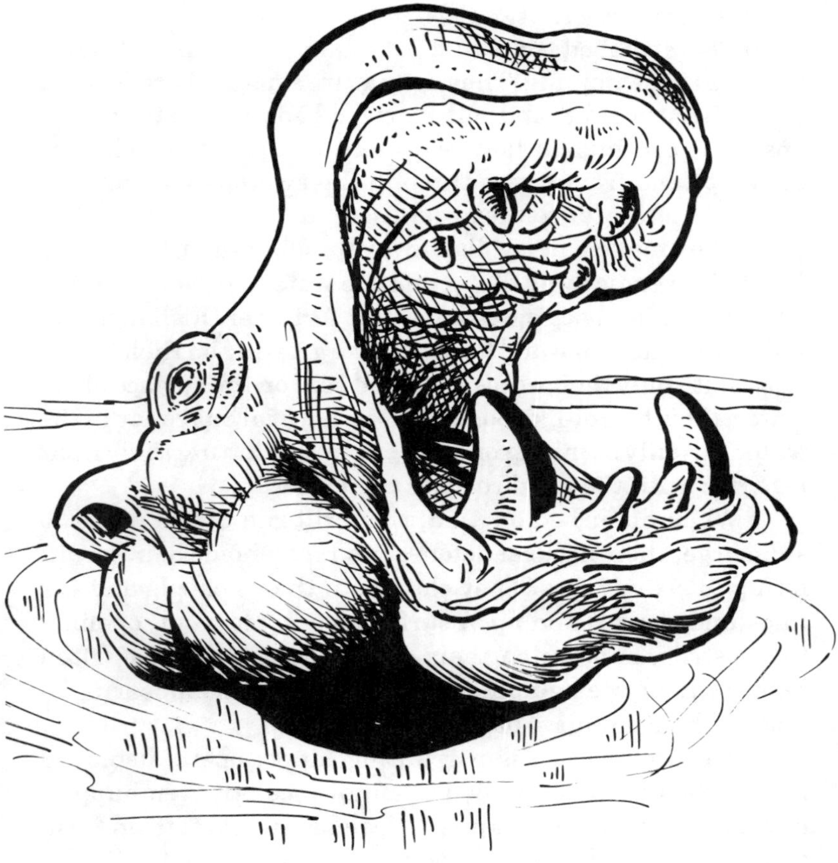

## THE AQUATIC HIPPO

Amphibious rolypoly hippos spend most of the day in the water, only courageous enough to show their unsightly bodies at night when ambling off to graze. Features of their aquatic lifestyle are numerous.

Their webbed feet assist in walking on the muddy river beds and in swimming. They are nature's natural dredgers as they displace sand and silt in river beds and estuaries to ensure a continuous flow of water. The paths which they stamp to and from rivers through the swamps increase the flow of fresh water to the swamps.

They make a noisy display by flapping their tails sending their organic dung flying into the water, spreading nutrients for fish and acting as a natural fertilizer. Fish also will swim with the hippo and feed off algae growing on their skins.

With only their noses, eyes and ears on the surface of the water, their barrel-like bodies have a natural buoyancy in the water, usually standing on the bottom and letting their front legs rise until the head reaches the surface.

When disturbed on land, they will run to the water to submerge, their natural defense, and may hold their breath for up to six minutes. They close both their nostrils and ear flaps underwater and upon surfacing will blow out, opening the nostrils, and twitch their ears to open the flaps. Often babies will be seen gulping for breath before disappearing to rest on their mothers' backs.

A content hippo is a grunting hippo; open, displayed jaws are a sign of aggression or annoyance. An even happier hippo is an animal who is able to feed his sweet tooth on fresh green grass at a bush camp or nearby sugar cane field!

# ZAIRE

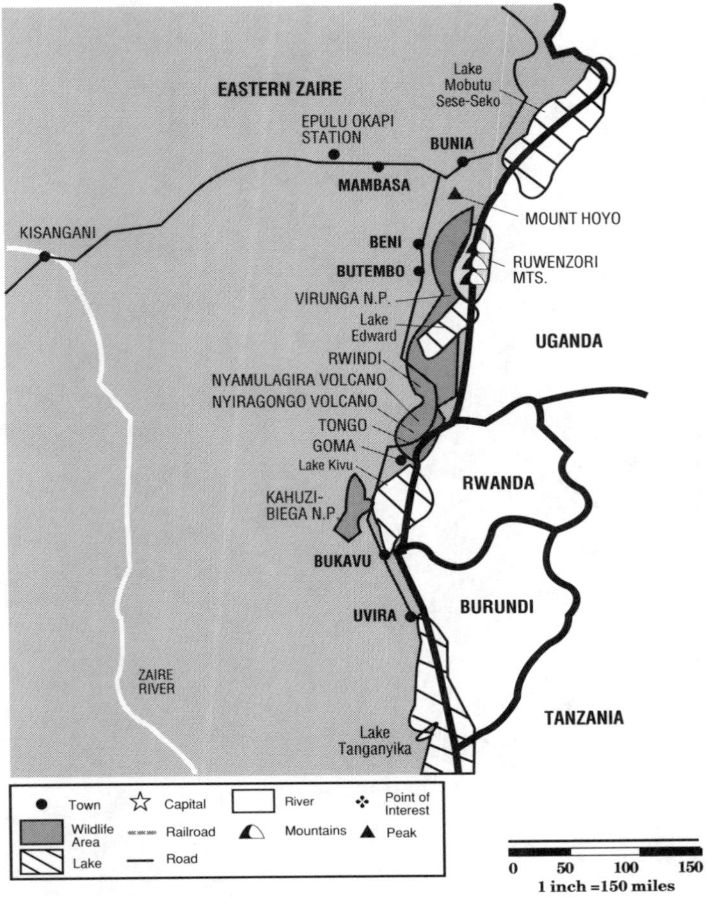


FACTS AT A GLANCE

| | |
|---|---|
| AREA: | 905,000 SQUARE MILES |
| APPROXIMATE SIZE: | U.S.A. EAST OF THE MISSISSIPPI RIVER OR TEN TIMES THE SIZE OF GREAT BRITAIN |
| POPULATION: | 33 MILLION (1992 EST.) |
| CAPITAL: | KINSHASA (POP. EST. 3,500,000) |
| OFFICIAL LANGUAGE: | OFFICIAL: FRENCH<br>NATIONAL: SWAHILI, TSHILUBA, KOKONGO, LINGALA |

# ZAIRE

The Republic of Zaire, formerly the Democratic Republic of the Congo, is the third-largest country in Africa. The name Zaire comes from the Kikongo word *nzadi*, meaning "river". The Congo or Zaire River, the tenth longest river in the world, winds 2880 miles through the Zaire basin, the world's second-largest drainage basin (the Amazon is the largest), and finally empties into the Atlantic ocean.

Of all the countries listed in this guide, Zaire is closest to "Tarzan's Africa." One can very easily imagine him swinging on a vine right in front of you as you travel through this country, visited more by adventurers than tourists.

Kivu Province, the most beautiful region of Zaire, holds the country's most exciting attractions. This province is situated along the western borders of Rwanda and Uganda in the region of the great lakes: Lakes Tanganyika, Kivu, Edward (Idi Amin), and Mobutu (Albert). This is an important agricultural area with large tobacco, coffee, tea and banana plantations. There are no paved roads in Kivu Province.

Due to the altitude, the region has an agreeable Mediterranean-type climate. In general, the best time to visit eastern Zaire is during the dry seasons from December-February and mid-June-August.

Of the 200 or so tribal or ethnic groups, four-fifths are Bantu. Physically, tribal groups range from the Tutsi, some of the tallest people on earth, to pygmies. About 80 percent of the population is Christian with the balance having Muslim or traditional beliefs.

What is now Zaire remained virtually unknown until Henry Morton Stanley traveled from East Africa to the mouth of the Congo (Zaire) River (1874-1877). Belgian King Leopold the Second claimed what became the Congo Free State as his personal property until he ceded it to Belgium in 1907, and it was renamed the Belgian Congo. Zaire achieved independence on June 30, 1960.

Zaire is a country of gigantic untapped resources. Fifty percent of the land is arable and scarcely two percent is under cultivation or used as pasture. The country holds 13 percent of the world's hydroelectric potential. Copper accounts for about half of the country's exports, followed by petroleum, diamonds and coffee.

## WILDLIFE AND WILDLIFE AREAS

Eight reserves cover 15 percent of the country's area. Virunga National Park is one of the finest reserves in Africa and contains the world's largest concentration of hippo. Over 1,000 species of birds have been recorded in Zaire, many in the Virunga National Park. In addition, Zaire is also a home of the rare okapi (antelope).

Like Rwanda, gorillas are a major attraction in Zaire. Mountain gorillas may be visited in Virunga National Park and eastern lowland gorillas may be seen in Kahuzi-Biega National Park.

The parks and reserves in Zaire are much less crowded than the ones in East Africa. During my latest visit, there were only four visitors staying at Virunga National Park's Rwindi Lodge, and I was the only visitor to Mt. Hoyo and the Ruwenzori Mountains in two weeks.

The world has not yet discovered that these are among the continent's finest attractions, making a visit here all the more inviting and adventurous. However, travel on your own is very difficult and often exasperating, even if you know French.

# THE NORTHEAST

## GOMA

Goma is the tourist center for eastern Zaire and the administrative center for Virunga National Park and Nyiragongo and Nyamulagira Volcanoes. Fortunately tourism has done little to change this typical African town. Goma is situated on the northern shores of Lake Kivu, one of the most beautiful lakes in Africa, with Mt. Nyiragongo (volcano) forming a dramatic backdrop to the north.

Three boats per week depart Goma for Bukavu across Lake Kivu.

Le Nyira is a good restaurant in town. Goma has an international airport. Air charters are available.

ACCOMMODATIONS - FIRST CLASS: * *Hotel Karibu* has rooms with private facilities and is located six miles outside of Goma on Lake Kivu.

TOURIST CLASS: * *Hotel des Grand Lacs* also has rooms with private facilities. * *Masques Hotel* is located in town and has rooms with private facilities.

## NORTH OF GOMA

On the drive from Goma northward one passes over the dramatic Kabasha Escarpment to Butembo. The route from the Kabasha Escarpment to Beni is one of the most beautiful in Africa and is properly named the "Beauty Route." The road passes through many picturesque villages, coffee, tea and banana plantations — the Africa that many of us have pictured in our minds.

# VIRUNGA NATIONAL PARK (PARC NATIONAL DES VIRUNGA)

Virunga National Park, previously called Albert Park, is the oldest reserve in Africa. It is the best game park in Zaire and is one of the finest and least-known parks in all of Africa. With approximately 4600 square miles in area, it is one of the largest on the continent as well. Altitudes range from 3000 feet on the grassy savannah to 16,794 feet in the Ruwenzori mountains, resulting in a tremendous variety of topography, flora and fauna.

Virunga is about 185 miles long and 25 miles wide and is divided into several sections, each requiring separate entrance fees. From south to north: the Nyiragongo and Nyamulagira volcanoes and Tongo, Rumangabo Station (Bukima), Djomba Gorilla Sanctuary, Rwindi, the Ruwenzori Mountains, and Mt. Hoyo. Guides are compulsory and their services are included in the park entrance fees.

## VOLCANOES

The region around Goma is a highly volcanic area of constant activity. On my first visit here, I discovered that a new volcano had been born recently, and we hiked ten miles into the bush to see it. In the event of an eruption, we camped uphill from the volcano, which was scarcely 300 feet high and watched the fabulous fireworks all night. For some unknown reason, a new volcano usually pops up in this active region about every other year between December and April. I just missed visiting another lava-filled caldera in 1984, which cooled a few weeks before my arrival.

In the southern part of the park near Goma lie the active volcanoes of Nyiragongo and Nyamulagira, which do not require technical mountaineering skills to climb. If the volcanoes are active at the time of your visit, you may want to spend a night near the crater rim to enjoy the remarkable fireworks display.

The best time to climb is December-January and June

when the weather is clearest. February, July and August are also good.

## NYIRAGONGO

Nyiragongo (11,384 ft./3470 m.) erupted in 1977, spewing out miles of molten lava which destroyed villages within its path. I visited the area three months later and could still feel the heat radiating from the newly hardened lava.

Nyiragongo can be climbed in one day if you begin climbing early in the morning. The guide and porter station is located at Kibati (6400 ft./1950 m.), eight miles north of Goma on the Rutshuru road. Hike four to five hours through forest and Afro-alpine vegetation and past lava flows to the summit. Have lunch on the crater rim while watching sulfurous gases escape from the crater below. Allow two to three hours to return to Kibati before dark.

It is better to take two days for the climb, overnighting at a hut (in poor condition) about a 30-minute walk below the summit. At dawn the next morning, hike to the crater rim and enjoy breathtaking views of Lake Kivu, Goma and the surrounding countryside.

## NYAMULAGIRA

If you would like to see wildlife, this is the better of the two volcanoes to climb. An armed guide accompanies each group, and porters may be hired. With luck, you will see forest elephant, chimpanzees, buffalo and antelope.

Nyamulagira (10,023 ft./3055 m.) is best climbed in three days. On the first day, hike about six hours through dense upland jungle, passing numerous lava flows to a basic lodge at 8200 feet (2500 meters) altitude. Water is available at the lodge but must be purified.

On Day Two you reach the tree line after about an hour's hike and the crater rim about an hour after passing the tree line. The crater itself is about a mile and a half in diameter.

Within the crater is a blowhole with a huge 1300-foot diameter shaft. Descend into and explore the crater, then return to the same lodge you slept in the night before. Hike down the mountain on the third day.

Nyamulagira is reached via Kakomero (5900 ft./1800 m.), 24 miles north of Goma.

ACCOMMODATIONS - CAMPING: Campsites are available at the Nyamulagira base camp.

## TONGO

Located north of Goma about nine miles west of the main Goma/Rutshuru road is Tongo, presently the best place in Zaire to see chimpanzees. The trek from Tongo Camp is rather arduous; only those in good walking condition should undertake the trek to visit these fascinating primates in their own environment.

## DJOMBA GORILLA SANCTUARY

The Djomba Gorilla Sanctuary covers much of the Zaire side of the Virunga Mountains, which are shared with Rwanda and Uganda.

Here, three groups of mountain gorillas have been habituated to man's presence. Each group is named after its leader (a silverback) and may be visited by up to six persons each at a time. National Parks guides must accompany each group.

Djomba Camp is the base from which gorilla trekking begins. To reach Djomba (sometimes spelled Jomba), drive about 40 miles north from Goma past Nyiragongo and Nyamulagira volcanoes. Two miles before reaching Rutshuru, turn right and continue 19 miles to Park Headquarters. From there, visitors must hike for 30-45 minutes to Djomba Camp. Porters are available to carry luggage.

Two gorilla groups, Oscar (Rugendo) and Marcel

(Rugabo), are the closest of the three groups to Djomba Camp and are most often visited by international guests. These two groups are normally found in less than one or two hours, but occasionally it can take as long as four or five.

The Oscar and Marcel groups are most always found at lower altitudes than the mountain gorillas of Rwanda, and the terrain is not as steep as in Volcano National Park in Rwanda. The gorilla search, therefore, is usually less physically demanding here than in Rwanda. In addition, trekkers may visit with the gorillas up to two hours at Djomba, allowing plenty of time to enjoy the experience, whereas in Rwanda visits are limited to one hour. However, Djomba is more difficult (and more expensive) to reach than Volcano National Park.

The Faida group lives at higher altitudes than the Marcel and Oscar groups, and the trek can be very demanding. In addition, the Faida group spends part of its time in Uganda and cannot be tracked over the border.

Buffalo and elephant are also present in the sanctuary, so keep an eye out for them. For a description of gorillas and gorilla trekking in general, see "Volcano National Park" in the chapter on Rwanda.

Permits must be purchased in advance for the Marcel and Oscar groups. Permits for the Faida group are not sold in advance since it spends part of its time in Uganda.

ACCOMMODATION - CLASS B/C: * *Djomba Camp* has several cabins, each with two double rooms with private facilities and a shared sitting room with fireplace.

CLASS F: A self-service hut is available with two bedrooms (12 beds total). Bring your own food.

CAMPING: Campsites are available.

## RUMANGABO STATION (BUKIMA)

Mountain gorillas may also be seen at Rumangabo Station, which is closer to Goma than Djomba. However, two days are required to visit the gorillas here. To reach Rumangabo, drive 28 miles north of Goma on the Goma-Rutshuru road and turn off to Park Headquarters. From here a park guard will lead you to the village of Bukima where you spend the night. Your gorilla trek to see the Bukima (Zunguruka) group begins the following morning. As with the Djomba Gorilla Sanctuary, reservations must be made in advance.

ACCOMMODATION - CLASS D: A small lodge with basic facilities is available.

## RWINDI

Continuing north towards Rwindi are the **Rutshuru Waterfalls** and **Maji Ya Moto** hot-water springs, both near Rutshuru.

Rwindi is the chief game-viewing region of Virunga National Park. Predominantly composed of savannah plains and swamps, Rwindi has the greatest concentrations of hippo in the world (about 23,000). Lion in Rwindi are known for their unusual ability to kill hippo.

The Kabasha Escarpment rises up to 6000 feet above the plains below and provides a dramatic backdrop for wildlife which includes elephant, buffalo, hippo, lion, hyena, jackal, waterbuck, reedbuck, bushbuck, topi, Thomas kob, Defassa kob, crocodiles and numerous aquatic birds.

The fishing village of Vitshumbi, located on the southern shores of Lake Edward (Lake Idi Amin), is worth a stop. Visit the fishery to enjoy the taste of delicious barbecued tilapia with pilipili (hot sauce).

Most game viewing is from minibuses with roof hatches. Vehicles must stay on the park tracks. The main road from Goma to Butembo passes right through the park.

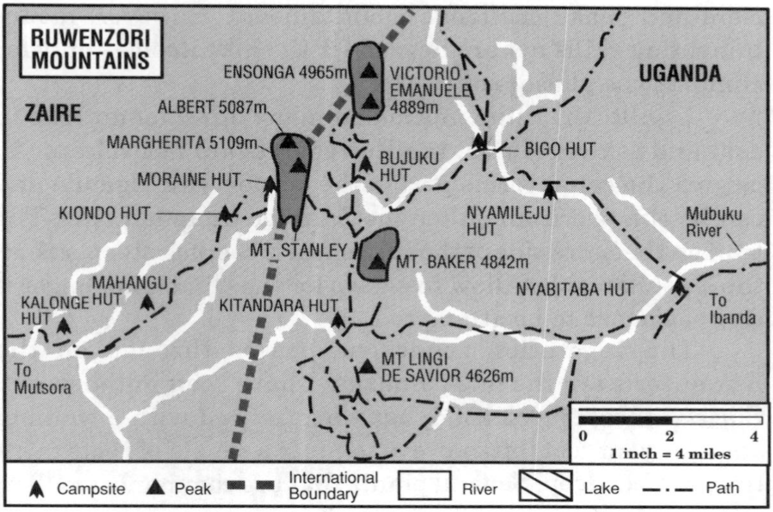


The best time to visit is during the dry season. Roads and tracks are poor in the rainy season. Rwindi Lodge, park headquarters and camping sites are located at Rwindi, 81 miles north of Goma.

ACCOMMODATION - CLASS C: * *Rwindi Lodge* has rondavels with private facilities (130 beds total) and swimming pool.

CAMPING: Camping is not allowed.

## RUWENZORI MOUNTAINS

The third highest mountains in Africa (behind Mts. Kilimanjaro and Kenya), the "Mountains of the Moon" are the highest *mountain chain* on the continent. Permanently snow-covered over 14,800 feet (4500 meters), these jagged mountains are almost perpetually covered in mist.

The mountain chain is approximately 60 miles long and 30 miles wide, and the highest peak, Margherita, is 16,762 feet (5109 meters) in altitude. A number of permanent glaciers and peaks challenge mountaineers. However, mountaineering skills not are needed for the hike itself — only for climbing the glaciers or peaks.

Unlike Mt. Kilimanjaro and many other mountains in east and central Africa, the Ruwenzoris are not volcanic in origin. The range forms part of the border with Uganda and can be climbed from either the Zaire or Ugandan side. The trail on the Zaire side of the Ruwenzoris is much steeper than the Ugandan side. Allow five days for the climb and longer if any peaks are to be attempted.

The vegetation zones one passes through on the Ruwenzoris are the most amazing I have seen in the world. Colorful mosses look solid, but when probed with a walking stick (or your foot) often prove to cover a tangle of roots more than six feet deep. Several plants that are commonly small in other parts of the world grow to gigantic proportions.

Park Headquarters are located at the village of Mutsora, two miles from Mutwanga, which is 30 miles east of Beni. From the road junction near Beni, drive 28 miles east to Mutwanga, then two miles to Mutsora.

### The Butawu Route

The Butawu Route is the only route regularly used on the Zaire side of the Ruwenzoris. All other routes are so overgrown with vegetation that they are virtually impossible to climb.

On the first day, it takes five to six hours of hiking from the park headquarters at Mutsora (5600 ft./1700 m.) through small fields of bananas, coffee, and other crops to reach Kalonge Hut (7015 ft./2135 m). The hut sleeps 16 persons, and there is room for tents nearby.

On the second day, one passes through areas with giant stinging nettles and bamboo forest over 100 feet high. Soon you come to a resting spot where offerings are left for the mountain gods. Your guide will expect you to leave something, (i.e., a few coins).

At about 8500 feet (2600 meters), the sides of the slick, muddy path become lined with spongy mosses and heather 25 feet tall. After about five hours of hiking (actually the most difficult part of the climb), one reaches Mahangu Hut (10,860 ft./3310 m.). The hut has room for 16 persons, and there is room for camping.

The third day one finally hikes past the upper tree line at about 12,500 feet (3800 meters) and enters a zone of giant groundsels over 16 feet high and giant lobelia over 25 feet high. Before completing the five-hour hike to Kiondo Hut (13,780 ft./4200 m.), you hike along an open ridge with fabulous views of Lac Noir (Black Lake). Kiondo Hut has room for 12, and there is room for tents nearby.

On Day Four of the hike, the Butawu Route continues on to Wasuwameso Peak (14,600 ft./4450 m.) for some fabulous views of Mt. Stanley. Climbers then return to Kiondo Hut and continue on down to Kalonge Hut for the night.

Alternatively, take a fabulous hike past Lac Vert (Green Lake) and Lac Gris (Grey Lake) to Moraine Hut (14,270 ft./4350 m.) at the foot of the glaciers. The hike to Moraine Hut from Kiondo Hut takes about five hours round-trip and requires a short bit of easy rock climbing with fixed ropes. Then return to either Kiondo Hut or Mahangu Hut for the night.

If you hike to Moraine Hut, be sure to return to Kiondo Hut early. My guide insisted there was plenty of time to reach Moraine Hut and return to Kiondo Hut the afternoon of the third day. We were so late returning we were forced to return in the dark. Had I not brought a flashlight, we might still be up there.

On the fifth day, return to Mutsora — hopefully for a hot bath and a soft bed!

Many hikers prefer camping at Grey Lake instead of using dilapidated Moraine Hut, which leaks. There is space for only one tent near Moraine Hut. Experienced mountaineers may press on to conquer the glaciers and peaks of the Ruwenzori from either location. Allow a minimum of six or seven days total for the climb if you wish to attempt any summits.

For information on climbing the summits and glaciers,

I recommend the *East Africa International Mountain Guide* by Andrew Wielochowski (1986) and *Guide to the Ruwenzori* by Osmaston and Pasteur (1972), both published by West Col Productions in England.

The best time to climb is from December-February; June-August is also good. To reach the Ruwenzoris, travel north from Goma through Butembo, and just before Beni turn east 28 miles to Mutwanga. Park headquarters are at Mutsora, about 1.5 miles from Mutwanga.

A guide at no charge is required; porters are available for a small fee. Both guides and porters expect cigarettes in addition to a tip. The guides know the path and where to find water en route — but little else. All guides speak French; an English-speaking guide may not be available. Guides who speak English tend to know only a few words.

Guides are not equipped for or experienced in glacier or rock climbing. Your group must be self-sufficient. There are no mountain rescue teams; bring a comprehensive medical kit.

Huts have fireplaces, bunk beds and wood stoves. Guides and porters love to smoke and often share the huts with you; consider bringing your own tent. Also, bring a warm sleeping bag, mattress, food, fuel, and enough water to last two days. Most of the windows are broken; you may wish to bring some plastic with which to cover them.

See "Mt. Kilimanjaro" in the chapter on Tanzania for a more extensive equipment checklist and other preparations. Mt. Kilimanjaro is higher, but the trail up the Ruwenzoris is much steeper, slicker and more difficult to negotiate.

ACCOMMODATION - TOURIST CLASS: See "Butembo" or "Beni" below.

CLASS F: Rooms are available at a basic lodge at Park Headquarters.

CAMPING: Camping is allowed at Park Headquarters.

## ISHANGO

The Ishango region of Virunga National Park is situated at the northern end of Lake Edward (Idi Amin). This seldom-visited region of the park is predominantly open savannah similar to the Rwindi area and the southern shores of Lake Edward. Wildlife is also similar to what you find in the Rwindi region, except there are no elephant. Water birds are prolific, especially where the Semliki River empties into Lake Edward.

From Beni, travel east past the turnoff to the Ruwenzori Mountains and onward toward the Ugandan border to Kasindi. Then turn right (south) and continue to Ishango.

ACCOMMODATIONS: None.

CAMPING: Campsites are available.

## MT. HOYO

Fifty-seven miles north of Beni and 12 miles south of Komanda, take the track to the east, uphill for nine miles to the colonial-style Mount Hoyo Lodge (Auberge du Mount Hoyo).

Halfway up this track, I came upon a line of millions of safari ants crossing the road. Thousands of ants had joined their legs and formed a "cocoon" across the road, protecting those that crossed beneath.

Mt. Hoyo has many attractions. The Cascades of Venus (l'Escaliers de Venus) is a stepped waterfall in a thick jungle setting of natural beauty. The cascades and the grottoes (caves) with stalagmites and stalactites can be easily visited in a half-day hike. Black and white colobus monkeys, chimpanzees and the rare okapi may be seen in the forest.

A very interesting excursion is to join a few Balese (pygmy) hunters on a mock antelope hunt. Armed with their bows and arrows, groups of up to three visitors follow these hunters through thick jungle vegetation in search of game.

A pygmy family in front of their hut near Mt. Hoyo.

The pygmies whistle to attract their "prey." Here, they proved the advantage of being small — effortlessly walking under vines and limbs, while I had to crawl on my hands and knees.

We feasted on honey which they fished from a bee's hive in a tree trunk with their arrows; and they enjoyed another delicacy — termites from a large mound.

Be sure to visit a pygmy village while in the area. Villages along the main roads have become a bit "commercialized," so if you have time, have a guide take you to a village off the beaten track.

ACCOMMODATION - CLASS C/D: * *Mount Hoyo Lodge (Auberge du Mount Hoyo)* has rooms with private facilities and good views of the jungle below.

CAMPING: Campsites with basic shower and toilet facilities are available.

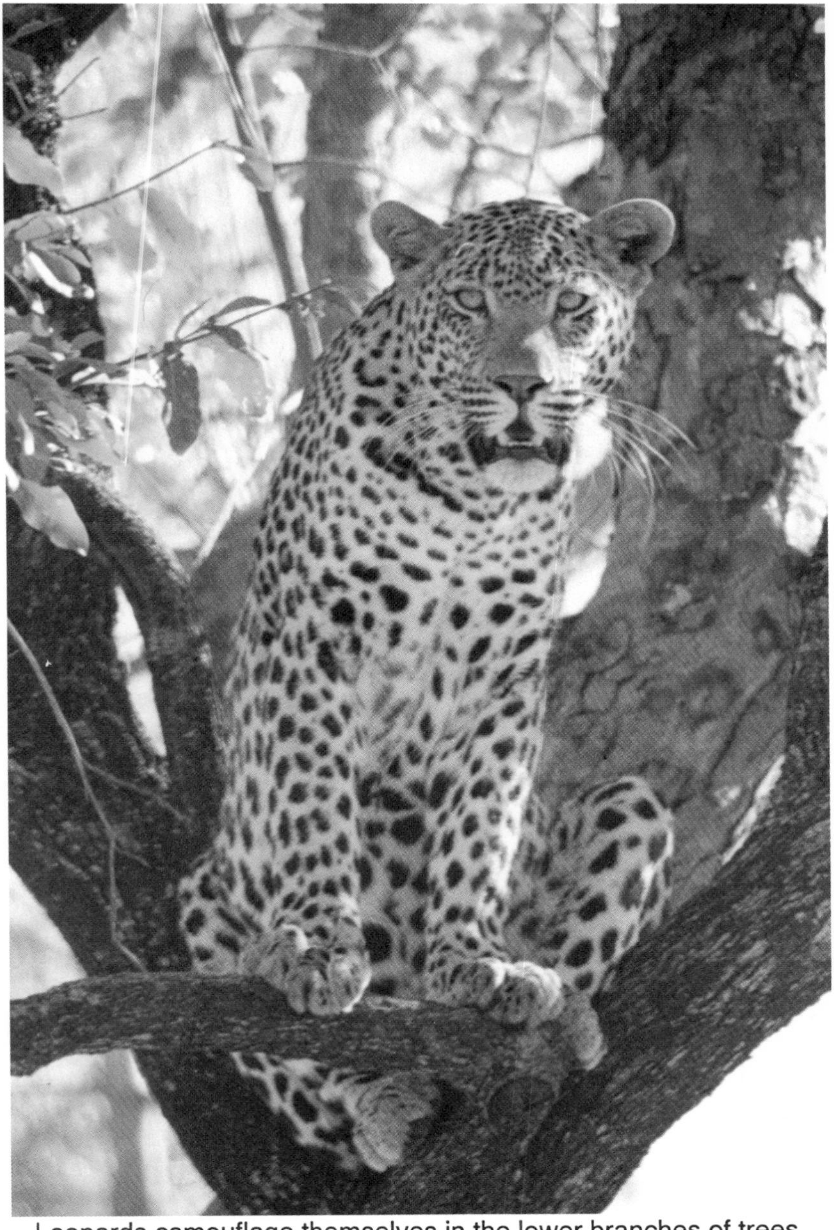

Leopards camouflage themselves in the lower branches of trees.

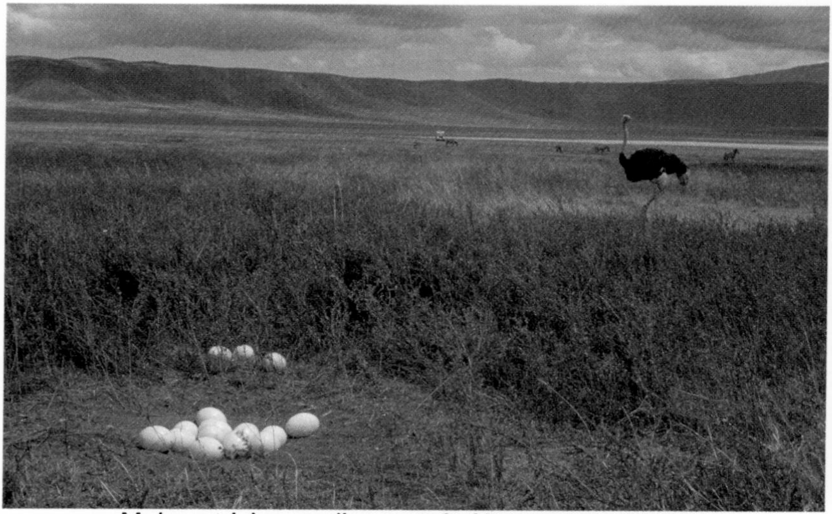

Male ostrich guarding nest in Ngorongoro Crater.

Burchell's zebra stallions fighting for territory.

A battle of wills . . . they both wanted the sandbank, but the hippos won!

Red-billed oxpeckers enjoy a symbiotic relationship with black rhino.

Lion cubs provide great entertainment on safari.

Silverback mountain gorilla in Volcano National Park, Rwanda.

Wildlife roams freely through many camps in Zimbabwe, Zambia and Botswana, as this couple discovered!

Remote rustic bush camp, Damaraland Wilderness Reserve, Namibia.

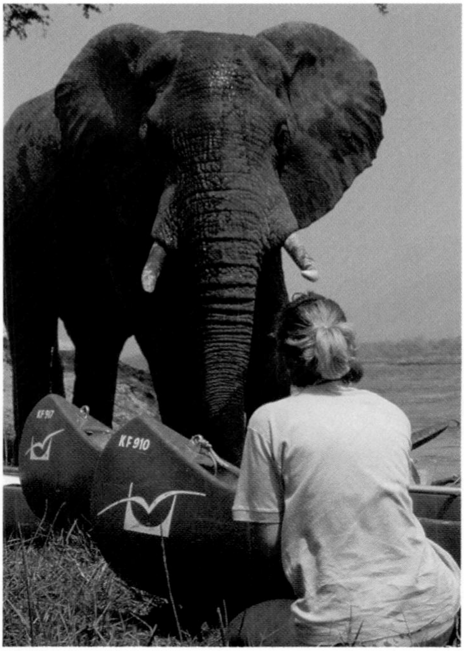


Left:
A close encounter on canoe safari along Mana Pools National Park, Zimbabwe.

Below:
A mock charge by a bull elephant on a walking safari.

The night before . . .

. . . The morning after.

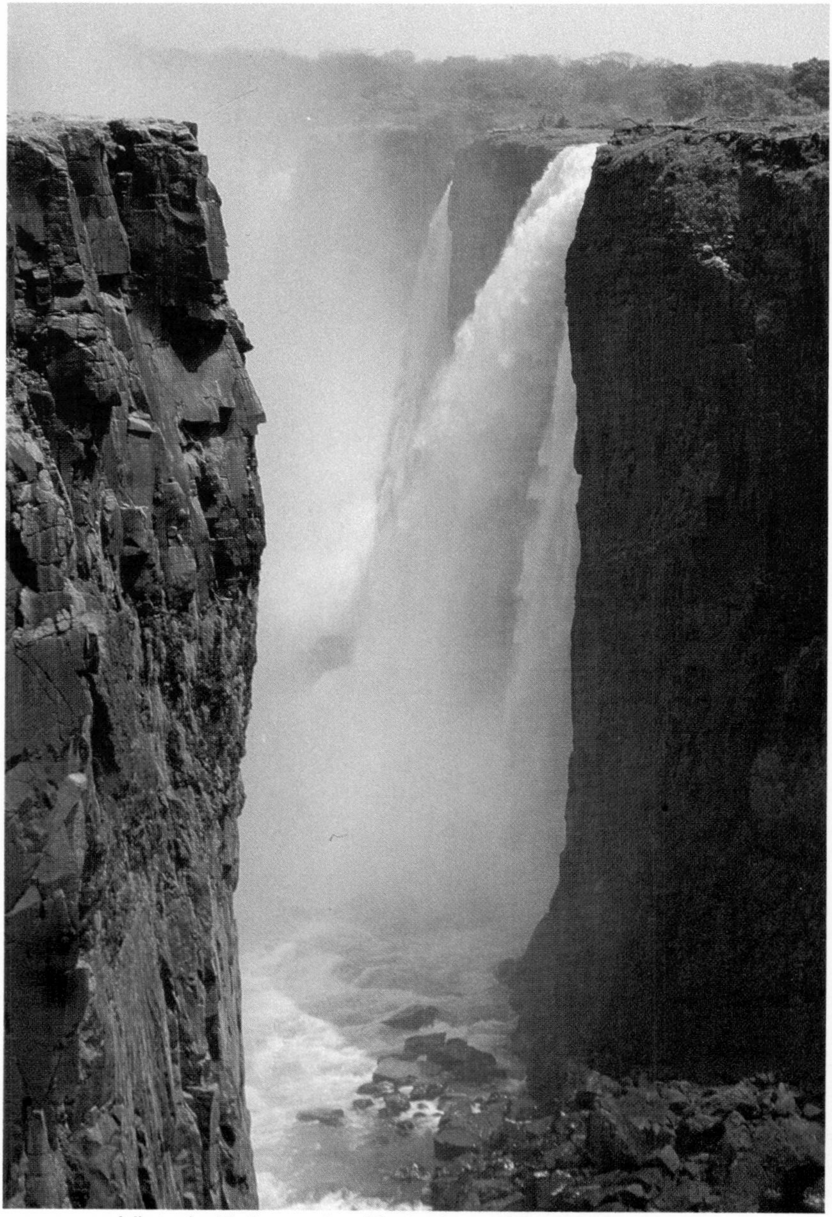

Victoria Falls on the Zimbabwe / Zambian border.

## LOYA RIVER

The Loya River crosses the main road a few miles south of the turnoff to Mt. Hoyo. Take a ride in a piroque (dugout canoe) through the thick green Ituri Forest, past artificial dams created for fishing, and thick jungle. The Loya River flows into the Ituri River, which travels deep into the Ituri Forest.

Visit a pygmy village before returning. Be sure to bring a gift (i.e., pens or tobacco), especially if you wish to take pictures.

## BUTEMBO

This busy village with a population of over 100,000 is situated in the highlands along the "Beauty Route" just north of the equator, about halfway between Goma and Bunia. Many banana, coffee and tea plantations are in the area. Travelers driving from Rwindi often spend the night here before continuing on to Mt. Hoyo or the Ruwenzori Mountains.

ACCOMMODATION - TOURIST CLASS: * *Auberge* has rooms with private facilities. * *Kikyo Hotel* has rooms with private facilities.

## EPULU OKAPI STATION

At the Okapi Station at Epulu, you may see the rare Okapi antelope (ten at present), roaming several large pens set in natural surroundings. In addition, fourteen primate species have been seen in the forests near Epulu.

An interesting excursion for the adventurous is to go hunting with pygmies and camp in the forest for a night or two. The pygmies will build you a shelter for the night or you may bring a tent.

Pygmy villages seldom visited by overseas visitors may also be visited by hiking into the jungle with a guide.

The Epulu Okapi Station is situated on banks of the

Epulu River about a six-to-seven-hour drive from Mt. Hoyo in the dry season (December-February and June-August), which is the best time to visit. Roads are often impassable in the rainy season. From Mt. Hoyo, drive north to Komanda, then west past Mambasa to Epulu. Alternatively, charter a plane to Mambasa and try to hire a vehicle for the 50-mile drive to Epulu.

ACCOMMODATION - CLASS F: Three rondavels and a guesthouse (20 beds total) with an ablution block with toilets and showers (cold water only).

CAMPING: Campsites are available.

## THE SOUTHEAST

## KAHUZI-BIEGA NATIONAL PARK

This 2300-square-mile mountain sanctuary, located 17 miles northwest of Bukavu, is dedicated to preserving the eastern lowland gorilla (*Gorilla gorilla graueri*). Searching for these magnificent, rare and endangered animals is recommended only for travelers in fairly good physical condition.

There are three groups of habituated gorillas, one with 11 members, one with 24 members, and one with 27 members.

The search for gorillas usually takes less than an hour of hiking to altitudes from 7000 to 8200 feet through dense upland jungle and bamboo forests. However, it occasionally takes three or four hours to locate the gorillas. The park also includes swamp, woodland and extensive equatorial rain forest. The highest point in the park is Mt. Kahuzi at 10,853 feet.

On my visit to the park, I was the only tourist there to search for gorillas. I was accompanied by a guide and several cutters wielding pangas. As our search progressed, we found gorilla lairs where they had spent the previous night.

After four hours of following their trail and cutting our

way through dense tropical foliage, we finally located them. The silverback (dominant male) was one of the largest I have seen — estimated by the guide to weigh over 400 pounds. Hanging vines and branches that blocked our view were cut until the silverback pounded his chest and charged — stopping just short of us and establishing his well-earned territory. In the background an adult female and her young offspring were curiously watching us.

Other wildlife present in the park includes elephant, giant forest hog, duiker, chimpanzee and colobus monkeys.

The park is managed by the Frankfurt Zoological Society. At present, there is a limit of eight people that may visit a gorilla group at one time. Children under 15 years of age are not allowed to visit the gorillas.

Daytime temperatures average 50-65° F., and yearly average rainfall is high — about 70 inches. The heaviest rainfall is in April and November. The best time to visit the park is in the dry season. Bring waterproof light hiking boots (you may have to wade through water), a sweater, waterproof cover jacket, lunch, snacks and a canteen.

To reach the park, go north from Bukavu along the western side of Lake Kivu for 13 miles to Miti, then turn left (west), traveling for four miles to Station Tshivanga, the Park Headquarters.

ACCOMMODATION - CLASS B: * *Mbayo Lodge* has seven rooms (doubles) and is located on a tea plantation six miles from the park gate. Gorillas are sometimes seen on the plantation.

CAMPING: Campsites are available at Park Headquarters.

## BUKAVU

Bukavu, the region's capital, is situated on the southern shores of Lake Kivu near the Rwanda border. Bukavu is the nearest city to Kahuzi-Biega National Park.

Boats for Goma depart Bukavu and cross beautiful Lake

Kivu to Goma three times per week.

ACCOMMODATION - FIRST CLASS: * *Orchids Safari Club*, located on the shores of Lake Kivu, has 14 rooms (doubles) with private facilities. Cruises on Lake Kivu are offered.

## CENTRAL AND WESTERN

### ZAIRE RIVER

Exploring the Zaire River by riverboat from Kinshasa to Kisangani is truly an adventure into the dark continent. The boat is slow, taking about 12 days upstream and eight downstream for the 1000-mile voyage — if no complications arise. You may also cruise from Lisala to Kisangani: this trip takes three to five days.

The riverboat is actually a motor boat with several barges tied on, with a dining room and bar on each barge. Local tribesmen paddle out to meet the riverboat in their dugout canoes, latch hold, and sell monkeys, crocodiles, huge juicy pineapples and other tropical fruits. One passes through the "mainstream" of Zairian life on this river.

Deluxe and first-class cabins are recommended for all but the most rugged of travelers. This riverboat is only for those with flexible schedules; it is not uncommon for it to be a week or more "off schedule."

### KINSHASA

Situated in western Zaire near the mouth of the Zaire (Congo) River, Kinshasa is the country's capital. Points of interest include the Presidential Gardens and Zoo, the central market, and the National Academy of Fine Arts. Thieves Market is a good place to shop for malachite and wood carvings.

One of the greater attractions of this city are the numerous live bands playing the music of Zaire in clubs. Zaire music is extremely popular throughout most of sub-Sahara Africa.

The airport is 18 miles from Kinshasa. More travelers reach Eastern Zaire from Nairobi (Kenya) or Kigali (Rwanda) than from Kinshasa.

ACCOMMODATION - DELUXE: * The *Inter-Continental Hotel* is centrally located near the World Trade Center and has 510 air-conditioned rooms with ensuite facilities, swimming pool, tennis courts, squash, health club, casino and disco.

FIRST CLASS: * *Hotel Le Memling* has 212 rooms with ensuite facilities.

# ZAMBIA

## THE LONESOME LEOPARD

This shy, solitary, nocturnal and secretive creature is an independent animal who moves silently and by its intelligence can adapt to any environment. Its presence is widespread, but sightings are uncommon; though for the persevering person, there are some signs to look for.

Leopards may wake early in the morning, tails hanging from beneath a branch, to watch their prey from a tree before descending to commence a short stalk, chase and pounce on the animal, and finally give the death bite. Their phenomenal neck strength and claws both are used to drag their meal, step by step, back up the tree. Later in the morning, they may find an open sunny spot on a rock outcrop to warm and groom themselves.

Leopards are natural swimmers and often supplement their diet with fish and other river species and can be seen taking a drink at a river in the late afternoon. If baboons are nearby, they will always give away the leopard's presence. The elusive leopard will never be undetected by wary baboons in the trees above. They will move through the branches chattering and barking, creating a uncontrolled noise loud enough to deter a leopard attack.

It is not uncommon for a leopard to initiate an attack on a baboon troop, only to be attacked itself and driven up the tree, chided by baboons above and below, finally finding peace once the baboons move off. Hyrax will also give away the presence of leopard hiding in rocky outcrops.

One of the biggest thrills on a safari is to hear and recognize the sound of the leopard's sawing grunt in the dead of the night and perhaps the chance to sight them on a night game drive.

# ZAMBIA

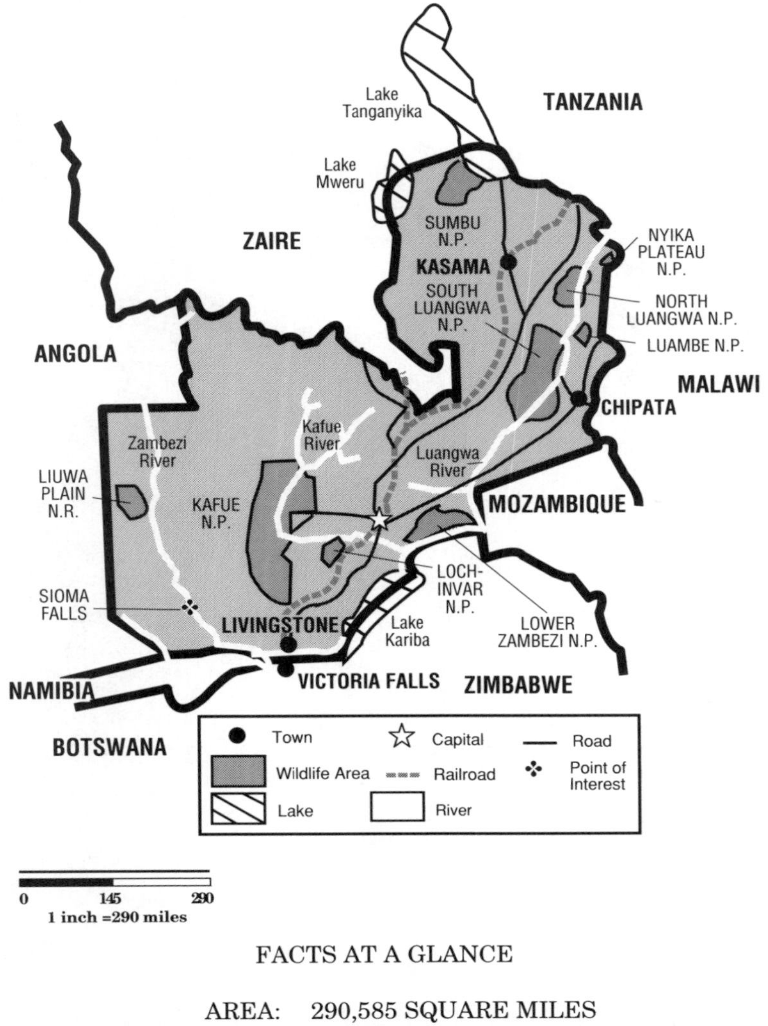


FACTS AT A GLANCE

| | |
|---|---|
| AREA: | 290,585 SQUARE MILES |
| APPROXIMATE SIZE: | LARGER THAN TEXAS OR FRANCE |
| POPULATION: | 7 MILLION (1992 EST.) |
| CAPITAL: | LUSAKA (POP. EST. 800,000) |
| OFFICIAL LANGUAGE: | OFFICIAL: ENGLISH |

# ZAMBIA

A sparsely populated country rich in wildlife, Zambia was named after the mighty Zambezi River which flows through southern Zambia. The Zambezi River is fed by its Kafue and Luangwa tributaries. The three great lakes of Bangweulu, Mweru and Tanganyika lie in northern Zambia, and Lake Kariba lies along the southeastern border adjacent to Zimbabwe.

The country is predominantly a high plateau ranging in altitude from 3000-5000 feet, which is why it has a subtropical rather than a tropical climate. April-August is cool and dry; September-October is hot and dry; and November-March is warm and wet. Winter temperatures are as cool as 43° F. and summer temperatures as warm as 100° F. The dry season, with clear sunny skies, occurs May-October.

The Zambian people are predominantly composed of Bantu tribal groups who practice a combination of traditional and Christian beliefs. English is the official language and is widely spoken. Seventy-three other languages and dialects are also spoken. In contrast to most African countries, over 40 percent of the population live in urban areas, due mainly to the copper mining industry.

Cecil Rhodes obtained mineral right concessions from the chiefs in 1888 of what was proclaimed Northern Rhodesia, which came under British influence. In 1953 Northern Rhodesia, Southern Rhodesia and Nyasaland (now Malawi) were consolidated into the Federation of Rhodesia and Nyasaland. Northern Rhodesia succeeded from the Federation in 1963 and achieved its independence on October 24, 1964, as the Republic of Zambia.

Zambia's economy is based primarily on copper from the government-owned mines in the "copper belt" near the Zaire border. The price and subsequent production of copper has declined since 1975; this has brought on hardship and forced the economy to diversify. More emphasis is now being placed on developing agriculture (exporting fruit, coffee, sugar) and the tourism industry as a greater source of foreign exchange.

With new elections in 1991, Zambia now has a multiparty political system.

## WILDLIFE AND WILDLIFE AREAS

Zambia provides fabulous options for the wildlife adventurer, including both night and day game drives by open vehicle, walking safaris using remote bush camps, old-fashioned portered walking safaris like those undertaken by early explorers, mobile tented safaris, canoe safaris and white-water rafting.

Zambia boasts 19 gazetted national parks covering over 24,500 square miles, and with the 34 game management areas adjacent to the parks, Zambia has set aside 32 percent of its land to the preservation of wildlife. However, many national parks and reserves are not open to the general public.

Zambia's two major parks are South Luangwa National Park and Kafue National Park. South Luangwa is the more popular of the two, largely due to its high concentration of elephant and other game. Kafue National Park is seldom visited by international travelers. The game is generally more scattered, but many of the species, such as greater kudu and sable antelope, are said to be substantially larger than elsewhere in the country. The red lechwe, unique to Zambia, is found in Kafue.

Going on safari in Zambia is different. In Kenya and Tanzania visitors are often rushed from park to park with only one or two nights in the same park. In Zambia the emphasis is on experiencing the bush and wildlife by participating in walking safaris and night safaris (the biggest attractions) as well as day game drives in open vehicles.

Zambia is excellent for walking safaris, which are operated in South Luangwa (my first choice), North Luangwa and Kafue National Parks. Most of the camps offer daily walks, and nearly all of them offer day and night game-viewing drives.

Fishing for tigerfish, lake salmon and Nile perch is excellent in Lake Tanganyika, Lake Kariba, and the Kafue River and is best April-November.

Visitors who have their own vehicles must be in the camps by nightfall and therefore cannot conduct night safaris on their own. Guests must not leave the roads in search of game or walk in the park without the company of an armed wildlife guard. I've been told that crocodiles in Zambia are responsible for more deaths than automobile accidents.

The best time to visit South Luangwa and Kafue National Parks is July-September, followed by June and October. Game viewing is fairly good November, April and May in the eastern part of the park near Mfuwe Airport, where camps are open year-round. December-March is the hot and humid rainy season when foliage becomes thicker, making wildlife more difficult to spot.

## THE NORTH AND NORTHEAST

## SOUTH LUANGWA NATIONAL PARK

The natural beauty, variety and concentration of wildlife make this huge 3500-square-mile park one of the finest in Africa. Game is so prolific Luangwa is called "The Crowded Valley." The park has one of the highest concentrations of elephant on the continent.

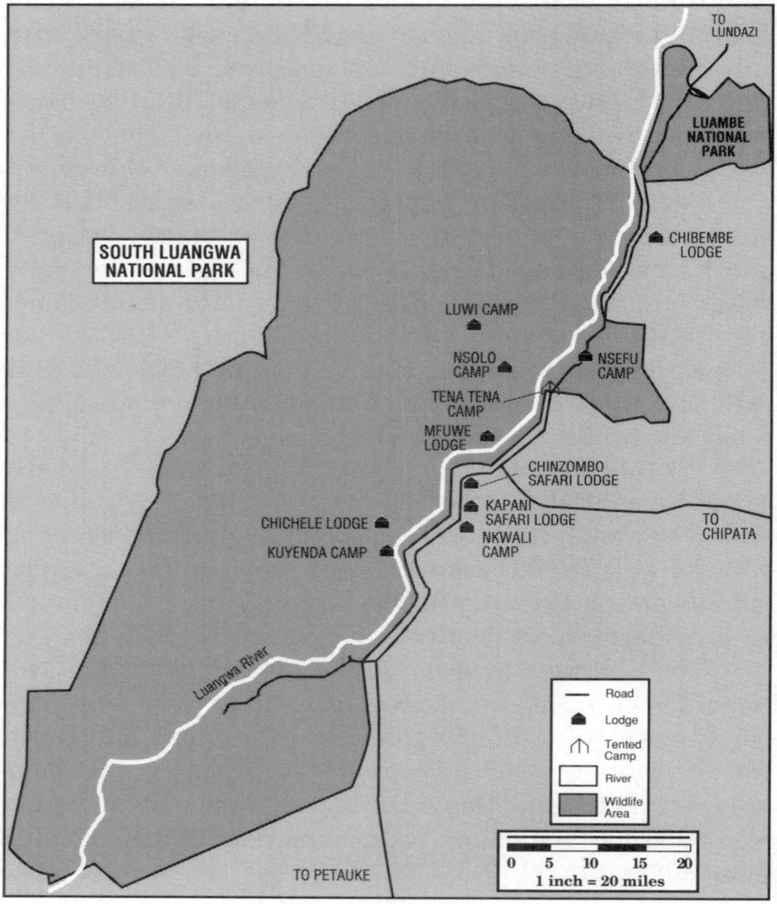


South Luangwa is home to savannah, wetland and forest animals. The southern regions are predominantly woodland savannah with scattered grassy areas. Leopard, kudu and giraffe are numerous. To the north the woodlands give way to scattered trees and open plains where wildebeest and other savannah animals dominate the scene.

Thornicroft's giraffe are indigenous to the park. Lion, hyena, buffalo, waterbuck, impala, kudu, puku and zebra are plentiful. Small herds of Cookson's wildebeest may be seen.

This is the best park in Zambia to see hippo completely out of the water. A few black rhino are present but are seldom seen. Leopard are most commonly sighted July-October and are frequently seen on night game drives. We saw at least one on each night drive during my recent visit.

Hippos and crocs abound in the muddy Luangwa River, a tributary of the Zambezi which runs along much of the park's eastern boundary and then traverses the southern part of the park.

Over 400 species of birds have been recorded, including sacred ibises, saddle-billed storks, yellow-billed storks, Egyptian geese, spur-winged geese, fish eagles, crowned cranes and long-tailed starlings. The best time for bird watching is November-April.

A real advantage of this great park is that visitors can experience day and night game drives in open vehicles as well as participate in walking safaris ranging in length from a few hours to three or more days.

In the central eastern part of the park, we saw lion, a pack of 21 African wild dogs, civet, buffalo, wildebeest, common waterbuck, greater kudu, puku, impala, crocs, hippos mating and fighting, Thornicroft's giraffe, elephant, zebra, monitor lizard, warthog, and the everpresent baboons and vervet monkeys. Just before sunrise, elephants can sometimes be seen crossing the Luangwa River.

Driving from Mfuwe Airport to the north of the park, we sighted two African wild dogs, a spotted hyena, wildebeest, impala and warthog. As we were sipping whiskeys by the camp fire that night, we listened to baboon, hyena and hippo noises and watched honey badger (ratel) pass by within 20 feet of us.

## Night Game Drives

There is no better park in Africa for night game drives than South Luangwa. On my most recent visit, the night game drive started out slowly until we almost ran over a lion lying in the middle of the road. What a shock! He was a member of a pride of seven that was hunting in thick bush. We followed them for awhile until the driver was afraid that we might accidentally get caught in the middle of the hunt and become the hunted!

We then followed a leopard at close range (20 feet) which all but ignored our presence. We had quite a thrill when the leopard jumped high into a bush after two doves that must have been sleeping. Other sightings on the night game drives included spotted hyena, Pel's fishing owl, several more leopard and lion, and a number of genet and civet.

Wildlife seen on one week's safari to South Luangwa included baboon, buffalo, bushbuck, civet, eland, elephant, large-spotted genet, Thornicroft's giraffe, hippo, honey badger, spotted hyena, impala, greater kudu, four leopard, over 20 lion, puku, vervet monkeys, warthog, common waterbuck, African wild dog, gnu, Burchell's zebra, banded mongoose, white-tailed mongoose, crowned crane, African darter, fish eagle, goliath heron, marabou stork, sacred ibis, long-tailed glossy starling, brown snake eagle and many other birds.

There are few all-weather roads in the park north of Mfuwe, so most of the northern camps are closed from November 1-June 1. In May and early June the grass is still high. The northern part of the park is usually closed December through May.

Guests of most camps usually have a game drive or walk in the early morning, and in the afternoon, take either a day game drive departing about 3:30 p.m. and returning at dusk, or a late afternoon/night game drive, departing after 4:00 p.m. and returning around 8:00 p.m. Schedules will, of course, vary from camp to camp. Be sure to sign up for the option of your choice when checking in or as soon as possible thereafter.

## Walking Safaris

Walking safaris are the highlight of many visitors' trips to Africa and are certainly one of my favorite ways of experiencing the bush. For those who would enjoy walking three to seven miles per day at a reasonable pace and wish to experi-

The beginning of an afternoon walk from a bush camp in South Luangwa National Park.

ence nature up close, walking safaris are highly recommended.

Walking safaris are only conducted from June-October during the dry season when the foliage has thinned out enough for safe walking. Walks may last from a few hours to four or more days, depending on the camps visited. Guests are accompanied by a naturalist and an armed game scout from the national parks. Children under the age of 12 are not allowed on walks.

Most camps offer morning walks to their guests. Many camps have their own bush camps catering to a maximum of six or seven guests, set in remote regions of the park, in which walking is the main activity. However, bush camps are also excellent for those who do not want to do a lot of walking, but wish to simply relax and experience isolation in the bush.

Facilities in bush camps vary from comfortable chalets with ensuite facilities to simple huts with one shower and one long-drop toilet for the camp (see "Accommodations" below for details). From bush camps, groups of up to six or seven adults (depending on the camp) may participate in morning and afternoon walks.

Some camps offer programs where guests may walk from one bush camp to another. Your luggage is carried ahead to the next bush camp by vehicle or by porters who walk separately from the group. Guests usually carry only their cameras and a little water. The terrain is fairly flat, but often rugged. Food is prepared by a resident cook, and camps are stocked with cold drinks, wine and liquor. Huts are cleaned by the staff, and laundry service is available.

On the first morning of a recent four-day walking safari, we walked about two hours, and then our tea-bearer made hot tea. Our guide showed us how to make fire with a piece of wood, a stick and dried elephant dung. On the walk he did an excellent job answering our endless questions about spoor (footprints), animal droppings, flora and fauna of the bush.

After another one-and-one-half-hours' walk, we reached our first camp. Scenically situated on the banks of the Luangwa River, there were more than 40 hippo in the water below and numerous crocs on the far shore.

After much-welcomed cold drinks, lunch, and a short siesta, we regrouped at 3:30 p.m. for tea. At 4:00 p.m. we set off for another walk and returned just before dark (about 5:45 p.m.). After everyone had a hot shower, dinner was served. Then we sat around the campfire, listening to the mysterious sounds of the night and gazing up at millions of stars.

Hippo, lion, hyena and elephant often came into camp at night. So, it's not a good idea to leave your hut after everyone has gone to bed.

One night we were awakened by an elephant silhouetted in the moonlight and standing next to our hut. One of the group took a flash photo and spooked it, and it ran out of camp. But I would have loved to have watched it longer, to have more fully experienced this encounter with the wildlife that is Africa.

On an afternoon walking through an area with high golden grass, I commented to our guide that a lion could be 20 feet from the path and we might not see it. Just as the guide agreed with me, we turned around and there was a large female lion on the path not 50 feet behind us. Once the lion knew we were all aware of her presence, she ran off. That was our first lion sighting!

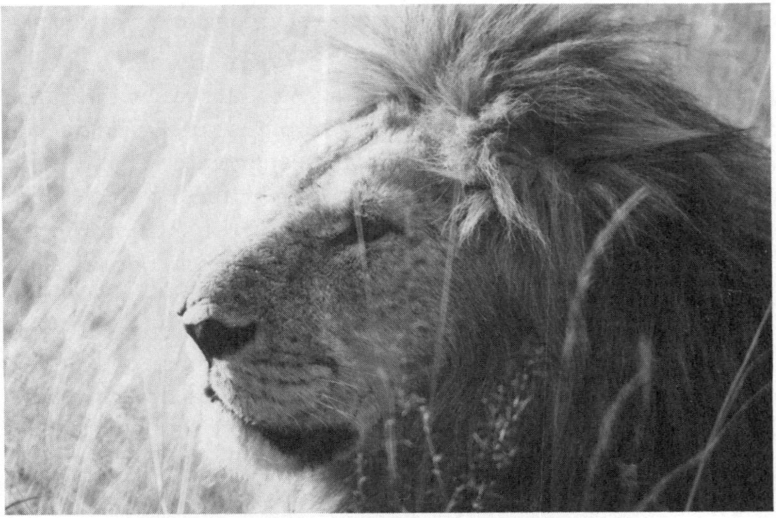

Lion are sometimes encountered on walking safaris.

The following morning we walked to our next bush camp, then had another walk in the afternoon. Two days later we returned to main camp, having seen numerous herds of impala, Burchell's zebra, puku, elephant and buffalo, along with Thornicroft's giraffe, baboons and lion. Most importantly, we felt a sense of accomplishment from experiencing the bush on more intimate terms in the way that Livingstone, Stanley and other early African explorers confronted the challenge of the continent — on foot!

I suggest that you stay at least one or two additional nights in the park to go on day and night game drives by open vehicle; this will give you the opportunity to see many species that you might have not seen on your walking safari.

Mfuwe Airport is about an hour flight from Lusaka. South Luangwa's main gate is 433 miles from Lusaka; driving takes about ten hours and is not recommended. Some international visitors fly into Lilongwe, Malawi, and are transferred by road to Mfuwe via Chipata.

ACCOMMODATION: Bush camps are listed under main camps with which they are associated.

ACCOMMODATION IN CENTRAL SOUTH LUANGWA (Open Year-Round) - CLASS A: * *Kapani Safari Lodge* is operated by Norman Carr—the man who introduced walking safaris to Zambia. This exclusive camp has four large double chalets (16 beds) with ensuite facilities, private veranda and refrigerator, a large swimming pool, and a library/video room where you can watch wildlife videos or even plug in your video recorder and view the footage shot during your safari. The cuisine is superb. Kapani is a 45-minute drive from Mfuwe airport and offers day and night game drives, walks, and visits to traditional villages and a crocodile farm.

Kapani also operates two bush camps: Nsolo Camp and Luwi Camp. Escorted walks may be taken from both camps, and guests may walk from Luwi Camp to Nsolo Camp. A sample five-night program could include two nights at Kapani, one at Luwi Camp, walk to Nsolo Camp and stay for two nights.

* *Nsolo Camp* (CLASS A/B) is situated near a permanent water hole in an isolated region of the park about a 90-minute drive from Mfuwe Airport. A maximum of six guests are accommodated in four comfortable cottages with ensuite facilities. Walking safaris are the prime activity; game viewing from a hide overlooking a water hole, and day and night game drives are also offered.

* *Luwi Camp,* (CLASS B/C), located a comfortable morning's walk upstream from Nsolo Camp, has four bamboo huts accommodating a maximum of six guests, with a shared hot shower and flush toilet facilities. A large hippo pool is located nearby. Walking safaris are offered.

CLASS A/B: * *Chinzombo Safari Lodge* is located on the eastern bank of the Luangwa River across from the park. The camp has nine rondavels (18 beds) with ensuite facilities and swimming pool. Day and night game drives, morning walks, and visits to local villages are offered. Chinzombo has a bush camp: * *Kuyenda Camp* (CLASS B/C) has reed and grass huts (six beds). Walks and game drives are offered.

CLASS B: * *Nkwali Camp,* situated just outside the park and open ten months of the year, has six chalets (12 beds) and offers day and night game drives and walks.

CLASS C: * *Mfuwe Lodge* is set on a picturesque lagoon and has rooms with ensuite facilities and swimming pool, and offers day and night game drives. * *Chichele Lodge,* set high on a hill overlooking the Luangwa River, has rooms with ensuite facilities (most with air-conditioning). Day and night game drives and morning walks are offered.

ACCOMMODATION IN NORTHERN SOUTH LUANGWA (Usually open June-October/November) - CLASS A: * *Tena Tena,* the only tented camp in South Luangwa, is located on the banks of the Luangwa River inside the park. Accommodations consist of six large tents (12 beds), each under a thatched roof, with ensuite facilities.

CLASS B: * *Nsefu Camp* is located near the Luangwa River one- to one-and-one-half-hours' drive from Mfuwe Airport and has six attractive brick and thatch rondavels (12 beds) with private facilities. Day and night game drives and morning walks are offered.

CLASS B/C: * *Chibembe Lodge,* located just outside the park on the banks of the Luangwa River, has rustic chalets with private facilities (40 beds) and swimming pool. Day and night game drives, morning walks, and four-day walking safaris using rustic bush camps (CLASS D) are offered.

CAMPING: Camping is not allowed in the park except with a licensed tour operator.

## NORTH LUANGWA NATIONAL PARK

As the name implies, this largely undeveloped 1790-square-mile park lies north of South Luangwa National Park in the upper Luangwa Valley.

Mark and Delia Owens, coauthors of *Cry of the Kalahari*, are conducting wildlife research here, and are working to reduce poaching and create an infrastructure to attract tourists.

The park lies between the 4600-foot-high Muchinga Escarpment on the west and the Luangwa River on the east, with altitudes ranging from 1640-3610 feet. Vegetation includes miombo woodland, scrubland and riverine forest.

Wildlife includes lion, leopard, elephant, buffalo, zebra, eland, kudu, Cookson's wildebeest, impala, bushbuck, hippo and crocodile. Nearly 400 species of birds have been recorded, including bee-eaters, ibises, storks and waterfowl.

Walking is allowed in this seldom-visited park. You will virtually have the park to yourself. In fact, it is doubtful you will encounter any other groups on your visit.

The rainy season is November-April. The best time to visit is July-October.

ACCOMMODATION: None. Mobile tented safaris are available.

CAMPING: Campsites are available.

## LUAMBE NATIONAL PARK

This undeveloped, 98-square-mile savannah and woodlands park is located just northeast of South Luangwa National Park. Luambe has many of the same species and features of South Luangwa National Park, but lacks first-class tourist facilities to accommodate visitors.

ACCOMMODATION: Self-service bandas are available.

CAMPING: Camping sites are available.

## NYIKA PLATEAU NATIONAL PARK

Located in northeast Zambia on the border with Malawi, this 31-square-mile park includes the small Zambian portion of the Nyika Plateau. This is a good park to visit for a keen naturalist or anyone wishing to escape the summer heat of the valleys below. Due to the high altitude, night temperatures sometimes drop below freezing May-September.

Montane grassland and relic montane forest dominate the scene. A great variety of orchid and butterfly species are present along with Moloney's monkey, blue monkey, civet and a number of other small mammals. Leopard, serval, bushbuck, reedbuck, blue duiker and klipspringer are present but rarely seen. Several species of birds not found elsewhere in Zambia may be seen. The best time for bird watching is November-June.

ACCOMMODATION - CLASS D/F: A self-service lodge is available.

## SUMBU NATIONAL PARK

Sumbu National Park borders the huge inland sea of Lake Tanganyika in the extreme north of Zambia. Visitors come to this 780-square-mile park mainly for fishing and water sports. This part of Lake Tanganyika is reputedly bilharzia-free, but be sure to check for its current status.

Forest and wetland wildlife species are plentiful. In fact, visitors are often accompanied to the sandy beaches by wildlife guards. Elephant, lion, buffalo, eland, puku, roan antelope, blue duiker and Sharpe's grysbok may be seen. The shoreline is inhabited by hippo, crocodiles and water birds. Savannah dominates the park inland.

Day and night game drives in open vehicles, guided walks, and day and night game viewing by boat for crocodiles are available.

Fishing for goliath tigerfish, vundu (giant catfish), lake

salmon and Nile perch in Lake Tanganyika is excellent, especially November-March. The Zambia National Fishing Competition at Kasaba Bay is held every March or April, depending on the water level. Boats are available for hire.

ACCOMMODATION - CLASS C: * *Kasaba Bay Lodge* has 18 chalets (doubles) with private facilities and swimming pool, located a few hundred yards from the beach. The lodge offers fishing, game viewing and boating. * *Ndole Bay Lodge,* located just outside the park, has chalets (18 beds) with facilities ensuite; game viewing, fishing and boating are available. * *Nkamba Bay Lodge,* 15 miles from Kasaba Bay in the park on a hill overlooking the beach, has ten chalets (doubles) with ensuite facilities. Activities include fishing, boating and game viewing.

## THE SOUTH AND WEST

### LUSAKA

Lusaka, the capital of Zambia, has little to offer the international tourist. Sights include the Luburma Market, the Munda Wanga Botanical Gardens and Zoological Park with over 400 different species of plants and a small zoo, and Chief Mungule's Village. Wood carvings made by local craftsmen can be seen at Kabwata Cultural Center.

There is a duty-free shop in town that only takes foreign currency; this shop has liquor and other items you may be unable to find in other stores, since shopping is limited. The airport is 16 miles from the city.

ACCOMMODATION - DELUXE: * *Pamodzi Hotel,* a 480-bed, air-conditioned hotel with facilities ensuite, swimming pool, and casino. * *Lusaka Inter-Continental Hotel* is an air-conditioned hotel with 402 rooms with facilities ensuite, 24-hour room service, three restaurants, casino, and swimming pool.

FIRST CLASS: * *Ridgeway Hotel,* an air-conditioned, 215-bed hotel with facilities ensuite, casino and swimming pool.

TOURIST CLASS: * The *Andrews Motel* is a 250-bed, air-conditioned motel with swimming pool.

## LOCHINVAR NATIONAL PARK

Lochinvar is a bird watcher's paradise with over 400 species recorded. In addition, the park is host to about 30,000 Kafue lechwe (their stronghold), 2000 blue wildebeest, and 700 zebra. Greater kudu, bushbuck, oribi, hippo, side-striped jackal, reedbuck, and common waterbuck are also present.

Kafue lechwe are unique to the Kafue Flats and are related to the red lechwe of the Busanga Swamps of Kafue National Park.

Bird watching is good year-round and is best November-May. Water birds such as the wattled crane are especially abundant. Other bird species include fish eagles. The park also encompasses part of Chunga Lake, which is fished by villagers living outside the park boundaries.

The park is open year-round and is located 145 miles southwest of Lusaka, 30 miles northwest of Monze off the Lusaka-Livingstone road. A four-wheel-drive vehicle may be necessary in the rainy season.

ACCOMMODATION - CLASS C: * *Lochinvar Lodge* has rooms with ensuite facilities.

## KAFUE NATIONAL PARK

Kafue National Park is one of the largest in Africa, covering 8650 square miles, making it two and one-half times the size of South Luangwa National Park and half the size of Switzerland.

Kafue has the largest number of different antelope species of any park in Africa. However, game is more difficult

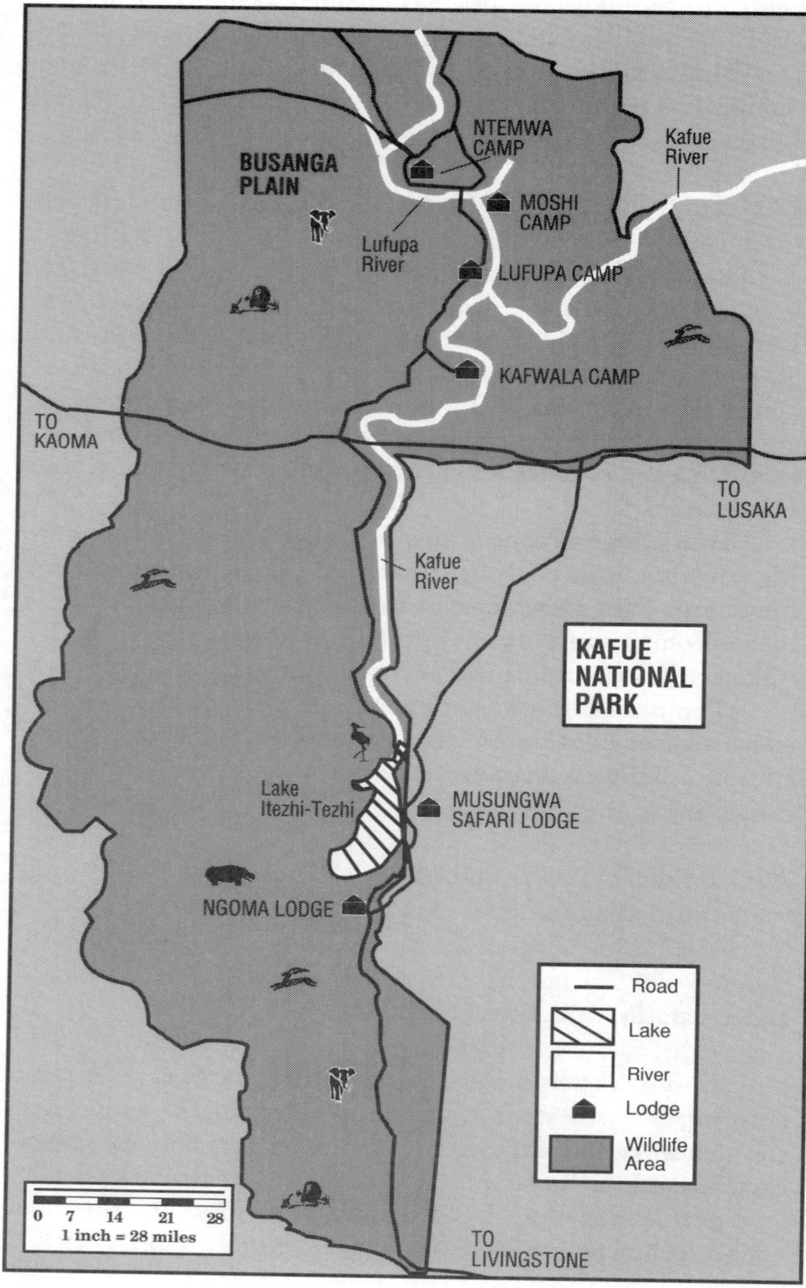
KAFUE NATIONAL PARK
BUSANGA PLAIN
NTEMWA CAMP
Kafue River
MOSHI CAMP
Lufupa River
LUFUPA CAMP
KAFWALA CAMP
TO KAOMA
TO LUSAKA
Kafue River
Lake Itezhi-Tezhi
MUSUNGWA SAFARI LODGE
NGOMA LODGE
Road
Lake
River
Lodge
Wildlife Area
0 7 14 21 28
1 inch = 28 miles
TO LIVINGSTONE

to see here than in South Luangwa, since much of Kafue, especially the southern area, is clothed with a double-canopy forest. It is seldom visited by international travelers.

The southern and central parts are open all year while the northern area is only open during the dry season, June-October/November. Game is especially difficult to spot in the rainy season.

Game drives in this park are sometimes a combination of riding in a vehicle and walking, according to the wishes of the group.

On daylight game drives in the south of the park, we found elephant, impala, warthog, hippo, sable antelope, Burchell's zebra, wildebeest and buffalo. Night game drives produced sightings of impala, oribi, hundreds of spring hares, greater kudu, buffalo, serval, bushbuck, duiker, spotted hyena, Burchell's zebra, elephant, Defassa waterbuck and bushbabies.

Lake Itezhi-Tezhi, formed as the result of a hydroelectric dam constructed at the southern end of the Kafue Flats, provides fishing, bird watching and boating opportunities for visitors.

The Busanga Plains and marshes in the north have a greater number and variety of wildlife species. Wildlife is easier to spot here than in the dense woodland savannah in the south. This region is characterized by mopane and miombo forests, rock hills, open plains, marshes and riverine forests. The Kafue River runs through the northern part of the park and along its east central border.

Large herds of rare red lechwe may be seen on the Busanga Plains. Sitatunga may be found in the Busanga Swamps on the northern border of the park. Buffalo, elephant, puku, wildebeest, impala, roan antelope, sable antelope, kudu, waterbuck, leopard, lion, hyena and cheetah are also present. The Kafue Flats are an excellent location to spot many of the park's more than 400 recorded species of birds.

There is little to be seen on the four-hour, 170-mile drive from Lusaka, so those with limited time may wish to charter a plane.

ACCOMMODATION IN SOUTHERN KAFUE (Open Year-Round) - CLASS B: * *Hippo Camp* is a small camp (eight beds) with a two-story pontoon boat used for day trips. * *Musungwa Safari Lodge* (46 beds) is located just outside the eastern boundary of the park. The lodge has a swimming pool, and most rooms have private facilities. Sunset cruises, river trips, and game drives are offered.

CLASS C: * *Ngoma Lodge* has a swimming pool and airstrip. Each two rooms share facilities.

ACCOMMODATION IN NORTHERN KAFUE (Open June-October/November) - CLASS C: The following four camps specialize in walk-ride safaris and offer night game drives. Most chalets have private showers and toilets. * *Moshi Camp* ia situated on a hill. * *Ntemwa Camp* is the most northern riverside camp on the Lufupa River and is also the most comfortable (six beds). * *Kafwala Camp* overlooks the Kafwala Rapids. * *Lufupa*, situated in the center of the northern region near the confluence of the Kafue and Lufupa Rivers, also offers good fishing and game viewing by boat.

## LIUWA PLAIN NATIONAL PARK

Located in southwestern Zambia, this remote 1400-square-mile park of open plains contains large numbers of wildebeest along with lion, hyena, and spectacular numbers of migrating birds.

Wildlife, however, should be considered a plus and not the main reason for traveling to this seldom-visited park, which is more suited for bird watchers and for those looking to travel in a remote wilderness area and to meet Africans who have had little contact with tourists.

ACCOMMODATION: None. Mobile tented safaris are available.

## SIOMA FALLS

Sioma Falls, located a six-hour drive and 185 miles upstream (northwest) of Victoria Falls, is a magnificent series of nine horseshoe-shaped falls stretching across the one-and-one-half-mile-wide Zambezi River. The best time to visit is July-January.

ACCOMMODATION: None. Mobile tented safaris are available.

## MOSI-OA-TUNYA (VICTORIA FALLS) NATIONAL PARK

Called Mosi-oa-Tunya (the smoke that thunders), Victoria Falls should not be missed. Visitors may walk along the Knife Edge Bridge for a good view of the Eastern Cataract and Boiling Pot.

A "Sunset Cruise" is a very pleasant experience; hippo and crocodiles are often seen. Fishing for tigerfish on the Zambezi River is best from June-October (September is best) before the rains muddy the water.

The falls are located about three miles from Livingstone. See the chapter on Zimbabwe for a detailed description of the falls.

### White-Water Rafting

The Zambezi River below Victoria Falls is one of the most exciting white-water rafting experiences in the world. Numerous fifth-class rapids (the highest class runable) make this one of the most challenging rivers on earth. One-, two-, three- and seven-day trips are operated on the Zambezi River below Victoria Falls from the Zambia and/or Zimbabwe side of the Zambezi River. No experience is required; just hang on and enjoy the ride!

The one-day trip is rated as the wildest commercially

run one-day trip in the world. Rafts with up to eight riders and one oarperson disappear from sight as they drop into deep holes and crash into waves over 12 feet high, being further dwarfed by sheer cliffs which often rise hundreds of feet on both sides of the canyon.

Hippo and crocs are more frequently seen further downstream on multiday trips. Klipspringer and other wildlife can be seen on the banks, especially during the dry season.

Camp is made on sandy river banks, and all meals are prepared by the staff. These multiday trips are not for those who wish to be pampered. There are no facilities en route. One-day trips are operated March, April, and mid-June-December, and the longer trips from July-December only.

For the one-day trip, I would suggest you wear a swimsuit and take a hat and sunglasses with something to tie them onto yourself, short-sleeved shirt, sunscreen, tennis shoes (tackies) or Tevas (a type of sandal), polypropylene undershirt and fast-drying nylon shorts. During Winter (June-August) also bring wetsuit booties, heavy polypropylene underwear, a wool sweater and rainsuit. For the longer trips, get a checklist from your tour operator.

Plans are underway to build a dam to relieve some pressure off the Kariba Dam downstream. Such a dam would flood the gorge and make these river trips a thing of the past. Go now while there are still rapids to run!

ACCOMMODATION - FIRST CLASS: * *Mosi-Oa-Tunya Inter-Continental Hotel*, a 200-bed hotel with air-conditioning, swimming pool and three restaurants, is a five-minute walk from Victoria Falls.

CLASS A/B: * *Tongabezi Camp*, situated on the Zambezi River 15 miles upstream from Victoria Falls, is an exclusive 14-bed camp with large tents with private facilities, a honeymoon house, and swimming pool hewn out of rock. Canoeing, game viewing by boat and overnight tented safaris on islands in the Zambezi River are offered.

TOURIST CLASS: * *Rainbow Lodge*, in Mosi-oa-Tunya National Park, has traditionally styled rondavels and rooms with air-conditioning (104 beds) and ensuite facilities. * The *New Fairmount Hotel* is a small hotel with air-conditioned rooms (168 beds) with private facilities, swimming pool and casino.

## LIVINGSTONE

Livingstone is a small town of about 80,000 inhabitants, five miles from Victoria Falls. Driving from Lusaka takes five to six hours (295 miles) and flying takes a little over an hour.

The Livingstone Museum is the National Museum of Zambia and is renowned for its collection of Dr. Livingstone's memoirs. Other exhibits cover the art and culture of Zambia. The Maramba Cultural Center exhibits bandas from various districts in Zambia and presents colorful costumed performances by Zambian dancers. The Railway Museum has steam engines and trains from the late 1800s and 1900s.

**Livingstone Zoological Park** is a small fenced park near Livingstone covering 25 square miles. It is stocked with greater kudu, white rhino, impala, and other wildlife. The best time to visit is from June-October.

ACCOMMODTION: See Mosi-oa-Tunya (Victoria Falls) National Park.

## LAKE KARIBA

Lake Kariba is one of the largest man-made lakes in the world — 180 miles long and up to 20 miles wide (see "Lake Kariba" in the Zimbabwe chapter for full details). The Zimbabwe (southern) side of the lake is more developed than the Zambia (northern) side of the lake. Canoe safaris are offered downstream of Kariba Dam.

## SIAVONGA

Siavonga is a small village situated on Lake Kariba just west of Lake Kariba Dam.

ACCOMMODATION - TOURIST CLASS: * *Mauchinchi Bay Lodge* is a 60-bed lodge with swimming pool. Boating and fishing are offered.

## LOWER ZAMBEZI NATIONAL PARK

Located along the Zambezi River across from Mana Pools National Park (Zimbabwe), the Lower Zambezi National Park extends approximately 20 miles inland between the Chongwe River on the west and the Musensensai River mouth, 55 miles downstream.

Wildlife is relatively sparse with the main attraction being canoe safaris on the Zambezi River. Walks are also offered.

ACCOMMODATION - CLASS B: * *Chongwe Camp* is a tented camp (16 beds) with tents under thatch and facilities ensuite, situated on the banks of the Luangwa River. * *Chifungulu Island Camp* has tents with private facilities. * *Masungu Camp* has tents with facilities ensuite.

# ZIMBABWE

## THE ENDANGERED BLACK RHINO

This poor-sighted, bad-tempered mammal has been under intense poaching in the last few years due to the high price its hair-like horn fetches in the Yemen and Far East markets. The horn is used for dagger handles, which are a sign of wealth in the Yemen, and for medicinal purposes in the Far East. To encourage its conservation, various policies have evolved besides ending the demand.

A program to dehorn the rhinos has begun in some reserves, which should deter any poaching, as the value of the rhino is in its horn. This, however, could affect the rhinos' behavior as they use their horns for defense. Studies of dehorned rhinos are being conducted in Hwange National Park.

National Parks have also employed antipoaching teams who patrol the parks, giving protection to the rhino and arresting suspected poachers within the park. As rhinos are creatures of habit, returning to the same drinking holes every day, they can be found very easily by poachers.

So as not to be detected, black rhino may visit their drinking holes at night. This pattern of drinking at night can interfere with their much-loved midday mud-wallow, where they will lie down in the mud to cool off.

The relocation of the black rhino into private game reserves involves tracking the animals for a distance and darting them with a sedative drug. Rhinos usually have the noisy red- or yellow-billed oxpecker acting as their sentry, warning them of human approach and will run off, which makes it difficult for the darter to get close enough to shoot. Once under sedation, they will be moved to their new homes.

The black rhino is exciting to track and generally may be found on a morning's walk in certain reserves. Since the rhino has no natural enemy, there is no reason he should not survive.

# ZIMBABWE

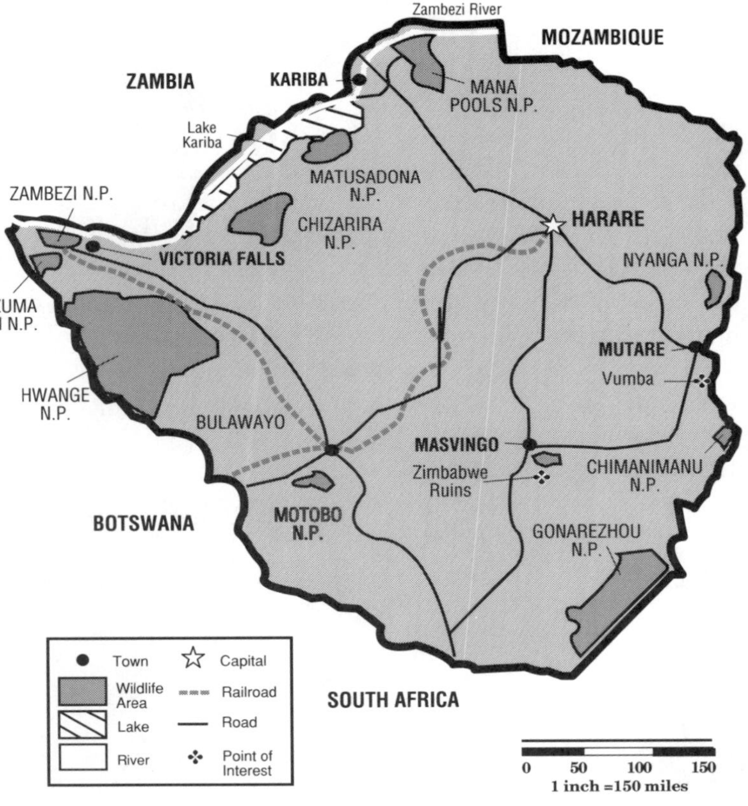


FACTS AT A GLANCE

| | |
|---|---|
| AREA: | 151,000 SQUARE MILES |
| APPROXIMATE SIZE: | CALIFORNIA OR ONE AND A HALF TIMES THE SIZE OF GREAT BRITAIN |
| POPULATION: | 9 MILLION (1992 EST.) |
| CAPITAL: | HARARE (POP. EST. 800,000) |
| OFFICIAL LANGUAGE: | OFFICIAL: ENGLISH<br>OTHER: SHONA AND SINDEBELE |

# ZIMBABWE

Thought by some to be the land of King Solomon's mines, Zimbabwe (previously called Rhodesia) is a country blessed with good farmland, mineral wealth, beautiful and varied landscapes, and excellent game parks.

Most of Zimbabwe consists of a central plateau 3000-4000 feet above sea level. The highveld, or high plateau, stretches from southwest to northeast from 4000-5000 feet with a mountainous region along the eastern border from 6000-8000 feet in altitude.

The Zambezi River runs along the northeastern border, and the Limpopo River along the southern border. The Zambezi Valley is an extension of the Great Rift Valley. The southern edge of the Zambezi Valley is formed by the Zimbabwean escarpment. The Zambian escarpment, situated north of the Zambezi River, forms the northern edge of the Zambezi valley.

The climate is moderate and seasons are reversed from the northern hemisphere. Winter days (May-August) are generally dry and sunny with day temperatures averaging 59-68° F. Summer daytime temperatures average 77-86° F. with October being the hottest month. The rainy season is November-March.

The major ethnic groups are the Mashona and Ndebele. About 50 percent of the population is syncretic (part Christian and part traditional beliefs), 25 percent Christian, 24 percent traditional, and one percent Hindu and Muslim. English is understood by about half of the population.

In the first century, the region was inhabited by hunters related to the Bushmen. Cecil Rhodes and the British South Africa Company took control in 1890, and the area was named Southern Rhodesia, which became a British Colony in 1923. Unilateral Declaration of Independence (UDI) from Britain was declared by Prime Minister Ian Smith and the white minority on November 11, 1965. Officially Zimbabwe became independent on April 18, 1980.

Zimbabwe has one of the most widely diversified economies in Africa, consisting of industry, mining and agriculture (in which they are self-sufficient). Main foreign exchange earners are tobacco, minerals, agriculture and tourism.

## WILDLIFE AND WILDLIFE AREAS

Adventurers wishing to do more than view wildlife from a vehicle should seriously consider a safari in this country. Zimbabwe offers the greatest variety of methods of wildlife viewing in Africa, including day and night game drives in open vehicles, boat game drives, walking, canoeing, kayaking, white-water rafting and travel by houseboat.

Zimbabwe has excellent and well-maintained parks and reserves. The country's three premier reserves, which also rate as three of the best reserves in Africa, are Hwange, Mana Pools and Matusadona National Parks.

Hwange National Park is famous for its huge elephant population (over 25,000) and numerous large pans. Matusadona National Park, located along the southern shores of beautiful Lake Kariba, has an enormous buffalo population and the country's largest concentration of black rhino. Mana Pools on the Zambezi River has one of the highest concentrations of wildlife of any park on the continent during the dry season.

Many of the safari camps are able to offer very personalized service because they cater to only six to 16 guests. Accommodations and food are excellent.

Instead of driving to the reserves, many people fly to the parks, taking advantage of Air Zimbabwe's daily flights connecting Kariba, Victoria Falls, Hwange, Bulawayo, Masvingo and Buffalo Range. There are also a number of overland safaris available.

Game viewing is by open landrover, and walking is allowed with a licensed guide. Night game drives are conducted in some areas adjacent to the reserves.

# THE WEST

## VICTORIA FALLS NATIONAL PARK

Dr. David Livingstone became the first white man to see Victoria Falls on November 16, 1855, and named them after his queen. In his journal he wrote, "On sights as beautiful as this, Angels in their flight must have gazed."

Victoria Falls is approximately 5600 feet wide, twice the height of Niagara Falls, and one and one-half times as wide. It is divided into five separate waterfalls: Devil's Cataract, Main Falls, Horseshoe Falls, Rainbow Falls and Eastern Cataract, ranging in height from 200-355 feet.

Peak flood waters usually occur around mid-April when 150 million gallons per minute crash onto the rocks below, spraying water up to 1650 feet in the air. At this time (March-April) so much water is falling that the spray makes it difficult to see the falls. May-February is actually a better time to see them, keeping in mind that they are spectacular any time of the year.

Victoria Falls and the Zambezi River form the border between Zambia and Zimbabwe. The banks of the 1675-mile-long Zambezi River, the only major river in Africa to flow into the Indian Ocean, are lined with thick riverine forest. Daytime and sundowner cruises operate above the falls where hippo and crocs may be spotted and elephant and other wildlife may be seen coming to the shore to drink.

Fortunately the area around the falls has not been

commercialized, and there are unobstructed views from many vantage points connected by paved paths. Be prepared to get wet as you walk through a luxuriant rain forest surrounding the falls, a result of the continuous spray. A path called the Chain Walk descends from near Livingstone's statue into the gorge of the Devil's Cataract, providing an excellent vantage point.

**Spencer's Creek Crocodile Ranch** has specimens up to 14 feet in length and weighing close to 1000 pounds. The **Craft Village** in the middle of town is very interesting with living quarters and other structures representing traditional Zimbabwean life of the country's major tribes. **Big Tree** is a giant baobab over 50 feet in circumference, 65 feet high and 1000-1500 years old. The **African Spectacular**, presented every night at the Victoria Falls Hotel, features tribal dancing at its finest.

The **"Flight of Angels,"** a flight over the falls in a small plane, is highly recommended to acquire a feeling for the true majesty of the falls. Game-viewing flights upstream from the falls along the Zambezi River and over Victoria Falls National Park are also available. It is best to reserve seats in advance.

The falls can also be viewed from Zambia. Zambian visas for day visits are available at the border for most nationalities, but in case of change, it is better to obtain a visa in advance.

Generally speaking, the falls are more impressive and the accommodations and tourism infrastructure are better on the Zimbabwean side.

The Zambezi River offers one of the most exciting (if not the most exciting) **white-water rafting** trips in the world. Rafting trips are available July-late December/January (depending on the water level of the river) in the gorges below Victoria Falls from both the Zimbabwean and Zambian sides of the river. The Zambezi River is rated fifth class (the highest class runable). Around 9:00 a.m. rafters take a short walk down to the river's edge where the rafting safari begins. For many travelers, it is a highlight of their safari (see chapter on Zambia for details). Rafters must be 16 years of age or older to participate.

"Flight of the Angels" over Victoria Falls.

**Kayaking Safaris** (white-water canoeing) are a great way to explore the upper Zambezi from near Kazungula to just above Victoria Falls; these safaris are offered June-October. Adventurers pass numerous hippo, crocs and other wildlife as they paddle two-man expedition kayaks on a three-day/two-night safari.

No previous kayaking experience is necessary. However, the tricky part is that two of the most difficult rapids are the second and third rapids encountered, which doesn't allow much time for training! Most kayaks (including ours) flip once — an experience in itself!

A crew traveling in a landrover sets up camp ahead of the group. Participants sleep under the stars (beware of lions). There are no shower or toilet facilities at the camps. Under special arrangement, safari companies can arrange a more deluxe tented program with shower and toilet tents.

ACCOMMODATION - DELUXE: * *Elephant Hills*, the newest and most prestigious hotel in the area, overlooks the Zambezi River about a mile upstream from Victoria Falls. The hotel has 270 rooms and suites with facilities ensuite, exotic swimming pool, squash courts, tennis courts, 18-hole championship golf course, casino, three restaurants and a conference center. * *Victoria Falls Hotel* has maintained much of its colonial elegance with its colonial architecture, spacious terraces and colorful gardens. The hotel has 138 air-conditioned rooms and suites with private facilities, swimming pool, tennis courts, and conference facilities, and is only a ten-minute walk from the falls. * *Ilala Lodge* is a small 15-room (30 beds) thatched lodge with ensuite facilities located close to the falls, with swimming pool and popular restaurant.

FIRST CLASS: * *Makasa Sun Hotel* is a modern hotel situated adjacent to the Victoria Falls Hotel with 97 air-conditioned rooms and suites with ensuite facilities, casino, swimming pool and tennis courts.

TOURIST CLASS: * *Rainbow Hotel* is located near Victoria Falls Village and has 48 air-conditioned rooms with private facilities and swimming pool. * The *A'Zambezi River Lodge*, one of the largest buildings under traditional thatch on the continent, is located one and one-half miles from town on the banks of the Zambezi River. The lodge has a swimming pool and 83 air-conditioned rooms. * *Sprayview Hotel* is a budget hotel a little more than a mile from the Falls.

CLASS F & CAMPING: * *Victoria Falls Rest And Caravan Park* has small hostel, camping and caravan sites.

ACCOMMODATION NEAR VICTORIA FALLS - CLASS A: * *Westwood Camp* is a 45-minute drive from Victoria Falls and is situated on a 120,000-acre private concession bordering the Zambezi National Park. Westwood caters to a maximum of eight guests in thatch and stone chalets (doubles) with private facilities situated on the banks of the Zambezi. Day and night game drives, walking, kayaking, boating and fishing are offered. * *Imbabala Camp,* located on private land on the banks of the Zambezi River only a mile from the Botswana border, has nine chalets (doubles) with private facilities and swimming pool. Day and night game drives by vehicle, boat game drives and fishing are offered.

CLASS B: * *Masuwe Lodge* is a tented lodge located five miles from Victoria Falls on a private game concession. Activities include game drives into Zambezi National Park, along with night drives and walks on the concession land.

CLASS D: See "Zambezi National Park."

## ZAMBEZI NATIONAL PARK

Victoria Falls National Park includes Victoria Falls as well as 215-square-mile Zambezi National Park. The park is located west of the falls and extends for 25 miles along the Zambezi River.

Zambezi National Park is well known for its abundance of sable antelope. Among other species are white rhino, black rhino, elephant, zebra, eland, buffalo, giraffe, lion, kudu, and waterbuck.

Day safaris are offered from Victoria Falls. Fishing is very good for tigerfish, tilapia, and giant vundu (giant catfish). There are 30 sites along the river for picnicking and fishing (beware of crocodiles). Since the game reserve does not have all-weather roads, parts of it are usually closed during the rains from November 1-May 1.

ACCOMMODATION - CLASS D: * *Zambezi National Park Lodges,* scenically situated on the banks of the Zambezi, consist of 15 self-service lodges, each catering to a maximum of six people.

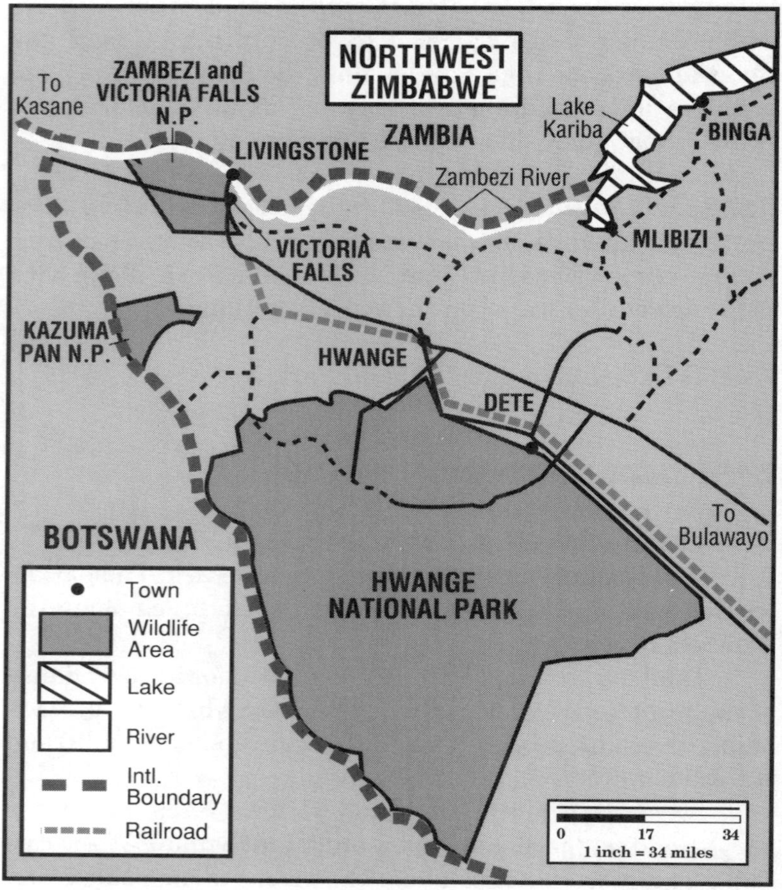


## KAZUMA PAN NATIONAL PARK

Located north of Hwange National Park in the Matetsi Safari Area, Kazuma Pan National Park is a small park that has a series of pans that flood in the rainy season. The eastern part of the park is wooded with more water and a greater variety and concentration of wildlife than the western side of the park, which is predominantly grasslands. Lion, cheetah and rhino are often seen. The park is open to campers who are self-contained. Walking is allowed with a licensed guide. There are no facilities.

# HWANGE NATIONAL PARK

Hwange (previously called Wankie) is Zimbabwe's largest national park and famous for its large herds of elephant. Other predominant species include buffalo, giraffe, zebra, wildebeest, sable antelope, white and black rhino, cheetah, wild dog, and bat-eared fox. This is also one of the best parks on the continent to see sable antelope.

Hwange is slightly larger than the state of Connecticut, covering 5600 square miles. The park is located in the northwest corner of the country just south of the main road between Bulawayo and Victoria Falls. Hwange boasts over 100 species of mammals and 400 species of birds.

The park ranges from semidesert in the south to a plateau in the north. The northern part of Hwange is mudstone and basalt, and the southern part is Kalahari sand veld. The park has an average altitude of 3300 feet. Winter nights can drop to below freezing, and summer days can be over 100° F., while average temperatures range from 65-83° F.

There are no rivers and only a few streams in the north of the park, but boreholes (wells) provide sources of water year-round for wildlife. During the dry season, these permanent water holes (pans) provide an excellent stage for guests to view wildlife performing day-to-day scenes of survival.

Generally, there are no seasonal animal migrations. The best time to see wildlife is during the dry season from July-October when the game concentrate near permanent water. Game viewing is good June and November, fair in April, May and December, and poor during the rainy season from December-March when the game is widely dispersed.

Game viewing is usually very good within ten miles of Main Camp and Park Headquarters. Wildlife commonly seen nearby include elephant, giraffe, zebra, greater kudu, impala, buffalo, sable antelope, wildebeest, tsessebe, black-backed jackal, lion, hyena, and cheetah. Rhino may also be seen. We saw a very large male lion with a full mane guarding a buffalo kill while a jackal darted in and out, snatching morsels as dozens of vultures waited their turn.

Moonlight game viewing occurs from one or two nights

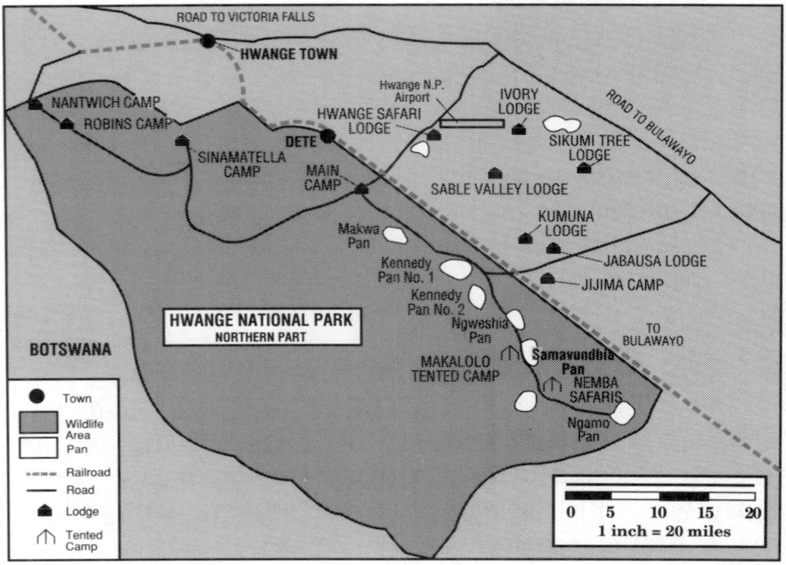


before and after a full moon when park staff escort guests to the Nyamandhlovu (meaning "meat of the elephant") Platform near main camp. Morning walks with a national park game scout are also available.

The area around Sinamatella Camp in the northern part of the park is good for spotting kudu, elephant, giraffe, impala, hippo, klipspringer, warthog, lion, hyena, and leopard. The Bumbusi Ruins, the third largest ancient stone buildings in Zimbabwe, are located behind Bumbusi Camp, 15 miles northwest of Sinamatella Camp.

The northwestern part of the park near Robins Camp is known for its large lion population. Other species often seen include impala (which attract the lion), buffalo, kudu, sable antelope, roan antelope, waterbuck, elephant, giraffe, reedbuck, tsessebe, lion, side-striped jackal, cheetah, and hyena.

Hwange has 300 miles of roads, some of which are closed during the rainy season. All-weather roads run through most of the park. Some roads near the main camp are tarmac, which detracts a bit from the feeling of being in the bush.

Elephant in camp, the resident guide reassures a guest.

Vehicles must keep to the roads and visitors are not allowed to leave their vehicles unless escorted by a licensed professional guide, or at the hides, game-viewing platforms and at fenced-in picnic sites. Open vehicles are allowed.

An airstrip is available for small aircraft at Main Camp. The closest rail station is Dete Station, 15 miles from Main Camp.

ACCOMMODATIONS: Sable Valley Lodge, Sikumi Tree Lodge, Kanondo Tree Camp, Ivory Lodge and Hwange Safari Lodge are all located in 60,000-acre Dete Vlei (private reserve) bordering Hwange National Park, a 15-30-minute drive from Hwange Airport; guests of these camps enter the park through the main gate. Jabulisa Lodge, Jijima Camp and Kumuna Lodge are located on private reserves; guests enter the park through Kennedy Pan. Makalolo Tented Camp and Nemba Safaris are located in an exclusive area deep within the park, about a two-and-one-half-hour "game drive" from the airport. Only guests of these two camps are allowed in this region of the park. Mobile tented camp safaris are also available.

CLASS A: * *Sable Valley Lodge* overlooks a water hole and accommodates up to 16 guests in luxury thatched lodges with ensuite facilities. Day game drives and walks are offered. * *Sikumi Tree Lodge* has nine thatched chalets (doubles) set in mangwe trees and two family chalets set closer to the ground (24 beds), all with private facilities and swimming pool. Activities include day game drives and walks.

CLASS A/B: * *Makalolo Tented Camp* is situated in the Makalolo Wilderness Area, a remote region of the park teeming with game. Only guests of Makalolo and Nemba Safaris (see below) are allowed in this part of the park, guaranteeing exclusivity. Tents with private facilities accommodate a maximum of 14 guests. The camp offers day and night game drives and walks. * *Nemba Safaris* is a 14-bed tented camp with ensuite facilities situated in the remote Inquasha Wilderness area of the park. Day game drives and walks are offered. * *Jabulisa Lodge* is a refurbished 1920s farmhouse with thatched cottages (14 beds) with ensuite facilities on a private reserve a 20-minute drive from the park. Game drives are offered. * *Jijima Camp* is a luxury tented camp (16 beds) with ensuite facilities situated on a private reserve about a 20-minute drive from the park.

CLASS B: * *Hwange Safari Lodge* has 100 double rooms with private facilities, swimming pool and an elevated game-viewing platform with bar. Game drives are offered in large trucks and open vehicles. * *Kumuna Lodge* has 14 thatched rondavels with swimming pool on an 80,000-acre private game ranch adjacent to the park. Game drives, walks, horseback riding and fishing are offered.

CLASS D, F & CAMPING: There are six *National Park Camps — Main Camp, Sinamatella Camp, Robins Camp, Bumbusi Camp, Lukosi Camp, Deka Camp* and *Nantwich Camp* — all of which have lodge accommodation. Some rooms have private facilities. Ablution blocks are available for campers and for people in rooms without private facilities.

# THE NORTH

## HARARE

Formerly called Salisbury, Harare is the capital and largest city. It is one of the cleanest and most modern cities on the continent. Points of interest include the National Art Gallery, Botanical Garden, Houses of Parliament and the Tobacco Auction Floors (the largest in the world). Mbare Msiki Market is good for shopping for curios.

A beautiful park adjacent to the Monomotapa Hotel features a large variety of brilliant flora. Harare Botanical Gardens has indigenous trees and herbs.

Harare's best restaurants include Tiffany's, L'Escargot, La Chandelle, La Fontaine, The Bamboo Inn, and Pino's Restaurant — famous for its fresh prawns from Mozambique. Jackets for men and dresses for women are appropriate attire (but are usually not required) for the top restaurants.

A short drive from Harare are the Larvon Bird Gardens, Ewanrigg Botanical Gardens and Lake McIlwaine Game Park. Imire Game Park Farm has Bushmen paintings, an animal orphanage, and is well stocked with wildlife.

ACCOMMODATION - DELUXE: * *Meikles Hotel* has 269 rooms and suites with ensuite facilities, swimming pool, sauna, and traditional old-world atmosphere. * *Sheraton Hotel* has 325 air-conditioned rooms and suites with ensuite facilities, swimming pool, tennis courts, sauna and gym. * *Monomotapa Hotel* has 214 air-conditioned rooms with ensuite facilities, swimming pool and convention facilities. * *Cresta Jameson Hotel* has 128 air-conditioned rooms and suites with facilities ensuite and swimming pool.

FIRST CLASS: * *Holiday Inn* has 205 air-conditioned rooms with ensuite facilities, swimming pool and the popular Harper's Night Club.

TOURIST CLASS: * *Oasis Hotel* has 84 rooms (including five

family rooms) and swimming pool. * *Bronte Hotel* has 108 rooms and swimming pool.

ACCOMMODATION - NEAR HARARE - CLASS A: * *Mwanga Lodge,* located on a game ranch 27 miles northeast of Harare, has six luxury A-frame thatched cottages nestled beneath a large granite outcrop. Activities include game drives and walks. * *Thetford House* is a lovely estate home with four guest rooms (some with private facilities) set in beautiful gardens with swimming pool 19 miles from Harare. Activities include horseback riding on the game ranch and visits to a dairy farm, tobacco farm, ostrich farm, and Bushmen paintings. * *Landella Lodge* is an 18-bed lodge located 20 minutes by road from the airport, with swimming pool, tennis court, horseback riding and temporary membership in the Ruwa Country Club (18-hole golf course). * *Pamuzinda Safari Lodge,* located 53 miles from Harare, is a private game ranch with 12 luxury bungalows (doubles) and swimming pool, situated on the banks of the Saruwe River.

## LAKE KARIBA

Sunsets over the deep blue waters of Lake Kariba dotted with islands are rated among the most spectacular in the world. This, one of the largest man-made lakes on earth covering over 2000 square miles, was formed in 1958 by damming the Zambezi River. The lake is 180 miles long and up to 20 miles in width and is surrounded for the most part by untouched wilderness.

When the dam was completed and the waters in the valley began to rise, animals were forced to higher ground, which quickly became islands soon to be submerged under the new lake. To save these helpless animals, Operation Noah was organized by Rupert Fothergill. Over 5000 animals, including 35 different mammal species, numerous elephant and 44 black rhino, were rescued and released in what are now Matusadona National Park and the Chete Safari Area.

Lights from commercial kapenta fishing boats are often

Sunset on Lake Kariba — nesting darter and cormorants.

seen on the lake at night. Fishing is excellent for tigerfish, giant vundu, bream, cheesa, and nkupi. October is the optimum month for tigerfishing and November-April for bream. Birdlife is prolific, especially waterfowl.

The Lake Kariba Ferry usually takes 22 hours to cruise from Mlibizi to Kariba Town. If you are thinking of taking a vehicle through Zimbabwe from Victoria Falls to Kariba, this ferry will save you over 775 miles of driving.

## KARIBA (TOWN)

Kariba is the major gateway to both Matusadona and Mana Pools National Parks. Many people fly here from Harare, Victoria Falls or Hwange and are then transferred by aircraft, boat or vehicle to their respective camps. This is a good place to meet Zimbabweans on vacation.

Kariba Dam, one of the largest in Africa, is a short distance from town. Water sports (beware of crocodiles and hippos) and cruises on the lake are available.

ACCOMMODATION - TOURIST CLASS: * *Caribbea Bay*

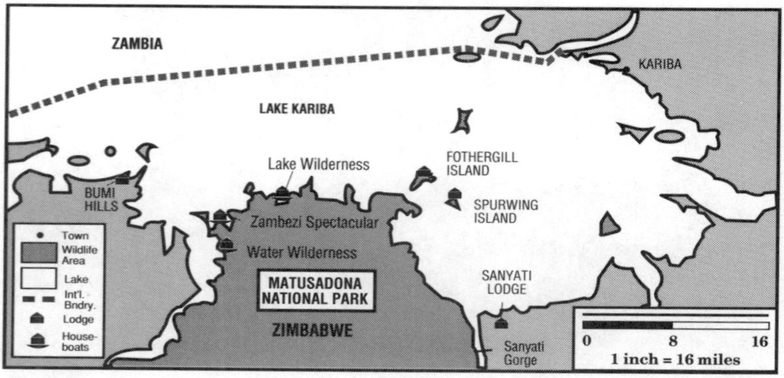


*Resort,* located on the shores of Lake Kariba, is a Sardinian-style resort with 43 rooms (some air-conditioned) with ensuite facilities, two swimming pools, popular poolside bar and casino. * *Lakeview Inn* has 52 air-conditioned rooms with private facilities and swimming pool overlooking Lake Kariba. * *Cutty Sark Hotel* has 65 air-conditioned rooms with facilities ensuite and swimming pool.

CAMPING: * *M.O.T.H. Campsite* is located just below the Lakeview Inn.

## MATUSADONA NATIONAL PARK

Situated on the southern shore of Lake Kariba and bounded on the east by the dramatic Sanyati Gorge and the west by the Umi River, this scenic 600-square-mile park has an abundance of elephant, kudu, impala and buffalo — especially along the shoreline in the dry season (May-October). Other game includes lion, sable antelope, roan antelope and waterbuck. This is one of the best parks in Africa to see black rhino while on escorted walks. For those looking for excitement in the bush, encountering black rhino on a walking safari is a unique experience not to be missed! Leopard are occasionally spotted in the Sanyati Gorge.

Game viewing by boat near shore and walking safaris are popular. Fishing is excellent but beware of crocodiles.

Guests of Water Wilderness on Lake Kariba visit each other and the dining houseboat by canoe.

Several-day walking safaris and private tented safaris with professional guides are another great way to experience the bush. Houseboats complete with captain, staff, and professional guide provide private parties great freedom and comfort in exploring the region.

ACCOMMODATION - CLASS A: * *Water Wilderness*, situated in an isolated area of the lake within the park, consists of four houseboats (doubles) with ensuite facilities, moored near the dining houseboat. Guests of each houseboat are given a canoe for transport among the houseboats. Game drives by boat and morning walks are conducted. Black rhino are often seen on walks. * *Zambezi Spectacular*, located in a secluded area of the lake within the park, has three houseboats (doubles) with facilities ensuite, moored near the central dining houseboat. Game walks, canoeing and sunset boat cruises are offered. This is also a good area for black rhino. * *Sanyati Lodge* is an exquisite 12-bed camp with great food, situated on the side of a hill at the mouth of the Sanyati Gorge, with privately set luxury chalets with private facilities, made of stone and thatch. Game viewing by boat and by vehicle is offered. Fishing in the gorge (especially for tigerfish) is excellent. * *Bumi Hills Lodge,* located on the western outskirts of the park on a hill overlooking the lake, has 20 well-appointed luxury rooms with ensuite facilities and swimming pool. Walks, game drives by vehicle and boat, and fishing are offered.

CLASS B: * *Spurwing Island* is a comfortable 40-bed camp with thatched chalets with private facilities and tents with shared facilities and swimming pool. Walks, game drives by vehicle and by boat and fishing are offered. * *Fothergill Island Safari Camp* has 25 Batonka lodges (doubles), most with facilities ensuite, and swimming pool. Game viewing on foot, by boat and by vehicle are offered. Due to the fluctuating water level of Lake Kariba, Fothergill is often connected to the mainland by a peninsula.

CLASS C: * *Lake Wilderness* has two houseboats with shared facilities, accommodating up to eight guests each, and a few smaller houseboats (doubles). Walks, game viewing by boat and vehicle are offered.

ACCOMMODATION ON LAKE KARIBA WEST OF MATUSADONA NATIONAL PARK - CLASS A/B: * *Sijarira Camp* is located on the shores of Lake Kariba in the Sijarira Forest Reserve below Chizarira National Park. Accommodation is in Batonka-style chalets (with private facilities) built on stilts. Activities include game cruises on the lake, game drives, walks and lazing around the swimming pool. Access is by charter aircraft or by boat from Binga, which is a five-hour drive from Victoria Falls.
CLASS D: The National Park has three self-service camps — *Ume, Mbalabala* and *Muuyu;* each camp may be booked by one party only.

CAMPING: The two National Park Campsites, *Tashinga* and *Sanyati,* have ablution blocks.

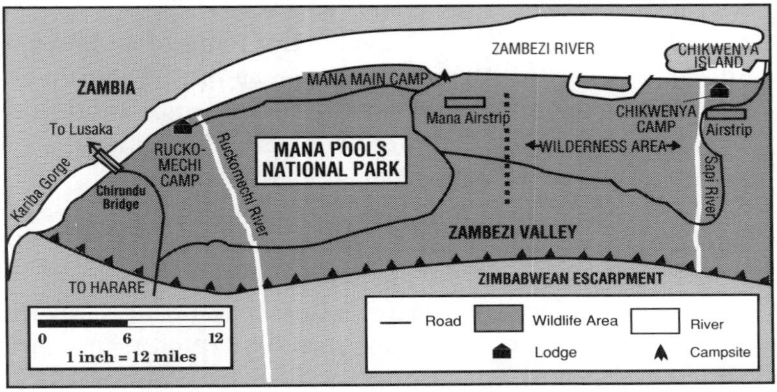


# MANA POOLS NATIONAL PARK

During the dry season, Mana Pools National Park has one of the highest concentrations of wildlife on the continent. The park is situated on the southern side of the Zambezi River downstream (northeast) of Lake Kariba.

This 965-square-mile park is uniquely characterized by fertile river terraces reaching from the slow-moving Zambezi River inland for several miles. Small ponds and pools such as Chine Pools and Long Pool were formed as the river's course slowly drifted northward. Reeds, sandbanks, and huge mahogany and acacia trees near the river give way to dense mopane woodland to the park's southern boundary along the steep Zambezi Escarpment.

Mana Pools National Park covers part of the Middle Zambezi Valley, which is home for 12,000 elephant and 16,000 buffalo (with herds of over 500 each).

Species commonly seen in the park include kudu, zebra, eland, impala, bushbuck, lion, leopard, jackal, hyena, and crocodile. Large pods of hippo are sometimes seen lying on the sandbanks soaking up the morning sun. Occasionally spotted are wild dog and the rare nyala. Large varieties of both woodland and water birds are present.

**Canoe Safaris**

For the adventurous traveler, this is one of the best ways to experience the African bush and is one of my favorite safaris on the entire continent. In fact, a canoe safari along Mana Pools National Park is *the* highlight for almost everyone who does a canoe trip as part of their safari.

Traveling silently by canoe, you can approach closely to wildlife which has come to drink along the shore. Most importantly, you actively participate in the adventure!

Canoe safaris, lasting from three to nine days, covering different stretches of the river, and operated from Kariba Dam downstream for up to 159 miles past Mana Pools National Park to Kanyemba near the Mozambique border, are available. Only one canoe group of a maximum of eight guests is allowed on any stretch of the river at one time. From below Kariba Dam canoeists pass through the Kariba Gorge on the way to Chirundu. From Chirundu to Mana Pools, the portion of the river along Mana Pools National Park is best for wildlife viewing. No motorized boats are allowed on this stretch of the river, making it all the more attractive. Downstream (east) of the park, one passes through the rugged Mupata Gorge on the way to Kanyemba.

Three different "levels" of canoe safaris are available. Budget (participation) canoe safaris do not have a support vehicle on land. Camping is often done on islands in the Zambezi where there are no facilities. Participants sleep in sleeping bags in small pup-tents or under mosquito nets, and everyone pitches their own tents and helps with the chores.

Landrover-backed (full service) canoe safaris have excellent guides and provide four-wheel-drive vehicle backup to the safari. Camp is set up before your arrival. Guests are accommodated in comfortable tents large enough to stand in with beds with mattresses, sheets and blankets. Shower tents (hot water) and toilet tents are set up for the group. Game drives may also be conducted from camp.

The best of all worlds (and the most expensive option) is to have a professional guide licensed to take you on walks as your escort on a landrover-backed canoe safari (described above); this will allow you to canoe, go on game drives by vehicle and walk. Unless your guide is licensed to take guests on walks, walking inland is limited to 50 meters (yards) from the riverbank.

During my most recent landrover-backed canoe safari along Mana Pools, I came the closest I have ever come to elephant. As we canoed past two large bull elephant walking along the river's edge, our guide instructed us to pull into shore about 50 yards downstream of them. The larger of the elephants continued walking toward us, eating apple ring acacia (*Acacia albida*) pods that had fallen from trees along the river.

Our guide and I crouched silently behind our canoe with the rest of the group doing the same behind us. The elephant came closer, and closer, and closer — until he was not more than *six feet* from us. One step more and he would have stepped into the canoe. What a thrill! Eventually he turned around and walked back down the shoreline from whence he came.

Several times we saw elephant swimming from the mainland to islands in the Zambezi in search of food. We also saw hundreds of hippo, buffalo, waterbuck and impala, dozens and dozens of elephant and crocodile along with lion and many other species.

On a previous canoe safari, a huge elephant walked out into the river in front of us and completely submerged underwater with the exception of its trunk waving in the air. When it came up, we were almost on top of it, and we paddled madly to get out of the way. When the elephant finally noticed us, it trumpeted loudly and began running through the water after us. Fortunately, it stopped after a few steps, and the mighty Zambezi moved us quickly downstream out of danger. What fun!

Your guide will instruct you on safety precautions to use on your canoe safari. Previous canoe experience is not necessary. However, spending at least a few hours in a canoe before your African safari would allow you to feel more comfortable canoeing in a foreign environment.

## Walking Safaris

The eastern part of Mana Pools has been designated as a wilderness area in which only walking and canoeing along its shores are allowed.

Recently we joined a three-night/four-day walking safari (full service) escorted by a professional licensed guide through the rich Mana Pools floodplains along the Zambezi River — an area teeming with wildlife. We encountered no one else during the entire four days. The only humans we saw were canoeists off in the distance paddling down the Zambezi River.

On the first day, we encountered a bull elephant that decided to charge us not once — but twice! On the first charge, it stopped about 30 feet from us, and on the second charge — about 15 feet. Keep in mind that as long as you do what your guide says there is little danger — only a big rush of adrenaline!

Shortly after the charge, we reached camp. Later, under a full moon, the same elephant approached our camp, and we walked out to meet it. The elephant trumpeted, then charged us again! This was the first time we had ever been charged by moonlight!

On the last day of the safari, we encountered so many breeding herds (females with their young) of elephant that we had to continuously backtrack and look for alternative paths between them in order to get to our pick-up point.

Because of the drought, most of the large elephant herds had broken up into several small ones. Our guide climbed several termite mounds, scouting out the area. We even found ourselves walking through "adrenaline grass" — thick golden grass often over seven feet in height that is so thick you would almost bump into a buffalo or elephant before seeing it.

Events like this are why walking safaris, and safaris in general, are so popular — you never know what is going to happen next!

Walking safaris like this one may sound a bit risky. They are, however, quite safe — as long as the safari is conducted by a fully licensed professional guide. Just use common sense and enjoy the adventure.

The best time to visit the park for one of the finest exhibitions of wildlife on the continent is at the end of the dry season (August-October) when elephant, buffalo, waterbuck and impala come to the river by the thousands to drink and graze on the lush grasses along its banks. Game viewing is also very good in June-July. During the rainy season, most large land mammals move away from the river toward the escarpment.

Many roads within the park are closed during the rainy season from November 1-April 30. Charter flights operate to two airstrips in the park. Petrol is not available in the park, and power boats are not allowed. Four-wheel-drive vehicles are recommended in the dry season and necessary in the rainy season.

ACCOMMODATION - CLASS A: * *Chikwenya Camp*, operated by Jeff and Veronica Stutchbury, is situated on the Zambezi River just outside the eastern border of the park. The camp has eight thatched lodges (doubles) with private facilities and offers walking and game viewing by vehicle and by boat. * *Ruckomechi Camp*, just outside the western boundary of the park, has eight comfortable chalets (doubles) and one chalet with two double rooms; all chalets have ensuite facilities. Day and night game drives, walks and canoeing are offered.

CLASS D/F: National Parks accommodations include *Musangu Lodge*, *Muchichiri Lodge*, and *Vundu Camp*.

CAMPING: * *Nyamepi Camp* has 29 caravan/camping sites and ablution blocks with hot and cold water. The exclusive camps, which are limited to one group at a time are *Mucheni Camp*, *Nkupe Camp*, *Ndungu Camp*, and *Gwaya (Old Tree Lodge) Camp*.

## CHIZARIRA NATIONAL PARK

This remote undeveloped park is situated on the Zambezi Escarpment overlooking the Zambezi Valley and the southern part of Lake Kariba. Chizarira covers 740 square miles of wild, untouched bush with plateaus, deep gorges, thick woodlands and floodplains.

Chizarira is a park for the adventurer more interested in experiencing the wilderness than in seeing huge herds of animals. Much of the park is heavily wooded. Walking is allowed if accompanied by a fully licensed guide; this is the best way to explore this seldom-visited park. Black rhino are often seen on walks.

The best view of Lake Kariba and the Zambezi Valley is from Mucheni View Point. Roads are rough; a four-wheel-drive vehicle is recommended year-round and is necessary in the rainy season. Petrol is not available in the park. The park is a day's drive from Matusadona National Park. Easiest access is by charter aircraft.

ACCOMMODATION - CLASS A: * *Chizarira Lodge* is a new lodge with eight thatched deluxe chalets with ensuite facilities and swimming pool. Activities include game drives, walks, and overnight walking trails.

CLASS F & CAMPING: There are three exclusive national park campsites, *Kasiswi Bush Camp, Mobola Bush Camp,* and *Busi Bush Camp,* each limited to one party (maximum 12 persons).

## THE EAST

## NYANGA NATIONAL PARK

Most of this beautifully forested and mountainous park lies above 6560 feet (2000 meters), rising to 8504 feet (2592 meters). Mt. Inyangani is the highest mountain in Zimbabwe.

Trout fishing, horseback riding, hiking and golf are just a few of the many sports enjoyed in this refreshing environment.

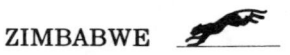

The park covers 127 square miles and is located near the Mozambique border north of Mutare.

ACCOMMODATION - FIRST CLASS: * *Pine Tree Inn* is a small country inn; rooms have facilities ensuite. * *Troutbeck Inn* has 74 rooms with ensuite facilities and offers horseback riding, trout fishing, lawn bowls, squash, tennis and golf. * *Montclair Hotel* has rooms with private facilities.

CAMPING: Numerous camping and caravan sites are available.

## VUMBA BOTANICAL GARDEN AND RESERVE

Located just south of Mutare, Vumba Botanical Garden is beautifully landscaped around a number of small streams. The garden also affords extensive views of Mozambique to the east.

The **Bunga Forest Botanical Reserve**, located adjacent to the botanical garden, has footpaths through unspoiled indigenous forests.

ACCOMMODATION - FIRST CLASS: * *White Horse Inn* is a small hotel (20 beds); rooms have private facilities.

CAMPING: Camp and caravan sites are available.

## CHIMANIMANI NATIONAL PARK

This rugged, mountainous park with deep gorges and numerous streams includes most of the Chimanimani Mountain Range, which rises to 7995 feet (2437 meters). This is an excellent park for hiking and backpacking. Eland, sable antelope and bushbuck are often seen.

ACCOMMODATION - CLASS F: A mountain hut is available for refuge.

CAMPING: Camping is allowed in the park.

## THE SOUTHEAST

## GREAT ZIMBABWE RUINS

These impressive stone ruins, located 11 miles from Masvingo, look distinctly out of place in sub-Saharan Africa where almost all traditional structures have been built of mud, cow dung, straw and reeds. The origin of these ruins is still not understood.

In 1890, Masvingo became the first settlement of whites in what is now Zimbabwe. The settlers first discovered the Great Zimbabwe Ruins in 1898.

The city which these ruins represent was at its prime from the thirteenth to the fifteenth centuries. The Acropolis or Hill Complex, traditionally the king's residence, is situated high on a granite hill overlooking the Temple (a walled enclosure) and the less complete restoration of the Valley complex.

ACCOMMODATION - TOURIST CLASS: * *Great Zimbabwe Hotel* is a country hotel, located a few minutes' walk from the ruins, with swimming pool and 45 rooms with private facilities.

## KYLE RECREATIONAL PARK

Located twenty miles southwest of Masvingo, this 85-square-mile park is a great place to go horseback riding among white rhino and a variety of other game. Pony trails are led by a park ranger into the fenced wildlife section of the park.

This 33-foot-high conical tower is part of the Great Zimbabwe Ruins.

ACCOMMODATION - CLASS C: See "Zimbabwe Ruins."

CLASSES D & F: * *National Park Lodges,* some with private facilities and others without, are available.

CAMPING: Camping and caravan sites with ablution blocks are located near the National Park office and at Sikato Bay Camp on the west bank of Lake Kyle.

## GONAREZHOU NATIONAL PARK

The second largest park in Zimbabwe, Gonarezhou borders the country of Mozambique in southeastern Zimbabwe and covers over 1930 square miles of bush.

Gonarezhou means "the place of many elephants" and is definitely elephant country. Other species commonly seen are lion, buffalo, zebra, giraffe, and a variety of antelope species. Nyala are regularly seen in riverine areas. Rarely seen are roan antelope, Lichtenstein's hartebeest and black rhino.

Elephant, rhino and buffalo have been heavily hunted and poached in this area. Visitors should approach these and other large mammals with extreme caution; these animals (especially elephants) have a justifiable grudge against man and are more likely to charge than in most other parks.

This park is off the beaten path and, as of this writing, international tourists are not allowed to visit; check the current status before venturing there. In spite of concentrated efforts, poaching is still a problem.

The park is divided into two regions, the Chipinda Pools section, which includes the Lundi and Sabi subregions, and the Mabalauta section. Game viewing is best in the Lundi subregion.

Gonarezhou is usually only open in the dry season, May 1-October 31. Winter temperatures are mild; however, summer temperatures can exceed 104° F.

From Masvingo drive southwest to Chiredzi, then continue either 36 miles to Chipinda Pools or 105 miles to Mabalauta Camp. Four-wheel-drive vehicles are highly recommended. No food or fuel is available at the park.

CLASS F: * *Swimuwini,* meaning "the place of baobabs," is located five miles from the Warden's Office and has three self-service chalets and an ablution block.

CAMPING: * *Chipinda Pools Camping and Caravan Site* and * *Chinguli* have ablution blocks. Seven remote campsites with basic facilities are also available. * *Mabalauta* has five camping/caravan sites.

ACCOMMODATION NEAR GONAREZHOU NATIONAL PARK - CLASS B: There are two facilities with a private airstrip situated on a 115-square-mile game ranch with elephant, buffalo, lion, black rhino, leopard, and a variety of antelope near Gonarezhou National Park. * *Induna Lodge* has five stone and thatch chalets (doubles) with private facilities, nestled in a rock amphitheater.

CLASS C: * *Kwali Camp* has 11 wood and thatch bungalows (doubles) with separate facilities (an ablution block).

## BULAWAYO

Bulawayo is the second largest city in Zimbabwe and holds the National Museum and Railway Museum — both well worth a visit.

Special **Steam Train Safaris** from Bulawayo to Victoria Falls lasting three days are available for the railroad enthusiast. The train stops at Hwange National Park for a day of game viewing; guests have the option of spending that night on the train or at Hwange Safari Lodge. There is also an overnight train to Harare.

**Chipangali Wildlife Orphanage**, 15 miles southwest of Bulawayo on the Esigodini/Beit Bridge road, cares for a variety of young animals, often including lion, leopard, genet, civet, elephant, and chimpanzee.

ACCOMMODATION - FIRST CLASS: * *Induna Lodge* has three rooms (eight beds) with private facilities, swimming pool, sauna, personalized service and excellent food. * *Churchill Arms Hotel* is a modern Tudor-style hotel with 50 rooms with ensuite facilities, located four miles from the city center. * *Bulawayo Sun Hotel* is located in the center of town and has

172 air-conditioned rooms with private facilities. * *The Castle*, built in 1906 by a professional castle builder from Scotland, has eight double rooms with private facilities and is located only a few miles from the city.

ACCOMMODATION NEAR BULAWAYO - CLASS A/B: * *Londa Mela Lodge*, located on a game ranch a half-hour's drive from the airport, has four thatched chalets (doubles) with facilities ensuite, swimming pool and game viewing platforms. Activities include day and night game drives, walks, horseback riding, canoeing and fishing.

## MATOPOS (MATOBO) NATIONAL PARK

Hundreds of kopjes supporting thousands of precariously balanced rocks give the 167-square-mile Matopos National Park one of the most unusual landscapes in Africa. This highly underrated park is divided into two sections — a general recreational area, where pony trails are very popular, and a game reserve.

Matopos National Park has the highest concentration of black eagles in the world. Leopard and jackal are the only predators.

Accompanied by a national park ranger in the game reserve, we walked near two white rhino and a baby which were eventually scared off when a herd of wildebeest stampeded nearby.

Cecil Rhodes was buried on a huge rock kopje called "View of the World" from which one has sensational panoramas of the rocky, barren countryside.

Nswatugi Cave **rock paintings** include images of giraffe and antelope. For Bambata Cave rock paintings, allow one and one-half hours for the hike. White Rhino Shelter rock paintings are also worth a visit.

ACCOMMODATION - CLASS A/B: * *Amalinda Camp*, set among enormous kopjes, has four tents under thatch with ensuite facilities. Activities include day and night game drives, walks, horseback riding and visits to Bushmen paintings. * *Matobo Hills Lodge* has ten thatched chalets (doubles) and swimming pool built into the rocks. Game drives, walks, horseback riding and visits to Bushmen paintings and local villages are offered.

FIRST CLASS: See Bulawayo.

CLASSES D & F: * *National Park* bungalows with and without ensuite facilities are available.

CAMPING: Camping and caravan sites with ablution blocks are available at *Maleme Dam* and *Toghwana Dam*.

# THE SAFARI PAGES

# THE SAFARI PAGES

We have endeavored to make the information that follows as current as possible. However, Africa is undergoing constant change.

My reason for including the following information, much of which is likely to change, is to give you an idea of the right questions to ask — not to give you information that should be relied on as gospel. Wherever possible, a resource has been given to assist you in obtaining the most current information.

## AIRPORT DEPARTURE TAXES

Call an airline servicing your destination, the tourist office, embassy, or consulate of the country(ies) in question for current international and domestic airport taxes.

International airport departure taxes must be paid in U.S. dollars or other hard currency, such as British Pounds or German Marks. Be sure to have the exact amount required — they will not give change. Domestic airport departure taxes are usually payable in local currency.

At the time of this writing, international airport departure taxes for the countries in this guide do not exceed U.S. $20; domestic departure taxes are usually under U.S. $5.

## BANKS

Barclays and Standard Chartered Banks are located in most of these countries.

## BANKING HOURS

Banks are usually open Monday-Friday mornings and early afternoons, sometimes on Saturday mornings, and closed on Sundays and holidays. Most hotels, lodges and camps are licensed to exchange foreign currency.

## CREDIT CARDS

Major international credit cards are accepted by most top hotels, restaurants, and shops. Visa and MasterCard are most widely accepted. American Express and Diner's Club are also accepted by most first-class hotels and many businesses.

## CURRENCIES

The currencies used by the countries included in this guide are as follows:
**Botswana** (1 pula = 100 thebe)
**Burundi** (1 Burundi franc = 100 centimes)
**Kenya** (1 Kenya shilling = 100 cents)
**Lesotho** (1 malote = 100 licente)
**Mauritius** (1 rupee = 100 cents)
**Namibia** (1 rand = 100 cents)
**Rwanda** (1 Rwanda franc = 100 centimes)
**South Africa** (1 rand = 100 cents)
**Swaziland** (1 lilangeni = 100 cents)
**Tanzania** (1 Tanzania shilling = 100 cents)
**Uganda** (1 Uganda shilling = 100 cents)
**Zaire** (1 Zaire = 100 makutas)
**Zambia** (1 kwacha = 100 ngwee)
**Zimbabwe** (1 Zimbabwe dollar = 100 cents)

The currencies of Lesotho and Swaziland are on par with the South African rand. The South African rand is widely accepted in Lesotho and Swaziland; however, the currencies of Lesotho and Swaziland are not accepted in South Africa.

Current rates for many African countries can usually be found in the financial section of large newspapers and in periodicals such as *Newsweek*. Call an airline that travels to the country you wish to visit and ask for the current rate of exchange.

## CURRENCY RESTRICTIONS

Most African countries require visitors to complete currency declaration forms upon arrival; all foreign currency, travelers checks and other negotiable instruments must be recorded. These forms must be surrendered on departure.

When you leave the country, the amount of currency you have with you must equal the amount with which you entered the country less the amount exchanged and recorded on your currency declaration form.

For most countries in Africa, the maximum amount of local currency that may be imported or exported is strictly enforced. Kenya, for instance, does not allow visitors to take any Kenyan currency into or out of the country. Check for current restrictions by contacting the tourist offices, embassies or consulates of the countries you wish to visit.

In some countries, it is difficult (if not impossible) to exchange unused local currency back to foreign exchange (i.e., U.S. dollars). Therefore, it is best not to exchange more than you feel you will need.

## CUSTOMS

**Australian Customs:**

Contact the offices below for current information:
The Collector of Customs, Sydney, NSW 2000;
tel: (02) 20521
The Collector of Customs, Melbourne, Victoria 3000;
tel: (03) 630461

**Canadian Customs:**

For a brochure on current Canadian customs requirements, ask for the brochure "*I Declare*" from your local customs office, which will be listed in the telephone book under "Government of Canada, Customs and Excise."

**New Zealand Customs:**

Two of the several customs offices are listed below. Contact them for current information:

Box 29, Auckland; tel: 773 520
Box 2098, Christchurch; tel: 799 251

**United Kingdom:**

Contact the office below for current information:
HM Customs and Excise, Kent House, Upper Ground, London SE1 9PS

**U.S. Customs:**

Travelers to the countries included in this guide may qualify for additional allowances through the Generalized System of Preferences (GSP). Contact your nearest customs office and ask for the leaflet "GSP & The Traveler" and for the usual duty-free allowances currently allowed. This information is available from the U.S. Customs Service, P.O. Box 7407, Washington, D.C. 20044; tel: (202) 566-8195.

For current information on products made from endangered species of wildlife that are not allowed to be imported, contact *Traffic* (U.S.A.), World Wildlife Fund, 1250 24th Street N.W., Washington, D.C. 20037; tel: (202) 293-4800 and ask for their leaflet "Buyer Beware" for current restrictions.

## DIPLOMATIC REPRESENTATIVES OF AFRICAN COUNTRIES

**In Australia:**

**Kenya:** 474788/474722/474688 or 474311
Sixth Floor, QBE Building, 33-35 Ainslie Ave., P.O. Box 1990, Canberra ACT 2601, Australia

**Mauritius:** 281-1203 or 282-4436
Hampton Circuit, Yarralumla, Canberra ACT 2600, Australia

**In Canada:**
**Burundi:** (613) 236-8489
151 Slater St., No. 800, Ottawa, Ontario, K1P 5H3, Canada
**Kenya:** (613) 563-1773/4/5/6
Suite 600, 415 Laurier Ave. East, West Ottawa, Ontario, K1N 6R4, Canada
**Lesotho:** (613) 236-9449
202 Clemow Ave., Ottawa, Ontario, K1S 2B4, Canada
**Rwanda:** (613) 722-5835
1221 Sherwood Dr., Ottawa, Ontario, K1Y 3V1, Canada
**Tanzania:** (613) 232-1509
50 Range Rd., Ottawa, Ontario, K1N 8J4, Canada
**Uganda:** (613) 233-7797
170 Laurier Ave. West, Suite 601, Ottawa, Ontario, K1P 5V5, Canada
**Zaire:** (613) 232-3983
18 Range Rd., Ottawa, Ontario, K1M 8J3, Canada
**Zambia:** (613) 563-0712
130 Albert St., Suite 1610, Ottawa, Ontario, K1P 5G4, Canada
**Zimbabwe:** (613) 237-4388
112 Kent St., Place de Ville, Tower B, Ottawa, Ontario, K1P 5P2, Canada

**High Commissions in The United Kingdom:**
**Botswana:** (071) 499-0031
6 Stratford Place, London W1N 9AE, England
**Kenya:** (071) 6362371/5
45 Courtland Place, London W1N 4AS, England
**Lesotho:** (071) 373-8581
10 Collingham Road, London SW5 0NR, England
**Mauritius:** (071) 5810294/5
32/33 Elvaston Place, London SW 7, England
**South African Consulate:** (081) 9446646
No. 5 & 6, Alt Grove, London, SW19 4DZ, England
**Swaziland:** (071) 581-4976/7
58 Pont St., London SW1, England
**Tanzania:** (071) 499-8951
43 Hertford St., London W1 8DB, England

**Uganda**: (071) 839-5783/0
Uganda House, 58/59 Trafalgar Square, London WC 2N 5DX, England
**Zaire**: (071) 23-57122
Swix 8, HH, 26 Chesham, London 2, England
**Zambia**: (071) 589-6655
2 Palace Gage, Kensington, London W8 5NG, England
**Zimbabwe**: (071) 8367755
429 Strand, London WC 2R OSA, England

**In The United States**:
**Botswana**: (202) 244-4990/1
Suite 7M, 3400 International Drive, N.W., Washington, D.C. 20008
**Burundi**: (202) 342-2574
Suite 212, 2233 Wisconsin Ave. N.W., Washington, D.C. 20007
**Kenya**: (202) 387-6101
2249 R Street N.W., Washington, D.C. 20008
**Kenya Consulates**:
9100 Wilshire Blvd., #111, Beverly Hills, CA 90212
(213) 274-6635
424 Madison Ave., New York, NY 10017
(212) 486-1300/3
**Lesotho**: (202) 797-5533
251 Massachusetts Ave. N.W., Washington, D.C. 20008
1601 Connecticut Ave. N.W., Washington, D.C. 20009
**Mauritius**: (202) 244-1491/2
Suite 134, 4301 Connecticut Ave. N.W., Washington, D.C. 20008
**Rwanda**: (202) 232-2882/3/4
1714 New Hampshire Ave. N.W., Washington, D.C. 20009
**Rwanda Consulate**: (708) 439-9090
10 Gould Center, Suite 707, Rolling Meadows, IL 60008
**South Africa**: (202) 232-4400
3051 Massachusetts Ave. N.W., Washington, D.C. 20008
**South Africa Consulate**: (213) 657-0200
50 N. La Cienega Blvd., Suite 300, Beverly Hills, CA 90211
**Swaziland**: (202) 362-6683

3400 International Dr. N.W., Suite 3M, Washington, D.C. 20008
**Tanzania:** (202) 939-6125
2139 R Street N.W., Washington, D.C. 20008
**Uganda:** (202) 726-7100/3
5909 16th Street N.W., Washington, D.C. 20011-2896
**Zaire:** (202) 234-7690
1800 New Hampshire N.W., Washington, D.C. 20009
**Zambia:** (202) 265-9717
2419 Massachusetts Ave. N.W., Washington, D.C. 20008
**Zimbabwe:** (202) 332-7100
1608 New Hampshire Ave. N.W., Washington, D.C. 20009

**Missions to the United Nations or Consulates in New York:**
**Botswana:** (212) 889-2277
103 East 37th St., New York, NY 10016
**Burundi:** (212) 687-1180
336 East 45th St., New York, NY 10017
**Kenya:** (212) 421-4740
424 Madison Ave., New York, NY 10017
**Lesotho:** (212) 661-1690
204 East 39th St., New York, NY 10016
**Mauritius:** (212) 949-0190/1
211 East 43rd St., New York, NY 10017
**Rwanda:** (212) 696-0644
124 East 39th St., New York, NY 10016
**South Africa:** (212) 213-4880
333 East 38th St., New York, NY 10016
**Swaziland:** (212) 371-8910
866 United Nations Plaza, Suite 420, New York, NY 10017
**Tanzania:** (212) 972-9160
205 East 42nd St., New York, NY 10017
**Uganda:** (212) 949-0110
Uganda House, 335 East 45th St., New York, NY 10017
**Zaire:** (212) 754-1966
77 Third Ave., 25th Floor, New York, NY 10017
**Zambia:** (212) 758-1110
237 East 52nd St., New York, NY 10022

**Zimbabwe:** (212) 980-9511
128 East 56th St., New York, NY 10022

## DIPLOMATIC REPRESENTATIVES IN AFRICA

**Australian High Commissions:**

**Kenya:** tel: 334666/7
Development House, Moi Ave., P.O. Box 30360, Nairobi, Kenya

**Mauritius:** tel: 208 1700
Rogers House, John Kennedy St., Port Louis, Mauritius

**South Africa:** tel: 3254315
Fourth Floor, Mutual and Federal Center, 220 Vermuelen St., Pretoria 0002, South Africa, or tel: 232160
Tenth Floor, 1001 Colonial Mutual Building, 101 Adderby St., 8001 Cape Town, South Africa

**Tanzania:**
Seventh and Eighth Floors, NLC Investment Bldg., Independence Ave., P.O. Box 2969, Dar es Salaam, Tanzania

**Zambia:** tel: 229371
Ulendo House, P.O. Box 35395, Lusaka, Zambia

**Zimbabwe:** tel: 794591/4
Third Floor, Throgmorton House, Samora Machel Ave. & Julius Nyerere Way, P.O. Box 907 (45341), Harare, Zimbabwe

**Canadian High Commissions:**

**Kenya:** tel: 334033
Comcraft House, Haile Selassie Ave., P.O. Box 30481, Nairobi, Kenya

**Mauritius:** tel: 208-0821
c/o Blanche Birger Co., Ltd., Port Louis, Mauritius

**South Africa:** tel: 287062
Nedbank Plaza, 856 Kingsleys Center, Deatrix St., Arcadia, Pretoria 0007, South Africa

**Tanzania:** tel: 20651
Pan African Insurance Bldg., P.O. Box 1022, Dar es Salaam, Tanzania

**Zaire:** tel: 22706
Édifice Shell, B.P. 8341, Kinshasa, Zaire

**Zambia:** tel: 228811
Cairo Road, P.O. Box 31313, Lusaka, Zambia
**Zimbabwe:** tel: 793801
45 Baines Ave., P.O. Box 1430, Harare, Zimbabwe

**United Kingdom High Commissions:**
**Botswana:** tel: 52841/2/3
Private Bag 0023, Gaborone, Botswana
**Burundi:** tel: 23711
British Liaison Office, 43 Ave. Bubanza, B.P. 1344, Bujumbura, Burundi. Permanent staff in Kinshasa, Zaire
**Kenya:** tel: 335944
Bruce House, Standard St., P.O. Box 30465, Nairobi, Kenya
**Lesotho:** tel: 313961
P.O. Box MS 521, Maseru 100, Lesotho
**Mauritius:** tel: 686-5795
King George V Ave., Floreal, P.O. Box 186, Curepipe, Mauritius
**Namibia:** tel: (61) 223022
British Liaison Office, 116A Lentwein St., Windhoek, Namibia
**Rwanda:** tel: 75219
Honorary Consul, Ave. Paul VI, B.P. 351, Kigali, Rwanda
Permanent staff in Kinshasa, Zaire
**South Africa:** tel: 3319011/4
Consulate: Fifth Floor, Nedbank Mall, 145 Commissioner St., P.O. Box 10101, Johannesburg 2001; South Africa
tel: 3052929/20
Tenth Floor, Fedlife House, 320 Smith St., P.O. Box 1404; Durban 4001, South Africa
**Swaziland:** tel: 42581
Alister Miller St., Private Bag, Mbabane, Swaziland
**Tanzania:** tel: 29601
Hifadhi House, Samora Ave., P.O. Box 9200, Dar es Salaam, Tanzania
**Uganda:** tel: 257054/9 and 257301/4
10-12 Parliament Ave., P.O. Box 7070, Kampala, Uganda
**Zaire:** tel: 21327
191 Ave. de l'Équateur, Fifth Floor, B.P. 8049, Kinshasa, Zaire
**Zambia:** tel: 228955
Independence Ave., P.O. Box RW 50050, Lusaka, Zambia

**Zimbabwe:** tel: 793781 or 728716
Stanley House, Stanley Ave., P.O. Box 4490, Harare, Zimbabwe

**United States Embassies:**
**Botswana:** tel: 267 353982/3/4
P.O. Box 90, Gaborone, Botswana
**Burundi:** tel: 23454
B.P. 1720, Ave. du Zaire, Bujumbura, Burundi
**Kenya:** tel: 254 2 334141
Embassy Building, Haile Selassie & Moi Avenues, P.O. Box 30137, Nairobi, Kenya
**Lesotho:** tel: 266 312666
P.O. Box MS 333, Maseru 100, Lesotho
**Mauritius:** tel: 208-2342
Rogers Bldg., Fourth Floor, John Kennedy St., Port Louis, Mauritius
**Namibia:** tel: 254 61 229791
Ausplan Bldg., 14 Lossen St., P.O. Box 9890, Windhoek 9000, Namibia
**Rwanda:** tel: 205 755601/2/3
Blvd. de la Révolution, B.P. 28, Kigali, Rwanda
**South Africa:** tel: 27 12 284266
Phibault House, 225 Pretorius St., Pretoria, South Africa
Consulate: tel: 27 11 3311681
11th Floor, Kine Center, Commissioner & Kruis Sts., P.O. Box 2155, Johannesburg, South Africa
**Swaziland:** tel: 268 46441/2/3/4/5
Central Bank Bldg., Warner St., P.O. Box 199, Mbabane, Swaziland
**Tanzania:** tel: 255 51 375012/3/4
36 Laibon Road (off Bagamoyo Rd.), P.O. Box 9123, Dar es Salaam, Tanzania
**Uganda:** tel: 256 41 259791/2/3/4/5
British High Commission Bldg., 10/12 Parliament Ave., P.O. Box 7007, Kampala, Uganda
**Zaire:** tel: 243 12 258812/3/4/5/6
310 Ave. des Aviateurs, Kinshasa, Zaire
**Zambia:** tel: 260 1 214911

Independence & United National Aves., P.O. Box 31617, Lusaka, Zambia
**Zimbabwe:** tel: 263 14 794521
172 Rhodes Ave., P.O. Box 3340, Harare, Zimbabwe

## DUTY-FREE ALLOWANCES

Contact the nearest tourist office or embassy for current duty-free import allowances for the country(ies) which you intend to visit. The duty-free allowances vary; however, the following may be used as a *general* guideline: One litre of wine and one litre alcoholic beverage, two cartons of cigarettes or 50 cigars or 8¾ oz. of tobacco, and a small quantity of perfume.

## ELECTRICITY

Electric current is 220-240 volt AC 50Hz.

## GETTING TO AFRICA

**By Air:**
Most travelers from North America flying to the countries listed in this guide must pass through Europe. Air fares and air routings to Africa are continuously changing. For special discount air fares, I suggest you call The Africa Adventure Company at 1-800-882-9453 (U.S.A. and Canada), 305-781-3933 or FAX 305-781-0984.

**By Road:**
From Egypt to Sudan and Ethiopia to Kenya and southward; trans-Sahara through Algeria, Niger, Nigeria or Chad, Cameroon, Central Africa Republic, Zaire, Rwanda and eastern and southern Africa. Allow several months. Roads are very bad.

**By Ship:**
Some cruise ships occasionally stop at Kenyan, Tanzanian and South African ports.

## GETTING AROUND AFRICA

See each country's map for details on major roads, railroad lines and waterways.

**By Air:**

Capitals and major tourist centers are serviced by air. There is regularly scheduled air service to the following destinations within Africa:

**Botswana:** Maun, Francistown, and Selebi Phikwe.
**Burundi:** Domestic charter service only.
**Kenya:** Kisumu, Malindi, Mombasa, Lamu, and Nairobi. Charter services are available to Amboseli, Masai Mara, Nyeri, Nanyuki, Samburu, Lake Turkana, and Lamu.
**Lesotho:** Maseru, Qacha's Nek, Semonkong, Thaba Tseka, and other towns.
**Mauritius:** Rodrigues Island.
**Namibia:** Windhoek, Katima Mulilo, Keetmanshoop, Lüderitz, Swakopmund, and Tsumeb (near Etosha National Park).
**Rwanda:** Gisenyi and Ruhengeri.
**South Africa:** Bloemfontein, Cape Town, Durban, East London, George, Johannesburg, Kimberley, Port Elizabeth, Upington, and Windhoek.
**Tanzania:** Kilimanjaro International, Dar es Salaam, Kigoma, and Zanzibar.
**Uganda:** Arua, Kasese, Gulu, and Mbarara.
**Zaire:** Goma, Bukavu, Kisangani, Lubumbashi, and Kinshasa.
**Zambia:** Chipata, Lusaka, Livingstone (Victoria Falls), Mfuwe (South Luangwa National Park), and Ndole.
**Zimbabwe:** Buffalo Springs, Bulawayo, Harare, Hwange, Kariba, Masvingo, and Victoria Falls.

**By Road:**

Major roads are tarmac (paved) and are excellent in Namibia, South Africa and Zimbabwe. Most major roads are tarmac in fair condition in Botswana, Kenya, Rwanda, Swaziland, and Zambia, and poor in Tanzania and Uganda. Burundi, Lesotho, and Zaire have very few tarmac roads.

Many dirt roads (except in Namibia) are difficult and many are impassable in the rainy season (especially Zaire), often requiring four-wheel-drive vehicles.

Petrol and diesel are readily available in Botswana, Kenya, Lesotho, Mauritius, Namibia, South Africa, Swaziland, and Zimbabwe; may be difficult to obtain in Burundi, Rwanda, Tanzania, and Zambia; and very difficult to obtain in Zaire.

**Taxis** are available in the larger cities and at international airports. **Service Taxis** travel when all seats are taken and are an inexpensive but uncomfortable means of long-distance travel. **Local Buses** are very crowded, uncomfortable, and are recommended only for the hardiest of travelers. Pick-up trucks (matatus in East Africa), often crammed with 20 passengers, luggage, produce, chickens, etc., are used throughout the continent. Be sure to agree on the price before setting off.

**By Rail:**

Trains in South Africa are excellent (especially the Blue Train and Rovos Rail). The "Lunatic Express" from Nairobi to Mombasa in Kenya and the steam train from Bulawayo to Victoria Falls are also good. See the chapters on Kenya, South Africa, and Zimbabwe for details.

Otherwise, train travel is slow and not recommended except for those on an extreme budget on long journeys. Train travel is possible from Arusha (Tanzania) through Zambia, Zimbabwe, Botswana to Cape Town, South Africa. Railway lines are depicted on the maps of each country in this guide.

**By Boat:**

Steamer service on Lake Tanganyika services Bujumbura (Burundi), Kigoma (Tanzania), Mpulungu (Zambia), and Kalemie (Zaire) about once a week; steamers on Lake Victoria service Kisumu (Kenya) and Musoma and Mwanza (Tanzania) and Kampala-Port Bell (Uganda).

## HEALTH

**Malarial risk** exists in all countries covered except

Lesotho, so be sure to take your malaria pills as described before, during and after your trip. Contact your doctor, an immunologist, and the Centers for Disease Control in Atlanta for the best prophylaxis for your itinerary. Use an insect repellent. Wear long-sleeve shirts and slacks for further protection.

**Bilharzia** is a disease that infests most lakes and rivers on the continent. Do not walk barefooted along the shore, wade or swim in a stream, river or lake unless you know for certain it is free of bilharzia. Bilharzia does not exist in salt water.

If you must get in the water, as with canoe or kayak safaris, do not get out of the canoe where there are reeds in the water. A species of snail is involved in the reproductive cycle of bilharzia; these snails are more often found near reeds and in slow-moving water. Follow your guide's instructions and your risk of contracting the disease will be minimized. If you feel you may have contracted the disease, go to your doctor for a blood test. If diagnosed in its early stages, it is easily cured.

**Tap water** is safe in many of the larger cities; but to be safe, it should not be drunk. Wear a hat and bring sunblock to protect yourself from the tropical sun. Drink plenty of fluids and limit alcohol consumption at high altitudes.

For further information, obtain a copy of *Health Information for International Travel* from the U.S. Government Printing Office, Washington, D.C. 20402.

## INSURANCE

Be sure your medical insurance covers you for the countries you plan to visit. Acquire additional insurance for emergency evacuation should your present policies not include it.

Travel insurance packages often include a combination of emergency evacuation, medical, baggage, and trip cancellation — all of which are highly recommended. The peace of mind afforded by such insurance far outweighs the cost. Ask your Africa travel specialist for information on relatively inexpensive group-rate insurance.

## MAPS

Before going on safari, obtain good maps for each country you intend to visit. This will increase your awareness of the areas you want to see and enhance your enjoyment of the trip. For a free catalog of difficult-to-find country maps, regional maps, and mountain maps, see p. 486.

It is best to purchase maps before arriving in Africa as they are not readily available.

## METRIC SYSTEM OF WEIGHTS AND MEASURES

The metric system is used in Africa. The U.S. equivalents are:

| | |
|---|---|
| 1 inch — 2.54 centimeters (cm.) | 1 cm. — 0.39 inch |
| 1 foot — 0.305 meters (m.) | 1 m. — 3.28 feet |
| 1 mile — 1.6 kilometers (km.) | 1 km. — 0.62 miles |
| 1 square mile — 2.59 sq. km. | 1 sq. km. — 0.3861 sq. mile |
| 1 quart liquid — 0.946 liter (l.) | 1 l. — 1.057 quarts |
| 1 ounce — 28 grams (g.) | 1 g. — 0.035 ounce |
| 1 pound — 0.454 kilograms (kg.) | 1 kg. — 2.2 pounds |

Temperature

| | |
|---|---|
| −20° C. = −4° F. | 15° C. = 59° F. |
| −15° C. = 5° F. | 20° C. = 68° F. |
| −10° C. = 14° F. | 25° C. = 77° F. |
| −5° C. = 23° F. | 30° C. = 86° F. |
| 0° C. = 32° F. | 35° C. = 95° F. |
| 5° C. = 41° F. | 40° C. = 104° F. |
| 10° C. = 50° F. | |

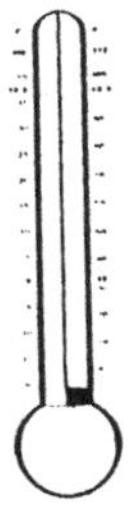

Converting Centigrade into degrees Fahrenheit: Multiply Centigrade by 1.8 and add 32.

Converting Fahrenheit into degrees Centigrade: Subtract 32 from Fahrenheit and divide by 1.8.

## MONEY

One way to receive additional funds is to obtain additional travelers checks with your American Express or other credit card. Other options include having money sent by telegraph international money order (Western Union), telexed through a bank or sent via international courier (i.e., DHL).

## PASSPORT OFFICES

To obtain a passport in the U.S.A., contact your local post office for the passport office nearest you. Then call the passport office to be sure you will have everything on hand which they will require.

## SEMINARS ON AFRICA

The Africa Adventure Company
(305) 781-3933 or 1-800-882-9453
P.O. Box 2567
Pompano Beach, FL 33072
Seminars by Mark Nolting, author of this guide.

## SHOPPING

If you like bartering, bring old clothing to trade for souvenirs. This works particularly well at roadside stands and in small villages, although the villagers are becoming more discerning in their tastes.

The following are some ideas of what to shop for:

**Botswana**: Baskets and carvings are sold in Maun, Kasane and the Mall in Gaborone. Also consider products made from karakul fleece, pottery, tapestries, and rugs. There are curio shops in many safari camps, hotels and lodges.

**Burundi**: Crafts available in numerous shops.

**Kenya**: Makonde and Akomba ebony wood carvings, soapstone carvings, colorful kangas and kikois (cloth wraps). In Mombasa, Zanzibar chests, gold and silverwork, brasswork, Arab jewelry, and antiques.

**Lesotho**: Basotho woven carpets are known worldwide, tapestry-weaving and conical straw hats.
**Mauritius**: Intricately detailed, handmade model sailing ships of camphor or teak, pareos (colorful light cotton wraps), macrame wall hangings, and Mauritian dolls.
**Namibia**: Semiprecious stones and jewelry, karakul wool products, wood carvings, and beadwork.
**South Africa**: Diamonds, gold, wood carvings, dried flowers, and wine.
**Swaziland**: Beautiful handwoven tapestries, baskets, earthenware and stoneware, and mouthblown, handcrafted glass animals and tableware.
**Tanzania**: Makonde carvings and Meerschaum pipes.
**Uganda**: Few shops for tourists.
**Zaire**: Wood carvings, malachite, copper goods, semiprecious stones, and baskets.
**Zambia**: Wood carvings, statuettes, semiprecious stones and copper souvenirs.
**Zimbabwe**: Carvings of wood, stone and Zimbabwe's unique verdite, intricate baskets, ceramicware and crocheted garments.

## SHOPPING HOURS

Shops are usually open Monday-Friday from 8:00/9:00 a.m.-5:00/6:00 p.m. and 9:00 a.m.-1:00 p.m. on Saturdays. Shops in the coastal cities of Kenya and Tanzania often close midday for siesta. Use the shopping hours given above as a general guideline; exact times can vary within the respective country.

## THEFT

The number one rule in preventing theft on vacation is to leave all unnecessary valuables at home. What you must bring, lock in safety deposit boxes when not in use. Theft in Africa is generally no worse than in Europe or the U.S.A. One difference is that Africans are poorer and will steal things that most American or European thieves would consider worthless.

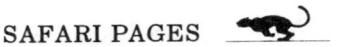

## TIME ZONES

**EST+7/GMT+2**
Botswana
Burundi
Lesotho
Namibia
Rwanda
South Africa
Swaziland
Zaire (Eastern)
Zambia
Zimbabwe

**EST+8/GMT+3**
Kenya
Tanzania
Uganda

**EST+9/GMT+4**
Mauritius

## TIPPING

A ten-percent tip is recommended at restaurants for good service where a service charge is not included in the bill except in Zambia where tipping is against the law. For advice on what tips are appropriate for guides, ask the Africa specialist booking your safari.

## TOURIST INFORMATION

In addition to the addresses below, information may also be available through embassies or consulates of the countries in question. See **DIPLOMATIC REPRESENTATIVES** above.

**Offices in Africa:**
**Botswana:** (267) 53024/3314
Division of Tourism
Private Bag 0047, Gaborone, Botswana
**Burundi:** (257) 222023, 222202
National Office of Tourism
Liberty Ave., P.O. Box 902, Bujumbura, Burundi
**Kenya:** (254 2) 331030
Ministry of Tourism and Wildlife
Utalii House, P.O. Box 30027, Nairobi, Kenya
**Lesotho:** (266) 32-3760
National Tourist Board

P.O. Box 1378, Maseru 100, Lesotho
**Mauritius**: (230) 201-1703
Government Tourist Office
Emmanuel Anquetil Bldg., Jules Koenig St., Port Louis, Mauritius
**Namibia**: (254 61) 26571
SWA Directorate of Trade and Tourism
Private Bag 13297, Windhoek 9000, Namibia
**Rwanda**: (250) 76514/15
Office Rwandais du Tourisme et des Parcs Nationaux (ORTPN), B.P. 905, Kigali, Rwanda
**South Africa**: (271 2) 471131
Tourism Board
Mellyn Park Office Block, Private Bag X164, Pretoria 0001, South Africa
**Swaziland**: (268) 42531
Government Tourist Office
Swazi Plaza, P.O. Box 451, Mbabane, Swaziland
**Tanzania**: (255 51) 27671
Tourist Corporation
Maktaba St., P.O. Box 2485, Dar es Salaam, Tanzania
Zanzibar: (255 51) 32344
Tanzania Friendship Tourist Bureau
P.O. Box 216, Zanzibar, Tanzania
**Uganda**: (256 41) 32971/4
Ministry of Tourism and Wildlife
P.O. Box 4241, Kampala, Uganda
**Zaire**: (243 12) 30070 or 30022
Office National du Tourisme
Avenue des Orangers 2A/2B, B.P. 9502, Kinshasa/Gombe, Zaire
Office National du Tourisme, Blvd. Mobutu, B.P. 242, Goma, Zaire
Also contact Sabena Airlines for information.
**Zambia**: 22908/90
National Tourist Board
Century House, Cairo Road, P.O. Box 30017, Lusaka, Zambia
321487/321404
Tourist Centre

Mosi-oa-Tunya Road, P.O. Box 60342, Livingstone, Zambia
**Zimbabwe:** (263 4) 793666/7/8/9
Tourist Development Corporation
P.O. Box 8052, Harare, Zimbabwe

**Offices in Australia:**
**South Africa:** 231 6166
AMEV-UDC House, 115 Pitt St., Sydney, NSW 2001
**Zambia:** 231 2172
68 Pitt Street, Level 12, Sydney, NSW 2000

**Offices in Canada:**
**South Africa:**
Suite 1001, 20 Eglington Ave. West, Toronto, Ontario, M4R 1K8

**Offices in the United Kingdom:**
**Kenya:** 3553144
25 Brooks Mews, Davis St., London W1Y 1LG, England
**Lesotho:** 242 3131
433 High Holborn House, 52 High Holborn, London WC1V 6RB, England
**Mauritius:** (71) 584-3666
3233 Elvaston Place, London SW7 5NW, England
**South Africa:** 439 9661
Regency House, I-4 Warwick St., London W1R 5WB, England
**Swaziland:**
58 Pont St., Knightsbridge, London SW1, England
**Tanzania** 499 7727
77 South Audley St., London W1Y 5TA, England
**Zambia:** (081) 5896343
2 Palace Gate, Kensington, London W8 5NG, England
**Zimbabwe:** 629 3955
Collette House, 52-55 Piccadilly, London W1V 9AA, England

**Offices in the United States:**
**Kenya:** (212) 486-1300/3
Office of Tourism (213) 274-6635
424 Madison Ave., New York, NY 10017

Doheny Plaza, Suite 111,
9100 Wilshire Blvd., Beverly Hills, CA 90212
**Mauritius:** (212) 239-8367
Government Tourist Information Service
15 Penn Plaza, 415 Seventh Ave., New York, NY 10001
**South Africa:** (213) 641-8444
Office of Tourism (SATOUR) (212) 838-8841
9841 Airport Blvd., Suite 1524, Los Angeles, CA 90045
747 Third Ave., 20th Floor,
New York, NY 10018
**Zambia:** (212) 308-2155/2162/2171
National Tourist Board
237 East 52nd St., New York, NY 10022
**Zimbabwe:** (800) 621-2381, (212) 332-1090
Tourist Office
1270 Avenue of the Americas, Suite 412, New York, NY 10020

## TRAVELERS CHECKS

American Express, Thomas Cook's, MasterCard and Visa Traveler's Checks are widely accepted. Stay away from lesser-known companies; you may have difficulty cashing them.

## VACCINATIONS

Check with the tourist offices or embassies of the countries you wish to visit for current requirements. If you plan to visit one or more countries in endemic zones, (i.e., in Africa, South America, Central America, or Asia), be sure to mention this when requesting vaccination requirements. Many countries do not require any vaccinations if you are only visiting their country directly from the U.S.A., Canada or Western Europe; but if you are also visiting countries in endemic zones, there may very well be additional requirements.

Then check with your doctor and preferably an immunologist, or call your local health department or the Centers for Disease Control, Atlanta, GA 30333, tel: (404) 639-3311, for information. They may very well recommend some vaccinations in addition to those required by the country you will be visiting.

Make sure you are given an International Certificate of Vaccinations showing the vaccinations you have received.

Malarial prophylaxis (pills) are highly recommended for all the countries included in this guide except for Lesotho. However, international travelers must at least pass through South Africa in route to Lesotho.

## VISA REQUIREMENTS

Travelers from most countries must obtain visas to enter many of the countries included in this guide. Apply for visas with the closest diplomatic representative well in advance and check for all current requirements (see **DIPLOMATIC REPRESENTATIVES** above).

### VISA REQUIREMENTS CHART

| Traveling to | AUS | CAN | NZ | UK | USA | Requirements / Restrictions |
|---|---|---|---|---|---|---|
| Botswana | No | No | No | No | No* | *Maximum visit of 90 days. |
| Burundi | Yes | Yes | Yes | Yes | Yes | Onward ticket; sponsorship for business visa. |
| Kenya | Yes | No | No | No* | Yes | *UK citizens of Asian origin need visa. Visitor's pass issued upon arrival. |
| Lesotho | No | No | No | No | No | |
| Mauritius | No | No | No | No | No | Maximum 3-month stay. |
| Namibia | No | No | No | No | No | |
| Rwanda | Yes | Yes | Yes | Yes | Yes | |
| South Africa | Yes | Yes | Yes | No | Yes | Letter from employer for business visa. |
| Swaziland | No | No | No | No | No | |
| Tanzania | No* | No* | No* | No* | Yes | *Visitor's pass required. For business visa, letter of invitation. |
| Uganda | No | No | No | No | Yes | Letter from company for business visa. |
| Zaire | Yes | Yes | Yes | Yes | Yes | Certified sponsorship letter from government for business visa. |
| Zambia | No | No | No | No | Yes | |
| Zimbabwe | No | No | No | No | No | Require a return ticket. |

**WARNING:**

Visitors with South African visas stamped in their passports may be refused entry into some African countries, i.e., Tanzania. Call the embassies of the countries you wish to visit for current information. The U.S. Passport Office often will issue you a second passport in these circumstances.

If you need a visa for South Africa, you may be able to avoid future problems by asking the South African Embassy/ Consulate to issue you a "loose-leaf" visa.

**WILDLIFE ASSOCIATIONS**

African Wildlife Foundation, 1717 Massachusetts Ave. N.W., Washington, D.C.; tel: (202) 265-8394.

David Shepherd Conservation Foundation, Winkworth Farm, Hascombe, Godamling, Surrey GU8 4JW, England; tel: Hascombe 220.

Digit Fund/Morris Animal Foundation, 45 Inverness Dr. East, Englewood, CO 80112, U.S.A. Following Dian Fossey's murder at Christmas, 1985, this organization has continued her work of protecting, studying and providing veterinary care for the gorillas.

Fauna and Flora Preservation Society, c/o Zoological Society of London, Regents Park, London NW1 4RY, England.

World Wildlife Fund, 1250 24th Street N.W., Washington, D.C. 20037; tel: (202) 293-4800.

# SAFARI GLOSSARY

**ablution block** - a building containing showers, toilets and sinks, most often with separate facilities for men and women.
**adaptation** - the ability, through structural or functional characteristics, to improve the survival rate of an animal or plant in a particular habitat.
**age (approx.) - mammals**
1) adult - eight years and older
2) juvenile - three to eight years
3) infant - zero to three years

**arboreal** - living in trees.
**banda** - a basic shelter or hut, often constructed of reeds, bamboo, grass, etc.
**boma** - a place of shelter, a fortified place, enclosure, community (East Africa).
**browse** - to feed on leaves.
**calving season** - period when young of a particular species are born. Not all species have calving seasons. Most calving seasons occur shortly after the rainy season commences. Calving seasons can also differ for the same species from one park or reserve to another.
**camp** - camping sites; also refers to lodging in chalets, bungalows or tents in a remote location.
**caravan** - a trailer.
**carnivore** - an animal that lives by consuming the flesh of

other animals.
**carrion** - remains of dead animals.
**diurnal** - active during the day.
**gestation** - duration of pregnancy.
**grazer** - an animal that eats grass.
**habitat** - an animal or plant's surroundings that has everything it needs in order to live.
**habituated** - an animal that has been introduced to and accepted the presence of human beings.
**herbivore** - an animal that consumes plant matter for food.
**hide** - a camouflaged structure from which one can view wildlife without being seen.
**kopje** - (pronounced kopee) - rock formations which protrude from the savannah, usually caused by wind erosion (Southern Africa).
**koppie** - same as kopje (East Africa).
**kraal** - same as "boma" (Southern Africa).
**mammals** - warm-blooded animals that produce milk for their young.
**midden** - usually an accumulation of dung in the same spot as a scent-marking behavior.
**nocturnal** - active by night.
**omnivore** - an animal that eats both plants and animals.
**pan** - hard-surfaced flatlands that collect water in the rainy season.
**predator** - an animal that hunts and kills other animals for food.
**prey** - animals hunted by predators for food.
**pride** - a group or family of lions.
**rondavel** - an African-style structure for accommodation.
**ruminant** - mammals that have complex stomachs and therefore chew the cud.
**rutting** - behavioral pattern exhibited by male species over a time period that mating is most prevalent, e.g., impala, wildebeest.
**savannah** - open grassy landscape with widely scattered trees.
**scavenger** - an animal living from carrion or remains of animals killed by predators or that have died from

other causes.
**species** - a group of plants or animals with specific characteristics in common, including the ability to reproduce among themselves.
**spoor** - a track (i.e., foot print) or trail made by animals.
**symbiosis** - an association of two different organisms in a relationship that may benefit one or both partners.
**tarmac** - asphalt-paved roads.
**territory** - the home range or domain which an animal may defend against intruders of the same or other species.
**tracking** - following and observing animal spoor by foot.
**tribe** - a group of people united by traditional ties.
**troop** - a group of apes or monkeys.
**ungulates** - hoofed animals.
**veld** - a Southern African term for open land.
**wallow** - the art of keeping cool and wet, usually in a muddy pool, i.e., rhinoceros, buffalo and hippopotamus.

## LATIN/SCIENTIFIC NAMES OF MAMMALS, REPTILES, BIRDS AND TREES

### MAMMALS

| | |
|---|---|
| Aardvark (Antbear) | *Orycteropus afer* |
| Antelope, Roan | *Hippotragus equinus* |
| Antelope, Sable | *Hippotragus niger* |
| Baboon | *Papio anubis* |
| Baboon, Chachma | *Papio ursinus* |
| Bongo | *Boocercus eurycerus* |
| Buffalo | *Syncerus caffer* |
| Bushbaby, Greater | *Galago crassicaudatus* |
| Bushbuck | *Tragelaphus scriptus* |
| Bushpig | *Potamochoerus porcus* |
| Caracal | *Caracal caracal* |
| Cheetah | *Acinonyx jubatus* |
| Chimpanzee | *Pan troglodytes* |
| Civet | *Viverra civetta* |
| Colobus, Black and White or Guereza | *Colobus guereza* |
| Dikdik, Kirk's | *Rhynchotragus kirki* |
| Dog, African Wild | *Lycaon pictus* |
| Duiker, Grey Bush | *Sylvicapra grimmia* |
| Eland, Patterson's | *Taurotragus oryx* |
| Elephant, African | *Loxodonta africana* |
| Fox, Bat-eared | *Otocyon megalotis* |
| Gazelle, Grant's | *Gazella granti* |
| Gazelle, Thomson's | *Gazella thomsoni* |
| Gemsbok or Oryx | *Oryx gazella* |
| Genet | *Genetta tigrina* |
| Giraffe, Masai | *Giraffa camelopardalis tippelskirchi* |
| Giraffe, Reticulated | *Giraffa camelopardalis reticulata* |

| | |
|---|---|
| Giraffe, Rothschild's | *Giraffa camelopardalis rothschildi* |
| Gorilla | *Gorilla gorilla* |
| Hare, African | *Lepus capensis* |
| Hare, Spring | *Pedetes capensis* |
| Hartebeest | *Alcelaphus buselaphus* |
| Hippopotamus | *Hippopotamus amphibius* |
| Hog, Giant Forest | *Hylochoerus meinertzhageni* |
| Hyena, Brown | *Hyaena brunnea* |
| Hyena, Spotted | *Crocuta crocuta* |
| Hyena, Striped | *Hyaena hyaena* |
| Hyrax, Bush | *Dendrohyrax brucei* |
| Hyrax, Rock | *Procavia johnstoni* |
| Hyrax, Tree | *Dendrohyrax arboreus* |
| Impala | *Aepyceros melampus* |
| Jackal, Black-backed | *Canis mesomelas* |
| Jackal, Golden | *Canis aureus* |
| Jackal, Side-striped | *Canis adustus* |
| Klipspringer | *Oreotragus oreotragus* |
| Kongoni | *Alcelaphus buselaphus* |
| Kudu, Greater | *Tragelaphus strepsiceros* |
| Lechwe | *Kobus lechwe* |
| Leopard | *Panthera pardus* |
| Lion | *Panthera leo* |
| Mongoose, Banded | *Mungos mungo* |
| Mongoose, Dwarf | *Helogale parvula* |
| Mongoose, Slender | *Herpestes sanguineus* |
| Mongoose, White-tailed | *Ichneumia albicauda* |
| Monkey, Patas | *Erythrocebus patas* |
| Monkey, Vervet | *Cercopithecus aethiops* |
| Nyala | *Tragelaphus angasi* |
| Oribi | *Ourebia ourebi* |
| Oryx, Fringe-eared | *Oryx beisa* |
| Pangolin, Temminck's Ground | *Manis temmincki* |
| Porcupine, Crested | *Hystrix africae-australis* |
| Ratel | *Mellivora capensis* |
| Reedbuck, Mountain | *Redunca fulvorufula* |
| Rhinoceros, Black | *Diceros bicornis* |
| Rhinoceros, White | *Ceratotherium simum* |

| | |
|---|---|
| Serval | *Leptailurus serval* |
| Sitatunga | *Tragelaphus spekei* |
| Steenbok | *Raphicerus campestris* |
| Topi | *Damaliscus korrigum* |
| Tsessebe | *Damaliscus lunatus* |
| Waterbuck, Common | *Kobus ellipsiprymnus* |
| Waterbuck, Defassa | *Kobus defassa* |
| Wildebeest | *Connochaetes taurinus* |
| Zebra, Burchell's | *Equus burchelli* |
| Zebra, Grevy's | *Equus grevyi* |
| Zorilla | *Ictonyx striatus* |

**REPTILES**

| | |
|---|---|
| Chameleon | *Chamaelo dilepis* |
| Crocodile, Nile | *Crocodylus niloticus* |
| Monitor, Nile | *Varanus niloticus* |
| Python | *Python sebae* |

**BIRDS**

| | |
|---|---|
| Barbet, d'Arnaud's | *Trachyphonus darnaudi* |
| Bustard, Kori | *Ardeotis kori* |
| Crane, Crowned | *Balaearica regulorum* |
| Darter, African | *Anhinga rufa* |
| Eagle, Bateleur | *Terathopius ecaudatus* |
| Eagle, Fish | *Haliaeetus vocifer* |
| Eagle, Martial | *Polemaetus bellicosus* |
| Flamingo, Greater | *Phoenicopterus ruber* |
| Flamingo, Lesser | *Phoenicopterus minor* |
| Guinea Fowl, Helmeted | *Numida meleagris* |
| Heron, Goliath | *Ardea goliath* |
| Ibis, Sacred | *Threskiornis aethiopicus* |
| Lourie, Grey | *Corythaixoides concolor* |
| Nightjar, Dusky | *Caprimulgus fraenatus* |

| | |
|---|---|
| Ostrich | *Struthio camelus* |
| Roller, Lilac-breasted | *Coracias caudata* |
| Sand Grouse, Yellow-throated | *Ptercoles gutturalis* |
| Secretary Bird | *Sagittarius serpentarius* |
| Spoonbill, African | *Platalea alba* |
| Spurfowl, Grey-breasted | *Francolinus rufopictus* |
| Starling, Superb | *Spreo superbus* |
| Stork, Marabaou | *Leptoptilos crumeniferus* |
| Vulture, Egyptian | *Neophron percnopterus* |
| Vulture, Hooded | *Neophron monachus* |
| Vulture, Nubian | *Torgos tracheliotus* |
| Vulture, Ruppell's | *Gyps rueppelli* |
| Vulture, White-backed | *Gyps africanus* |
| Vulture, White-headed | *Trigonoceps occipitals* |

**TREES**

| | |
|---|---|
| Candelabra Tree | *Euphorba candelabrum* |
| Stinkbark Acacia | *Acacia clavigera* |
| Umbrella Acacia | *Acacia tortillis* |
| Wait-a-bit Thorn | *Acacia mellifera* |
| Whistling Thorn | *Acacia drepanolobium* |
| Wild Date Palm | *Phoenix reclinata* |
| Yellow-barked Acacia or Fever Tree | *Acacia xanthophloea* |

## SUGGESTED READINGS

### Wildlife - General:

*A Field Guide to the Birds of East and Central Africa*
J. G. Williams, 1967, (Collins, London).

*A Field Guide to the Mammals of Africa*
H. Diller, 1977, (Collins, London).

*Among the Elephants*
Iain and Ona Douglas-Hamilton, 1975, (Viking). Elephant research at Lake Manyara National Park, Tanzania.

*Conservation and Wildlife Management in Africa*
Edited by R. H. V. Bell and E. McShane Caluzi, 1984, (World Wildlife Fund, Washington, D.C.). Research.

*Elephant Memories*
Cynthia Moss, 1988, (Fawcett Columbine, New York).

*Field Guide to the Larger Mammals of Africa*
Jean Dorst and Pierre Dandelot, 1970, (Collins, London).

*Golden Shadows, Flying Hooves*
George B. Schaller, 1973, (Knopf). Personal study of the lions of the Serengeti.

*Gorilla: Struggle for Survival in the Virungas*
Michael Nichols, 1989, (Aperture Press). Color photo book.

*Newman's Birds of Southern Africa*
Kenneth Newman, 1983, (Southern Book Publishers).

*Safari: The East African Diaries of a Wildlife Photographer*
Gunter Ziesler and Angelika Hofer, 1984 (Facts on File, New York).

*The African Safari*
P. Jay Fetner, 1987, (St. Martin's Press, New York). Lots of photos and information on wildlife.

*The Chimpanzees of Gombe, Patterns of Behavior*
1986, (Harvard University Press, Cambridge, MA). Chimpanzee research.

**Africa - General:**

*African Expedition Gazette*
One Penn Plaza, Suite 100, New York, NY 10119. Quarterly newspaper devoted exclusively to safari adventure travel. One-year subscription: $25.00 in U.S.A.; $35.00 internationally.

*No Man's Land: The Last of White Africa*
John Heminway, 1983, (Harcourt Brace Jovanovich). Remarkable account of one man's journey through Africa.

*North of South*
Shiva Naipaul, 1979, (Penguin).

*The Besieged Desert*
Richard Reardon, (Harper Collins).

*The Blue Nile*
Alan Moorehead, 1962, (Harper & Row).

*The Making of Mankind*
Richard Leakey, 1981, (Michael Joseph).

*The Tree Where Man Was Born*
Peter Matthiessen, 1972, (E. P. Dutton, New York).

*The White Nile*
Alan Moorehead, 1960, (Harper & Row).

*Trees of Southern Africa*
Keith Coates Palgrave, 1977, (Struik Publishers, Cape Town, South Africa).

*West with the Night*
Beryl Markham, 1983, (North Point).

**Botswana:**

*Cry of the Kalahari*
Mark and Delia Owens, (Houghton Mifflin Co., Boston).

*Newman's Birds of Southern Africa*
Kenneth Newman, 1983, (Southern Book Publishers).

*Okavango: Jewel of the Kalahari*
Karen Ross (Macmillan Publishing Co., New York).

*Okavango, Sea of Land, Land of Water*
P. Johnson and A. Bannister, 1977, (Struik Publishers, Cape Town, South Africa). Large photo book.

*The Bushmen*
P. Johnson, A. Bannister and A. Wallenburgh, 1979, (Struik Publishers, Cape Town, South Africa). Large photo book.
*The Heart of the Hunter* (series)
Laurens Van der Post, 1980, (Harcourt Brace Jovanovich).
*The Lions and Elephants of the Chobe*
Bruce Aitken, (Struik Publishers, Cape Town, South Africa).

**East Africa:**

*A Field Guide to the Birds of East and Central Africa*
J. G. Williams, 1967, (Collins, London).
*Field Guide to the National Parks of East Africa*
John G. Williams, 1967, (Collins, London).
*Guide to Mt. Kenya and Kilimanjaro*
Edited by Iain Allen, 1981, (Mountain Club of Kenya, Nairobi, Kenya). Rock and ice routes.
*No Man's Land: The Last of White Africa*
John Heminway, 1983 (Harcourt Brace Jovanovich). Remarkable account of one man's journey through Africa.
*The Tree Where Man Was Born*
Peter Matthiessen, 1972, (E. P. Dutton, New York).

**Kenya:**

*Born Free*
Joy Adamson, 1960, (Harcourt, Brace and World, New York).
*Out of Africa*
Isak Dinesen, 1937, (Vintage Books).
*Shepherds of the Desert*
David Keith Jones, 1984, (Elm Tree Books, London).
*The Flame Trees of Thika*
Elspeth Huxley, 1959, (Morrow).
*The Lunatic Express*
Charles Miller, 1971, (Macmillan).
*The Marsh Lions*

Brian Jackman, 1982, (Elm Tree Books).

**Namibia:**

*Namibia: Africa's Harsh Paradise*
A. Bannister and P. Johnson, 1978, (Struik Publishers, Cape Town, South Africa). Large photo book.
*Skeleton Coast*
Amy Schoeman, 1984, (Macmillan South Africa). Pictorial and informative.
*The Besieged Desert*
Richard Reardon, (Harper Collins).

**Rwanda:**

*Gorillas in the Mist*
Dian Fossey, 1989, (Penguin Books).

**South Africa**

*Lightning Bird: One Man's Journey into Africa*
Lyall Watson, 1983, (Touchstone, S&S)
*My Chocolate Redeemer*
Christopher Hope, 1989, (Heinemann, U.K.).
*My Traitors Heart*
Rian Malan. An Afrikaner's story of Africa.
*The Covenant*
James A. Michener, 1980, (Random House).
*The Heart of the Hunter* (series)
Laurens Van der Post, 1980, (Harcourt, Brace, Jovanovich).
*The Last Wilderness*
Nicholas Luard, (Macmillan, U.K.).
*When the Lion Feeds* (series)
Wilbur Smith, (Pan Books, U.K.). African adventure fiction.

**Tanzania:**

*Barefoot over the Serengeti*

David Read, 1979. Autobiography about growing up in the northern Serengeti/southern Masai Mara.

*Golden Shadows, Flying Hooves*
George B. Schaller, 1973, (Knopf). Personal account of the author's famous study of the lions of the Serengeti.

*Kilimanjaro: The White Roof of Africa*
Harald Lange, 1985, (The Mountaineers Books, Seattle, WA). Large photo book.

*Sand Rivers*
Peter Matthiessen, 1981. A walking safari in the Selous Game Reserve.

*Serengeti Shall Not Die*
Bernard and Michael Grzimek, 1960, (Hamish Hamilton, London).

*The Chimpanzees of Gombe, Patterns of Behavior*
1986, (Harvard University Press, Cambridge, MA). Chimpanzee research.

**Uganda:**

*Mountains of the Moon*
Patrick Synge, 1986, (Hippocrene Books). Travel in Uganda in 1934.

**Zaire:**

*Guide to the Ruwenzori*
H. A. Osmaston and D. Pasteur, 1972, (West Col Productions, Reading, Berks, U.K.). Rock and ice routes.

*The Forest People*
Colin Turnbull, 1962, (Doubleday). On pygmies of the Ituri Forest.

*The River Congo*
Peter Fobath, 1977, (Harper & Row). History.

**Zambia and Zimbabwe:**

*Guide to the Wildlife of the Luangwa Valley*
Norman Carr, (BP Zambia Ltd.).

*The Leopard Hunts in Darkness*
Wilbur Smith, 1986, (Fawcett).
*Zambezi*
L. Watermeyer, J. Dabbs and Y. Christian, 1988, (Albida Samara Pvt. Ltd., Harare, Zimbabwe). Large photo book.
*Zambezi — A Journey of a River*
Michael Main, 1990, (Southern Book Publishers).
*Zambezi — The River of the Gods*
J & F Teede, 1991, (A. Deutsch England).

# INDEX

— D —



— E —

— F —



— G —



— H —



— I —

—J—



—K—



—L—

— N—

— O —



— P —



— Q —



— R —



— S —

# ANIMAL INDEX

-E-



-F-



-G-



-H-



-I-



-J-

-K-



-L-



-M-



-N-



-O-



-P-

-R-



-S-



-T-



-V-



-W-



-Z-

# BIRD INDEX

## ABOUT MARK NOLTING, AUTHOR & AFRICA EXPERT

Mark Nolting wanted adventure. He found it as an Olympic sportscaster, international businessman, oil engineer, and Hollywood actor. But it wasn't until he traveled through Africa that he found the excitement he was looking for.

Nolting heads up The Africa Adventure Company, Pompano Beach, Florida. He is the author of two award-winning books, *Africa's Top Wildlife Countries* and *Travel Journal Africa*.

Known as the "Travel Expert of Africa Travel" in the industry, Nolting arranges tours and advises travelers who want to go on African safari.

It all began in 1975. Nolting had graduated from Florida State University the year before with a degree in business administration and minors in chemistry, physics, math and biology. For a year and a half, he had worked for a South Florida marketing firm. But the call of the wild beckoned.

"One morning," said Nolting, "I just woke up and realized I wanted to travel around the world. And I decided, If I don't go, I'll always regret it, and if I don't go now, I never will."

Two weeks later, he departed for Luxembourg. During the 1976 Winter Olympics in Innsbruck, Austria, he worked for ABC Sports. Next he found a job in middle-management with the world's third-largest mail order catalog house, located in West Germany.

But Nolting wasn't trying to become a European businessman. He was out to see the world. Although his itinerary called for him to head for India, Nepal and the Far East, he took a six-month detour through Africa — and hitchhiked across the Sahara Desert.

Mostly, he caught rides with trucks being ferried across the desert. Once he rode with some accidental tourists. He continued on through Central and East Africa, staying with natives in mud huts, learning the culture. He toured several parks and reserves and fell in love with the "safari experience."

Then he found his way to the Mideast and was fast-tracked through a program for oil drilling engineers. He eventually came back to the United States — Los Angeles. It occurred to Nolting that he'd never tried acting. So he decided to give it a shot and wound up working for four years.

Yet the yearning to travel more through Africa was still with him. He couldn't shake the memory of the wildlife and the spectacular terrain he had seen there. And so, once again, he was off, heading for Africa, a purpose in mind.

He returned to Africa and traveled for two years through 16 countries, from Cairo to Cape Town, gathering material for his books and established contacts with various safari companies and tour guides. On his return to the United States in 1985, he wrote his books and established The Africa Adventure Company.

His many visits have included touring the antiquities of Egypt and SCUBA diving off the Sinai Peninsula; crossing Lake Nasser and the deserts of Sudan; experiencing the multitude of lodge safaris and authentic African mobile tented safaris to the wildlife reserves of Kenya and Tanzania; climbing Mt. Kenya, Mt. Kilimanjaro in Tanzania and the Ruwenzoris in Zaire; visiting the beautiful Kenyan coast; gorilla trekking and mountain climbing in Rwanda; hunting with pygmies, gorilla trekking and game viewing in Zaire; and taking the ferry from Bujumbura (Burundi) to Kigoma (Tanzania).

In southern Africa his adventures have included walking safaris from bush camp to bush camp and night game drives in Zambia; one- and seven-day white-water rafting safaris (5th class) on the Zambezi River; viewing Victoria Falls at different times of the year; kayak safari upstream of Victoria Falls; canoeing safaris on the lower Zambezi River; walking with top professional guides and game viewing by boat and open vehicle in Zimbabwe; flying safaris to the major reserves of Botswana; mokoro safaris in the Okavango Delta; a fly-in safari to the Skeleton Coast and visiting Etosha Pan and other parks in Namibia; driving the Garden Route, sightseeing in Cape Town, visiting the private reserves and parks in South Africa; pony trekking in Lesotho; traveling through Swaziland; and holidaying in the beautiful island country of Mauritius.

Mark continues to travel to Africa yearly to update information and explore new areas. Hard-to-find information on Africa is always at his fingertips, and he loves to take the time to talk to people about the adventures that can be found in Africa.

The Publishers

THE AFRICA ADVENTURE COMPANY

Dear Adventurer:

Mark Nolting, president of THE AFRICA ADVENTURE COMPANY, has spent over 15 years exploring and researching the African continent. This valuable experience is reflected in his award-winning book, *Africa's Top Wildlife Countries,* in which Mark chronicles every aspect of the safari experience, and in *Travel Journal Africa,* a diary, phrasebook, and wildlife guide.

His tour company, THE AFRICA ADVENTURE COMPANY, offers this same attention to detail when helping to plan your safari. Unlike other companies whose brochures might highlight only a few standardized tours, Mark promises — and delivers — a much more personalized approach.

This book contains difficult-to-find information on various national parks and wildlife reserves, different types of safaris, accommodation, and transportation available, and a full range of adventure activities in 14 African countries.

Mark and his friendly staff will combine their intimate first-hand knowledge of each African country with your ideas to choose a safari, whether a group tour or tailor-made itinerary, to precisely fit your needs and personal expectations.

"The key," says Mark, "is to understand the personal experience an individual wants to have in Africa and to match that experience with the optimum itinerary specifically designed to the client's needs, wants, and desires. This can best be accomplished only if the person advising the client has extensive on-site experience in **all** the top safari countries. No amount of office training can substitute for actually having been there."

"Once we have a good feeling for what our clients want," continues Mark, "we then recommend the African countries which can best provide that experience, along with the best parks and reserves. Only then do we pick a few tour options or create special itineraries for our clients to consider with specific hotels, lodges, camps, or mobile tented accommodations, and safari activities that we feel would be of greatest interest to them. Doing anything less would be compromising the best interests of our clients."

"The main allure of Africa is that you can find adventure there still," says Nolting. "When you go on safari, you never know what you're going to see or what's going to happen. Every safari is exciting. It doesn't matter if you go on tented safari, a hot-air balloon ride, walking safari, canoe safari, fish for marlin, climb Mt. Kilimanjaro, or go white-water rafting. With the right assistance and guidance from an expert in Africa travel, there's no finer adventure."

Prices of tours begin around $3,000 per person (land and air from New York) for a 12-day lodge safari to over $300 per person per day for a private lodge/mobile tented safari. Whatever your cup of tea may be, dispense with the uncertainties of traveling to Africa.

Save yourself and your energies for the adventure of your Africa trip . . . let Mark and the friendly staff of THE AFRICA ADVENTURE COMPANY go to work for you, just as they have done for many happy, satisfied 'safariers'.

It's easy to start planning your safari. Call toll free (from U.S.A. and Canada), 1-800-882-9453 (1-800-882-WILD). You'll soon be off to Africa!

Sincerely,

THE AFRICA ADVENTURE COMPANY

First Union Bank Bldg./Suite 900
1620 S. Federal Hwy., Pompano Beach, FL 33062 USA
Tele: (305) 781-3933 Fax: (305) 781-0984

## WHAT OTHERS SAY ABOUT THE AFRICA ADVENTURE COMPANY

"I had been fantasizing about a trip to Africa for over 20 years, but never in my wildest dreams did I expect it to be as exhilarating as it was. The sights and sounds of the untamed African wilderness will live with me forever.

"I have traveled to many parts of the world, but never have I experienced a vacation that surpassed both the promotional literature and my own expectations. From the booking of the trip (to Botswana) to the arrival back home, everything was perfect. My only worry is that my next trip will be anticlimactic. Thanks for the memories, Africa Adventure Company!"

John Craig
Ansonia, CT

"The arrangements you made for our East Africa safari were superb. The guides, food, accommodations and itinerary exceeded my highest expectations and gave me the freedom to experience the bush without concern. We would like to return to Africa this year. What are our options for a trip in July or August?"

Roseanne Belsito, Ed.D.
Ft. Lauderdale, FL

"I could never have done my fabulous African safari trip without your help. So a great big thank you! I've had many different kinds of experiences and have grown from them enormously. My favorite safaris (of my two-month trip) were the landrover-backed/canoe safari along Mana Pools National Park, the mobile tented program through Zimbabwe, safari to the Caprivi Strip in Namibia, and South Luangwa National Park in Zambia. Everyone I showed my itinerary to was *very* impressed. Many thanks for a trip of a lifetime!"

Maureen Gale
Devon, England

"On our private tented and lodge safari to Tanzania, we saw a leopard in a tree in Tarangire (our favorite park) and several prides of lion in Ngorongoro Crater, along with tons of other wildlife. The food was wonderful — we even had fresh baked bread in camp every day! It was our most memorable vacation. We had a blast!"

George and Ona Harris
Mooresburg, TN

"What I was especially surprised by on my safari was the wonderful diversity of the parks that were included on my mobile tented program to Zimbabwe. The food was great, and our guide was very knowledgeable about the wildlife and culture. It took me awhile to get used to the sounds of the African night, but I came back missing them!"

Nancy Kenney
Morgan Hill, CA

"We had a trip of a lifetime. Everything came off without a hitch, from Nairobi to Mt. Kilimanjaro to the Crater to the Masai Mara. One thing we must share is the phrase we so often said to another, 'I'm so glad we weren't on a group tour.'

Our mountain guide and porters were wonderful; Stephan really knew his birds and mammals whilst in the Crater, Tarangire and Arusha National Parks. The Masai Mara was a fantastic way to end the trip as 'they treat you right at Governor's Camp.'

It truly was a remarkable trip. Needless to say, your company comes highly recommended. Thanks for a great Africa Adventure."

Annie Kurz and Al Chambard
Redmond, WA

# *Travel Journal AFRICA*

## by MARK NOLTING

Expanded and revised second edition

*Travel Journal AFRICA* is the perfect companion for an African safari. Before, during and after an African vacation, you will proudly show this book to your family, friends and travel companions.

This handsome 192-page travel journal is printed in rich brown ink. Its durable yet flexible gold-stamped, rich leatherette cover will stand up against the roughest of conditions. The 5 ½" X 8 ½" size fits easily, handily into a safari jacket pocket or tote bag.

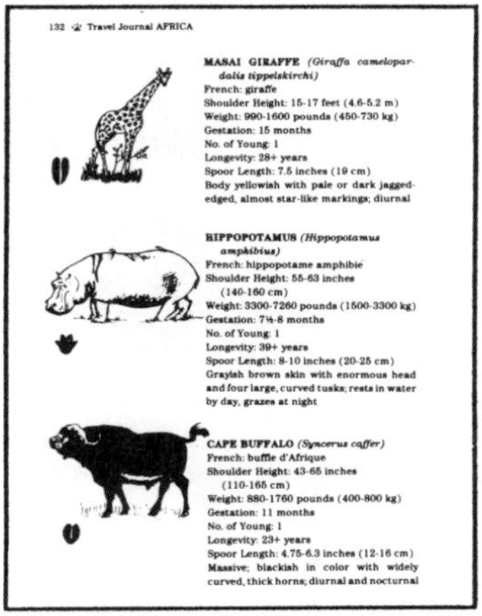

132 Travel Journal AFRICA

**MASAI GIRAFFE** *(Giraffa camelopardalis tippelskirchi)*
French: giraffe
Shoulder Height: 15-17 feet (4.6-5.2 m)
Weight: 990-1600 pounds (450-730 kg)
Gestation: 15 months
No. of Young: 1
Longevity: 28+ years
Spoor Length: 7.5 inches (19 cm)
Body yellowish with pale or dark jagged-edged, almost star-like markings; diurnal

**HIPPOPOTAMUS** *(Hippopotamus amphibius)*
French: hippopotame amphibie
Shoulder Height: 55-63 inches (140-160 cm)
Weight: 3300-7260 pounds (1500-3300 kg)
Gestation: 7½-8 months
No. of Young: 1
Longevity: 39+ years
Spoor Length: 8-10 inches (20-25 cm)
Grayish brown skin with enormous head and four large, curved tusks; rests in water by day, grazes at night

**CAPE BUFFALO** *(Syncerus caffer)*
French: buffle d'Afrique
Shoulder Height: 43-65 inches (110-165 cm)
Weight: 880-1760 pounds (400-800 kg)
Gestation: 11 months
No. of Young: 1
Longevity: 23+ years
Spoor Length: 4.75-6.3 inches (12-16 cm)
Massive; blackish in color with widely curved, thick horns; diurnal and nocturnal

## VALUABLE JOURNAL FEATURES INCLUDE:

Over 125 illustrations of mammals, reptiles, birds, and trees allow for easy identification while on safari. Adjacent to each animal illustration is the name in English, Latin and French, weight range, gestation period, number of young, longevity and general description to help the African traveler become an instant authority!

ORDER FORM

Please rush me . . .

__________ Copies of *TRAVEL JOURNAL AFRICA* @ $12.95 each.

__________ Copies of *AFRICA'S TOP WILDLIFE COUNTRIES* @ $15.95 each.

Make checks and money orders payable to Global Travel Publishers, Inc. Mail to Global Travel Publishers, Inc., P.O. Box 2567, Dept. B, Pompano Beach, FL 33072, U.S.A., or call (305) 781-3933 or toll-free 1-800-882-9453 (1-800-882-WILD) and charge to Visa/MasterCard.

_____ Check/M.O. Enclosed _____ Visa _____ MasterCard

Card No. ______________________________ Exp. ____/____

Telephone Day: (___) __________ Home: (___) __________

Signature ______________________________________

Name __________________________________________

Company _______________________________________

Street Address __________________________________

City ____________________ State _____ Zip __________

*TRAVEL JOURNAL AFRICA* @ $12.95 $__________

*AFRICA'S TOP WILDLIFE COUNTRIES* @ $15.95 $__________

Purchase Total $__________

Sales Tax * (See next page) $__________

Shipping & Handling ** (See next page) $__________

TOTAL $__________

* Florida residents add 6% sales tax.
** For items shipped within the U.S.A. or Canada, add $3.00 for one item, $1.00 for each additional item for shipping and handling. Overseas orders add $3.00 for each item surface; for airmail add $8.00 for the first item, $5.00 for each additional item.

_____ We would like your Africa travel expert, Mark Nolting, to personally plan and book our vacation, expedition, business, group or incentive trip. We understand there is no charge for this service. We have enclosed a description of what we have in mind or will call (305) 781-3933 or toll-free 1-800-882-9453 (1-800-882-WILD) soon to discuss it.

_____ We would like Mark Nolting to speak to our club, organization, business, etc. We have enclosed a brief description of our request.

Name: ______________________________

Company: ______________________________

Address: ______________________________

______________________________

Telephone No.: ______________________________

# NOTES

# NOTES

# NOTES

# NOTES